Grandmothering While Black

Grandmothering While Black

A TWENTY-FIRST-CENTURY STORY
OF LOVE, COERCION, AND SURVIVAL

LaShawnDa L. Pittman

UNIVERSITY OF CALIFORNIA PRESS

University of California Press
Oakland, California

© 2023 by LaShawnDa Pittman

Library of Congress Cataloging-in-Publication Data

Names: Pittman, LaShawnDa, 1972- author.
Title: Grandmothering while black : a twenty-first-century story of love,
     coercion, and survival / LaShawnDa L. Pittman.
Description: Oakland, California : University of California Press, [2023]
     | Includes bibliographical references and index.
Identifiers: LCCN 2022041391 (print) | LCCN 2022041392 (ebook) |
     ISBN 9780520389953 (cloth) | ISBN 9780520389960 (paperback) |
     ISBN 9780520389977 (ebook)
Subjects: LCSH: Grandparents as parents—United States—21st century. |
     African American grandmothers—Social aspects—21st century.
Classification: LCC HQ759.9 .P47 2023 (print) | LCC HQ759.9 (ebook) |
     DDC 306.874/508996073—dc23/eng/20220913
LC record available at https://lccn.loc.gov/2022041391
LC ebook record available at https://lccn.loc.gov/2022041392

Manufactured in the United States of America

32 31 30 29 28 27 26 25 24 23
10 9 8 7 6 5 4 3 2 1

With love and gratitude to my grandmothers,
Ida Wells and Warnella Henderson Wells

Contents

Acknowledgments

I'm grateful to a large number of people for their support, encouragement, and advice over the course of data collection and analysis and as I completed this book. I began this project as a graduate student at Northwestern University. My dissertation committee, which included Aldon D. Morris, Celeste Watkins-Hayes, Dorothy E. Roberts, and Jennifer A. Richeson, provided incredible support and mentorship as I completed my dissertation, obtained predoctoral and postdoctoral fellowships, and secured my first professorship. I am especially grateful to Aldon D. Morris for his ongoing mentoring and guidance. While in Evanston, Cheryl Y. Judice, Pat Vaughn Tremmel (and too many to name) provided love, laughs, and encouragement when I needed them most.

Mario Renzi and Michael Blackie provided inspiration and encouragement during my time at Hiram College as a predoctoral fellow. As did the "OBs"—Liz Piatt, Stacey Blount, and Anisi Daniels-Smith. Kerry Ann Rockquemore and Mary Tuominen offered wise counsel, gave me tools to navigate academia as a first-generation college graduate, and rooted for my success. As a postdoctoral fellow at the University of Michigan's National Poverty Center, Sheldon H. Danziger, Sandy K. Danziger, and Kristin S. Seefeldt provided the space, expertise, and encouragement needed to move this work forward. The community created by Sean Joe and the Emerging Scholars Interdisciplinary Network was also invaluable, especially the write-on-sites that emerged with Chandra Alston and Brandon Respress.

This research also benefited from the support of the Ford Foundation, the US Department of Health and Human Services, Office of Planning, Research, and Evaluation's Child Care Research Scholars Grant, the National Science Foundation (NSF), the University of Wisconsin's Institute for Research on Poverty, and a Hedgebrook Writing Residency. I appreciate the support provided by Deirdre Oakley as my NSF mentor. Akinyele Umoja, I am grateful for the love, reunion, and realness during my full circle back to Georgia State University as an NSF postdoctoral fellow.

My colleagues at the University of Washington have provided an outpouring of friendship, mentorship, and community as I've completed this book project. Words cannot express how much I appreciate the mentorship and friendship of Alexes Harris, Sonnet Retman, Scott Allard, and Sarah Elwood. Thank you for reading chapter drafts and providing critical guidance as I secured a book contract and responded to reviewers. Vicky Lawson, Chandan Reddy, Jennie Romich, and Heather Hill provided substantial support during the earliest drafts of this book and beyond. Antonia Randolph, Monica White, and Chavella Pittman, thank you for the love and for being a part of my brain trust for "all the things Black women navigating the academy." I thank Judy A. Howard and George I. Lovell, Divisional Deans of Social Sciences, for providing resources necessary to complete this book. I am also deeply grateful for the Simpson Center for the Humanities. Kathy Woodward, Rachel Arteaga, and the First Book Fellowship group offered resources, support, and feedback to complete the manuscript.

I am immensely thankful for the wonderful community of scholars and friends provided by Women Investigating Race, Ethnicity, and Difference (WIRED), my colleagues in the American Ethnic Studies (AES) Department, and the Black Faculty Collective, especially the camaraderie and encouragement provided by LaTaSha Levy, Carolyn Pinedo-Turnovsky, Juan C. Guerra, Linh Nguyen, Rick Bonus, Jang Wook Huh, Tyina Steptoe, Dafney Blanca Dabach, Carrie Freshour, Manka Varghese, Ileana M. Rodríguez-Silva, Suhanthie Motha, Hedy Lee, Angela B. Ginorio, Valerie Curtis-Newton, and Wadiya Udell. Thank you to the AES staff—Anjélica Hernández-Cordero, Ellen Palms, and Lorna T. Hamill—for their behind-the-scenes contributions to this work. Cameron Macdonald thank you for lighting my path (again) by affirming that this was one book and not several chapters in a larger book project. Sylvia Wells, Ray Nimrod, Marika Lindholm, and Molly Barber: thank you for your generosity and care. I am thankful for Karen Hartman's presence at our write-on-sites and her encouragement as this book became two books and then one again. Thank you for going on the journey with me.

Thanks to Naomi Schneider, my editor at the University of California Press, for taking an interest in this project and for your patience. I'd like to thank copy editor Dawn Hall, production editor Jeff Anderson, and editorial assistant LeKeisha Hughes at the University of California Press for their hard work in helping to complete the final stages of this manuscript. I also appreciate the copyediting of Kate Brubeck, which came with grace and lush language and improved the manuscript greatly. Additionally, Jim Gleeson, Dorothy E. Roberts, Latrica E. Best, Shirley Hill, and an anonymous reviewer offered thoughtful reader reports that helped me fine-tune the book before publication.

Of course, I am indebted to the women who graciously allowed me to learn at their knees and who offered their stories for the benefit of my research. Their collective wisdom and honesty fed me throughout the research and writing process. Their resilience and love continue to inspire me. I only hope that I have amplified their voices enough to shine a light on their remarkable beauty, complexity, and perseverance as they raise a second and third generation. I still pray for them and their families. I am also deeply grateful for the community fostered by the Seattle and King County Mayor's Council on African American Elders and kinship caregiver community—thank you Barb Taylor, Cynthia A. Green, Karen Winston, Alesia Cannady, and Mary Mitchell for helping me to continue this work.

Finally, I am thankful for the love and encouragement provided by my parents, aunts, uncles, siblings, nieces, nephews, and cousins. I am also grateful for the love and support provided by my friends and the Hooks, Gay, and Merritt families. I am forever indebted to the people who have cared for my mind, body, and spirit—Susan R. Alterman, Graham Fowler, Johnny Kest, Lisa Price, Julie Onofrio, Keri Shaw, James Lord, Marnonette Marallag, Rachel Griffith, Amana Brembry Johnson, Jack Kornfield, Tara Brach, and my mindfulness sangha.

Introduction

Sylvia exemplifies many of the Black[1] women raising their grandchildren in skipped-generation households (consisting only of grandparents and grandchildren) who are featured in this book. Compelled to raise two-year-old Zoe, the forty-one-year-old grandmother experienced a transformation in the role meanings and expectations she associated with grandmotherhood, confronted the paradox of fulfilling the social and legal functions of motherhood without the legal rights to do so, and grappled with the financial and personal costs of raising another generation. When I interviewed Sylvia, she had been raising Zoe almost since the day she was born (see table 1 at the end of the chapter). Although Sylvia came from a long line of intensive grandmothering (the assumption of responsibilities and aspects of child-rearing typically associated with parenting),[2] she still vacillated between disbelief and dismay at her situation. She had been fifteen years old when her mother, Eleanor, left her substance-abusing father. Unable to provide for her eleven children without support from her husband, Eleanor had moved her family into Robert Taylor Homes public housing in Chicago. She made do by combining public assistance with contributions from her parents, who not only helped with Sylvia and her siblings but also provided them refuge. By doing what they could to buttress their daughter's single-mother status in public housing and to ensure the welfare of their grandchildren, Sylvia's grandparents shaped her early ideas about the place and importance of grandparents.

Eleanor, too, engaged in intensive grandmothering—Sylvia raised her children in the same public housing projects where she came of age, and while she didn't lose the father of her three oldest children to drug addiction, she did lose him to the drug trade (he was serving a twenty-year prison sentence for drug dealing). As a young, unmarried mother, Sylvia stayed home with Eleanor. When her oldest child was almost school age, Sylvia rented an apartment near her mother in Robert Taylor Homes.

History repeated itself when Sylvia's nineteen-year-old daughter Shanice remained home after the birth of her first child—three generations of Black mothering shaped by an intersection of personal, cultural (e.g., expectations of motherhood), and structural (e.g., poverty, racial and gender inequality) forces. Although Sylvia was still raising her two younger children, she anticipated providing parenting support to her young, unmarried daughter, who lacked a place of her own. While her family's custom of intensive grandmothering prepared Sylvia for a multifaceted and hands-on role as a grandmother, it did not prepare her for raising a newborn.

Before Shanice left three-month-old Zoe in Sylvia's permanent care, Sylvia tried following her own mother's example by providing her daughter with parental guidance. However, unlike the dynamic between Sylvia and Eleanor, Sylvia's advice created friction, as has been documented in other studies on the dynamics between young Black mothers and their mothers.[3] When Shanice moved out, Sylvia shifted from providing parenting support to assuming a surrogate parent role.

Sylvia was blamed by her family and friends for assuming Shanice's parenting responsibilities. "Because she got a mama who doin' it for her,' that's what a lot of people say." Nevertheless, her dilemma—the choice between raising her granddaughter or risking her safety by letting her be with her mother—elaborates the manifestation of coercion: "They don't understand. I'm not finna make her take my grandbaby nowhere that it ain't safe . . . just so I can say she with her mommy. Then I'm still worried. . . . What's happening? What's goin' on? That ain't gonna help me. I'd be outside on the bus looking for them. Nah, I'll be super worried about my grandbaby." This dilemma was further complicated by Sylvia's contradictory emotions:

> Hmm. Well, I love my grandbaby. I love her to death. I tell people, "I love her dirty Pamper." . . . And I wouldn't let her go nowhere or let nobody hurt her. So, I enjoy raising her. . . . Even though it's stressful, but I still love her. But she wouldn't be nowhere else, and she won't never go in the [child welfare] system.

Sylvia cared for Zoe because she loved "her to death," but also because, given the circumstances (e.g., a mother who walked away, safety concerns, fear of Zoe ending up "in the system" [child welfare system]), she didn't feel she had a choice.

Notwithstanding her ambivalence about raising her granddaughter, Sylvia did not lack clarity about legalizing their relationship. Because she was invested in Shanice eventually reclaiming her child, Sylvia maintained her private kinship arrangement by devising strategies to access child-rearing institutions, despite her lack of legal authority. Although Sylvia did not have to worry about school, she did need to procure medical services and the child's WIC (Women's, Infants, and Children supplemental nutrition program) benefits. So, Sylvia became Zoe's WIC proxy by writing a letter permitting herself to access formal resources, signing her daughter's name, and getting the document notarized. She also strategized how to use Zoe's medical card for doctor's appointments. "Well they ask me, 'Is you the grandmother?' and I say, 'Well I don't know where she [the mother] at and she's sick and I got the medical card and I got my ID, so' . . ."

Compounding these challenges, Sylvia had been unable to work since assuming care for Zoe. Since the jobs she qualified for were insufficient to pay her living expenses and childcare, she, like many young poor parents, made the difficult choice between working a low-wage job and paying for childcare or remaining home with her non-school-aged grandchild. However, Sylvia could not apply for subsidized childcare because her daughter received the child's public assistance and the state provides aid for a child to only one caregiver. When parents refuse to relinquish children's resources, grandmothers must provide proof of physical or legal custody to get the resources their grandchildren deserve. Many grandmothers in these circumstances feared pursuing legal guardianship because they did not want the mother to retaliate by removing the child from their custody. So, the decision to forgo resources to protect grandchildren was complicated and coercive, preventing some grandmothers from receiving the cash assistance for which they were eligible. Because Sylvia had no cash income, her saving grace was Section 8 and Supplemental Nutrition Assistance Program benefits. In addition, she relied on her extended family and her partner to make ends meet.

Since Sylvia's expectation of grandmotherhood had been of a peripheral or, at most, a supporting role to Shanice, she struggled with depression, feeling trapped—literally at home with her granddaughter day in and day out. Although Zoe was a happy child, her separation anxiety compromised Sylvia's ability to take breaks; to care for Zoe, Sylvia gave up not only working but also other parts of her life, including time with family and friends, and prioritizing her intimate relationship. As Sylvia waited and hoped that her daughter would get herself together and take care of her child, she exercised agency to determine *how* she and Zoe waited, in this case, in a private kinship arrangement that provided an avenue to one day regain control of the direction of her life.

Grandmothering While Black: A Twenty-First Century Story of Love, Coercion, and Survival[4] interrogates how racial, gender, and economic inequality shape mothering among women like Eleanor, Sylvia, and Shanice and how effects of those inequalities are passed on to their children, necessitating intensive grandmothering and skipped-generation households among African Americans. This book investigates how role meanings and expectations of grandmotherhood among Black women are influenced by the unique cultural and structural forces that shape Black families. Furthermore, it illuminates the family circumstances and dynamics, as well as the public policies, that have contributed to morphing the traditional roles of Black grandmothers into a parenting role devoid of the legal obligations and rights held by parents. *Grandmothering While Black* examines the ways in which Black grandmothers experience what I call "coerced mothering" across a range of caregiving arrangements, and their strategies for managing legal marginalization vis-à-vis parents and the state. It also delves into the costs of grandparent caregiving and the coping strategies grandmothers use to reduce the financial and personal price they pay for parenting another generation. Finally, the book addresses the following questions: *Why* are largely poor, Black women like Sylvia taking on surrogate parenting roles despite the gravity of their personal struggles? *What* meanings and expectations do these women associate with the grandmother role? *Why* and *how* do Black women's traditional grandmother roles morph into surrogate parenting? *What* challenges do today's Black grandmothers face that distinguish their grandparent caregiving experiences from those of their mothers and grandmothers? *How* do they manage the demands of caregiving, including their lack of legal rights, challenges to making ends meet, and inability to prioritize their personal lives?

To understand the experiences of grandparents raising grandchildren in skipped-generation households, from 2007 to 2011 I conducted in-depth interviews with seventy-four Black grandmothers. I also completed participant-observation sessions in caregiving-prominent sites (e.g., doctor's visits, welfare office appointments, school and day-care center meetings, appointments with caseworkers, and so on). The average age of grandmothers was fifty-five years, they were raising an average of 1.81 grandchildren for an average of 5.25 years, and had an average of 3.51 children. Eighteen were married, twenty-three were divorced, four were in long-term partnerships, four were separated, six were widows, and the rest were single. At the time of data collection, twenty of the women reported annual household incomes higher than $15,000 and the rest were impoverished. The federal poverty level (FPL) during the years of data collection for families of two, three, four, and eight were $13,690, $17,170, $20,650, and $34,570, respectively. Seventeen of the twenty women who reported income above the FPL had incomes of approximately 1.5 times the FPL, and three had annual household incomes more than two times the FPL. Twenty-six of the women were working at the time of recruitment, fourteen were retired, and the rest were unemployed.

Over my four-year course of interviews and ethnography with these women on Chicago's South Side, my research questions and my understanding of their experiences evolved. For starters, they faced graver adversities than previous research documented, and they faced more adversities than the women themselves expected. Furthermore, despite coming from families steeped in intensive grandmothering and grandparent caregiving, most women had little context for their own caregiving, which departed significantly from that of their historic counterparts, including women in their own families. In the span of a generation, their grandchildren's circumstances, the increased demand to legalize relationships with grandchildren, and the symbolic and actual threat of their grandchildren ending up in the child welfare system had changed.

This book is critical to any understanding of not only Black grandmothers raising their grandchildren but also the complex kinship care (see table 2 at the end of the chapter[5]) system within which they must do so. When I finished collecting data, I understood that categorizing these families as skipped-generation households was a woefully inadequate expression of these grandmothers' experiences. Because of the implications for their legal rights and responsibilities, access to resources and services, and degree of privacy and autonomy, it was critical to identify and specify their caregiving arrangements (e.g., private, legal guardianship, kinship foster care, subsidized guardianship, adoption, and such) with their grandchildren. I argue that, within any of these caregiving arrangements, grandparents have only what I refer to as "quasi-legal rights"—that is, grandparents have no inherent or pre-given legal rights to their grandchildren, but rather must rely on and share any legal rights they obtain with parents and the state. For this reason, by theorizing the quasi-legal rights that frame grandparents' caregiving arrangements, *Grandmothering While Black* highlights the centrality of the legal system in delineating the possibilities and limits of Black grandmothering, especially the precariousness of the complex kinship care system within which they raise their grandchildren.

When grandmothers are coerced into increasing their child-rearing responsibilities beyond their desired level of intensity and their capacity to sustain, implications for the economic, social, mental, and physical well-being of not only these women but also of the generation of children in their care come into question. Indeed, both become canaries in the coal mine. Aspects of their experiences portend the future for other grandparents: the tension between their role meanings and expectations for grandparenthood and their lived experience, the negotiation of caregiving arrangements with parents and the state, and the array of strategies they implement as they negotiate parenting responsibilities for their grand-

children, navigate child-rearing institutions, manage interpersonal relationships, and meet their grandchildren's economic needs. As I highlight
how enduring US practices of racial, gender, and class discrimination in
public policy making contribute to the insurmountable challenges these
women must confront, I also impart lessons about the implications
of these policies for grandparents raising grandchildren in skipped-
generation households from other racial and ethnic groups. Specifically,
why skipped-generation households experience higher poverty rates compared to other families, are systematically excluded from already inadequate public assistance programs, and must devise innovative practices to
protect and care for their grandchildren without the legal rights to do so.

STUDYING GRANDPARENT CAREGIVING

More grandparents are currently raising their grandchildren than at any
other time in American history.[6] Researchers, policy makers, practitioners
(e.g., nonprofit employees, social workers, caseworkers, mental health and
health care providers, attorneys, and so on), and community organizers
and leaders have sought to understand the prevalence and demographic
characteristics of grandparent-headed households (children living in a
grandparent's home, with or without a parent) as well as the factors contributing to this increase. They have also investigated the form and function of different types of grandparent-headed households and how such
families fare within and outside of the child welfare system, as well as the
social, economic, and health vulnerabilities these families experience.

Prevalence and Demographic Characteristics

The share of US children living in a grandparent's household has more
than doubled from 3.2 percent in 1970 to 8.4 percent in 2019 (74 percent live in three-generation grandparent-headed households and 26 percent in skipped-generation households).[7] A recent paper published by
social welfare policy professors Mariana Amorim, Rachel Dunifon, and
Natasha Pilkauskas shows that these point-in-time estimates *under*esti-
mate the number of children who live with their grandparents at some

point and downplay the magnitude and importance of coresidence with grandparents in American children's lives.[8] The authors found that nearly 30 percent of US children live with grandparents at some point.[9] Approximately 5 percent of these children will live in skipped-generation households and 24.6 percent will live in three-generation households.[10]

Both three-generation and two-generation living arrangements are more prevalent among racial and ethnic minorities. In 2019, approximately 2.5 million grandparents reported responsibility for their grandchildren's needs.[11] Although African Americans comprise only 13 percent of the US population, in 2019 they accounted for 20.2 percent of grandparent-headed households (down from 24 percent in 2010 and 28 percent in 2000).[12] They are more likely than other racial and ethnic groups to raise grandchildren in skipped-generation households.[13] One in ten Black children ends up in a skipped-generation household, double the rate of the next highest group (Latinos, at 5 percent).[14]

Contributing Factors

Reasons for the increase in grandparent-headed households (and in skipped-generation households in particular) are attributed to three leading factors: (1) generational needs, specifically the support needs of the parent generation, (2) changes in social welfare policies, and (3) changes in child welfare system policies and practices. The first reason includes unprecedented sociodemographic trends—such as increases in single parenthood, declining marriage rates, rising divorce rates, increasing life expectancy, and declining birth rates—that have changed family life and increased the need for grandparent involvement among all racial and ethnic groups. However, African American grandparents in the twenty-first century are more likely than their predecessors and other racial and ethnic groups to be part of kinship networks composed of single-parent female-headed households. Between 1960 and 1980, the number of Black children living with a single parent increased from 9.9 to 20.5 percent, compared with 5.1 to 7.1 percent for White children.[15] In 2017, 65 percent of Black children were being raised by single parents, compared with 24 percent of White children.[16]

Generational needs also emerge from the social problems the parent generation contends with, including economic factors such as unemployment and underemployment, concentrated poverty, and racial discrimination in the labor market and earnings. Research has also identified parental death, mental and physical health issues, teen pregnancy, and child abuse and neglect as additional reasons for increasing numbers of grandparents raising their grandchildren.[17]

Previous research has identified causal connections between specific social problems and the rise in grandparent caregiving among African Americans, including the crack-cocaine epidemic of the 1980s and 1990s[18] and subsequent criminal justice policies that fueled mass incarceration.[19] Similarly, the opioid epidemic (1999 to the present) triggered a rise in grandparent caregiving. Initially, it hit rural and suburban, largely White communities, but later disproportionately affected American Indian/Alaska Native and African American communities.[20] As the number of incarcerated mothers more than tripled from 1985 to 2000, foster care caseloads more than doubled, compelling grandparents to care for as many as two-thirds of their grandchildren.[21] Studies that focus on the minor children of incarcerated women, including though not limited to those in the foster care system, indicate that approximately half of these children are being raised by their grandparents, and most often maternal grandmothers.[22] Further contributions to the overrepresentation of African Americans among grandparent-headed households include state-sanctioned violence (e.g., police brutality), residential segregation, and the HIV/AIDS epidemic.

The second reason relates to social welfare reforms, such as the 1996 Personal Responsibility and Work Opportunity Act, which aimed to move mothers from welfare to work and required unmarried teenage mothers to live with an adult (usually a parent). Economists Christopher Swann and Michelle Sylvester demonstrate that while previous literature often points to the AIDS and crack-cocaine epidemics as the principal causes of the increase in foster care caseloads during the 1980s, the most important factors were higher rates of female incarceration and decreases in welfare benefits.[23] Since the mid-1970s, neoliberalism has characterized US economic and social welfare policies. Social work professor Mimi Abramovitz is among many researchers and policy makers to show that it "has transformed social welfare policy in ways that undermine the delivery of social services, increase poverty and inequality, and create serious hardship for many individuals and families."[24] What this has meant for struggling parents is that if they cannot adequately rear their children, the government is absolved of assisting them. If government help is given, irresponsible behavior is blamed for the family's predicament and used to justify minimal assistance and practices that monitor, regulate, and control the lives of the poor.

The third reason the number of grandparent-headed households has increased is attributed to child welfare system policies and practices, specifically, shifts toward kinship rather than nonrelative foster care. In the late 1970s and 1980s, as more children entered foster care, states began to consider kin a viable option within the child welfare system.[25] Congress passed a series of laws that played a key role in altering states' use of kin as foster parents (see the appendix). All of these policies maintained a preference for "relatives first" when child welfare agencies determined children could not safely remain with parents. When the Illinois Department of Children and Family Services (DCFS) was established in 1964 it built on the state's preexisting practice of placing state wards with relatives. In its early years, kinship care never accounted for more than 15 percent of all the children in the department's custody.[26] However, between 2019 and 2020, kinship care accounted for 46 to 57.1 percent of Illinois's total foster care population.[27]

Kinship Foster Care

As increasing numbers of grandparents raise grandchildren within the child welfare system, scholars have focused on racial disproportionalities and disparities in the child welfare system, especially among African American and American Indian/Alaska Native children.[28] Researchers have also investigated how children and caregivers fare in different caregiving arrangements.[29] Much of this research focuses on the superiority of kinship caregivers over other types of placements in providing children a secure environment,[30] reducing their likelihood of multiple placements and reentry in the foster care system,[31] and increasing opportunities to maintain contact with their birth parents and to preserve racial and ethnic community ties and identities.[32] More recently, these findings have been complicated by research into children's experience of kinship diversion compared with that of formal foster care.[33]

Another area of research has focused on resource and service disparities between kinship and nonrelative foster care and on identifying the
service needs of kinship care families.[34] Other researchers and policy
makers have debated the degree to which kinship care should be held to
the same standards as traditional foster care and whether kinship care is
comparable to care provided by nonrelatives.[35]

In addition, research focuses on pathways to specific caregiving
arrangements (informal versus formal) rather than on how child welfare
system involvement influences caregivers' behavior (e.g., decision-making
processes) and the meaning and expectations grandparents associate with
their roles. A notable exception is the work of social work professor James
Gleeson and colleagues who discuss children's pathways to informal caregiving as well as caregivers' motivations for providing this care.[36] Human
development and family studies professors S. Yvette Murphy, Andrea
Hunter, and Deborah Johnson explore how the formalized relationship
between the child welfare system and African American custodial grandmothers is transforming the meanings and practices related to intergenerational caregiving in African American families.[37]

Social and Economic Vulnerabilities

A growing interest among researchers, policy makers, and social service
providers working with grandparent-headed households is to understand
their family situations, needs, and concerns. Previous research has found
that three-generation households tend to form in response to financial
difficulties, a need for childcare, illness, divorce, adolescent childbearing,
and in some instances, the grandparents' desire to help their children and
grandchildren. By contrast, skipped-generation households are frequently
the result of parental substance abuse and addiction,[38] incarceration,
death, mental illness, youth, and child abuse and neglect.[39]

Researchers have also investigated the economic disparities experienced
by caregivers and their charges across all racial and ethnic backgrounds.[40]
Compared to other family types, skipped-generation households are the
most economically disadvantaged. Two-thirds of children in these families
live in households with incomes less than 200 percent of the poverty line
(half of these are below 100 percent of the poverty line).[41] In 2019,

skipped-generation households headed by grandmothers were over three times more likely than those headed by both grandparents and seven and a half times more likely than those headed by grandfathers to live in poverty.[42] Grandmothers heading skipped-generation households are more likely than those in other family structures to be on public assistance, to be unemployed, to care for more children, to be single, and to receive subsidized childcare.[43]

Despite their economic disadvantage, grandparents in skipped-generation households significantly underuse public assistance, even when eligible. Researchers have focused on identifying the obstacles to formal support these caregivers face.[44] The compromised mental and physical health among caregivers[45] and the children they support[46] has also been documented, including that grandparents living in skipped-generation households appear to be particularly susceptible to poor health.[47] The prevalence and increased likelihood of intellectual and developmental disabilities and health problems among children in the care of these grandparents has also garnered attention.[48]

UNDERSTANDING BLACK GRANDMOTHERS RAISING THEIR GRANDCHILDREN IN THE TWENTY-FIRST CENTURY

Unanswered Questions

One limitation of studies focused on grandparent caregiving is influenced by the way research is reported. Nearly all of this scholarship has been published in peer-reviewed academic journals and edited volumes. Collectively, the numerous articles about some facet of grandparent caregiving in the post–civil rights era have increased understanding of the phenomenon. Additionally, this body of scholarship has strengthened the interdisciplinary field of grandparent studies, demonstrating its intersections with areas including carework, child welfare, aging, race and ethnicity, gender, poverty, public policy, and public health. However, at best, each contribution provides merely a snapshot or overview of a single aspect of caregivers' lives. Few books have focused on the whole lives of grandparents raising their grandchildren.

An exception is the work of Rachel Dunifon, professor of policy analysis and management, whose book captures the complexity of grandfamilies (skipped-generation households) with adolescent children in New York. She interviewed fifty-nine families—both grandparents and grandchildren—from diverse racial and ethnic groups, seeking to get "under the roof" of these families to understand their nuanced relationships. Dunifon elucidated what led to their family's formation, how grandparents and youth define their roles, the role of parents, and policies and programs addressing grandfamilies' needs.[49]

Grandmothering While Black centers the experiences of the group most overrepresented among skipped-generation households in the United States—Black grandmothers. Black children who live with a grandparent are more likely to live with a grandmother and a single parent or a grandmother and no parent than are other children who live with a grandparent.[50] This book explores the sociological factors that cause African Americans' overrepresentation among these families while simultaneously situating their experiences in a city (Chicago) where Black children make up the bulk of children taken into state custody, forcing some Black grandmothers to navigate the child welfare system to care for their grandchildren. Consequently, it remedies the second limitation of grandparent caregiving studies, which is the failure to adequately address the impact of an increasingly complex kinship care system on grandparent caregiving. Insufficient attention has been paid to how grandparent caregiving is transformed by the multiplicity of caregiving arrangements that caregivers can occupy, specifically, what compels families to choose one form of care over another.

The third limitation of existing research on grandparent caregiving is inattention to the role of coercion in caregiving and the impact of grandparent caregiving on grandmothers' role expectations and meanings, as well as their personal lives. Sociology professor Dorothy Ruiz, who has examined Black grandmothers living in three-generational and skipped-generation households in North Carolina, found that among the dominant themes in her work the majority of the women (60 percent) had mixed feelings about caring for their grandchildren, seeing the role as both a burden and a blessing due to "a lack of financial support, their own failing health, the need for respite care, the permanence of childcare responsibilities, and inadequate housing."[51] Another 20 percent reported no problems and truly enjoyed caring for their grandchildren. Twenty percent reported not enjoying or wanting the surrogate parent role and feeling trapped and very angry about their grandchildren being thrust onto them by the child welfare system or their own children. Similarly, public health scholars Meredith Minkler and Kathleen Roe, who explore the experiences of Black women in Oakland raising a grandchild, grandniece, or grandnephew in response to the crack-cocaine epidemic, found that although the women "willingly and lovingly accepted full-time caregiving as an alternative to having their grandchildren neglected or removed from the family and placed in foster care, many expressed anger, resentment, and depression over the prospect of 'second-time around' parenthood under these circumstances."[52] These "circumstances" referred to the parent's crack-cocaine addiction.

. . . . .

Three theoretical perspectives are central to understanding the experiences of Black grandmothers raising their grandchildren in the twenty-first century: coerced care, a feminist theory of caring, and role theory. Each of these concepts illuminates the complexity and gravity of raising a second and, in some cases, third generation in a skipped-generation household.

Coerced Care and Coerced Mothering

Centering the mixed feelings identified in the aforementioned studies, this book begins by exploring how coercion manifests in grandmothers' caregiving experiences. Sociologist Evelyn Nakano Glenn defines coercion as "physical, economic, social or moral pressure used to induce someone to do something."[53] In the case of grandparent caregiving, the most relevant form of coercion is status obligations—the duties assigned to all those in a given status, in this case, grandmothers.[54] The issue of coercion is highly germane to Black grandmothers' caregiving, as the demands of family life and state's use of kinship care force grandmothers to assume more responsibility for their grandchildren than they anticipate or desire. The added layer of state intrusion into the family lives of Black grandmothers has contributed to their fear of losing their grandchildren to the system, which is an additional form of state coercion that was not experienced by their historic counterparts and is not experienced to the same degree as grandmothers from other racial and ethnic groups, with the exception of American Indian/Alaska Native grandmothers.

Nakano Glenn refers to the social organization of care as "the systematic ways in which care for those who need it is allocated and how the responsibility for caring labor is assigned."[55] As the social organization of care for children who are not being cared for by their parents consists predominantly of the private households of grandparents and other relatives (as opposed to nonrelatives providing foster care or institutional settings), I show that grandmothers experience coerced care in four interrelated ways that Nakano Glenn identifies: their status position (which compels them to take on a disproportionate amount of their grandchildren's caregiving); the lack of alternatives (or only negative ones) for their grandchildren; grandmothers' loss of aspects of their identities and personhood; and the difficulty of "opting out," either temporarily or permanently, once they have assumed responsibility for their grandchildren.[56] In addition, however, I argue that the support needs of the parent generation and involvement of the child welfare system create two coercive forces beyond those Nakano Glenn outlines: (1) being subject to parental autonomy and prerogatives to direct the care of the children in question and (2) being at the mercy of the child welfare system's treatment of dependency relationships (e.g., making children wards of the state, enforcing state supervision, and being limited by nominal assistance relative to nonrelative foster care).

In this book, I argue that grandmothers experience coerced mothering not only when they are compelled to provide care, but also when they must perform the social and legal functions of motherhood. Parents and the state have a legal obligation and the prerogative to act in a child's best interest; grandparents have neither. I specify "mothering" rather than "parenting" because women are primarily responsible for raising children. Furthermore, because coerced mothering compels grandmothers to legalize their relationship with their grandchildren or to devise strategies in lieu of legalization the conditions of coerced mothering force grandmothers into the public realm (e.g., courts, the child welfare system, welfare offices, medical and educational sectors), where their vulnerabilities as surrogate parents are amplified. There is an urgent need to understand grandmothers' experiences of coerced mothering, since not only must grandmothers navigate child-rearing institutions that favor parent-child families; their legal relationship with their grandchildren also increasingly determines whether they can access such institutions, as well as what, if any, resources and services they receive to provide care. Finally, coerced mothering is a particularly important concept to consider because it considerably constrains and directs women's choices, reinforces that they are predominantly responsible for providing unpaid care, and transforms their role expectations and meanings.

Caregiving and the Legal System

This book foregrounds the ways in which the legal system both facilitates and constrains grandparent caregiving in skipped-generation households. It builds on Berenice Fisher and Joan Tronto's argument about the nature of caring and the primary social modes of caring in our society (e.g., the household, the market, and the bureaucracy). In their seminal chapter, "Toward a Feminist Theory of Caring," the authors reconceptualize caring as "comprehensive (including both the public and private), integrated (not based on the separation of spheres), and feminist (speaking to the ways in which caring often entails and perpetuates the oppression of women)."[57] They maintain that caring is a process with four intertwined phases: caring about, taking care of, caregiving, and care-receiving.[58] Caring is also a process involving certain ability factors—namely, time, material resources, knowledge, and skill. The phases of caring do not fit together neatly, and ability factors may contradict or complement each other. I explore the ways in which grandparents' legal rights relative to parents and the state have transformed with the child welfare system's increased reliance on kinship care as a service to children receiving out-of-home care; child-rearing institutions' increased need for proof of legal rights; grandparents' increased use of legal guardianship as a form of "private child protection"; and the increased use of the *parens patriae* ("parent of the nation") doctrine by the state, especially among Black families.[59] According to the *parens patriae* doctrine, the state (comprising federal and state governments) has a right and a duty to override parental autonomy and to act as a surrogate parent where necessary to provide protection for neglected or abused children.[60]

Caregiving, which is the focus of this book, refers to the hands-on work of maintaining and repairing our world. It involves more continuous and denser time commitments than taking care of, which can be accomplished by using paid or unpaid labor. The knowledge involved in caregiving is also more extensive than that of taking care of, requiring a carer to be able to adapt her strategies to moment-to-moment and day-to-day conditions and to improvise with available resources.[61] This adaptability requires experience, skills, and judgment.

Fisher and Tronto demonstrate that a shortage of time, knowledge, skill, or resources impedes the caregiving process and argue that women are often unable to provide adequate care because of their frequent lack of control over the caring process and their household's dependence on the marketplace and on bureaucracy. I extend their theory about the nature of caring and the primary social modes of caring in our society by focusing on how the caregiving process is dependent on the legal system. In the case of grandparent caregivers, their lack of legal rights means that their ability to provide care is contingent on the permission of parents or the state and shaped by child-rearing institutions requiring proof of legal authority.

PARENT'S AND STATE'S RIGHTS

The state regulates how families form and function, passing laws that reinforce the primacy of parent-child families even though such laws fail to reflect how actual families operate. The United States Supreme Court has long established parents' fundamental decision-making rights concerning their children's care, custody, and control.[62] Similarly, the laws affecting grandparents' ability to legalize their relationship with their grandchildren have changed very little in over a century; the bulk of grandparent caregiving, regardless of race and ethnicity, has occurred in private kinship arrangements. Grandparents' visitation rights expanded with the passage of state legislation supporting visitation statutes from the 1960s through the 1980s, and a subsequent constriction of visitation rights occurred in the 2000s with the *Troxel v. Granville* decision.[63] Ultimately, parents and grandparents can arrange privately who has custody of or time with children. But if a dispute arises, the rights of the parents take precedence. If a grandparent seeks custody over parental opposition, the grandparent generally must show that the parent is unfit or has failed to protect the child's welfare.[64]

Grandparents are increasingly doing just that. Recent scholarship is documenting the unprecedented use of legal guardianship, which involves a legal custodial relationship with one's grandchildren, as a form of private child protection among grandparents and other relatives from all racial and ethnic backgrounds.[65] Although legal guardianship for minors originated in colonial law for an entirely different purpose—to protect legal orphans who had inherited property—it has been transformed from a probate tool to its contemporary use in keeping children out of foster care and within the family. As the problems plaguing the parent generation and an increased demand for legalization by child-rearing institutions drive more grandparents to legalize their relationship with their grandchildren, it is important for researchers, policy makers, and practitioners—specifically, nonprofit, community, legal, and social service workers—to understand the ways in which their use of legal guardianship differs from that intended by lawmakers.

Unlike grandparents, the state has the legal authority to declare a parent unfit and to take a child into state custody. Like grandparents, it too has increased the use of its power to do so, especially among Black families. Beginning in the late 1980s, Black children were taken into state custody in droves—largely due to the state's punitive response to the crack-cocaine epidemic. The enormous growth in foster care caseloads was concentrated primarily in cities with sizeable Black communities.[66] Social work professor Mark Testa points out that the significant disparities in Illinois foster care placement between Black children and White and Latino children "cannot be interpreted as a linear outgrowth of the deteriorating circumstances of parents and children."[67]

> Many of the adverse conditions that weakened the primary group structures of African Americans in the 1980s also affected white and Hispanic families. . . . Yet neither white nor Hispanic families in Illinois experienced anywhere near the growth in foster placements that blacks did.[68]

States increasingly came to rely on relatives to care for children they deemed unable to remain with parents. In 2007, when data collection for this study commenced, 24 percent of children in foster care nationwide were in relative or kinship foster care. In 2019, this number had risen to 32 percent, with ten states between 40 and nearly 50 percent.[69] The drastic increase in children placed in kinship foster care suggests that many more states can be expected to privilege kinship foster care over other types of placements. Significantly for this study, the majority of kinship foster parents are grandparents.[70]

SCHOOLS AND MEDICAL CARE

In the last fifty years, health care and education systems have institutionalized legal guardianship and parental consent, demonstrating that both systems are structured to serve parent-child families. In response to the challenges faced by private kinship caregivers, California started the consent law trend when it passed its combined educational and health care consent law in 1994. In 2019, only twenty-four states had both educational and health care consent laws.[71] Four states had only educational consent laws,[72] and fifteen states had only medical consent laws.[73] Consents vary widely in grandparent permissions and in duration.

In most districts, only parents and legal guardians can enroll children in school. So, unless grandparents live in a state with educational consent laws or know that such laws exist in their state, they face increasing difficulty enrolling children in school. Without a consent law, relative caregivers can bypass some of the more stringent requirements (e.g., determining a student's residence based on legal custody, a certified copy of the child's birth certificate) by invoking the federal McKinney-Vento Homeless Assistance Act (42 U.S.C. 11431), which requires states to review and revise policies to ensure the immediate enrollment of homeless children and youth.[74] Illinois residents can also take advantage of the Illinois Education for Homeless Children Act (105 ILCS 45/1-1 or IEHCA), which requires school districts to assist homeless families by giving students options regarding school choice, providing transportation to and from the school of origin, and providing homeless prevention services, among other things.[75] But not every student who lives with a caregiver will qualify for McKinney-Vento services. Eligibility determinations are made on a case-by-case basis, depending on whether the child lacks a fixed, regular, and adequate place to live.[76]

In Illinois, relatives caring for children that McKinney-Vento does not define as homeless may use an Affidavit of Enrollment and Residency.[77] However, relatives receiving public aid benefits for the child are disqualified. In these cases, the caregiver can provide proof of documentation such as a birth certificate or court order—neither of which is easy to obtain—to enroll a child in school. Again, in order to take advantage of these policies and practices, grandparents or school personnel must know that they exist.

Relative caregivers' ability to enroll children in school is further complicated by the ways in which the education system has become a potential site of criminalization for low-income families seeking better education for their children. Local property taxes are used to fund the bulk of spending on public education, which means that wealthier areas with higher property values have more resources for their children's education. It also explains why educational consent laws are less common and more controversial to enact than health care consent laws. With the disparities in educational services between districts, "stealing school," or "boundary-hopping" (students zoned for one school district but attending school in another), has garnered not only more media attention but also more criminalization by school districts.[78] Statistics on the prevalence of enrollment fraud are scant. And while it is not new, boundary-hopping is a growing phenomenon throughout the country, one that historically would have resulted in disenrollment of the student, not school districts seeking criminal charges against parents. In recent years, school boards have adopted tougher measures to stop enrollment fraud, many districts now spending tens of thousands of dollars each year to purge these students from their enrollment lists.[79] States' legislative and prosecutorial approaches to punishing this practice vary, but increasingly involve a combination of financial penalties, community service, and imprisonment.[80] The overrepresentation of poor mothers *and* grandmothers among those prosecuted in high-profile cases involving enrollment fraud has been well documented.[81]

The increased traction of these punitive policies and practices has implications for nonparents enrolling children in school. Since the often fluid nature of grandparent caregiving arrangements means that children *may* in fact spend time with parents on weekends, during summers, or holidays, their habits may reflect this fluidity, not fraudulent behavior. So, requiring proof of legal custody or guardianship may prevent children who are being raised by relative caregivers from attending school.[82]

In addition to overcoming these obstacles, grandparents raising their grandchildren in skipped-generation households also struggle to obtain medical care for the children in their care. Changes in case law have necessitated consent practices in general, and parental consent in particular. As a result, grandmothers experience increased difficulty obtaining medical care for their grandchildren than did previous generations.[83] Although medical consent laws exist in some states and may alleviate some barriers to consenting to medical treatment, they are not a panacea.

Black Grandmothers' Role Expectations and Meanings

Roles are patterned and characteristic social behaviors associated with a social position.[84] Role expectations in the context of my work may be viewed as the rights, duties, and rules associated with a role as perceived by self (the grandmother) and others (e.g., grandchild, parent). How women experience and enact the grandmother role is also shaped by their role identity, which is the meaning they associate with the role. Role identity is composed of three subdimensions: essence, salience, and emotional investment.[85] Essence refers to the substantive meaning women attach to the grandmother role. Salience is a cognitive concept and indicates the relative importance of the grandmother role in a woman's role repertory. Emotional investment refers to the feelings grandmothers have about being a grandmother.[86]

The grandmother role exists even before a woman occupies that social position and derives from the accumulated experience of past occupants of the role, shaped slowly as past and current generations adapt to the demands of their environments. Socialization into the grandmother role is the process by which role-associated expectations are transmitted to women and to others, beginning early, through observational learning, and continuing across the life course as women accrue experience.[87]

Prior to assuming the grandmother role, women in this study learned from the women in their families to associate responsibility with Black grandmotherhood, fostering role expectations of what I refer to as "anticipatory responsibility"—the expectation held by grandmothers and the Black community of duty to or accountability for a grandchild's well-being. By linking responsibility to the grandmother role, the women in their families also shaped women's future role expectations.

Socialization in Black families illustrates two features of Black grandmotherhood that influenced how the women in my study conceptualized the role across the life course. First, the line between motherhood and grandmotherhood was blurred and fluid, and the roles shared common characteristics.[88] Second, socialization within Black families and communities that linked grandmotherhood to responsibility demonstrated that mothers alone are not responsible for children's upbringing. In response to the precarity of life experienced by Black families historically and contemporarily, Black grandmothers have anticipated the need to support and care for their grandchildren.

By addressing the relationship between systemic stability and conformity to expectations internalized during socialization, structural role theory suggests that roles are the main mechanisms linking individuals to social structures, and that individuals are under continuous and heavy pressure outside and inside themselves to conform to social expectations.[89] Thus, grandmothers may adhere to role expectations that are both internally driven and induced by the state, the Black community, and Black families, which all seek to mold the convention of Black grandmotherhood for their benefit and based on their expectations. By contrast, structural symbolic interactionism emphasizes the ways in which individuals define interactive situations, use their definitions to organize their own behavior in the situation, and respond to conflict among competing definitions. In other words, it shows that social behavior is the product of not only role-playing but also of role-making.[90] This book shows that while grandmothers may adhere to externally driven role expectations, they also define and negotiate their own grandmothering experiences.

Prominent scholars of Black grandparenthood have urged future scholars to investigate not only parental surrogacy but other aspects of grandparenthood that have received scant attention among African American grandparents, including role meanings and role expectations.[91] Some explicitly state that surrogate parenting "should not be viewed as the normative grandparental role among older black Americans."[92]

I address this gap in previous research by exploring these basic aspects of grandmotherhood among those Black grandmothers who are raising their grandchildren. Because these women are raising grandchildren, it is often assumed that they themselves see their expected role as that of surrogate parent. Indeed, for some grandmothers, they do.[93] However, when given a choice, many of the grandmothers I interviewed would prefer *not* to raise their grandchildren. Focusing on women's role expectations and meanings illuminates the impact of coercion on disrupting Black grandmothers' role expectations and transforming their role identities.

DESIGN OF STUDY

This study examines grandmothers raising grandchildren in skipped-generation households rather than those raising grandchildren in multigenerational households. Grandmothers raising grandchildren in skipped-generation households are burdened with navigating child-rearing institutions and negotiating relationships with parents and the state in ways that other caregivers are not—not to mention assuming primary responsibility for meeting children's material and nonmaterial needs. Moreover, understanding how some families end up in the child welfare system and not others, as well as their experiences of state involvement, increases knowledge of the influence of state-level policies and practices on grandparent caregiving. To analyze these complexities, I leverage in-depth interviews and ethnographic observations with Black grandmothers raising grandchildren in Illinois, investigating the factors that compel, constrain, and support Black grandmothers' efforts to ensure the safety and well-being of their grandchildren.

My recruitment of Black grandmothers maximized the contrast among women providing care through various caregiving arrangements (see the appendix): I mailed information packets about the study to Chicago-area social service agencies, religious institutions, and childcare providers that provide services to this population; I also posted flyers advertising the study in targeted communities and relied on word of mouth; finally, I gathered a snowball sample, with participants leading me to other Black grandmothers in skipped-generation households.

After eligibility screening, all women participated in one in-person interview that lasted approximately three hours, for which they received $50. If they chose to, they also participated in one observation session at a site relevant to the caregiving experience, for which they received $25. Women were eligible to participate in the study if they (1) self-identified as Black; (2) spoke English; and (3) self-identified, at the time of recruitment, as primary caregivers to at least one grandchild or great-grandchild under the age of eighteen with no parents living in the home; (4) were living in the greater Chicago metropolitan area; (5) were not hospitalized or incarcerated; and (6) had been caring for their grandchildren for at least six months.

In interviews with these grandmothers, I asked about their relationships with parents, parental involvement, custody-related issues, child welfare system involvement and experiences, decision-making concerning caregiving arrangements, and supports or impediments to their access to child-rearing institutions, resources, and services. I also asked about stressors and how grandmothers coped with the demands of caregiving, including family conflict, fulfilling their grandchildren's day-to-day needs, barriers to institutional access, and inadequate receipt of formal and informal support. Most of my interviews took place in grandmothers' homes and I conducted sixteen participant observation sessions.

My choice to study Black grandmothers—rather than grandmothers from other racial and ethnic backgrounds or experiences among a range of grandmothers—was informed by several factors. First, while Black grandmothers are overrepresented among both grandparent-headed households and skipped-generation households, the two books[94] that have been written about Black grandmothers acting in this capacity, although significantly increasing understanding of Black grandmothers serving as surrogate parents, hardly capture either the vastness of their caring labor or the diversity among their experiences. Because they are more likely than all other grandparents to be caring for grandchildren in skipped-generation households, Black grandmothers are at the forefront of restructuring their carework in ways that reflect significant changes in caregiving arrangements since the 1980s. I also selected Black grandmothers because they are especially aware of and influenced by numerous multifaceted structural and institutional changes affecting families. I sought to understand their responses to these changes and to demonstrate that there is no monolithic Black-grandmother experience of surrogate parenting.

Second, despite the fact that Black grandparents have had to contend with racial disproportionalities and disparities in the child welfare system that grandparents from other racial and ethnic groups have not (with the exception of American Indian/Alaska Native, who also have tribal protections), no book has to my knowledge centered their experiences of child welfare system involvement. However, not only is it important to understand the experiences of Black grandmothers at a time when African Americans continue to be overrepresented within the child welfare system, but it is also vital to do so in Illinois in particular, a place where Black families, especially poor Black families, have been especially hard hit by the concentration of the child welfare system in their communities.[95] Indeed, at one point, Illinois had one of the highest per capita rates of children in foster care in the nation—the majority of whom were Black. In 2007, when data collection for the study commenced, Black children made up 61 percent of the number of children in out-of-home care in Illinois. Although that number has decreased to 42 percent, Black children (who are only 15 percent of the general child population) are still more likely than all other groups to populate Illinois's foster care system.[96] Twenty-nine of the grandmothers I studied have had direct experience with the child welfare system, including in other states.

The intersection of the grandmothers most likely to be grandparent caregivers and the concentration of child welfare systems in poor Black communities begs examination. I selected the subset of Black grandmothers raising their grandchildren to participate in this study because of their disproportionate rates of skipped-generation households and high rates of poverty. While most of the grandmothers lived in or near predominantly African American, urban neighborhoods with concentrated or high poverty (at least 40 percent of residents live at or below the poverty line)—the very communities within which the child welfare system is most concentrated[97]—additional Chicago South Side neighborhoods were added to the study as data collection evolved.

Finally, the complexity of types of care indicates that grandmothers may experience multiple caregiving arrangements while caring for a grandchild. I wanted to explore how Black skipped-generation house-holds are shaped by and shape this variability in caregiving arrangements. Children's routes to care and the processes that shuttle them into caregiving arrangements that may offer more or fewer services and supports has consequences for families already struggling financially. Black grand-mothers' experiences of increasingly nuanced and complex caregiving arrangements are also of interest because of the tendency of scholarship to oversimplify contemporary women's experiences by comparing them with those of women from earlier historical periods that predate the current range of caregiving arrangements.

In order to demonstrate the evolution of the structure of surrogate parenting among contemporary Black grandmothers, I provide data on the number of grandmothers in specific caregiving arrangements at the time of the interview and the number of grandmothers who have had any experience of specific caregiving arrangements over the period of their caregiving experience. At the time of the interview, grandmothers provided care to 134 children in thirty private kinship arrangements, seventy-one legal guardianships, three kinship diversion arrangements, sixteen kinship foster care arrangements, four subsidized guardianships, ten kinship adoptions, and one private adoption. As they cared for grandchildren, grandmothers in this study had experience with each type of care: thirty-one with kinship foster care, ten with kinship adoption, four with subsidized guardianship, one with private adoption, seventy-one with legal guardianship, eighteen with kinship diversion, and seventy-one with private kinship care.

I used grounded theory, which involves constructing hypotheses and theories by collecting and analyzing data, to identify and make sense of the themes that emerged as significant to the study population. I then used a deductive approach to extend and deepen Nakano Glenn's social organization of care and Berrick and Hernandez's caregiving arrangements framework.

Despite coercive circumstances, the situations I observed during my interviews and ethnographic data collection reflected a preponderance of love, once again reflecting the complexity of grandmothers' experiences. The predominantly nuanced and resilient attitudes and actions of my study participants may reflect self-selection; grandmothers who were abusing their grandchildren most likely would not have agreed to be interviewed.

While seventy-four women generously shared their experience for this study, space has constrained me to focus on those stories that most poignantly convey the findings that shed light on the complex issues addressed in each chapter. Each chapter, therefore, follows the journeys of only a fraction of the number of women interviewed. However, I intentionally feature different women in each chapter to demonstrate the diversity of their experiences and the depth and diversity in the data collected.

THE ROADMAP FOR *GRANDMOTHERING WHILE BLACK*

Chapter 1 demonstrates the distinctive challenges Black mothers faced as they provided for their children's physical needs and devised parenting strategies that prepared their children for success and protected them from the world beyond their front doors. It examines two aspects of mothering that distinguish Black mothers' experiences from those of other women: (1) their increased likelihood of being primary breadwinners and working outside of the home, and their experience of significant racial wage disparities despite their high labor force participation rates; and (2) their significant housing challenges compared with other mothers, including being more segregated and isolated and raising their children in or near concentrated poverty. The chapter examines the effects of these racial, gender, and class inequalities across generations and introduces four ways mothers interpreted how their adult children "turn out": by providing context, weighing the opportunities they provided their children, centering their own and their children's responses to life's struggles and opportunities, and self-blaming.

Chapter 2 illustrates the meanings and expectations Black women associated with the grandmother role. It argues that the socialization of Black women into the grandmother role across their life course and the societal context of Black family life contributed to their sense of anticipatory responsibility. It shows that grandmothers interpreted their responsibility for their grandchildren in different ways, including peripheral involvement; helping parents with children; and, under certain circumstances, serving as surrogate parents. The chapter identifies the generational needs that make it necessary for Black grandmothers to play a larger role in their grandchildren's lives than they anticipated. Finally, it shows that beyond offering their caring labor, women attached deeper meaning to their grandmothering, including prioritizing and protecting their grandchildren, nurturing them as a part of their lineage, and equipping them with the tools necessary to achieving success.

Chapters 3 and 4 present the ways grandmothers experienced coerced mothering within various caregiving arrangements, examining parental and state coercion of women into providing care beyond their role expectations and desires. The chapters explore the strategies grandmothers used to confront their legal marginalization vis-à-vis parents and the state, including using punitive institutions to overcome their lack of legal authority and resolve family conflict, "taking" and "keeping" their grandchildren from parents to ensure their safety and well-being (chapter 3), adhering to DCFS rules and regulations to get *and* keep their grandchildren in their care, and accommodating, resisting, and maximizing their child welfare system involvement (chapter 4). Chapter 3 examines grandmothers' experiences of coerced mothering within informal kinship care, where the bulk of grandparent caregiving takes place. Chapter 4 examines coerced mothering among grandmothers raising grandchildren within formal kinship care.

Chapter 5 examines the impact of caregiving on grandmothers' fragile financial status and the economic survival strategies they used when the ends did not meet. As grandmothers strategized to satisfy their family's income and housing needs, the inequitable resources and services within the kinship care system exacerbated their financial strain. As a result, grandmothers engaged in risk-negotiation strategies in three policy settings critical to grandparent-headed households and low-income households broadly: subsidized child care, cash assistance, and subsidized housing. Their economic survival strategies transformed their prevailing meanings of grandmotherhood, as the role also included negotiating risks, brokering deals, navigating safety net programs, and making enormous financial sacrifices.

Chapter 6 foregrounds the toll of grandparent caregiving on women's personal lives, including restricting their freedom, impairing their romantic relationships, and impeding their retirement. I also demonstrate how grandparent caregiving contributed to or exacerbated their physical and mental health issues, and that women coped with the costs associated with grandparent caregiving by relying on their social support networks and religious coping. I give voice to the rewards associated with raising a grandchild, including grandmothers' desires for companionship and intimacy, an opportunity to reparent, and a sense of purpose.

The conclusion provides insights based on Black grandmothers' positionality as canaries in the coal mine, illuminating their experiences and providing critical information about grandparent caregiving in the twenty-first century, including: (1) how surrogate parenting affects not only women's grandmotherhood but also their personhood; (2) the ways in which the racial geography of the child welfare and criminal justice systems concentrates them in poor communities of color, especially Black communities, forcing families living in these communities to use these systems to resolve family conflict and crises. I discuss the debates among scholars, activists, and policy makers about reforming, defunding, and abolishing the police and the child welfare system; and (3) how US public policy can make a difference for grandfamilies at large.

Table 1 Demographic and Caregiving Arrangement Information

Study participant name	Age	Marital/dating status	Children	Grandchildren/ great-grandchildren	Grandchildren raising	Kinship care arrangements
Sylvia	41	Single (dating)	4	1	1	Private
Angela	45	Single	2	2	2	Private
Susan	69	Divorced	8	10/4	2	Private
Dorothy	50	Divorced (dating)	2	1	1	Private
						Legal guardianship
Otha	68	Divorced	1	3/1	2	Private
						Legal guardianship
Cassandra	47	Single	6	9	1	Private
Kathleen	48	Single	4	9	1	Private
						Legal guardianship
Helen	48	Partnered	3	3	1	Kinship diversion
						Legal guardianship
Shalonda	41	Married	3	5	1	Private
						Legal guardianship
Donna	54	Divorced	5	20/1	2	Licensed kinship foster care
Laverne	54	Married	3	9/1	5	Private
						Legal guardianship
Barbara	41	Divorced	3	1	1	Kinship diversion
						Legal guardianship
Victoria	38	Single (dating)	3	1	1	Private
Rose	41	Divorced	3	4	2	Private
Pearl	76	Divorced	4	14/uncounted	3	Private
						Kinship diversion
						Legal guardianship

Name	Age	Marital status				Arrangement
Tamara	51	Engaged	4	48/uncounted	4	Unlicensed kinship foster care Adoption
Martha	63	Divorced	5	9/11	4 (great-grandchildren)	Private adoption/(GC#2–4) Private
Eliza	63	Married	4	12	6	Legal guardianship Private Kinship diversion Legal guardianship
Bobbie Joe	54	Divorced	1	1	1	Legal guardianship (joint custody)
Kathryn	49	Divorced	3	5	1	Private
Judy	51	Married	7	13	1	Private
Virginia	81	Married	2	4/3	2 (great-grandchildren)	Legal guardianship/(GC#2) Private
Sonya	45	Married	2	2	1	Private
Miriam	62	Separated	12	18/5	2	Kinship foster care Private/(GC#2) Private
Maxine	50	Divorced	3	2	2	Legal guardianship
Beulah	58	Divorced	2	10	2	Private
Nancy	50	Separated	4	10	1	Legal guardianship Kinship diversion
Faith	48	Divorced	3	5	1	Legal guardianship Kinship foster care (different state)
Lottie	58	Married	3	9	3	Legal guardianship Private
Lena Bell	65	Widowed	4	12/5	2	Legal guardianship Licensed kinship foster care Adoption

Table 1 (Continued)

Study participant name	Age	Marital/dating status	Children	Grandchildren/ great-grandchildren	Grandchildren raising	Kinship care arrangements
Cora	63	Married	4	8/10	2	Private Licensed kinship foster care Adoption
Lonna	51	Single	3	6	1	Unlicensed kinship foster care Subsidized guardianship
Opal	81	Widowed	7	11/uncounted	1	Licensed kinship foster care Adoption
Nell	63	Divorced	4	10	2	Licensed kinship foster care Subsidized guardianship
Sandy	58	Single	4	13	1	Private
Cheryl	52	Divorced	4	8	5	Private Legal guardianship
Grace	50	Single	2	3	1	Private
May	58	Divorced	4	5	1	Private Legal guardianship
Ruby	69	Single	3	5	1	Licensed kinship foster care
Gloria	54	Single	3	7	3	Kinship diversion
Ida	69	Married	2	4/12	1 (great-grandchild)	Licensed kinship foster care
Eloise	60	Married	3	2	2	Unlicensed kinship foster care
Latoya	42	Married	2	2	1	Unlicensed kinship foster care
Bertha	75	Divorced	1	2/3	1 (great-grandchild)	Unlicensed kinship foster care Subsidized guardianship
Viola	69	Widowed	4	12/uncounted	3 (great-grandchild)	Unlicensed kinship foster care

Frances	1	67	Married	9	2	Kinship diversion / Legal guardianship
Alice	1	54	Married	1	1	Licensed kinship foster care
Josephine	3	52	Divorced	3	2	Private
Louise	7	81	Widowed	10 + a son with "a bunch of 'em [kids] but I don't know how many he got" / uncounted	1	Unlicensed kinship foster care / Licensed kinship foster care
Janet	2	57	Married	3	1	Unlicensed kinship foster care
Carolyn	7	40	Divorced	4	1	Private
Lenora	1	51	Single	2	2	Legal guardianship
Nicole	1	50	Single	8	3	Private / Legal guardianship / Private
Michelle	3	47	Divorced	1	1	Legal guardianship / Kinship diversion
Velma	2	71	Married	4/12	1 (great-grandchild)	Legal guardianship / Licensed kinship foster care / Adoption
Connie	4	60	Single	13	1	Legal guardianship
Mavis	5	59	Separated	13	1	Legal guardianship
Chandra	5	40	Single	3	3	Private
Natalie	2	48	Married	2	2	Legal guardianship / Kinship foster care (different state) / Legal guardianship

Table 1 *(Continued)*

Study participant name	Age	Marital/dating status	Children	Grandchildren/ great-grandchildren	Grandchildren raising	Kinship care arrangements
Claudette	63	Divorced	8	32/4	1	Private
Pamela	52	Partnered	1	4	3	Legal guardianship
Marian	74	Divorced	5	6/2	1 (great-grandchild)	Legal guardianship
Joan	49	Separated	2	6	3	Private
Sharon	70	Divorced	5	11/2	2	Legal guardianship
Jacky	48	Married	4	2	2	Legal guardianship
Joyce	36	Single	4	14	2	Legal guardianship
Vivian	53	Single	6	13	2	Private
Brenda	58	Widowed	2	6	1	Private
Norris	57	Widowed	4	8	2	Private
Regina	49	Partnered	2	4	3	Legal guardianship
Denise	42	Separated	3	2	1	Private
Waneda	51	Single	5	2	1	Legal guardianship
Penny	55	Divorced	5	10	2	Private
Rachel	49	Married	3	2	1	Legal guardianship

Table 2 The Five-Tiered System of Kinship Care

Caregiving arrangement	Role of state in caregiving arrangement	Legal rights/ reversibility	Resources provided	Services provided	Screening and/or assessment of caregiver prior to placement?	Ongoing review of placement/ caregiving?
			Tier 1			
Licensed kinship foster care	Mandated	Custodial rights/Yes. Juvenile court's emphasis on reunification with the birth parent.	Full foster care board rate	Services available, though uneven implementation.	Same screening/ assessment standards as traditional foster care.	Monthly caseworker visits
Licensed subsidized guardianship (kinship guardianship, KinGAP)	Mandated	Custodial & legal rights/ Yes. Birth parent can petition juvenile court.	Guardianship payment (equivalent to foster care).	Not typically, though some jurisdictions offer post-permanency services.	Same screening/ assessment standards as traditional foster care.	Annual form completed by caregiver to attest to child's continued residence in the home.
Kinship adoption	Mandated	Parental rights/No	Adoption subsidy (equivalent to foster care).	Not typically, though some jurisdictions offer post-permanency services.	Some screening/ assessment as foster care.	None

Table 2 *(Continued)*

Caregiving arrangement	Role of state in caregiving arrangement	Legal rights/ reversibility	Resources provided	Services provided	Screening and/or assessment of caregiver prior to placement?	Ongoing review of placement/ caregiving?
Voluntary placement agreement	Mandated	Custodial rights/Yes, Child welfare worker can return child following successful completion of case plan or safety plan. Child must be returned home within 6 months or formally placed in foster care, guardianship/ adoption.	Full foster care board rate (or equivalent) once approved as a foster parent and/or if the child is federally eligible.	Services available, though uneven implementation.	Same screening/ assessment standards as traditional foster care.	Monthly caseworker visits
Tier 2						
Unlicensed kinship foster care	Mandated	Custodial rights/Yes, Juvenile court's emphasis on reunification with the birth parent.	State standard of need— higher than TANF child-only payments but lower than the foster care payments.	Services available, though uneven implementation.	Screening and assessment may be relaxed.	Monthly caseworker visits
Unlicensed subsidized guardianship (kinship guardianship)	Mandated	Custodial & legal rights/ Yes. Birth parent can petition juvenile court.	State funded option (lower payments than licensed).	Not typically, though some jurisdictions offer post-permanency services.	Yes	Annual form completed by caregiver to attest to child's continued residence in the home.

Tier 3

Legal guardianship (Probate legal guardianship, civil legal guardianship)	Mediated	Custodial & legal rights/ Yes. Birth parent can petition probate court	TANF child-only; TANF family grant if income eligible.	Uneven implementation/ Referral to community agencies/Kinship Navigator programs/ Caregiver support groups.	Some screening & assessment	None
Private adoption	Mediated	Parental Rights	Social Security benefits; Federal adoption tax credit; TANF child-only; TANF family grant if income eligible.	None, though some states and local jurisdictions operate Kinship Navigator programs/ Caregiver support groups.	Some screening & assessment	None

Tier 4

Private arrangements (informal kinship care, private kinship care)	None/ Independent	None/Yes, typically via negotiation/agreement between caregiver and birth parent.	TANF child-only; TANF family grant if income eligible.	None, though some states and local jurisdictions operate Kinship Navigator programs/ Caregiver support groups.	No	None

Table 2 (Continued)

Caregiving arrangement	Role of state in caregiving arrangement	Legal rights/ reversibility	Resources provided	Services provided	Screening and/or assessment of caregiver prior to placement?	Ongoing review of placement/ caregiving?
			Tier 5			
Kinship diversion (voluntary care, state-mediated care)	Mediated	None/Yes, typically via negotiation/agreement between caregiver and birth parent.	TANF child-only; TANF family grant if income eligible.	Referral to community agencies/Kinship Navigator programs/ Caregiver support groups.	Varies by state	Varies by state, but often none

State-Mandated Care: the state (1) initiates the kinship care arrangement, (2) imposes mandated responsibilities on kin caregivers and parents, and (3) extends certain rights to the caregiver. State-Mediated Care: mediated arrangements pursued by a relative or by state agents. Recognized by the state through the decision of a probate or civil court judge. State-Independent Care: caregiving arrangements without child welfare system involvement.

1 Mothering While Black

As mothers, the women in this study experienced many firsts. They or their mothers were the first generations to move to Chicago from various parts of the South during the Great Migration. They or their mothers were the first to integrate White neighborhoods or to live in newly constructed Chicago public housing. They were the first to hold jobs from which centuries of slavery and racism had excluded Black women. They were often the first generation to attend or graduate from college, hoping to pave the way for their children. They were the first in their lineage of women to make it into the Black middle class. They were the first women in their families who did not end marriages by drifting into long-term separations, but began to divorce. They also led the wave of never-married Black mothers. And while they were not the first generation of Black mothers to contend with poverty, they or their mothers were the first to raise their children in or near concentrated urban poverty and its attendant social problems.

Ida, Marian, Louise, and Penny figure among these firsts. They also experience the distinctive challenges of Black mothers navigating interlocking systems of oppression (e.g., White supremacy, patriarchy, economic inequality) to "feed the physical needs of their children."[1] Their stories demonstrate the legacy of the effects of oppression, affecting their children's ability to

parent. They illustrate the parenting strategies Black mothers devise to prepare their children for success and protect them from anti-Black racism and
"the streets"—an umbrella reference to drug addiction, drug dealing, and
death caused by community violence and substance abuse. These mothers'
stories illustrate that Black women's mothering experiences are rich and
complex and vary based on age, socioeconomic status, personality, family
history, geography, the nature and quality of intimate relationships, and
parenting styles. What does not vary is that parenting doesn't end when children reach adulthood, yet little attention has been given to Black mothers'
perceptions of their adult children. This chapter considers Black mothers'
assessment of the factors that shape how their children "turn out," including
their own parenting, their adult children's agency and personal responsibility, and the society within which their children are raised and must live.

Historically, Black feminists have had to respond directly to harmful
stereotypes and theories explaining the overrepresentation of Black people among the poor and Black mothers' contributions to it—articulated by
the asphyxiating repercussions of Daniel Patrick Moynihan's words:

> There is no one Negro community. There is no one Negro problem. There is
> no one solution. Nonetheless, at the center of the tangle of pathology is the
> weakness of the family structure. Once or twice removed, it will be found to
> be the principal source of most of the aberrant, inadequate, or anti-social
> behavior that did not establish, but now serves to perpetuate the cycle of
> poverty and deprivation. . . . A fundamental fact of Negro American family
> life is the often reversed roles of husband and wife.[2]

The cultural link between destructive individual behavior and poverty
(e.g., the "tangle of pathology," the "culture of poverty," the "underclass")
ignores the structural forces that contribute to poverty. It also distorts
Black families' realities and denies them agency and desperately needed
systemic changes to combat racial, gender, and economic inequality. At
the same time, the stereotypes of "Black family pathology," "matriarchy,"
"welfare queen," and "the strong Black mother" distort Black mothers'
lived realities and deny them equal access to the resources and services
necessary to care for themselves and their children. My work showcases
Black mothers' experiences on their own terms and from their perspectives, privileging knowledge production among Black women.

FEEDING THE PHYSICAL NEEDS OF THEIR CHILDREN

In her work on the meaning of mothering among Black women, sociologist Patricia Hill Collins notes, "Black mothers pay the cost of giving up their own dreams . . . because many spend so much time feeding the physical needs of their children."[3] While this is true of many mothers, this section explores how Black mothers' work and housing experiences not only distinguish them from other women but also undermine their ability to improve family outcomes: Black mothers are more likely than all other women to work outside of the home and to be their family's primary breadwinner. In addition, they experience significant wage disparities despite their high labor force participation rates. Black mothers also face more significant housing challenges than other mothers, including more racial residential segregation and isolation and an increased likelihood of raising their children in or near concentrated poverty; moreover, they experience significant racial disparities in home buying.[4]

Finding and Maintaining Work

The Southern migrants in this study moved to Chicago during the Great Migration. As the Jim Crow racial caste system, disfranchisement, and racial violence escalated in the South, six million Black people left over the duration of six decades (1910–70). Ida, Louise, and Marian were among those Southern migrants to leave the South in search of a better life. The Great Migration marked a significant turning point for Black women because it facilitated desperately needed job changes. As scores of Black women left the South, they also left the informal economy of agricultural, personal, and household service workers. Their ability to do so was driven in part by wartime labor demands, institutional and policy changes (e.g., 1935 National Labor Relations Act, 1941 Fair Employment Practices Committee), and organized labor activism among Black workers.[5] Black mothers working to provide for their children in subsequent decades built on these wartime economic advances and increased access to higher income, higher status jobs, and educational opportunities.

As they raised their children, seventy-one of seventy-four women worked full-time, part-time, or intermittently. Mothers were less likely to work or worked only intermittently or part-time when they had health problems and additional caregiving responsibilities (e.g., caring for an aging parent, ill spouse or child, other family members), or when their children were non-school-aged. Based on their occupations, formal receipt of support, housing history, and marital status, the majority of mothers were working-class and poor. Mothers experienced upward and downward mobility based on their number of dependents and whether they were partnered and received financial support, lost and gained jobs, and acquired more education. Working-class and working-poor women worked in various occupations, including customer service, the hospitality industry, dry cleaning, building maintenance, janitorial services, retail, manufacturing, food service, social service, security, the nonprofit sector, education, and formal carework (e.g., nursing assistant, home-health-care aide, nurse, childcare provider). Eighteen women in this study were able to take advantage of the expanding Black middle class of the 1950s and 1960s. These middle-class mothers worked in higher-paying social service, health, and tech jobs. They also worked in the public sector (e.g., child welfare services, postal service, transportation). One middle-class mother and her husband owned a grocery store and then a laundromat before both ended up working in public transit, and another owned a hair salon. As they raised their children, ten middle-class mothers combined their incomes with their husbands', six divorced, and two remained single.

When possible, Black married couples in the United States strategize to keep women out of the exploitative and unequal labor market. But most Black families cannot survive without the financial contributions of Black women. Black feminists have long pointed out that the heteronormative, nuclear family maintained by men working and women taking care of the family is less accessible to Black families, largely because racial oppression has denied them sufficient resources. Even the Black middle class is more fragile than the White middle class; racism increases their susceptibility to downward mobility, compromises reproducing class status across generations, and causes income and wealth disparities (Black families have the lowest median and mean wealth of all racial and ethnic groups—less than 15 percent of White families, at $24,100 and $188,200, respectively, in 2019).[6] Therefore, the majority of Black mothers, regardless of their socioeconomic status, work outside of the home to provide for their children, including those in this study. When her children went to school full-time, sixty-nine-year-old Ida began working for a mail-order company, filling catalog orders:

I left to better myself and I always went back. There was something about Spiegel, I liked it. No boss over me. I can work as fast as I want and do what I wanted to do. . . . I was goin' back and forth to school. Learning some new trades and stuff.

During one of her hiatuses from Spiegel, Ida worked at the post office for eighteen months, one of several women in this study to do so. Similarly, eighty-one-year-old Louise worked in the public sector once all of her children were in school full-time. In 1967, she started working with the Head Start program, advancing from cook's aid to program director.

Black women participate in the labor force at higher rates than other women (except multiracial women, who also have a high labor-force participation rate).[7] Black women enter the labor market younger, continue working after marriage, and stay in the workforce longer than their White counterparts.[8] These racial differences have been driven by Black men's lower earnings and higher unemployment rates relative to White men, African Americans' lower nonlabor income (e.g., Social Security and other transfer payments associated with aging, disability, and economic hardship), a higher prevalence of female-headed households among Black people, and distinct social norms within Black and White communities about women's work.[9]

Black women as a group have labored more intensively than White women, yet they earn less. Even when considering and controlling for differences in productivity, education, industry, and occupation, studies consistently find persistent substantial differences in the racial wage gap across gender.[10] In 2019, the median annual earnings of Black women ages fifteen and older who work full-time, year-round was $43,209, compared with $53,731 for White women.[11] In 2020, the median household income for White households was $74,912, significantly higher than the $45,870 median income for Black households.[12] Since 80 percent of Black mothers are breadwinners in their families, this wage penalty[13] significantly affects Black families.[14]

Like many Black mothers, those in this study combined multiple jobs to take care of their children. Fifty-five-year-old Penny worked in customer service and sales in the nonprofit sector and insurance industry, respectively. "I worked. Maybe too much. I always had two jobs. I didn't have a college education. Get one of those and you have one job. If not, you will be working two jobs." Penny lost her job in insurance during the Great Recession of 2007. Valuing work, she took a coworker's advice and moved into private-duty carework. The care economy is one of the fastest-growing sectors of the US economy, yet wages for careworkers are not growing.[15] Careworkers are underpaid, undervalued, and underprotected, and are disproportionately African American and immigrant women.[16] Penny's experiences illustrate that while Black women working in the post–civil rights era have expanded the kinds of jobs available to them, especially among those with a college education, they continue to be oppressed by income and wealth disparities, overrepresentation in low-wage service and minimum- and sub-minimum-wage jobs, and underrepresentation in higher-paying, high-status professions (e.g., law, medicine, technology, executive, etc.).[17] Misogynoir, the unique discrimination Black women combat, significantly contributes to their occupational segregation.[18] Consequently, Black women are the only group (across race, ethnicity, and gender) more likely to work multiple jobs now than a decade ago.[19]

Given Black women's meager earnings and their families' reliance on their wages, it isn't surprising that when mothers are unable to rely on their incomes or a partner to make ends meet, they rely on or supplement their earnings with public assistance. Any resistance to taking a "handout" eventually waned as the mothers in my research were simply unable to survive on their earnings. Even women who had worked full-time for most, if not all, of their adulthood used subsidized housing or welfare at some point over the course of their motherhood. They combined work, public assistance, and financial support from a partner to survive, a strategy that recent scholarship indicates some Black mothers continue to use.[20] However, there is an important distinction between my research on grandmothers and research on recent generations of Black mothers: Most, though not all, of the mothers in my study who used public assistance did so before welfare reform and obtained Section 8 and other forms of subsidized housing before the freeze and wholesale decline of place-based subsidized housing. Some accessed welfare during the "man in the house" rules, which prevented adult males from residing with mothers and children who were receiving assistance.[21]

Although Black mothers are stigmatized for staying home with their children and relying on public assistance, some single mothers, like seventy-four-year-old Marian, did so anyway—aware that when choosing between avoiding punitive and dehumanizing social welfare policies and practices and providing for their children, being a good mother meant choosing the latter.

> I didn't want to get on aid because there's such a stigma attached. . . . But I swallowed my pride, quit my job, went down on 63rd and Cottage Grove. And the aid worker treated me like I was a dog. She could not believe that all of my children had the same father. . . . Each time she would ask for my baby's name and who's the father. . . . I was not treated very kindly. I did get the food stamps. And I did get a stipend. And back in that day, every month you had to fill out a form in order to continue to get food stamps and it was about six pages long. But I did it for two years because I knew I wasn't going to stay on it. That was a means to an end.

While Marian's experience occurred "back in that day," the paternalistic and punitive regulations associated with social welfare policy continue to plague the experiences of Black mothers needing formal support, including the increasing use of technology to intertwine the social welfare and criminal justice systems.[22]

Finding and Maintaining Housing

Black mothers must make particularly difficult choices about the best way to "keep a roof" over their children's heads, as they experience several housing constraints not experienced by other mothers. Consequently, in seeking to provide their children with the best housing and neighborhoods they can afford, some mothers I interviewed lived in multigenerational households with parents or other relatives, either permanently or until they could afford their own housing. Others lived in subsidized housing or relied on public assistance to offset the gap between the high cost of living and their earnings. All mothers based their housing decisions on several factors, such as affordability, safety, proximity to their social support systems, and the ability to provide their children access to cultural capital (e.g., educational and extracurricular opportunities). Black mothers across generations, including those in this study, contend with the negative impact of residential segregation and high-poverty neighborhoods on their ability to raise successful children. The stories and sociological context that follow contribute to research demonstrating how residential environments influence family outcomes.[23]

BLACK MOTHERING IN THE THROES OF SEGREGATED HOUSING

African Americans experience unprecedented and unique residential segregation and isolation. Black people are more segregated from White people than are Latinos, Asian Americans, and American Indians/Alaska Natives (Black-White segregation at the national level was 62 in 2019).[24] Moreover, Latinos, Asian Americans, and American Indians/Alaska Natives are highly segregated from African Americans.[25] Therefore, Black mothers are more likely than other mothers to raise their children in segregated neighborhoods. Predominantly Black neighborhoods, even if they are relatively advantaged, are unique in the degree to which they are spatially linked with communities of severe concentrated disadvantage.[26] What this means for Black mothers raising their children in predominantly Black neighborhoods is that even for nonpoor families, "they live in neighborhoods with lower socioeconomic status, higher crime, lower property values, more pollution, and more physical blight than whites with similar economic status."[27] Consequently, their children and partners are more likely than their White counterparts to experience the negative effects of residential segregation, including (1) being victims of violent, property, and drug-related crimes,[28] (2) participating in gang and criminal activity,[29] (3) being involved in the child welfare, criminal justice, and juvenile justice systems, (4) experiencing family disruption, joblessness, and disparities in health and health care, and (5) achieving lower levels of educational attainment.[30]

By the time Ida, Louise, and Marian arrived in Chicago, racial residential segregation and isolation had become a permanent structural feature of American cities. A number of housing policies and practices combined to produce residential segregation and isolation throughout the country, including those that created and perpetuated racial and economic zoning, redlining, white flight, and white fight.[31] Redlining was the direct result of intentional government policy refusing to back mortgages in areas they deemed economically hazardous, mapping out these "risky," mostly inner-city Black neighborhoods in red.[32] Prospective home buyers in a redlined neighborhood were universally denied mortgages, regardless of their financial qualifications. Between 1934 and 1962, the federal government backed $120 billion in home loans, with less than 2 percent going to non-Whites.[33] Racist housing policies and practices produced a racial suburbanization of America and forced Black people into a small number of city and suburban neighborhoods, spurring and accelerating racial residential segregation and isolation.

Chicago is among the worst cities in the country for racial residential segregation and isolation, those conditions worsening as Ida, Louise, Marian, and Penny raised their children. Between 1950 and 1970, Chicago saw an increase in its Black population from 14 to 33 percent.[34] Even as the ghetto swelled, residential segregation of Black people was perpetuated,[35] the ghetto expanding only within the city's South and West Side.[36] In 1930, the Black isolation index for Chicago was 70.4, and by 1970, it was 89.2.[37] When the Great Migration began in 1910, the Black-White segregation index in Chicago was 67, and by the time it ended in 1970, it was 92.[38]

When Ida came to Chicago in 1953 from Birmingham, Alabama, her family lived across from Englewood High School, which she attended. When she was twenty, she married U.Z., a kind, quiet man who had supported his family by working in industry. The newlyweds settled in West Englewood, a neighborhood with a small Black population dating back to the antebellum era. Their experience typified the pattern of White resistance many Black families encountered as they expanded the Chicago Black Belt through integration. Ida and U.Z. wanted to move in 1966, a year before they actually did, but they worried about racial violence and hostility. According to Ida, they moved "when they stopped fightin' and burning down garages and running people back out."

"There wasn't too many of us when we came here," she recalled. "The girl over here [a neighbor], she came in October. We came in November [1967] . . . it was a Puerto Rican family lived over there and one over here." It did not take long for their White neighbors to flock to the suburbs and for the shopping malls, Southtown Theater, Sears, Wieboldt's department store, and other businesses to permanently close their doors. "All the Black businesses we had; I mean gone. You can't get it back no more. And the

Black entertainment places. You can't get it back no more." In 1970, African Americans made up 48 percent of the residents in West Englewood. By 1980, it had risen to 98 percent—demonstrating the magnitude and expedience of white flight.[39] And to this day, West Englewood and Englewood remain predominantly Black.[40] Ida's experience of West Englewood's devolution mirrors research findings—it wasn't just that white flight was associated with White families and businesses moving to the suburbs in response to the changing racial composition of central cities,[41] it was what happened when African Americans lived in segregated neighborhoods. "They [couldn't] get home loans . . . they [didn't] have a decent tax base, there are no jobs. And then that [became] associated with Black space."[42]

"There wasn't no trouble until the gang members moved here," Ida said, recalling the exact moment in 1973, one Sunday when she looked out her window and "all hell start breakin' loose. . . . Cars was everywhere, all down there, all up our street." Thinking it was a funeral procession, she called her sister to ask who had died. But the cars lined up near the playground where her two young children played were there to buy drugs.

> I go, "Oh my God. Now, where the police at now?" See, they get the word where to go, 'cause I understand that people are comin' from the way north side, west side, suburbs. Comin' to certain areas to get their stuff. So now you can see where in a nicer neighborhood, where they don't have this stuff goin' on, they know where to go, and the poor neighborhood, to make it poor, to get the drugs. Now, the police know all this stuff goin' on. See, so every once in a while, they'll do a raid. What good is a raid? They go to jail for a few minutes, then they come out. But to get to the big person, they ain't tryin' to do that. Because that's big money.

As Ida astutely observed, the presence of open-air drug markets, where sellers and buyers do not know one another, not only fueled drug addiction and dealing in communities like hers, but impoverished her once working- and middle-class neighborhood—driving out businesses and residents.

Open-air drug markets are overrepresented in Black space and are used to justify overpolicing and punitive criminal justice policies and practices. The drugs responsible for turning Ida and U.Z.'s previously "nice," "quiet" neighborhood into an open-air, high-volume drug market were heroin in the 1970s and, in the mid-1980s through the 1990s, crack cocaine, both epidemics disproportionately affecting African Americans. When Ida explained that the criminal justice system was more likely to target low-level offenders than go after "the big person," she was referencing the dramatic uptick in Black incarceration rates associated with the "war on drugs" declared in 1971 by President Nixon, who dramatically increased the size and presence of federal drug control agencies and implemented measures such as mandatory sentencing and no-knock warrants. In 1986, the Reagan administration passed the notorious Anti-Drug Abuse Act, setting penalties one hundred times harsher for crack than for powder cocaine and imposing mandatory-minimum sentences. A person caught with 50 grams of crack would be sentenced to ten years in prison. For cocaine, the equivalent would be the possession of 5,000 grams.[43] The Anti-Drug Abuse Act also allocated millions of dollars to build prisons and invest in law enforcement.[44] Subsequently, the United States has the highest per capita incarceration rate in the world—due largely to racial disparities in drug penalties: the war on drugs has been waged disproportionately against African Americans despite similar rates of drug use and dealing to White Americans.[45]

Ida's son, Peter, was twenty-two when he and his girlfriend left home to go to the corner store on an errand for his mother and never returned. "He got shot in the back—him and his girlfriend. . . . They thought he was somebody else. The girl knew the guy that shot 'cause they shot her too." Ida recalled learning of Peter's murder from someone saying they'd seen it on the news.

> I got to the door, I just fell off. I couldn't go no further. I didn't see him. I just couldn't take it, so my neighbor was livin' over there, I don't know how she got over here. . . . But she said I was tryin' to go through the window up there. And so she grabbed me and they kept me from the hospital. But my husband and my daughter went to see if that was him.

This working-class family that did everything "right" except raise their two children in the "right" neighborhood lost their only son. "He would have been fifty," Ida said, still grieving after twenty-eight years. She hadn't recovered, but coped by thinking about her son as "being on vacation somewhere. 'Cause when I do think about it I cry." Black mothers deal with traumatic loss in myriad ways. Some verbalize and take action, adjudicating their grievances by making claims against the state (e.g., in instances of police brutality), while others express grief privately. Performance arts professor Rhaisa Williams distinguishes Black maternal grievance from grief, arguing that "grief is the incommunicable and often illegible underside to the verbalized, action-based, and adjudicating grievance."[46] It was grief, not grievance, that often characterized the mourning of Ida and other mothers who lost their children to the streets.

Ida and U.Z. demonstrate the spatial and economic organization of residential segregation and concentrated urban poverty. They were drawn to West Englewood because it was affordable and close to Ida's family, and because they liked the location (Chicago's mid–South Side) and housing stock. They could not control that their once "nice" neighborhood was now characterized by high poverty rates, unrelenting gunfire, turf wars, gang leaders arming children with sawed-off shotguns, and helicopters hovering overhead exhorting residents to "Go in the house! Go in the house!" Ida pointed out the house directly across the street, where her neighbor was shot while on his front porch, then the one next door, where "they beat him [a different neighbor] and threw him over the banister." The crime and violence drove her neighbors indoors, or worse, out of the neighborhood entirely, though many were assaulted, robbed, and murdered before they could do so. Her story panned out in facts: between 1980 and 1990, Englewood and West Englewood lost more than 20,000 residents combined.[47] With little to no recourse, Ida watched as her neighbors, who once sat on their front porches socializing and keeping watch over their community, abandoned their posts.

> I look at my neighbors, they in the house, they don't come out. . . . Come outside, sit on your porch. When I walk down the street, I wanna see somebody, if you missin', then I can see, "Have you seen Miss So-and-So, have you seen Mr. So-and-So. So we can get somebody to check on you." . . . I said, "Put the porch light on." That light right there is not enough . . . because I can sit here and nobody see me. But I put my porch light on, they [drug dealers] won't be out in front of my house, and my gate, on my porch.

Crime and disorder weaken social control, defined as "the effort of the community to regulate itself and the behavior of residents and visitors to the neighborhood,"[48] and diminish social capital, the capacity of social net-works and relationships to achieve important goals through connections to others. By living in or near concentrated poverty, Black mothers face threats to the social capital they and others work so hard to cultivate. As West Englewood became one of the most crime-ridden and impoverished neigh-borhoods in the Chicago area, Ida and U.Z. experienced firsthand the ero-sion of social capital through social isolation, alienation, and loss of life.

Ida, now sixty-nine, and U.Z. had been married for forty-nine years and were the backbone of their large extended family and for their "one daugh-ter, four grandkids, eleven great-grandkids, and one great, great grand." Asked if she ever considered moving, Ida replied, "This is my home. I put a lot into this place. . . . I got a little garden back there. You know, my flowers. . . . We done put all this in here. *You* go home," she said, meaning all the bad elements in Englewood: the dope dealers, gang bangers, and aggressive police. "I'm not goin' nowhere that I don't have to."

Marian's experience in Hyde Park provides a stark contrast to Ida and U.Z.'s experience of expanding the Chicago Black Belt in the 1960s by inte-grating historically White neighborhoods. When Marian and her husband moved to Chicago in the 1960s, she got a job as an administrative assistant in higher education and helped take care of their family. The middle-class couple and their five children moved to Hyde Park, which was once exclu-sively White, despite its proximity to the Black Belt. Supported by the University of Chicago, Hyde Park relied on racially restrictive covenants and urban renewal projects to keep African Americans out. According to the University of Chicago "Guide to the Hyde Park Historical Society Collection 1830–2009," these racist housing policies and practices sought to counteract the cycle of integration, white flight, and economic depression that materialized in other parts of the Chicago Black Belt. After the plan was carried out, Hyde Park's average income soared by 70 percent, and Black people unable to afford the newly rehabilitated areas left.

When Marian and her husband divorced, they became part of another national trend. Although the number of Black and White divorced women increased between 1940 and 1980, the increase occurred sooner and more steeply for Black women.[49] When Marian's marriage dissolved, she had five children to raise on her own and identified her husband's failing to provide financial support as a significant life event.

It wasn't emotional, but it left me in a crunch in terms of resources. I had to make decisions on how we were going to survive. And for a minute, that was kind of stressful. But my brothers stepped in and told me as long as they were there, I had no reason to worry about anything. And I didn't.

Like other mothers in this study, Marian's social support system helped with child-rearing.

When she appeared before the judge for her divorce, he was willing to expedite public housing for her.

Because I had so many children . . . he [the judge] said, "You can't afford to pay a mortgage and keep your kids in private school and live the lifestyle you're living. So I'll make you an emergency stay so you can move into public housing." And I told him, "No thank you." And he said, "How are you going to survive?" I said, "I'll work two and three jobs." And that's what I did.

Marian understood that location influences life chances and that raising her children in concentrated poverty would deprive them of adequate schooling, neighborhood safety, and social networks.

"I tried working two jobs. Actually three. And I fell out on one job and they took me to the emergency room and the doctor said, 'There's nothing wrong with you, other than you are just exhausted.'" After this incident, Marian adjusted to "taking a handout" when she realized she could not do it all on her own. She knew that if she wanted to truly get ahead, she would need to complete her education, and eventually used public assistance to attend school full-time and get her bachelor's degree. Later, she obtained a master's degree and she was ABD (all but dissertation) in her PhD program at the time of this interview. Although she experienced varying socioeconomic statuses, Marian succeeded in keeping her children in Hyde Park. "What can I say? I raised my children there . . . the school system was decent, the community was quiet and safe. And again, all of this was by choice, having come from where I come from."

BLACK MOTHERING AMID CONCENTRATED POVERTY

As White people gained greater access to federally backed home loans, Black people gained greater access to ever-expanding public housing projects. Federal, state, and local governments solved the urban housing crisis, including reduced housing stock for the poor, in part, by building public housing almost exclusively in the central city. Gradually, high-rise public housing complexes came to be referred to as "vertical ghettos" because of their architectural design and high poverty and crime rates.

Even as poverty rates remained relatively stable in metropolitan areas, the number of people living in high-poverty neighborhoods from 1970 to 1990 nearly doubled, from over four million to eight million people.[50] High-poverty neighborhoods are those where 40 percent of households live below the federal poverty line, and a defining feature of many of the remaining 60 percent is low or very low incomes. Between 2010 and 2014, almost fourteen million people lived in concentrated poverty in neighborhoods that continue to be segregated by race.[51] Despite a decline, the percentage of Black people living in high-poverty neighborhoods since the 1980s remains seven to ten times that of White people.[52]

Black mothers and their children disproportionately bear the brunt of the negative effects of living in or near high-poverty neighborhoods, including poorer physical and mental health outcomes, lagging school performance, substance abuse and addiction, early sex and parenthood, delinquency, and violence victimization and perpetration.[53] Additionally, poor neighborhoods may lack the social organization needed to demand better child- and family-related institutions (e.g., schools, child care providers, public libraries, recreational programs and activities, parks, religious institutions, and social service providers).[54] The greater needs of families may also overtax these institutions in poor communities.[55]

Numerous interrelated systems and structural forces, including spatial changes, changes in the country's urban political economy, and the impact of neoliberalism on the state's social provisions, have contributed to the isolation and concentration of poverty in Black space. Two spatial changes that contributed to concentrated poverty include: (1) increased spatial distance between poor and middle-class African Americans caused by an increase in the size of the Black middle class,[56] and (2) a shift in public housing away from working families having difficulty finding affordable private-sector housing and toward the poorest of the poor under the 1969 Brooke Amendment. The Brooke Amendment fixed the rent that any public-housing household could pay at no more than 25 percent of its income, concentrating poverty in public housing in the process.[57]

Consequently, in 2019, American Indians/Alaska Natives and African Americans were most likely to live in high-poverty neighborhoods (23.6 percent and 20.9 percent, respectively; compared with 17 percent for Latinos and 4.3 percent for White Americans).[58]

Significant declines in Black employment have resulted from deindustrialization, job suburbanization, and racial discrimination. Black men have been especially hard hit, resulting in a significant drop in their employment rates. Conspicuous racial discrimination in the postindustrial political economy has had significant consequences, including undermining Black men's ability to take care of their families, reach the "marriage bar" (the economic standard couples set before marrying), pay child support, and escape the informal and underground economies. With the structural changes to the economy have come seemingly insurmountable barriers to economic security for Black families, including unemployment rates twice as high as those of Whites[59] and higher temporary and permanent layoff rates, especially during recessions.[60] As African Americans have struggled, they have increased reliance on the social safety net. But by increasing economic insecurity, poverty, and inequality (including not passing policies to address racial discrimination in the labor market); privatizing social welfare services; and disciplining the poor, neoliberalism in US public policy contributes to the social problems Black families face and limits the resources available to address them. It is not surprising then that in 2019, 23 percent of Black children lived in concentrated poverty compared with 3 percent of White children.[61]

Louise knew intimately the difficulties associated with raising successful children amid the concentrated poverty found in public housing. When she left Mississippi in 1953 and took the City of New Orleans train to Chicago, she was twenty-six years old and separated from her husband. Louise was raising their four children on her own:

> My brother came first and then my sister came. And my sister had got a job, she was working downtown at a place called X Manufacturing Company and she put rhinestones and nail heads on dresses and shoes and things like that.

Her brother worked on the railroad. Louise's sister helped her get a job doing "piece work" and gave her a place to live, a commonplace arrangement among Southern migrants.

When Louise met Leo, the man she would later marry, she left her sister's place. Louise and Leo had three more children and were married for over forty years. The couple raised their children in Washington Park Homes, where they moved with their seven children in order to accommodate their large family on the meager income he earned in Chicago's manufacturing industry. "It was right on the lake front. There was nothing between us and Lake Shore Drive but the railroad tracks over there. . . . It . . . was a nice building. They had a solarium on the 14th floor . . . it was enclosed; they'd have dances up there. It was real nice." When she and Leo moved into Washington Park Homes in 1963, the community featured diverse family compositions and socioeconomic statuses, and more working and married families than when they left twenty years later.

For twenty years, Louise watched her community transform into something beyond any one person's or family's ability to overcome unscathed. She remembered things changing in the 1970s, a time line consistent with the passage of the Brooke Amendment to the National Housing Act. While construction of public housing was subsidized by the government, the day-to-day operations were supported by tenant rents. By the mid-1980s, tenant rent covered only 43 percent of public housing operating costs, down from 95 percent.[62] Louise was there when the Chicago Housing Authority (CHA) changed renter qualifications: "At one time they'd take any and everybody in CHA. They got where they had this law that said you had to take everybody regardless of what kind of background they had." CHA mismanagement and the withdrawal of resources also contributed to the demise of Chicago public housing.

> At first you could get your stoves or refrigerators when you needed 'em. Then it got to where it was kinda impossible to get a stove and a refrigerator. . . . They just didn't care whether you had one or not. Because see, they got to the attitude that you needed to buy. You needed to buy you a stove and a refrigerator and not worry them.

She was there when the gang violence spread and public housing complexes were flooded with drugs.

> They threw a boy out the window over there on . . . the 14th floor I think it was. . . . Them niggas was bad in all them buildings. The gang members and

things. . . . And it was a rivalry between them and them over there in the projects where I used to work.

Living amid gang activities became commonplace for many public housing residents, and the combination of gang violence, drug activity, a shift in residents' demographic makeup, and shrinking resources and services accelerated the decline of public housing projects not only in Chicago but also nationally.

Louise responded with activist mothering, defined as collective survival through community mothering practices.[63] She worked with the CHA in various capacities, including in the Community and Tenant Relations Aid program, which gave her and other tenants a vehicle for improving their communities: "A community tenant relations aide . . . is really [doing] social work because, see, you work with the families and the seniors and whoever. And your job is, like, to get the services for the people, families, that you work with." In her capacity as president of her building, she knew "all the presidents from all over CHA." She was also "on the advisory council at Washington Park."

Still, despite her efforts and those of other activist mothers, Washington Park continued to experience rapid decline. And, like so many other public housing residents, Louise and Leo were displaced by neighborhood deterioration. Due to disrepair, Louise and Leo's building was vacated in 1985, when seven hundred other families living in public housing were told by then CHA executive director Zirl Smith that they would be moved into other South Side CHA developments, rent-subsidized apartments in the private housing market, or nonsubsidized private-sector units.[64] But, according to Louise, it didn't happen like that: "They said they was gonna renovate the building and if anybody wanted to move back they could move back. But it wasn't like that. See we were out of the building from '85 until '90. I think it was eight or '99 or something when they imploded 'em." Louise, now eighty-one, and Leo used his retirement funds to buy a home. Although it would reduce the amount they had to live on in old age, they were still in a better position than most people dislocated through forced relocations during rehabilitation of deteriorated apartments and buildings as well as poverty deconcentration programs.[65]

These structural challenges to securing stable housing in safe communities profoundly shape Black mothering. The ability of Black mothers to meet their families' need for housing is impinged on by residential segregation and the concentration of poverty—deep structural inequalities resulting from decades of racially unequal housing policy, lending practices, and urban renewal strategies, and the private and public institutional strategies that enact them at every level of society in the United States.

PREPARING AND PROTECTING THEIR CHILDREN

Not only do neighborhoods affect parenting behavior (e.g., degree of punitiveness and authoritarianism, use of corporal punishment) and family dynamics, but parents and families also act as mediators between children and neighborhood environments.[66] Racism, poverty, and exposure to violence force Black mothers to combine preparing their children for success with protecting them from anti-Black racism and the streets. While church served a similar function for the majority of mothers, women in this study unanimously agreed that education was central to their children's ability to achieve success in adulthood, which is consistent with previous research that shows that, regardless of their socioeconomic status, African Americans highly value education.[67] Therefore, mothers used any resources at their disposal to keep their children in school and support their education. The most common practices were involvement at their children's schools, requiring homework before playtime, demanding school attendance and compliance with school rules, and strategizing to enroll their children in early and special needs education programs. Mothers also resorted to "stealing school" and forced their children to adhere to court-ordered school for truancy. In addition to using "conflict-anticipated" parenting to ensure that their children "got an education," mothers protected them by sending them "down South" during the summers so that children weren't left unattended during the workday. They confronted gang members directly when their children had run-ins with gangs. Others moved when their children, mostly sons, were pursued, harassed, and assaulted by gang members. And when her son was repeatedly "jumped" (beaten by gang members), one mother living in CHA housing

pursued and was granted Section 8 through the Victim Assistance program and was able to relocate. Mothers also kept their children in extracurricular activities, including sports, beauty pageants, and activities at
the local YMCA and with Big Brothers, Big Sisters.

To protect her children from anti-Black racism and the streets, and prepare them for success, Marian exemplified a culture-promoting, conflict-
anticipating parenting style—a style that psychology professor Jennifer
Rious and colleagues associate with high-warmth, high-cultural socialization, and high "hostility."[68] They argue that the intent and meanings of
socialization practices in some African American families may contravene
traditional definitions of "hostility" within parenting literature. Since culture determines what children perceive as "hostility," and it is different for
Black families than for other demographic groups, Rious and colleagues
reframe "hostility" as "conflict-anticipated." They found that Black adolescents who demonstrated the most favorable outcomes were those who
experienced this parenting style, perceiving that "their parents often demonstrate affection and care, while also engaging in strategies that include
criticism, threats, and cursing."[69] They also reported that their parents
frequently engaged in practices that foster racial pride.

As a single mother, Marian used this style to raise not just successful
children but three successful sons.

> Because my children grew up . . . in a time when they said, "A woman can't
> raise no boys, they going to end up in jail, on dope, or whatever." No they
> didn't, every last one of them went to college, because I was crazier than
> them. "You going to do what I say, when I say do it, or else I'm gonna kill you."

Marian's story spotlights the role of the child's gender in shaping mothers'
strategies. As a single parent of Black boys, she knew that she had to be
firm and demonstrate that she was willing to be even "crazier than them"
if and when they challenged her. Since the rate at which African Americans
are killed by police is more than twice as high as the rate for White
Americans,[70] and an overwhelming majority of people shot and killed by
police are male, Black mothers understood all too well the hypercriminali-
zation of Black boys and men. Consequently, they feared losing their sons
to the streets and to police violence. Interviews for this study were con-

ducted before the 2020 Black Lives Matter protest in response to the killing of George Floyd. And, although I did not focus explicitly on the racial-
socialization strategies mothers used to protect their sons from police
violence, they consistently shared that demanding compliance and respect
at home would teach compliance and respect in their interactions with
law enforcement, educators, and authority figures. This finding is consistent with other research on racial socialization of Black boys, which stresses
teaching them how to interact with police and how to present themselves
to avoid being stereotyped as a criminal or a "thug."[71]

Gender also affected mothers' treatment of male and female children,
in general, giving their sons more leeway to spend time outside of the
home. They kept tabs on them, but not as they did daughters, whom they
watched more closely and kept closer to the home front. When their own
efforts to manage behavioral issues failed, and mothers felt they needed a
male influence, they sent their adolescent sons to live with fathers who'd
been involved in their child's upbringing, and even those who had not.
Marian and other mothers also relied on their brothers, fathers, and other
men to serve this function.

Ida and U.Z. combined preparing their children for success and protecting them from anti-Black racism and the streets by transferring them
to a school in their maternal grandmother's neighborhood. As already discussed, stealing school is illegal. However, some parents in poor communities with inferior schools use it to improve educational outcomes for
their children. Ida and U.Z. were two such parents. Peter's being relent-
lessly pursued by the gangs that had taken over their community was Ida
and U.Z.'s primary motivation for transferring their son and daughter to a
different school. Peter had been beaten up many times for refusing to join
a gang—once, three times in one day.

> I had to transfer him from school. They [her children's] grades was goin'
> down. . . . Transferred 'em over by my mama house 'cause my mother lived
> across the street from the school. They grades popped up. . . . And some
> young man was in the class with my daughter, he had moved over this way,
> and told the teachers. . . . That teacher called my house, she said, . . . "You
> lied. They don't live here and they automatically being transferred back to
> Dewey." Well, there wasn't nothin' I could do.

Ida and U.Z. saw their children's grades plummet, improve, and plummet again.

> They went back [to their former school], they grades dropped back down. And it was so bad. Gang over here. Gang over there. The kids can't go nowhere. You know? Just like now, it's chaos now. These kids get shot. . . . If you in one [gang] you gonna be shot. If you not in one you get shot. They go around shootin', shootin'. The new kids comin' in fresh and they tryin' to take over someone territory. And it's just a mess.

Other than moving out of the neighborhood, teaching their children to stay clear of the gangs, and to stand up for themselves if somebody put their hands on them, there was little Ida and U.Z. could do to protect them.

Ida also illustrated mothers' involvement with their children's education, by "staying at" her children's school (meaning being present frequently) and by being on the school council. Even after her children were no longer in school, Ida continued these activities for the children in her community (another example of activist mothering): "I love kids. I love school. My first thing is, I love school. I didn't get to go to college. I took my nephew in and that took away my college stuff."

Mothers like Ida in this study went to great lengths to feed their children's educational needs, driven to address the imbalance between the education their children received and that received by White children. But Louise's story about the difficulty she and her husband had getting their youngest son, Al, to attend school demonstrated that mothers' efforts weren't always successful. Louise would make sure Al had "car fare and lunch money to go off to school. . . . At that time see they had truant officers in the school. . . . When I did go to court, the nigga had missed eighty-nine days in school." Louise later learned that Al was taking letters from the school out of the mailbox.

> So I went out there to court, it was up to Northeastern Illinois University. They had a center up there for juveniles. Okay. They sent him up there. . . . It was a school where they sent the kids with behavior problems. . . . You stayed a month before you could come out. See, you didn't visit, nobody visited you, and you couldn't come out. He must've been about twelve or fourteen or something.

When she couldn't make Al attend school, where she knew he would be safe, she took comfort in him being somewhere where she didn't have to "worry" about him.

In addition to ensuring their children's education, mothers tried to model the pursuit and prioritization of their own education. Many had grown up in families with parents and caregivers who had limited formal education, but nevertheless had stressed pursuing higher learning. So, for example, Marian used her public assistance to attend school full-time, taking her youngest child to class with her. Similarly, once her children were in school all day, Louise worked and attended college, majoring in family welfare and completing continuing education courses that allowed her to "learn how to work with the families and things." She later got a master's and doctorate in religious education. Ida's caregiving responsibilities took her away from "goin' for my own business degree and stuff like that. But I want to go do my little four years." And yet, she still found ways to demonstrate her love for learning. Penny, like Ida, did not get her degree, completing four years but being credited only "a year and a half of college" because of her intermittent enrollment. For Marian, Louise, and other mothers, the emphasis was not on just getting an education, but on using that education in service to the Black community, and on modeling the value of education to their children.

MOTHERS' PERCEPTIONS OF ADULT CHILDREN'S STRUGGLES

Despite the creative tactics of these mothers to meet their children's needs, and their sustained efforts to prepare their children for success and protect them from countless racial structural inequities, many saw one or more of their adult children struggle with life in general, and in their own roles as parents in particular. This section examines how Black mothers perceive and explain these adult children's struggles. These mothers interpret their adult children's parenting by providing context to their children's experiences, weighing the opportunities their children were (and weren't) provided, and evaluating their children's response to life's struggles and opportunities. Yet, sometimes, mothers blame themselves for their adult children's struggles.

It is important for several reasons to understand Black mothers' perceptions of their adult children. First, grandparenthood and parenthood are intertwined. How parents and grandparents perceive each other's parenting shapes the quality of their relationship in later life and the nature (e.g., access, frequency of communication) of children's relationships with their grandparents. Second, when grandparents raise their grandchildren, their assessment of their adult children's parenting affects whether grandparents facilitate or obstruct parents' participation in children's lives. Last, while structural constraints differentiate Black mothers' experiences from those of other mothers, their aspirations for their children are more similar than different; however, Black mothers and their children lack equal opportunity to fulfill those aspirations. As a result, Black mothers report higher levels of conflicting emotion toward their adult children than do White mothers.[72] Research finds that "parents of successfully launched adult children experience parental fulfillment and pride."[73] In contrast, "parents report strained relationships with children who have failed to achieve adult statuses, who are less successful, and who demand high, unreciprocated levels of support."[74] As a result, Black mothers' perceptions of their adult children's success may affect their own emotional well-being.

Ida exemplified mothers who analyzed adult children's struggles by the limits of their childhood—and in some cases adulthood—environments. Ida understood that her daughter Lola, fifty-one, was undoubtedly affected by the neighborhood she grew up in and the death of her brother. Although she grew up working class, Lola raised her four children in public housing, as a single mother. She had lived at home before she moved to the projects, and Ida blamed Lola's moving away and hiding things about "how she was living" and falling in "with the wrong people" for Lola's struggles. In other words, Ida could no longer buffer the harmful effects of the "wrong crowd" on her daughter, who was, after all, grown.

> The man she was with didn't want her to be tellin' things or whatever. But the oldest grandson told me. I went to the house one night. They lived in CHA on 35th and State Street. . . . They had no food. And I was always takin' little stuff. . . . I think the man had been stealin' the food stamps. Girl, I mean it was just somethin'. I bought her a dining room table. . . . I said, "He's no good for you and to these kids. He's stealin' from you. He's not

helpin' you bring in anything, and you can't go to work 'cause he won't help babysit." I said, "He run all your friends away."

Ida had tried unsuccessfully to intervene in her daughter's life. Lola eventually left her abusive relationship but not before developing a drug addiction; she entered a new relationship, but her fiancé had recently died. Ida's involvement with her daughter and grandchildren lessened the deleterious impact of Lola's substance addiction and abusive relationship on her four children. According to Ida, three of them were doing well. "One of 'em got two daughters, and one of 'em got two, a daughter and a son, and one of 'em got one son. So, they doin' pretty good." Unfortunately, Lola's only daughter had developed a drug addiction—it was this grand-child's child that Ida and U.Z. were parenting.

Like Ida, Louise also had to contend with the impact of concentrated poverty on her children. Despite her activist mothering, she couldn't shelter her sons from drug addiction and dealing. Neither Louise nor Leo had ever used drugs, but with drugs flooding their community, they couldn't keep them from seeping into their home, a lesson she learned from watching Al's struggle with his own drug addiction. Louise maintained that Al and some of his brothers were grown when they "went astray," and he was in his twenties when he served a couple of years in prison for drug dealing. Still, he was lucky by comparison to three of his brothers, who died of drug overdoses.

Although many mothers insisted that their children's destructive behavior emerged in adulthood, some discussed the negative influence of peers on their children's growth and development. While those associating with "the wrong crowd" shared some commonalities, such as defying parental and adult authority, and bucking social controls set by schools, churches, and other community institutions, mothers observed that, consistent with other research, gender affected children's behavior.[75] Negative peer influences for girls often meant premature sexual activity, teenage pregnancy, drug use, and dropping out of school. For boys, negative peer influence often involved truancy and illegal activity (e.g., gambling and underground-economy activities). For young women, drug use was most often associated with "bad" relationships, while for young men, it was more likely to evolve into drug dealing.

Marian typified mothers who considered their children's opportunities when assessing their adult success. She had sacrificed and made "choices" so that her children could benefit from living in Hyde Park. Although Marian understood that structural inequalities exist, she vehemently believed in individual agency, as demonstrated by the good choices she expected her children to make. She held high expectations and relied on culture-promoting, conflict-anticipating parenting strategies, and her five children lived up to those expectations. Marian insisted that she did not do this alone—her two brothers helped.

While Marian's adult children achieved as much as or more than she did, this wasn't the case for all mothers who assessed adult children's outcomes through this frame. These mothers struggled to understand the ways in which their adult children were not taking full advantage of opportunities. Sociology professor Mary Pattillo's work on Black middle-class families that live near high-poverty neighborhoods informs the ways in which "family strategies and circumstances interact with neighborhood options."[76] Like the parents in Pattillo's study, those in mine parented children who confronted "a diversity of local lifestyles," including "street" and "decent" culture in their neighborhoods and families. Nevertheless, some parents in my study refused to absolve their children of personal responsibility, even after considering the larger environment in which their children came of age.

In considering contributors to her daughter's struggles, Penny vacillated between her children's opportunities and her role. Penny and her two siblings were born and raised on Chicago's South Side by her single mother. Although her mother had obtained a master's degree, the furthest it took her was to a supervisory position at the post office. Still, it afforded her family a middle-class lifestyle—something that Penny had been unable to reproduce for her own family. Citing conflict with her mother, Penny left home immediately after high school and had five children, her first child with her husband, "right out of high school," and, during their seven-year marriage, one more child. When that relationship ended in the 1980s, Penny entered a nine-year relationship with the father of her third child, but never married. Her second marriage, to the father of her last two children, lasted a few years. Despite her relationship ups and downs, it was important to Penny to "give" her children both parents, as she had been raised without her father—in fact, she outstayed troubled relationships to keep her family intact. Penny was raised with the ethos: "You do your job, you take care of your family. . . . I . . . lived my whole life around my children. I went to work [full-time] and took care of my kids." The working-class mother relied on formal childcare to manage her work and family responsibilities.

As her children got older and her relationship faltered, Penny decided to leave Chicago for Atlanta: "Originally, I . . . was running away from a bad relationship. I know I'm grown, but I didn't know how to react to a bad relationship, so run. Get out of here because I didn't want to be in anything that was going to hurt me." Leaving her middle daughter in Chicago with the child's father to finish her last year of high school, she took her two youngest children and joined her oldest daughter in Atlanta. But this daughter was displaced from the dilapidated apartment complex she lived in when it was condemned, and Penny and her two youngest children moved into a shelter. Section 8 provided the footing she needed to stabilize her housing again. A subprime home loan[77] provided leverage to upgrade her housing:

> An opportunity came available for me to buy a house, and this is when they were doing the subprime, the stuff that's causing everybody to lose their house now. But I was able to buy it when I really didn't qualify, but a house is a house is a house is a house. So I took the opportunity and got the house.

Penny left her home to her children (they paid the rent) and returned to Chicago to care for her mother, who had Alzheimer's disease.

One of Penny's daughters, whom she described as a "pleaser" and a "cooperative passive child," had been in and out of jail over a four-year period. She was "an all 'A' student" who, on having children, lived with Penny in a multigenerational household before ending up in a toxic intimate relationship. Penny struggled to make sense of this outcome:

> So I'm lost. . . . I don't know where it broke down. She lived with me with the kids. I accepted her. I accepted them. We worked together to help her build her family. I enjoyed her family. I never made her feel like "you're not welcome." The encouragement was there. Do whatever you think you need to do, but let's go get you in school. . . . I know you know better than this and

why ain't you doing better than this?. . . What is that assault behavior? I didn't raise you with that, so I don't accept that this is how I am. . . . I kept you safe. I kept you in school. I kept you where these things wouldn't come to you, so when did this come to you? I can't account.

As Penny was forced by her daughter's behavior to raise another generation, she began to question her own parenting, even turning toward self-blame:

I think maybe if I was a good mom in the first place, I wouldn't have them [her grandchildren]. My own daughter would be doing what she's supposed to be doing with her kids. So I'm afraid to mess up another generation. I don't want to raise my grandchildren.

To sum up then, Black mothers' analyses of their adult children's struggles typically situated their family experiences in the larger milieu of multiple and systemic forms of oppression. They identified neighborhood disadvantage, specifically "the wrong crowd" and negative influences (e.g., open-air drug markets, gang violence), as well as the demands of combining work and child-rearing as culprits in undermining their ability to produce more successful family outcomes. Mothers who were inclined to weigh the opportunities provided by them (and others) to their children, considered the building blocks their children were given to succeed, including a quality education, a decent neighborhood, and a religious or moral foundation. These mothers expected their adult children to achieve as much as or more than they had. When children fell short, these women blamed their children's individual failure, specifically, their own poor choices and priorities. Mothers who prioritized how their family responded to what happened to them expected their children to function to the best of their capabilities and to persevere in the face of struggle. When their children faltered and did not rebound, depending on the reason, mothers expressed understanding and compassion. They also were inclined to feel that their own mothers "did the best she could." Finally, some mothers' past experiences with domestic violence, the underground economy, and an inability to prioritize their children in the face of work, intimate relationships, or personal struggles led them to take responsibility for their influence on their adult children.

CONCLUSION

The women in this study shed light on the richness and complexity of Black motherhood, providing a glimpse of "the core of Black family life" and "their essential character."[78] At this core are women like Louise, who raised her children in the projects because they were affordable for Black parents experiencing residential segregation and racial earning disparities in the 1960s. Louise lost some of her children to the streets. But it didn't stop her from being an activist mother and obtaining a PhD to improve her community for all Black families. At this core are women like Marian, who pivoted from getting divorced and, for a finite period, using welfare to raise five children to completing her bachelor's degree and creating the financial stability necessary to keep her children in a middle-class neighborhood. This single mother raised four Black sons and was willing to be "crazier" than they were to ensure that they attended college. At this core are women like Ida, who, with her husband, was able to integrate a historically White neighborhood and raise her children in a solid working-class family. As her community experienced white flight and became one of the most notoriously dangerous neighborhoods in the city, Ida protected her son Peter from gangs, drug use, or drug dealing. And when she lost him to a mistaken-identity murder, she channeled that grief into an even greater desire to change her community through activist mothering by pressuring state and local governments to pass laws and policies to address systemic racism. At this core are women like Penny, who tried to give her five children two parents even as her heart swelled and broke in time-limited intimate relationships. Penny, who captured the essential character of most Black families in stating "you do your job, you take care of your family."

Like their historic counterparts, Black mothers continue to experience significant disparities in income, wealth, and housing, despite how hard they labor. So, it isn't surprising that they are overrepresented among the poor, those using public assistance, and incarcerated women. Indeed, that fact is more of an indictment of America and misogynoir than of Black mothers.

These beleaguered but indomitable women use various parenting strategies to prepare their children for success and protect them from the world beyond their front doors. Ensuring their children's education enabled the mothers in this study to blend these two aspirations. While they used commonplace strategies (e.g., homework before playtime, staying involved at a child's school), they were driven to greater lengths by racism, poverty, and violence to support their children's educational success, including stealing school and supporting sending their children to truancy school.

And, like all parents, Black mothers must reckon with their role in shaping their children's lives—their early intimate relationships and motherhood, their fragile and sometimes violent marriages/partnerships and divorce, and their own personal struggles (e.g., substance addiction). Nevertheless, this reckoning cannot be divorced from the forces shaping Black family life in America, not to mention the controlling images that have long been associated with Black motherhood. For the majority of the women I interviewed, these realities and myths complicated that reckoning. Even those, like Marian, who weighed their adult children's opportunities and expected that their children achieve as much as or more than they had understood that "as much as or more" had a different meaning for White adult children, who had less to overcome. On the one hand, these mothers' meritocratic ideals were tempered by the realities of systemic racism; on the other hand, they were complicated by these women's belief that their adult children could achieve a modicum of success *because* of what they had been given by their parents and others, and because of the way paved for them. These mothers were unwilling to acknowledge the harmful impact of the environment in which their children came of age, feeling that they had inched up the starting line—an advantage that was not accessible to all African Americans. Indeed, raising children in concentrated poverty impairs socioeconomic mobility regardless of how hard a parent fights—a finding from this and other studies. Raising children in concentrated poverty also comes with immense grief, a feeling these mothers understood intimately and that is a defining feature of Black mothering.

It is important to note that the grief is not confined to what happens to their children in Black space; it follows Black mothers everywhere that their children's Black bodies take them in America. Everywhere that anti-Black racism manifests in their children's premature and violent deaths at the hands of police and White vigilantes and racists, the burden of this grief falls overwhelmingly to Black mothers. It is not surprising, then, that Black mothers must articulate their grief through grievance—an attempt to seek judicial redress.[79]

Black mothers like Mamie Till-Mobley demonstrated this grievance when she insisted on speaking out about her son Emmett's death at the hands of White racists and on an open-casket funeral, avowing, "I wanted the world to see what they did to my baby." After Emmett's death, Mamie continued a life of activism.

Black mothers like Lezley McSpadden articulated grievance when she was stirred to activism after her son Michael Brown was murdered by a police officer in Ferguson, Missouri, moving then-nascent Black Lives Matter solidly into national consciousness as a social movement. Black Lives Matter protests and Lezley's continued activism called out another facet of racist policing and structural racism: fines as a way of funding police departments, and violent arrests and incarceration for unpaid fines as racial violence and racialized impoverishment. Like Mamie, Lezley shared her family's experience by writing a book and sought to change the world for other Black families by founding an organization dedicated to education, justice, health, and family.

And finally, Black mothers like Gwen Carr expressed this grievance by relentless protesting to end state-sanctioned violence on losing her son, Eric Garner, to police violence in Staten Island, New York. Although George Floyd's mother had passed, Gwen stepped up to speak on her behalf.

None of these mothers got justice for the murder of their children. Yet they did not stop pursuing it, demonstrating that motherhood doesn't end when children die. Black mothering too often necessitates speaking and acting for both the living and the dead: for the living, so that no mother has to experience losing her child to state-sanctioned violence; for the dead, as they keep their children's memories alive.

Black mothers have long been iconic leading voices of protest against state-sanctioned violence directed at their children, speaking out publicly to catalyze protest, insist on structural change, and challenge the demonizing narratives that are circulated to blame Black people for the violence they experience—and that seek to legitimize the behavior of police, White racists, and so on. Black mothers have spoken at vital moments when protests and social movement come together, resulting in a shift in national consciousness around state-sanctioned violence in all its forms. When they do, they shape the narrative and appeal to the consciousness of all mothers in their insistence that "these children belonged to somebody!" "This was somebody's child!"

Black mothers like Mamie, Lezley, Gwen, Ida, Marian, Louise, and Penny speak and act in support of other grieving mothers who have lost their children to state-sanctioned violence, be it to police brutality or to "the streets," especially those whose grief is incommunicable and heartrending.

2 Black Grandmothering

Like so many of the grandmothers that I interviewed, sixty-eight-year-old Otha was born and raised in the South before migrating to Chicago. Otha grew up in a close-knit family composed of her parents, five siblings, and Otha's maternal grandmother, Edna. When I asked Otha who raised her she responded, "My parents and grandmother, my mother's mother."

> My mother's mother stayed with us . . . because her and her husband like they separated when she got old. So both of them got old and in that day and time, people could just like go and separate. So they separated and at that time they wasn't giving Social Security or anything. So some of your people had to take you in.

With no income and no partner, Edna moved in with her daughter and son-in-law. As Otha pointed out, without the cushion of social security benefits, she and countless other African Americans relied on family to fill this gap in the social safety net.[1] Otha's grandmother, Edna, was sheltered and cared for by her daughter's family and she, in turn, helped raise her grandchildren.

When Otha had her first and only child at eighteen, she remained at home with her parents. She did not have a lasting relationship with her child's father and relied on her parents for housing and help with her daughter, Tammy. She left their home when she married someone else at twenty-one. When Tammy became a single mother, she remained home with her mother as she raised her three children. Otha reflected on how they managed child-rearing responsibilities together, including getting the children to childcare: "She would take them there . . . and then I would go and pick them up. Or I would go home and start dinner and she'd go and pick them up." The mother and daughter coparented in much the same way that parents divide up child-rearing responsibilities.

Otha provided parental support until her daughter's sudden death from cancer.

> I was fifty-nine years old when my daughter died. The baby just made two weeks before she passed. And the other one was four. She was forty. She had lung cancer. She went in [to the hospital] on Sunday. She died on Tuesday.

Otha knew that her daughter would "be sick" and "tired all the time" but she did not know the gravity of her illness. Tammy did not tell Otha how sick she was: "I guess because she didn't wanna worry me or whatever. But she should have told me because she knew that if she passed away where were the kids gonna go?"

Otha shifted from helping her daughter with her children to raising them on her own.

> When she passed away, they just stayed with me. But then the Public Aid told me how to get legal guardianship. But a lot of people said that I was too old, that I should have DCFS come and get them. But I wasn't gonna do that.

Otha "wasn't gonna do that" despite having other expectations for grandmothering and old age. "My sister has a senior apartment over on 48th and Western. That's what I say, 'Ooh when I retire, I'm gonna get me a senior apartment and I'm just gonna live my life like I wanna live it.'" But being a grandmother to Otha meant, among other things, caring for her grandchildren similarly to how she cared for her own child.

OTHA: I didn't want none of my grandkids that I know of out there and I not know where they are. . . . I know they're my grandchildren, but it's like they're mine. But I know who I'm raising. But that's just the way I feel from the inside. It's like I'm raising my own. . . . I mean because it has to be something that you really want to do. It can't be nothing that you feel obligated to do, because it will hurt you really bad because you'll be all frustrated, you'll be depressed and everything. . . . Because I did have the choice. I didn't have to keep them.

LASHAWNDA: What made you feel like it was something you wanted to do?

OTHA: Because I don't want my family just scattered all around and I not know where they are.

Like so many of the women with whom I spent time, Otha was part of a long succession of grandmothers who played a parent-like role in the lives of their grandchildren. She was also like other women in this study in that her formative experiences shaped her role expectations of the grandmother role. Otha anticipated supporting her daughter, Tammy, in her role as a mother. Like Otha, Tammy's relationship with the fathers of her three children was fragile. However, unlike Otha, Tammy never married or had a long-term partner with whom she could share parenting responsibilities.

When Tammy died leaving behind two small children, Otha felt like she had a "choice" about whether she wanted to raise them. Otha's decision-making shows how her decision to parent another generation was shaped not only by her role expectations, and her willingness to adjust them, but also by the meaning she associated with being a grandmother, wanting to know "where they are" and raising them "like they're mine."

This chapter examines the cultural and structural forces that shape Black women's role expectations and meanings about grandmotherhood as well as how Black grandmothers engage in both role-taking as they adhere to externally driven role expectations and role-making as they define and negotiate their own grandmothering experiences. By centering Black women's role expectations and meanings for the grandmother role, this chapter mitigates normalizing and equating parental surrogacy with Black grandmothering and shows that these women may experience parental surrogacy as coercive.

When the support needs of the parent generation make it necessary for Black grandmothers to play a larger role in the lives of their grandchildren than they anticipated, they may experience role conflict. Role conflict occurs when the anticipated role enactment of the grandmother role differs from the unanticipated role enactment of the surrogate parent role. This chapter foregrounds how Black grandmothers adjusted their role expectations and grappled with role conflict. However, while Otha was able to adjust her role expectations for grandmotherhood, not every grandmother in this study was able to do so. Most grandmothers in my study experienced parental surrogacy as coercive. Consequently, they not only experienced role conflict but also coerced mothering.

ROLE EXPECTATIONS: ANTICIPATORY RESPONSIBILITY

A voluminous body of knowledge documents Black grandmothers' long history of intensive grandmothering and their deviation from the "traditional" grandparent role as defined by White experiences and expectations.[2] Even early grandparenthood research shows that Black grandmothers' roles differed significantly from those of their White counterparts because they were more likely to resemble the role of parents, but also because they were less likely to be constrained by norms of noninterference.[3] Studies of White American and European grandparents have identified a strong norm of noninterference, meaning they should not interfere with how their children were raising their grandchildren.[4] For White grandparents, a boundary around parental authority exists. But this boundary is, if not absent, then is at the least more permeable for Black grandparents, who rarely voice fears of interference.[5]

West African antecedents and slavery blended the mother and grandmother roles in ways that influenced the normative expectation of Black grandmotherhood. Although enslaved families could not replicate their African extended families, households were often "extended" beyond the nuclear family, which was highly vulnerable to disruption. Their familiarity with operating as an extended kinship group to ensure family upkeep and survival was a protective measure for enslaved Africans against the destabilizing effects of slavery on family formation and security.

Stripped of their rights and responsibilities for their children and faced with unrelenting labor demands, enslaved parents found it difficult, if not impossible, to devote time, energy, and resources to child-rearing. Instead, they relied on a cadre of older women and othermothers to care for children. Frequently, these fictive or biological grandmothers spent more time with children than parents were allowed.[6] When parents or children were forcibly separated, orphaned children were absorbed by family members or informally adopted by older women and othermothers.

These normative expectations continued after slavery as grandparents absorbed the bulk of responsibility for single mothers and children not in their parent's care. Census data beginning in the 1880s shows that African American families are more likely to live in extended households than those of Whites because of higher rates of single parenthood and parental absence among children.[7] Even when African Americans experienced high marriage rates (which they did before the 1960s), grandmothers still played an involved role. Studies of Black family life during the Jim Crow era consistently found that Black grandparents, especially grandmothers, assumed a more parental role in their interactions with their grandchildren than their White counterparts.[8] While the interconnectedness of these roles has ensured Black family survival, it has also been identified as a source of conflict for both grandmothers and mothers.[9] While some Black grandmothers in this and other studies embraced a grandparent role characterized by intensive grandmothering or surrogate parenting, the role expectations of others were characterized by more role differentiation (clear distinctions between the parent and grandparent role) than those of their foremothers or prior generations. Although they stepped in to care for their grandchildren when the need arose, the majority of the women I interviewed resisted the use of their caring labor as a panacea to systemic and systematic oppression or as a substitute for parental and state responsibility.

Regardless of race and ethnicity, grandmothering varies by historical period, family needs, quality of intergenerational relationships, parental demographic characteristics, proximity, and characteristics of the grandmother.[10] Yet across time and circumstance, Black grandmotherhood is characterized by anticipatory responsibility, which I define as the normative role expectation that grandmothers have a sense of duty to or accountability for their grandchildren's well-being.

Anticipatory responsibility means that when a new grandchild is born the grandmother is already expecting that she will be responsible for that child. It means that those responsibilities may be broader than those assumed in White families. Women interpret their responsibility for their grandchildren in different ways, and the behaviors associated with their role enactment vary.[11] Anticipatory responsibility does not mean (even though she may) that the grandmother expects to demonstrate her sense of duty and accountability to her grandchildren by raising them. A common, and anticipated, manifestation of anticipatory responsibility among the women in this and other studies involved the provision of parental support, including emotional and instrumental support (e.g., housing, childcare assistance, transportation, cash assistance, and such).[12] Many grandmothers were also actively involved with their grandchildren because they wanted to be, not always because they needed to be. I refer to the cultivation of these kinds of relationships as "peripheral involvement." Peripheral involvement included socializing activities (e.g., attending church, playing games, cooking together, crafting, traveling, and such) and educational and informational activities (e.g., transmitting values, socializing, and teaching children their family and racial/ethnic history, and so on). Such activities vary by frequency, consistency, and forms of communication (e.g., face-to-face interaction, telephone calls).

Anticipatory responsibility differs from family obligation in that family obligation delineates the extent to which family members, regardless of family status, feel a sense of duty to assist one another and to take into account the needs and wishes of the family when making decisions.[13] In contrast, anticipatory responsibility is unique to grandmothers, whose gender, age, and family status make them more responsible for their grandchildren than any other family member, except for parents. In other words, the status obligations associated with the grandmother role compel these women to provide care in ways not experienced by other family members.

Arguably, anticipatory responsibility could characterize the grandmothering experiences of all women, since gender norms contribute to the increased likelihood of grandmothers rather than grandfathers raising or helping to raise their grandchildren. But, anticipatory responsibility takes into account historical and cultural influences on how Black grandmothers (and other racial and ethnic minorities) actualize their roles as well as the structural realities of Black family life. While intensive grandmothering is beginning to characterize the experiences of White grandmothers, making it more normative among some White women (e.g., poor White grandmothers, White grandmothers whose adult children are engaged in intensive parenting), it has long defined grandmotherhood among women of color, regardless of socioeconomic status.[14]

PARENTAL SUPPORT NEEDS THAT COMPEL BLACK GRANDMOTHERS TO BECOME SURROGATE PARENTS

In addition to the generational needs already identified in chapter 1, Black grandmothers in this study encountered three parental circumstances that, because they expose grandchildren to actual or potential maltreatment, increased grandmothers' role in their grandchildren's lives beyond their expectations: teenage and single motherhood, substance-abusing parents, and parents with their own child-mistreatment history. While low-income Black families are harder hit by these issues than their middle-class counterparts, the fragility of the Black middle class makes them more susceptible to these issues than middle-class White families.

Single and Teenage Motherhood

Today, nearly half of all US-born children will spend some part of their childhood in a single-parent or cohabiting-parent household.[15] Single motherhood not only reproduces class inequities by decreasing children's material resources but also exacerbates racial inequalities (overrepresenting Black women) and increases gender inequalities as mothers incur more child-related costs than do fathers, and fewer fathers participate in family life.[16]

Research has established that children living with single mothers may be more likely to experience maltreatment than children living in married-parent households[17] and indicates that, compared to their married peers, single mothers may be more likely to be reported to child protective services (CPS).[18] Research on fathers and child maltreatment is mixed, with some studies finding that the presence of a father in the household is a risk factor for child maltreatment (fathers are disproportionately responsible for child abuse) and others finding that father absence increases children's risk of child maltreatment.[19] Poverty is also closely tied to maltreatment among single mothers,[20] as is maternal age.[21] Teenage pregnancy has significantly decreased in the last three decades, but in 2017 was still higher among Black (27.6 per 1,000 adolescent females) and Latina (28.9) adolescents than their White counterparts (13.4).[22]

The struggles of teenage and single mothers have been well documented by qualitative and quantitative social science research, including the roles of different sources of income (e.g., low-wage work, welfare benefits) and ungenerous US work-family policies (childcare provisions, paid maternity and parental leave) in perpetuating the feminization of poverty,[23] family instability,[24] job displacement,[25] and severe housing cost burden. Research has also documented the reliance of these young and single mothers on their social support networks to mitigate the impact of these difficulties on their parenting.[26] Yet research has shown the limits of these networks.[27]

In my study, grandmother-mother conflict revolved around: (1) family issues unrelated to child-rearing (e.g., grandmother's or mother's partners, household rules), (2) mothers not taking care of children or taking care of them inadequately, and (3) mothers' rejection of and resistance to parental guidance. On the one hand, the grandmother-mother conflict made multigenerational households difficult and, sometimes, impossible. On the other hand, living off welfare benefits or low-wage jobs made it difficult, if not impossible, for them to set up their own households and provide for their children. Grandmothers lamented being unable to "make" resistant teenage mothers' parent their children. Consequently, grandmothers felt compelled to mind their grandchildren to prevent maltreatment.

Substance Abuse and Addiction

Having a substance-using caregiver has been associated with higher CPS-referral and re-referral rates, and with higher substantiated case rates within the child welfare system than those of other families.[28] Substance use alone does not predict child maltreatment but can if it occurs with any of the following contributors to that risk: characteristics of the child (vulnerability, fragility); parental capability (ignorance of child development, few parental skills); home environment (poverty, dangerous living conditions, overcrowding, immediate stressors); social environment (social isolation, negative family and interpersonal relationships); and a history of maltreatment within the family.[29] Twenty-one parents in my study were grappling with substance addiction and two more were in recovery and rehabilitation. To further complicate the situation, substance addiction was often accompanied by intimate-partner violence or used to manage the symptoms of an untreated mental illness.

The United States has largely treated substance abuse and addiction as a public-safety rather than a public-health issue. The overcriminalization of drug use and possession reflects a political bias that results in mass incarceration instead of providing the health and social services that researchers and practitioners (e.g., addiction-focused health care professionals, educators, counselors, and such) have shown to be more effective and economical.[30] In 2010, the National Center on Addiction and Substance Abuse published its second report on substance abuse and addiction among the nation's prison population. They found that of the 2.3 million Americans in US jails and prisons, 1.9 million were substance involved and two-thirds reported substance abuse, compared to just 5 percent of the adult general population.[31] And yet, only about 10 to 15 percent of inmates with substance abuse and addiction disorders receive any treatment while incarcerated.[32] Despite increased recognition of the problem and its potential solutions, the nation has made no progress in mitigating substance abuse and addiction problems, and by extension the harm to affected individuals, their families, and their communities—in other words, to the legacy inherited by their children, with whose care Black grandmothers are burdened.

History of Being Mistreated as Children

A large body of literature suggests that parents with a history of childhood maltreatment have an increased likelihood of transmitting maltreatment to the next generation than parents without that history. The long-lasting relational effects of child maltreatment can impede parents' capacity to nurture and care for children, perpetuating "intergenerational cycles" of trauma.[33] Research also shows that child maltreatment is not randomly distributed, and parents with that history are more likely to be struggling with multiple challenges, including unintended pregnancies, antenatal and postnatal depression, contact with the criminal justice system, low employment, and difficulty transitioning to adulthood.[34] A recent study by psychology professor Kristin Valentino and colleagues examined the pathways that interrupt the intergenerational transmission of maltreatment among African American adolescent mothers. Their study revealed that among mothers with a child-abuse history, higher exposure to community violence and lower authoritarian-parenting attitudes (low parental supervision and monitoring) were associated with increased risk for intergenerational continuity of abuse.[35] Although the mediating mechanisms (e.g., social isolation/social support, intimate relationship quality, environmental context) related to intergenerational continuity of child maltreatment are not well understood, studies consistently find a strong link between maternal history of childhood victimization and children's risk of maltreatment.[36] That said, there is a dearth of sustaining evidence-based interventions for individuals, families, and communities experiencing intergenerational trauma, especially for African Americans—not to mention that concerns about inappropriate care and treatment, lack of access to services, and service delivery based on faulty assumptions and stereotypes govern African Americans' experience of mental health care and treatment.

The grandmothers featured across the next three chapters provide firsthand accounts of how cultural and structural forces influence Black grandmothering across the generations. Earlier generations of Black grandmothers provided parental support or stepped in as surrogate parents in response to poverty, parental death, work demands, desertion and migration, mutual aid networks, and marital separation. While contemporary grandmothers also provide parental support and surrogacy in response to these parental support needs, they are more likely than their historic counterparts to do so in response to teenage and never-married single motherhood, parental substance abuse, and parental history of childhood maltreatment.

ROLE IDENTITY: THE MEANING OF GRANDMOTHERHOOD

Otha's story demonstrates that the meaning women in this study attribute to the grandmother role is an important influence motivating grandmothers' role enactment. For these women, the essence of grandmotherhood included prioritizing and protecting their grandchildren, equipping them with the tools they need to achieve success, and nurturing them as a part of their lineage (see table 3 at the end of the chapter). Most of the women I interviewed expressed the substantive meaning of grandmotherhood according to more than one of these categories, but they tended to express one theme more dominantly than another. Importantly, while the meaning women associated with the grandmother role was related to their willingness to assume primary responsibility for their grandchildren, it applied to their relationship with all of their grandchildren, not just the one(s) in their care, as most women had grandchildren they were not raising.

As these Black women showed their love for their grandchildren through their caring labor and the meaning they associated with the grandmother role, they exhibited the complexity of their experiences consistent with Black feminist perspectives. Such perspectives situate how Black women express love in a larger context of systems of oppression and marginalization, careful not to romanticize or glorify Black motherhood and grandmotherhood by ignoring either the problems Black women face or how mothers and grandmothers demonstrate love differently from those idealized in popular culture.

The grandmothers I interviewed expressed being able to love their grandchildren in ways that differed from how they loved their children because, with time and experience, *they* were different, and the conditions and circumstances of their lives had changed. Many were free from abusive or otherwise unhealthy relationships, others were no longer employed and could devote more time and energy to their grandchildren, and still more had given up any behaviors that numbed them to the possibility and fullness of love, such as drinking, partying, drugs, and so. Despite managing the simultaneity of love and coercion, the Black grandmothers in this study demonstrated their love for their grandchildren in their willingness to provide care, as an extension of parenting and sometimes in place of it. However, they also exhibited their love as they prioritized and protected their grandchildren, nurtured them as a part of their lineage, and equipped them with the tools they needed to achieve success.

Prioritizing as Part of Grandmothering

Many grandmothers I interviewed stepped in to help parents with children or to raise them because, for them, prioritizing their grandchildren signified what it meant to be a grandmother. These grandmothers emphasized their grandchildren's importance regardless of their own lives and whether they were in parental care or foster care. They were concerned with ensuring that their grandchildren's material, emotional, educational, and spiritual needs were met. Providing these things when parents could or would not was a way for grandmothers to reinforce to their grandchildren that they were important. Grandmothers less concerned about grandchildren's basic needs focused on making sure they had not only "everything" they needed but also a lot of what they wanted. These women all expressed the importance of going out of their way to make sure their grandchildren felt special, some even talking about "spoiling" them. They stepped in as parents who either failed to prioritize their children or found themselves unable to because they were busy with school, work, and other parenting duties, or were managing grief, mental and physical illness, developmental disabilities, addiction, and unhealthy relationships.

Some grandmothers prioritized their grandchildren by ensuring that they had both what they needed and wanted. For example, born and raised in Chicago, fifty-four-year-old Bobbie Joe illustrates an example of prioritizing her grandchild in this way. Bobbie Joe grew up with her mother and her grandmother, Marilyn, in an upward extended multigenerational household (a multigenerational household headed by an adult child). Marilyn moved in with Bobbie Joe's mother to help her with Bobbie Joe and her brother after their father died, in the 1960s. It was an era when Blacks had higher mortality rates than Whites, the continuation of a historic trend that begin to decline (but did not achieve parity) in the 1960s and 1970s for both Black men and women.[37] The higher mortality rates of African Americans contributed to a parallel in their higher rates of widowhood.

Marilyn supported her daughter's desire to be "devoted to" her children and avoid bringing another man "around her children" to make ends meet by caring for her grandchildren while their mother worked full-time as a teacher. Some widowed and never-married mothers alike erred on the side of caution by not exposing their children to men who may mistreat them because they weren't their biological children. So, Marilyn's care-work also served a protective function. As the women shared child-rearing responsibilities, the connection between mothering and grandmothering was reinforced and signaled to Bobbie Joe that mothers alone weren't solely responsible for child-rearing.

Bobbie Joe was twenty years old and married when she had LeBron, her only child. She and her husband lived independently of their parents. When the marriage ended after a couple of years, Bobbie Joe continued to be self-sufficient, but, as a divorcée working two jobs, she relied heavily on her mother for childcare.

> My mother helped out quite a bit. When I worked two jobs, she would care for him. In fact, he would spend nights over there, he would go to church with her. Saturdays I went out, that was my time. . . . He adores my mother. He calls me "mom," but he calls her "mom" too.

LeBron expressed deep affection for the grandmother who helped raise him. Consistent with other studies, he was one of many family members among the women I interviewed who used terms of endearment conno-tating motherhood to refer to their grandmothers, signifying the blurred lines between motherhood and grandmotherhood. Among African Americans, the designation "grandmother" is a fluid one, often used inter-changeably with "mama" and freely given by family members and others to women who may not be biological grandmothers.[38]

Bobbie Joe's story also illustrates grandmothering in the context of noncrisis. Bobbie Joe's mother babysat her grandson so that her divorced, hardworking daughter could have a social life, but also so that she could spend time with the grandson with whom she shared mutual affection. Additionally, like many grandmothers I interviewed, her enactment of the grandmother role included making regular church attendance a part of her grandson's upbringing. These women talked about the significant role of grandmothers in fostering religious rituals, such as taking their grand-children to church, imparting lessons from the Bible, and teaching prayers and hymns.

Later on, Bobbie Joe was surprised when LeBron had his first child at twenty-one, while away at college. "When he told me, I was surprised. But

I was supportive and I sent money down and things for the baby and everything." Bobbie Joe also made clear the importance that women in her family placed on grandmothering by differentiating herself from the maternal grandmother of her granddaughter Cherelle.

> When the baby was born, she, the mom, didn't even come down. She had just got a new job—she said she wasn't taking the time off. Whereas when they called me and said, "Well, you're gonna be a grandmother today," I stopped whatever I was doing and went on down there.

Like many of the women I interviewed, she touched on anticipatory responsibility as the normative expectation held among African Americans when she referred to going to the hospital immediately upon learning of her granddaughter's birth, compared with the other grandmother's unwillingness to prioritize the birth of her newborn granddaughter or to provide ongoing support.

When Cherelle's parents asked Bobbie Joe to shift from playing a peripheral role in her life to a surrogate parenting role because they could no longer handle it, she agreed. According to Bobbie Joe, the unmarried couple was also not getting along. "I said, 'Okay.' Because I let him finish school." She was among several grandmothers I interviewed that cared for grandchildren so that parents could complete high school and college.

> Because for one thing they needed my help and I wanted her [Cherelle] to have a good life. I wanted her to enjoy everything that he [LeBron] did and more. And I felt that the only way that was gonna be done is if I took care of her. That may be a little selfish, but I just felt . . . if it would've been that she'd been with them, she would not have had an enriched life. And I was able to provide for her. I'm not talking about financial-wise. I'm talking about emotional-wise; the love and care that she gets from me. . . . She feels secure . . . and spoiled, don't get me wrong.

Bobbie Joe's rationale speaks to how both anticipatory responsibility ("they needed my help") and the meaning she attached to grandmotherhood ("I wanted her to enjoy everything that he did and more") influenced her decision. Although Bobbie Joe didn't anticipate raising her now twelve-year-old granddaughter, her desire to prioritize her in ways that she had been unable to prioritize her son because of competing work responsibilities and social activities also contributed to her willingness to adjust her role expectations.

While some grandmothers made efforts to be sure that their grandchildren's needs and wants were met, not all of them were able to afford to do so. However, their financial struggles did not stop these grandmothers from trying to demonstrate their prioritizing their grandchildren. Forty-five-year-old Angela was also raised by a widowed single parent. Angela was two years old when her mother died from a heart attack. Her paternal grandmother absorbed her son and his three children into her home in Cabrini Green housing projects. Of her upbringing, Angela shares, "My daddy and my grandmother raised me." By providing her son parental support, Angela's grandmother conveyed that child-rearing was not the responsibility of parents only.

In the late 1970s, Angela became pregnant at sixteen with her first child and at eighteen with her second. Her children's father refused to support her in raising their children. So when their son was three years old, Angela left him. "I broke up with their daddy and I never went back." She remained home with the father and grandmother who raised her. They helped Angela raise her children, too. She was nineteen years old when she moved into her own apartment in Cabrini Green. Although she lived independently, her father and grandmother continued to provide parental support. During our interview, Angela talked about never having to worry about childcare as she worked off and on while raising her children. In her family, motherhood and grandmotherhood were deeply intertwined. When Angela's grandmother died in 1990, she had been in her granddaughter's life for nearly thirty years and had helped raise her grandchildren and her great-grandchildren.

When her daughter, Jemele, became a mother at twenty-one, thirty-five-year-old Angela was there to cut her first grandchild's umbilical cord.

I cut the umbilical cord, her "honchos" come tracking me down. I'm like, "Y'all trackin' the one wrong down, ain't you?" [*Laughter*] You know, to let me know my daughter was in labor and meet her at the hospital. I'm like, "Do I look like the baby's daddy?" That's my first reaction. But I was there for her. Because me and my daughter is real tight. So I go to the hospital and it's a little big-headed boy.

As for other grandmothers, Angela's being present for her grandson Hakim's birth was an expression of the sanctity of the grandmother-grandchild bond. When I asked, "How did you feel being a grandmother?" Angela responded, laughing, "I was really more excited than [anything], you know, first grandbaby. You're making me a young grandmother but it's okay." Similar to women in other studies, the grandmothers I interviewed had expectations not only about actualizing their roles but also about the age at which they would or should do so.[39]

Jemele remained at Angela's home until she could set up her own household. Angela continued to cultivate her relationship with her grandson after her daughter "got her an apartment in Cabrini too," when she was about twenty-two years old. According to Angela, she saw her grandchildren every day when their mother moved out. When I interviewed Angela, she was caring for her grandchildren so that her daughter, who was no longer with the father of her two children, could work full-time and finish college. Angela demonstrated the relationship between anticipatory responsibility and Black grandmotherhood by stepping in when her daughter needed her.

Angela and Jemele devised an effective system of coparenting. Jemele took care of specific child-rearing responsibilities (e.g., combing hair, navigating child-rearing institutions when legal guardianship was needed) and Angela did the rest.

> I just like showing my daughter and my grandkids love. You can't buy love. I just like spending a lot of time with them showing them love. . . . It's a bind on us now because we used to like take 'em to the show or out to eat. We can't do that right now. And we try to explain. . . . We got them spoiled. [*Chuckles*]

Angela engaged in numerous and varied forms of grandmothering over the course of her grandchildren's lives, based on her family's needs and her personal circumstances. Despite her financial and emotional fragility, Angela did what she could to prioritize her grandchildren, treating them to little snacks on their way home from school until her Link card ran out. Angela's experience of caring for her grandchildren in the ways she could and grappling with the ways she could not, speak to their priority to her.

Angela did not associate grandmotherhood with raising her grandchildren beyond a finite period. When applicable, I asked each grandmother why she raised her grandchildren even when she did not want to or what made her feel like doing so was something she was supposed to do. Angela responded:

> It's not something you're *supposed* to do. Like I say, I done raised mine.
> I don't have nothing else to do right now. When I get back on my feet, believe me, I will be out tending my own business. [*Chuckles*]

Angela felt like she had the time and energy to raise her grandchildren temporarily as her daughter finished school, but did not feel it was something she was "supposed" to do.

Although she did not experience caregiving as coercive, Angela was not devoid of conflict about raising her grandchildren:

> I mean at first it was like you do get angry as a grandmother. It's like you gotta raise kids all over again. . . . I was kinda angry because I done raised mine and now I gotta help you raise yours. But as time went by it's beautiful, it's a beautiful thing.

Still, while she knew she was not "supposed" to raise them, in the sense that she was not obligated to, Angela also knew she would.

Over the four years that she had raised them, Angela worked with Jemele to prioritize the children. But not every grandmother participating in the study was able to do so. Some grandmothers were making up for what they saw as a failure by mothers and fathers to prioritize their own children. Such grandmothers prioritized their grandchildren by conveying to them that their needs were important even when others, including their parents, did not think so or affirm it.

Protecting as Part of Grandmothering

In contrast to prioritization, which involved making sure children came first, even over grandmothers or parents' personal needs and desires, protection involved ensuring children were safe. Women I interviewed unanimously equated protecting their grandchildren with grandmothering. However, some grandmothers foregrounded protection when the safety and welfare of their grandchildren were threatened due to actual or potential maltreatment. In such circumstances, protecting took precedence over other meanings women may have associated with the role of grandmothering, manifesting in their increased involvement with one or more of their grandchildren so that they did not have to "worry" about them.

Some grandmothers' protective function was triggered when they worried about their grandchildren being exposed to unsafe environments and unsavory people. Thirty-eight-year-old Victoria, who was born and raised in Chicago, was a case in point. When Victoria got pregnant with her first child it was by a man who refused to take any responsibility for their child or the subsequent nine children he fathered by different women. Victoria managed to survive by working at a fast-food restaurant and attending college. While she did, she lived with and relied on her parents for support with her daughter. It was while working at the fast-food restaurant that she met and started dating her boss, Raymond. Eventually, they had two children and moved into a CHA (Chicago Housing Authority) building. Victoria tried to build a life with Raymond. Although she was in a relationship with him for seventeen years, it did not translate into consistent, reliable support because Raymond battled substance addiction, making his economic, emotional, and instrumental contributions unpredictable.

When her oldest daughter Kaiya got pregnant with her first and only child, her relationship with her mother was so strained that Victoria was surprised that her daughter wanted her to be a part of her granddaughter's life at all. Their relationship was strained because Victoria had been unable to successfully control or discipline Kaiya as she became a teenager, causing friction between mother and daughter. Eighteen-year-old Kaiya and her baby were living with Roderick (the child's father) and his mother. Kaiya began to lean on Victoria in response to the difficulty she was having coparenting with Roderick. The agreement between Kaiya and Roderick was that he would keep Nia during the day while she worked. But Kaiya and Victoria both noticed that Roderick was not caring for Nia properly, one sign of which was her excessive crying that shushed when she got to her grandmother's house and another of which was his leaving Nia in the care of his eight-year-old sister. Victoria and Kaiya felt that it would be safer for Nia if she stayed at her house.

So I keep Nia because I think the environment at my house is safer and better for her. Because my daughter's working and she has to leave the baby there with her father and I don't think he takes care of her like he should.

Not only did Victoria's immediate action ensure her granddaughter's safety and keep Victoria from "calling or worrying about what's going on with her," but it also accompanied her doing what she could to support her daughter as she struggled to mature and get on her feet so that she could raise her own child. Victoria supported Kaiya as her parents had done with her. Victoria was dealing with a lot in her own life—she had been unemployed since getting diagnosed with HIV nearly four years ago, and she was raising two teenage daughters. Like many of the grandmothers I interviewed, Victoria challenged the notion that anticipatory responsibility was synonymous with parental surrogacy.

> I really don't feel like I'm supposed to [raise her granddaughter]. . . . I just kinda feel like if I didn't keep Nia then she would be kinda unsafe where she is. And my thing is I don't want something to happen. I don't want her to be a statistic before she's a person. Because how you think of statistics, you can just rattle those off and it's like you don't have any memory or any mention of it anymore. Whereas a person, you have the memories of them.

Like most grandmothers, Victoria interpreted anticipatory responsibility as providing parental support and temporarily raising grandchildren while parents got themselves together. Nia had been in her care for six months. By saying that she wanted her granddaughter to be a person before she was a statistic, Victoria captured what she felt Nia's foreseeable future would be without her intervening. Still, Victoria interpreted anticipatory responsibility as also having a choice about her degree of involvement. Not having a choice resulted in coerced mothering for grandmothers who felt that they didn't have a "choice" about parenting their grandchildren.

Victoria pushed back against others' perceptions of anticipatory responsibility, even as her mother weighed in about her role and responsibilities as a grandmother.

> Well, my mother just knew I was gonna be keeping her [Nia] and even thinks that I should go as far as when I move to put her on my lease. She

thinks I should put her and my daughter on my lease. And see my thing is
. . . I feel bad that she's [Kaiya's] positive, but it's like I want her to live on
her own and to be a mother.

Instead of adding her daughter and granddaughter to her lease and
cementing her current involvement, Victoria helped Kaiya come to terms
with being HIV positive so that she could become a more effective parent.
She also talked to her about the important role that getting an education
played in being able to care for herself and her daughter. Lastly, she hoped
that her daughter would awaken to the idea that Roderick—who not only
wouldn't care for his daughter but also wouldn't work—was not the best
for her and Nia.

Victoria worried about doing so much that her daughter might abdicate
her child-rearing duties in response—a form of what sociology professor
Madonna Harrington Meyer describes as enabling.[40] The grandmothers
participating in my study and their mothers, grandmothers, and other
women taking on caregiving roles described enabling as allowing parents to
shirk their responsibilities or being crutches rather than making them grow
up and into their responsibilities. Many enablers are not aware of the enabling role they play or can't afford to admit it without devastating the overall architecture of their lives. That being said, most of the women that I
interviewed felt that they were providing support in line with what parents
needed or that was necessary to ensure the safety and well-being of their
grandchildren. So, as Victoria helped her daughter "get herself together,"
she cared for her granddaughter in a private kinship arrangement.

Some grandmothers had strong feelings about children being mistreated in any way, which influenced their associating protection with
grandmotherhood. Like other grandmothers who had experienced the
turbulence that came from the loss of a parent during childhood, fifty-
eight-year-old May's experience of being ill-treated as a child influenced
the importance she placed on sheltering children from harm. When May's
father died, her mother had a nervous breakdown. May maintained that
her mother "forgot she had kids." Their father's background as a veteran
had allowed them to live well in Detroit. When, after the death of her husband, May's mother left the children alone in the house, some of her aunts
moved in and neglected them. A neighbor reported it and the six children

were dispersed across three different nonrelative foster homes. Eventually, some of May's mother's siblings rescued May and a sister she was in foster care with (leaving the other four children in foster care). According to May, not out of "the goodness of their hearts" but because "they couldn't let all that money go to waste. [*Laughs*] So, they came and got us and brought us to Chicago and raised us." May disclosed that they were neglected and mistreated by their relatives.

When May married the father of her first three children, she was committed to making the marriage work, even when he turned out to be abusive. "I stayed with this man," she explained, "in the sense that I wanted my kids to know who their parents were." Because he was in the military, May felt it was harder to get the help she needed to leave. As recounted about their men by many other women in my interviews, May's abusive husband subscribed to ideas about a woman's place, specifically, that she belonged in the home under his control.

> He didn't want me to work, he didn't want me to go to school. He wanted me to stay home. His thing was women belong in the kitchen barefoot and pregnant. When he come home, I'm supposed to have his pipe, his slippers, and food waiting for him.

The abuse was so bad that at one point May wanted to die. "Because I told him, I said, 'I'm tired, just kill me and get it over with.' . . . I can't do it no more. And I called DCFS and told 'em to come get my kids because I can't do it no more." It was DCFS that helped her put her violent husband out. May moved back home to Chicago while her husband was in jail for abusing her. She moved into public housing and got on public aid until she could get back on her feet. May chose Stateway Gardens because her sister lived there, and she stayed for about five years. After her stint in public housing, she moved to the city's east side. She got jobs in retail and went back to school. After divorcing her husband, May began and ended relationships and had her fourth and last child.

May was working, attending college, and caring for her ailing mother when she was compelled to increase her degree of involvement with her youngest of five grandchildren, McKayla, her youngest son's only child. According to May, McKayla's mother Jaya was caring for her inadequately, specifically regarding McKayla's hygienic and developmental needs (inconsistent school attendance) and repeatedly exposing McKayla to individuals and situations that severely compromised her safety.

> Because every weekend I would get this little girl and keep her and as soon as she hit my door you gotta go upstairs, you gotta take a bath. You gotta get out those nasty clothes you got on. . . . Girl, remember year before last when we had that zero-below weather? Zero-below weather, this girl got on capris. No socks, no underwear, a tank top, and a spring jacket. I'm freezing looking at her.

After this incident, May contacted DCFS to start the process of becoming her granddaughter's legal guardian so that if and when Jaya returned to get her, May would be able to stop her from doing so. She contacted DCFS three times before deciding to pursue legal guardianship on her own, motivated by the impetus to protect McKayla.

> I would do it again [take her granddaughter] in a heartbeat because my thing is, I was looking out for McKayla. Because I don't like to see kids being misused. That's my main goal . . . because they didn't ask to come here. They didn't. You don't misuse a child.

Just as May held role expectations about grandmotherhood, she had expectations about parenthood. "I already told my kids, look, you brought it [child] here, it's yours. You better take care of it." But May knew that her son, who was developmentally delayed, would not be able to care for McKayla on his own. May wasn't sure exactly why Jaya was unable to adequately parent her children: "I think she got a disability. She got something wrong with her." According to May, Jaya was often in toxic, abusive relationships. Jaya had the first of her four children as a teenager; one died when he fell into a bucket of water and drowned, two were being cared for by paternal grandparents, and one remained in Jaya's care. May was coerced to assume primary responsibility for McKayla, despite the expectations she held for the grandmother role: "I thought I was gonna be coming to pick her up, bringing her home, hanging out with her." McKayla had been in her grandmother's care for two years.

Protecting their grandchildren shifts from the philosophical to the real for those grandmothers whose grandchildren's well-being is threatened. And for another group of grandmothers, experiences shift from the real to the surreal when it is parents—their own children—whom they must protect their grandchildren from. Grandmothers are forced to grapple with how and why their children are failing to protect their offspring, or worse, with how and why their children are the perpetrators of harm to their offspring, and what if any role the grandmothers themselves have played. The answers to these questions are clearer when developmental disabilities, mental illness, and addiction are the culprit, as most grandmothers understand that these conditions make parents "not quite" themselves. The answers to these questions come with a heavier heart, and for some with a lot of anger, when parents not struggling with these afflictions abuse or allow others to abuse their children. Regardless of the reason or the person threatening their grandchildren's safety and welfare, neglect, mistreatment, and danger cause these grandmothers to intensify their degree of involvement with their grandchildren.

Nurturing Their Lineage as Part of Grandmothering

Some women's definition of grandmotherhood was rooted in biology and lineage. For these grandmothers, their grandchildren represented "a part of" them, they were their "children's children," and their "blood." At a basic level, these women equated lineage with family obligation—they felt inclined to care for their grandchildren in the same way that they cared for their children, who were also a part of them. Preserving their blood ties was a way to ensure the survival of their family. Still, others admitted that they couldn't absorb the immense responsibilities associated with raising another generation if those children were *not* their blood. Grandmothers like Otha, whose story begins the chapter, likened lineage to keeping their family intact and to being unable to rest knowing that their grandchildren were "out there" or "scattered" in the world somewhere, unknown and uncared for by them. Finally, lineage took on special meaning for grandmothers whose children had died. Assuming care for the grandchildren of deceased children was a way for these grandmothers to maintain a connection to their deceased child.

Some grandmothers equated lineage with a sense of family obligation. Fifty-four-year-old Laverne is a case in point. When her daughter, Trina, walked off and left her parents, Laverne and Leonard, to raise her five children, Laverne's belief in taking care of "blood, family" was part of what motivated her to take care of them. Laverne was born and raised in Chicago and during our interview talked about having three siblings but growing up in a house "full of kids." Laverne explained that her mother's loss of her mother as a child motivated her othermothering and her generous contributions to their extended family and the larger Black community: "She really takes to kids. . . . Because like she say, she didn't have a mama. . . . And you'd of thought my mama had a whole bunch of kids."

Laverne learned from her mother and other women in their family who modeled other and community mothering. Community mothers are generally women over forty years of age who have exhibited an ethic of care critical to the survival and well-being of their communities and who have "lived long enough to have a sense of the community's tradition and culture."[41]

> I was raised with family. And if something happens you just move over and keep on going. It's no big deal unless you make it out of one. We [Laverne and Leonard] still had two children at home so there's five of them [grandchildren], made me have seven. Just move on. My auntie had ten kids and she was always hollering she had room for one more.

Laverne underscored that observational learning happened not only when women witnessed their grandmothers assuming responsibility for children that weren't their own, but also when other women did so, including those dominant family figures within extended family networks.[42]

When Laverne and her husband of twenty-three years started raising their grandchildren thirteen years ago, they shifted from living with their daughter, Trina, and their five grandchildren in a multigenerational household and providing parental support to raising them in a skipped-generation household. Before leaving her children in her parent's care, Trina would come and go. When she was present, she helped her parents raise her children. But when her youngest child started kindergarten, Trina walked off and left her children for good. When asked why Trina wasn't raising her children, Laverne cried as she told me:

> That's my baby, that's my firstborn. I feel that I did a lot of stuff wrong. I was young, I couldn't teach her. And I showed her a lot of things that I shouldn't have showed her and it came back at me.

Laverne felt compelled to care for her grandchildren because they were "blood."

LAVERNE: I couldn't see me dragging 'em off to DCFS.

LASHAWNDA: Why not?

LAVERNE: I mean blood, family. You take care of family. You do what you gotta do.

She also wanted to keep the siblings together. When I asked if there was anything that she felt I did not address or missed in our interview, she said,

> I know a lot of people ask me why would I take them and the only answer that I can have for that is whatever their parents did, they didn't have anything to do with it and they deserve to be raised as sisters and brothers and know each other.

The desire not to split up siblings motivated quite a few grandmothers in the study to raise their grandchildren, and several grandmothers talked about being raised by family members committed to making sure that they had grown up with their siblings. Along these lines, grandmothers stressed the importance of making sure that all of their grandchildren knew each other, or at the very least knew about each other, including siblings outside of their family, specifically a mother's or father's other children.

Leaving a Legacy as a Part of Grandmothering

Some grandmothers felt responsible for giving the next generation the building blocks they needed to succeed and talked about "pouring into," meaning investing in, their grandchildren. For these grandmothers, their grandchildren represented their legacy. In this context, legacy is defined as transmitting knowledge, skills, time, and resources to the next generation. These grandmothers sought to positively affect their grandchildren as well as their families and the world, *through* their grandchildren. Thus, they did what they could to contribute to their grandchildren's accomplishments. They were often community mothers, committed to ensuring that all Black children had tools for successful living. Finally, in contrast to those who stressed prioritizing their grandchildren by giving them what they needed and wanted, including spoiling them, grandmothers who emphasized leaving a legacy were preoccupied with preparing their grandchildren for success in the external world. As such, they provided their grandchildren educational opportunities (e.g., paying for their grandchildren to attend private school, helping them pay for college, buying them cars on graduating) and cultural capital (e.g., paying for and participating in their grandchildren's extracurricular activities). These grandmothers also passed on strong religious and spiritual beliefs and practices and supported their grandchildren's psychological development by providing emotional support, teaching them healthy coping strategies, and connecting them to mental health care.

Fifty-eight-year-old Beulah exemplified how grandmothers cared deeply about leaving a legacy. Beulah ensured that her grandchildren had the best early learning and educational experiences possible when their mother failed to do so. She also made sure that their mental health and special education needs were met. Beulah was born and raised in Florida. Witnessing her mother serve as a surrogate parent and community mother shaped Beulah's relationship to her own role as a mother, grandmother, and community mother. Although Beulah's parents had ten children, they took in many more. Beulah explained the impact of her mother raising children who weren't hers on her own grandmothering and community mothering: "Like I say, going back to my mother and my father, which I tell you there was ten of us. . . . But it was always somebody else's kids there."

Beulah visited Chicago as a high school graduation gift from one of her brothers. She was twenty years old when she had "a summer relationship" with a young man. She ended up pregnant, but the relationship did not last. It was while working a government job that Beulah met her husband, who was also a government employee. Upon marrying, the couple had another child together and Beulah became what she referred to as a "desperate housewife."

> I stayed home for twenty years being a housewife, dealing with the school, dealing with the school counselors, dealing with all the things that housewives deal with. . . . I lived in Hyde Park. . . . My thought was that I wanted to deal with the kids that wasn't fortunate enough to experience what I had experienced.

As a community mother, Beulah not only raised her two daughters but about seven other girls as well.

Her belief in education inspired her to return to school to get her bachelor's degree, a decision her husband lived with rather than supported. Beulah persisted, feeling that, as a woman from her generation, she wanted to have a "voice" (equal rights) and wanted to teach her daughters and the women and girls she worked with to have a voice too. Beulah took her pledge to help women have a voice into the social services where she worked with domestic violence victims and young mothers.

After twenty years of marriage, Beulah and her husband separated because, according to her, they "outgrew each other." Despite their marital challenges, their shared obligation to their family paid off. Both of their daughters attended college. Their youngest daughter, Roxanne, followed in her parents' footsteps by working for the federal government. She had two children and was in a long-term relationship with their father. Their oldest daughter, Tricia, lived with Beulah in a multigenerational household when she became pregnant with her first child and, according to Beulah, "for almost eight years she didn't have but one child." When she met the father of her second child, she moved out and then "started just having kids, having kids, having kids, having kids." When the couple was "burned out" of their home, they moved in with Beulah until they could find housing. Before they moved, Beulah told her daughter that no school-aged child would leave her house if they weren't enrolled in school. "I say, I will fight you and take you to the cleaners. They will not leave this house. And that's how Mahogany [granddaughter] got here." Her grandson, Brayton, had never left his grandmother's house. When Beulah's daughter would not enroll the children in school or give Beulah guardianship so that she could do so, Beulah felt compelled to get legal guardianship of the children without her permission.

One way that Beulah satisfied the desire to leave a legacy was by "plugging" her grandchildren into "services," including early education, after-school care, private school programs, therapy, individualized education programs, medical care, university studies, and so on.

> I strongly bring in, I bring in a lot of services with Mahogany and Brayton, and give them tools. I use tools to say, "Hey you know you can call your uncle

or you can go to your mama's house. You know, go, go, go." To let them know don't rely on grandmother.

Beulah maintained that she did not think her daughter was incapable of raising her own children; after all, Tricia had six children in her care. "It's not that you [Tricia] have a mental health problem but you don't know where your priorities are. And when I say priorities, I say you don't meet no goals and stuff like that." Beulah raised the oldest two because she wanted them to have what she thought mothers were supposed to provide, and when the care of the children transferred to her, Beulah felt that her daughter was not providing them with those things. Showing her grandchildren how she felt they were supposed to be raised was important to Beulah: "Even if you're not with your mom . . . these are the things that mom have to do, that need to be in place to make sure that you have a secure, safe, and better life."

Grandmothers who defined grandmotherhood as leaving a legacy saw beyond what was possible in the present. They focused on preparing their grandchildren for the future, and for a future without them. These grandmothers linked building blocks such as formal and informal education, extracurricular and other activities associated with what sociologist Annette Lareau calls "concerted cultivation," not only to individual accomplishment, but also to family upkeep and survival, and to racial upliftment.[43] As Beulah put it, "Go, go, go . . . don't rely on grandmother."

CONCLUSION

We know that socialization—specifically observational learning of how grandmotherhood is enacted and childhood relationships with grandmothers—can powerfully influence the nature of the experience a girl will have as a grandmother, two generations later.[44] Yet previous research has paid little attention to the life histories of Black women, whose normative expectations of grandmotherhood, in the past and present, differ from those of their White counterparts. The influence of socialization is evident as women share that they learned during their grandchildhood, childhood, and motherhood that responsibility accompanies grandmotherhood, that motherhood and grandmotherhood are intertwined, and that mothers are not solely responsible for rearing children.

Black family life in the United States has created a context for the engaged and vital role played by grandmothers in West African ethnic groups. African cultural practices of grandmothering blended with the impact of slavery and Jim Crow–era structural inequities on Black families, strongly shaping African Americans' expectations about grandmotherhood. In the post–civil rights era, the institution of Black grandmotherhood has been affected by dramatic demographic, structural, institutional, and cultural changes and the persistence of social inequities and problems. All of which have contributed to efforts by the state and Black community to mold the institution of Black grandmotherhood to both benefit and resist interlocking systems of race, class, and gender oppression across historical periods.

But women define and negotiate their own experiences of what it means to have a sense of duty and responsibility for their grandchildren's well-being. They also make determinations about what their grandmothering will entail. While some Black grandmothers embrace a grandparent role characterized by intensive grandmothering or surrogate parenting, other grandmothers drew lines in the sand by insisting on having a "choice," refusing to take care of any more grandchildren, and signaling to parents that their surrogate parent roles were temporary. Not only did women negotiate the form and tenor of anticipatory responsibility for themselves, but also they used their conceptualization of anticipatory responsibility to judge and measure other Black grandmothers' involvement (or lack of) with their grandchildren. Lastly, by establishing anticipatory responsibility as the normative expectation for Black grandmotherhood, we can examine the mechanisms that facilitate this role expectation, how grandmothers conceptualize and negotiate their relationship to anticipatory responsibility, and within-group differences.

The role behavior of the women in this study was shaped by their role expectations and the meaning they held for grandmotherhood. In addition to using their carework to "step up" for their grandchildren when the need arose or "standing in the gap" where parents should be, grandmothers also prioritized and protected their grandchildren, nurtured them as a part of their lineage, and equipped them with the tools they needed to achieve success.

The grandmothers represented in this work talked freely and poignantly about their deep love for their grandchildren and about the varied strategies they used to show it—beyond helping parents with their children and being surrogate parents. From Victoria expressing that she kept her granddaughter safe in her home because she did not want her to be "a statistic before she's a person," to Laverne making sure that her grandchildren were raised together as "sisters and brothers" and Beulah making sure that her grandchildren had "tools," to Angela's daily ritual of using her Link card, her only income source, to buy her grandchildren snacks on the way home from school, these grandmothers wanted their grandchildren to feel that there was someone who would do everything possible for them, who would make sure that they felt loved. Remarkably, women did this even when they had struggled over their lifetimes with feeling a lack of love, especially for those abandoned or mistreated on the death or absence of parents, or worse, had been victims of domestic and structural violence. Rather than thwarting them, their own experiences of lovelessness increased their motivation to ensure that the next generation, their grandchildren, felt the presence and meaning of love in their lives.

Table 3 Black Grandmotherhood Role Meanings

Hallmarks of role meaning	Prioritization	Protection	Nurturing lineage	Leaving a legacy
Definition	Child-centered emphasis, regardless of personal needs or wants. Grandchild comes first whether with parent(s) or in foster care.	Shelter from harm. Keep grandchild safe, especially from child maltreatment.	Family obligation. Stressed biological relationship with grandchild and keeping family intact.	Contributing to a grandchild's accomplishments. Preoccupied with providing tools for external success.
Actualization of role meaning	Ensure grandchild's basic *needs* are met (material, emotional, educational, spiritual). Fulfill varying degrees of grandchild's *wants*.	Eliminate child welfare threat or remove grandchild from individual or environment threatening her/his safety and well-being.	Care for grandchild similarly to how they cared for own children. Raise siblings together.	Provide educational opportunities, cultural capital, and spiritual and psychological development.

3 How Grandmothers Experience and Respond to Coerced Mothering within Informal Kinship Care

At eighty-one, Virginia and Norman, her husband of fifty-eight years, were raising their two great-grandsons, Omar and Brandon. They had also raised the boys' mothers, Sydney and LeKeisha. As unique as Virginia's experience of caregiving was, she shared commonalities with other grandmothers, including what I term *coerced mothering* and decision-making about the most appropriate caregiving arrangement for her great-grandchildren, their mothers, and her and Norman.

Both Virginia and Norman anticipated active involvement with their grandchildren. As Norman put it: "I did whatever I had to do, what was necessary. My house has always been open to my grandchildren because I feel that any advice or opportunities that I could give them that could enhance their lives, I should." Viewing grandchildren as their legacy, Virginia and Norman felt responsible for providing the support they needed to succeed, including educational and extracurricular opportunities, spiritual guidance, and mental health services.

Virginia and Norman had worked their way into the Black middle class, employed as an RN and in industry, respectively. In 1962, Norman's veteran benefits secured them a new house on Chicago's Far South Side. Like many middle-class Black neighborhoods, Virginia and Norman's abutted poorer communities with destructive influences. Although their daughter merely dabbled in drugs, their son, Norman Jr., "was on drugs almost thirty years." His job paid for rehab twice before "finally he got himself together."

Unfortunately, Norman Jr.'s turnaround did not happen in time for him to raise his children. His oldest daughter, Sydney, was the first grandchild for whom Virginia and Norman assumed responsibility, due to parental substance addiction. As they had with their children, Virginia and Norman sent Sydney to private school, and as with their daughter, bought Sydney a car after she graduated from high school. Sydney didn't want to go to college, but Virginia insisted that she enroll "anywhere": "I think she might have gone two weeks. That was it. She wasn't interested. . . . What can you do?" Sydney was more interested in "following up behind" her boyfriends than in her own success. Virginia and Norman also sometimes cared for another of Norman Jr.'s daughters, LeKeisha, whose mother was incarcerated for drug dealing.

After raising their grandchildren, Virginia and Norman anticipated a break. But when Sydney became a mother at twenty-one and "just wouldn't take care of [Omar]," they found themselves coerced into providing care while she lived elsewhere, beginning and ending jobs and relationships, including an on-and-off relationship with Omar's father as he cycled in and out of prison for drug- and gang-related activity. Unlike her parents, Sydney wasn't challenged by substance addiction but refused parental responsibility. "I raised her," Virginia said, exasperatedly, "but she doesn't raise him. I have him. Isn't that a mess?" Virginia did not understand why someone who had "everything and didn't want for anything," wouldn't raise her child: "Don't care," she lamented. "Don't care."

Because no one else was willing to care for Omar, his beleaguered great-grandparents made sure that he stayed out of "the system" (child welfare system). Like many grandmothers, Virginia was hesitant to legalize her relationship with Omar because she upheld the primacy of the parent-child relationship. Even though she assumed parental responsibility, Virginia did not want to signal that she was trying to remove Sydney's parental rights. Virginia and Norman assumed legal guardianship only when Sydney entertained the idea of joining the military; Sydney never joined, but Virginia and Norman now had legal responsibility for their great-grandson.

Virginia and Norman felt unable to relinquish caregiving responsibilities, temporarily or permanently, as Sydney had long resisted parental responsibility and guidance. Like other grandparents in this study, they couldn't "make" Sydney spend time with Omar or assume responsibility for his welfare. As Virginia and Norman, eleven-year-old Omar's caregivers since birth, waited for improvement with Sydney, they had recently assumed responsibility for twenty-one-year-old granddaughter LeKeisha's four-year-old son Brandon, while she juggled work and school. LeKeisha had previously relied on her mother for child-rearing help, but, with her mother and stepfather incarcerated for drug trafficking, and LeKeisha and Brandon living in Washington, DC, away from their extended family, she was forced not only to put Brandon in day care twelve to fourteen hours a day but also to assume custody of her younger sister. "He [Brandon] was being I say, 'neglected,'" Virginia explained, "because [LeKeisha] was going to school and working, taking him to day care at six in the morning and picking him up at the maximum hour in the evening, which he was getting nothing." Concerned about the possible effects on Brandon's development, Virginia, Norman, and Brandon's paternal grandmother—all Chicago residents— agreed to share caregiving responsibilities until LeKeisha finished school, though Brandon's paternal grandmother had not done her part.

Virginia was conflicted about providing care rather than focusing on her own life. Although she, like many grandmothers I interviewed, felt it was God's will that she parent her grandchildren and great-grandchildren, she struggled.

> I know sometimes I feel discouraged, but God say he won't put more on you than you can bear. So this must be what he meant for me to do, is help these children. But like I say, what I would really like is to see not appreciation, but results. Let me see some fruits of my labor, that's all I ask. . . . I don't want nothing else.

In reality, Virginia did want something else—she and Norman wanted to sell their home, move to a retirement community, and take care of each other. However, she knew it was unlikely.

As for the legal aspects of parenting Brandon, Virginia and Norman were able to care for him privately, as they had Omar before obtaining guardianship. They enrolled him in the same private school their children and grandchildren had attended. Virginia had also recently gotten a medical card for Brandon: "They sent it to me and it's in my name and I also get what they call that TANF for clothing and whatever. I have a Link card that I get the $100 a month." Since they knew that they would likely raise Omar to adulthood, keeping their caregiving arrangement with Brandon private afforded them a chance of reuniting him with his mother.

As previously discussed, some grandmothers in my research experienced role conflict when the anticipated grandmother role differed from the unanticipated surrogate parent role. With her great-grandsons, Virginia not only experienced role conflict but, like many grandmothers, she experienced coerced mothering. Grandmothers experienced coerced mothering when they experienced the four interrelated aspects of coerced care (status obligation, lack of alternatives, loss of aspects of their personhood and identity, difficulty opting out), while at the same time being forced to fulfill the social and legal functions associated with motherhood.

This chapter focuses on how grandmothers in informal kinship care (e.g., private care, legal guardianship) experienced and responded to coerced mothering and how they negotiated with parents to provide care. The chapter begins by examining some of the legal issues that grandparents dealt with when they lacked parental rights: how their efforts to ensure their grandchildren's safety and well-being were circumvented by their legal marginalization; the ways in which the legal system highlighted differences between mothering and coerced mothering, as well as determined the *quasi-legal rights* that characterized their caregiving arrangements (see table 2 in the introduction); and how Black grandmothers often lacked access to nonpunitive institutions to get and keep their grandchildren in their care. The remainder of this chapter will demonstrate Black grandmothers' journeys to coerced mothering and the range of informal caregiving arrangements (tiers three and four of the five-tiered system of kinship care) it entails.

PARENTING WITHOUT PARENTAL RIGHTS

For most of the grandmothers in my study, their journeys to parental surrogacy begin when parents experience challenges that threaten their children's safety and well-being. Therefore, this chapter continues to bring attention to the effects of a wide-ranging set of social problems that make it difficult or impossible for Black parents to raise their children. I show that when this occurs, grandmothers intensify their involvement with their grandchildren and with their grandchildren's parent(s), who may be receptive or unreceptive to their interventions. When their efforts to support their grandchildren's parent(s) are insufficient, grandmothers are forced to shift into parenting their grandchildren. But they must do so without legal rights relative to their grandchildren and with limited (if any) access to nonpunitive institutions to obtain the legal rights they need to provide adequate care.

Narratives like Virginia's reveal the impact of the legal system on grandparents raising grandchildren. Political scientist Joan Tronto and educational philosopher Berenice Fisher foreground how women's caregiving is hampered by their household's dependence on the marketplace and bureaucracy. They argue that the political process that shapes caring in market and public sector bureaucracies (e.g., the child welfare system, schools, social service organizations, clinics) results in fragmented, inadequate caregiving.[1] I argue that, along with the household/community, market, and bureaucracy, the legal system both facilitates and constrains caregiving provided by legally marginalized caregivers. Grandparent caregivers' legal status relative to their grandchildren influences their ability (or inability) to provide care in market and public sector bureaucracies. Moreover, it is the legal system that highlights a crucial difference between coerced mothering and mothering. While motherhood comes with legal constraints, for example, shared custody with another parent or *parens patriae*, the legal rights associated with motherhood are a given and can only be disrupted with the mother's consent or when she is proven unfit. In contrast, the legal rights associated with coerced mothering are not a given. In fact, in many cases, grandmothers must fight for them. Consequently, because legal rights and caregiving arrangements are interlocked, grandmothers facing this dilemma cannot think about one without thinking about the other.

Women thus saddled with raising their grandchildren have at best what I refer to as *quasi-legal rights*, that is, they must rely on and share any legal rights they obtain with parents and the state. For instance, I distinguish between "taking" and "keeping" among grandmothers responsible for parenting their grandchildren in informal kinship care. *Taking* involves using the child welfare system to subdue parental rights (e.g., legal guardianship). Legal guardians are given enforceable legal rights—not as a full "parent," but in a legally defined role (see the appendix). Additionally, legal guardians are assigned specific duties by the courts, which may include care and protection and medical and educational rights. In contrast, *keeping* involves caring for grandchildren with no legal relationship (private care). The quasi-legal rights associated with informal kinship care complicates what it means for a woman to mother her grandchildren—to provide for their basic needs, to protect them from harm, and to make decisions on their behalf. In the absence of authorization from parents, grandmothers often face the anguish of having to prove their own children's unfitness. Or, lacking authorization from the state, grandmothers must become bureaucratic experts to access resources and services. Absent legal rights, grandmothers must depend on parents to navigate child-rearing institutions or on discretion and consistency from street-level bureaucrats[2] for access to resources and services for their grandchildren. This dependence on others for authority, access, discretion, and consistency, therefore, creates an obstacle course of inconsistency, and sometimes unattainability, for these grandmothers. It also creates fear among grandmothers in this and other studies, who are afraid that parents will reclaim their children.[3]

Women's narratives reveal that contemporary grandparent caregiving in informal kinship care is not simply a continuation of historical and cultural traditions within Black families. Virginia was able to care for her great-grandsons without the painful decision to involve Child Protective Services (CPS) or the police; however, that wasn't possible for many grandmothers in this study, who, without legal rights, had few options to challenge parental rights. The racial geography of the child welfare and criminal justice systems concentrates them in poor communities of color, especially Black communities. Without other options, families living in these communities are forced to use these systems to resolve family conflict and crises.[4] Policy makers have made CPS and the police (just one component of the carceral state) the most "widely available, well-funded, politically powerful institutionalized protective"[5] forces to address child maltreatment and crime within this country. And yet, racism and classism are deeply rooted in the history, policies, and practices of the child welfare and criminal justice systems, making them a tool of race-class control. Put another way, the systems "work the way they are supposed to." Consequently, it not surprising that there have been calls to go beyond reform, to abolish both systems and to reimagine "new, anti-racist means of keeping children, families, and communities safe and thriving."[6]

Paradoxically, even though the grandmothers whose stories are featured in this chapter successfully kept their grandchildren out of the system, some grandmothers with few resources relied on the system to keep their grandchildren in their care. Additionally, although low-income and poor families are overrepresented in the child welfare system, the particular fragility of the Black middle class meant that these grandmothers also lacked the means to hire a private attorney to "take" their grandchildren from parents who were unable to adequately care for them but resisted relinquishing custody. So, some of these grandmothers also used CPS to intervene on behalf of their grandchildren.

In addition to the range of legal complications already described, coerced mothering varied across but also within families, often affected by the nature of a grandmother's relationship with her grandchild. As a consequence, it was common for the same grandmother to have different caregiving arrangements with different grandchildren, and for caregiving arrangements to change over time. This often happened when grandmothers' strategies to resist their legal marginalization no longer worked and when parents' situations changed. For instance, while Virginia had legal guardianship of one grandson, she cared for the other privately. These different caregiving arrangements enabled her to access most, though not all, resources and services for her great-grandsons. It also allowed her granddaughters to maintain their parental rights. Finally, given that most of the great-grandmothers I interviewed were in their second round of coerced mothering, Virginia's experience also illustrates the insidious multigenerational cycle that reinforces coerced mothering as an inescapable social norm.

Black grandmothers face difficult decisions about *whether*, *how*, and *when* to intervene when their grandchildren experience or are at risk of child maltreatment. These women's stories reveal a submerged perspective, disclosing the otherwise invisible ways that social forces operate together—specifically, how social problems challenging Black families become forms of coercion forcing grandparents into caregiving roles, the lack of nonpunitive options for Black families dealing with family crisis and conflict, and grandmothers' lack of legal rights to act in their grandchildren's best interest—to transform Black grandmothers' role expectations and meanings.

MORPHING OF ANTICIPATORY RESPONSIBILITY INTO COERCED MOTHERING

Black grandmothers typically demonstrate anticipatory responsibility partly by supporting faltering parents. The grandmothers in my study, like those in other studies, did so by providing parental guidance, which involved modeling and correcting parenting, including teaching parents how to set appointments for their children (e.g., with medical providers, WIC, school staff), obtain resources, and bond with and care for their children.[7] Grandmothers also helped parents get jobs, provided childcare, and offered housing and other instrumental assistance.

A crucial aspect of grandmothers' role expectations was the gender of the parent. Both maternal and paternal grandmothers expected mothers to assume greater responsibility than fathers for their children, a gender bias that held mothers to a higher, and double, standard of parental accountability. When parents (predominantly mothers) failed to take grandmothers' contributions seriously or rejected them altogether, grandmothers struggled to thwart the deleterious effects of parental shortcomings on their grandchildren.

Finally, grandmothers shifted from anticipatory responsibility to coerced mothering in different ways. Some were provoked to suddenly increase responsibility for grandchildren after a series of incidents jeopardizing their safety and well-being tipped the balance. For other grandmothers, the shift was subtler; as the once-fluid line between Black motherhood and grandmotherhood hardened under the weight of parental breakdown, grandmothers became mothers by default. Yet, despite these circumstantial differences, these women shared a collective experience of coerced mothering.

In the stories that follow, I present a process that unfolds differently for every family, but that nevertheless reveals shared commonalities, including grandmothers' providing support aligned with their role expectations, parenting practices that jeopardize children's safety and well-being, family conflict that may or may not involve punitive institutions, and ratcheting up grandmothers' responsibility for grandchildren.

Provoked into Coerced Mothering

Grandmothers provoked into coerced mothering made the decision to increase their responsibility for their grandchildren—whether they wanted to or not—when the number and magnitude of incidents threatening their grandchildren's safety and well-being culminated in last-straw moments. Grandmothers differed about their threshold and tolerance for how many "chances" they gave parents to improve their parenting by integrating parental guidance or taking advantage of their instrumental support. These pivotal moments forced most grandmothers to decide not to relinquish custody of their grandchildren until parents could demonstrate adequate parenting. These determined and often distraught women did so even though they lacked legal rights, by using legal (e.g., CPS, DCFS, police) and nonlegal mechanisms (e.g., altercations) to erect a barrier between parents and children.

Mavis, fifty-nine, provides an example of this situation. Initially, Mavis cared for her newborn granddaughter, Anika, while her daughter, Vivica, attended college. They lived multigenerationally, with Mavis providing housing and childcare. This worked for Mavis: Vivica was doing something with her life and Mavis gave her the necessary support to lay a strong foundation for her and her new baby. But Vivica abandoned college and began to split her time between Chicago and Las Vegas, leaving Anika in Mavis's care. Mavis's status position as Anika's grandmother meant that she, more than anyone else, shouldered this responsibility. Her thrill-seeking daughter reminded Mavis of herself. The mother of five and grandmother of "twelve to thirteen grandchildren" confided that when she was younger, she too ran the streets and recognized that Vivica needed her community of women kinfolk to help with her child until she settled down. But, unlike Vivica, Mavis had participated when the women in her family, including the aunt who raised her, were helping her parent: "I was bringing money," she stated proudly, "putting it on the table." Mavis not only worked to feed and clothe her children but also washed and ironed their clothes and helped her aunt with utility bills.

Mavis's normative empathy faded as conflict between her and Vivica arose,[8] as it did for other grandmothers in this study. It is important to note that grandmothers did not expect their teenage or young adult daughters to know how to raise children or to do so without support. But they did expect them to be open to learning and to do their part (e.g., tend to children's day-to-day needs, sacrifice socializing and other activities to stay home with their children, work, and so on). Many grandmothers reported that trying to provide parental guidance to their daughters, as their own mothers and other women had done, too often resulted in conflict and the daughters' rejecting it. Some grandmothers had no choice but to marginalize mothers and assume parenting responsibilities after failed attempts to provide parental guidance, while others were thrust into coerced mothering when children were abandoned by their mothers.

The conflict between Mavis and Vivica that shifted Mavis from anticipatory responsibility to coerced mothering concerned Mavis's desire to protect Anika from her own mother's behavior. It wasn't just that Vivica pushed her mothering responsibilities onto her mother, but what her parenting looked like when she did it. For instance, when Vivica was in town and ostensibly spending time with her child, she frequently left her in the care of others, which infuriated Mavis. Given Mavis's concern, a concern expressed by many women caring for grandchildren who were too young to talk, she tried to educate Vivica about the risk to Anika when she was indiscriminate about where and with whom she left the child. But, during one of her visits to Chicago, Vivica went too far for Mavis—the last straw in a cumulative pattern of prior conflicts about Vivica's parenting.

One day she had took this baby over to the daddy's house and their house is so nasty. I got a church girl that live over there and she seen Anika walking down the hallway with one shoe, she was a toddler then, and a chicken bone in her hand. They had a mattress on the floor, no sheets on the mattress. House is filthy, a card table sitting on crates. . . . I said, "Hell no!" . . . I grabbed that baby, hit that downstairs, I said, "Never no more." . . . I told her [Vivica], "This baby is not going over to that nasty house no more. . . . She

[Anika's father's girlfriend] just as nasty and her kids older than Anika. But this girl got kids by him and you [Vivica] got a baby by him. What makes you think she's gonna treat your baby right? And this baby can't talk to tell you what somebody did to her." I said, "Girl, I will knock your ass out."

Mavis worried about the effect of Vivica's decision-making on Anika: "I done had this baby all her life. . . . I told her [daughter] she [granddaughter] not gonna be caught up in the system."

Vivica's repeated unwillingness to prioritize Anika reinforced that Mavis would be unable to relinquish being Anika's primary and sole caregiver. Eventually, the conflict over Vivica being a "drive-by mama," meaning she provided supplemental, sporadic parenting—when and how she wanted to—rather than primary, reliable parenting—when and how the child required—culminated in a call to the police.

She had came to the house to get her baby. And I wouldn't let her have her. So she called the police. "This my baby. I want to get her." I said, "You know what? She's worse than a drive-by shooter. She's a drive-by mama." But, by rights, she had the right to take her baby if she wanted to.

Mavis was confronted by the reality of how few people could adequately care for the three-year-old. Anika's father sold drugs and was in and out of jail, and his family's involvement was even more sporadic. So, like other women I interviewed who were strategizing alternative care solutions for their grandchildren, Mavis had a contingency plan that excluded the child's parents or other grandparents.

I've had two brain surgeries, three strokes. If I get to the point that I can't take care of that little yellow baby, my son, the twenty-nine-year-old one, he's next in line . . . to take care of Anika. And that daughter [the child's aunt] in there [living with Mavis].

Sixty-three-year-old Martha's story exemplifies how a parent's own history of child maltreatment undermined their parenting and provoked coerced mothering by grandmothers. Martha's sense of anticipatory responsibility kicked into high gear when she learned from her oldest daughter, Terri, that Kellen (a grandson whom Martha had raised) and his girlfriend, Erika, were abusing their one-and-a-half-year-old twins, Akram and Akria, and two-year-old Phallon. She was told of and later witnessed the parents neglecting, beating, and verbally abusing the children but did not live close enough to intervene. (Kellen and his family lived in another state.) Martha's middle daughter, Clarise, was Akram, Akria, and Phallon's grandmother, but refused to take responsibility for them, providing care "in spells"—when she wanted to be bothered with them, she would, and when she did not, she would not. Consequently, Martha was one of many great-grandmothers in this and other studies who experienced firsthand the result of caring being pushed up the generational ladder.[9] With Clarise unwilling to assume responsibility for her grandchildren and Erika estranged from her family, Martha saw no alternative but to increase her involvement with her great-grandchildren. But at that point, her intentions were only to help the young couple parent better.

Martha got an opportunity to intervene when Kellen asked if he could come home. She rented a truck, moved Kellen and his family into her home, gave them a room, and confirmed her suspicion of child abuse. But, Martha reasoned, Erika was also contending with intergenerational trauma.

> They was neglecting 'em. They was beatin' the little two-year-old girl. One time she [Erika] had whipped her so until that baby had bruises all on her back. . . . I think something's wrong with her [Erika] because she came up in the system. Everybody came up in the system is not bad, but . . . she was abused before she got in the system.

Since Erika had been sexually abused by her mother's boyfriend, Martha reasoned that she might not view her behavior as abusive. But when Martha tried to provide parental guidance, Erika made it clear that she did not want to be told how to raise her children. "I had to call the police on her," Martha disclosed, adding another dimension to the aforementioned reliance on the police as an interventionist parenting and grandparenting strategy, "because she had even threatened me."

The turning point for Martha from anticipatory responsibility to coerced mothering was when she could no longer keep her great-grandchildren safe in her capacity as their grandmother. Despite Martha's compassion for Erika, she could not permit child abuse: "And I talked to her, I pleaded with her. And I told her if they keep on, I was gonna call DCF on 'em. So, I did."

When, like so many grandmothers in this study pushed to using or threat of using punitive institutions to protect their grandchildren, Martha did call DCFS, Kellen and his family left her home. And when, a week later, they returned because they had no place else to go, Martha told them the children were welcome, but not Erika. Martha was already raising her five-year-old great-granddaughter Kennedy, but felt the circumstances left her no choice but to increase her involvement with her great-grandchildren.

> Now I have to tell you the honest truth, I don't want to raise no more kids forever and a day. I'm too old. . . . I just want them [Kellen and Erika] to get theyself together, get cleaned up, get jobs. . . . I want 'em to get they kids and love they kids and treat 'em right. But until then, I don't want 'em to have 'em. But I'm gonna have to know that they're doing what they need to do before they get those kids. I said, "My God, I'm gonna be dead raising great-grandkids."

In her refusal to relinquish custody (opt out of caring) until the parents could demonstrate that they could take care of the children without abusing them, Martha repeated what other women expressed—that their grandchildren "didn't ask to be here." Martha was also clear on the possible outcomes were she not to intervene, including the intergenerational transmission of trauma and abuse: "If somebody don't step up to the plate, they gonna end up dead or end up real bad. Because when you abuse a child, a child doesn't forget what you do." Nonetheless, her role expectation involved spending time with her great-grandchildren, not being primarily responsible for raising them. "I enjoy my great-grandkids," she maintained, but, "I would enjoy it better if they were coming to see me."

Coerced Mothering by Default

The fluid line between motherhood and grandmotherhood is a defining feature of Black women's experiences. So, when grandmothers' efforts to bolster a parent's parenting capacities failed, their parent-like involvement poised them for increased responsibility for their grandchildren. In contrast to grandmothers who were provoked by last-straw incidents, these women were negotiating a more subtle default process often associated with parents' (generally mothers') refusal or inability to parent. Grandmothers coerced by default described an inability to "make" mothers care for children: "I tried to make her be a mother. . . . But she wouldn't." "She just left the kids with me." "She would leave me with the kids . . . she never really wanted the responsibility." As when grandmothers were provoked into coerced mothering, conflict often ensued when parents rejected grandmothers' parenting support. When it did, some parents living in multigenerational households left with their children, only to determine they could not make it on their own and return their children to the grandmother's care. Other parents left without their children.

Fifty-year-old Grace was among those grandmothers who experienced coerced mothering by default—in Grace's case, when she was unsuccessful in imploring her teenage daughter with an intellectual and developmental disability to parent or help parent her children. Like other grandmothers in her situation, there was no final straw. As the conflict between Grace and her daughter, Rachel, swelled and deflated, and the child welfare system was called by and on Grace, she reluctantly found herself assuming some of Rachel's parenting "burden," despite years of resisting.

A survivor of child sexual abuse, a teenaged Grace had had two children, Rachel and a boy, before her stepfather was arrested and imprisoned for raping her. Despite being young and poor, Grace sought counseling for her family when her children reached adolescence. In addition to experiencing family trauma and being developmentally delayed, Rachel was, in Grace's words, a "problem child" who disobeyed and ran away from home.

> I was a single parent, trying to go to school, trying to work, and all those other things. And raising her and her brother . . . It was, I can say, a really heavy load. Okay? Trying to do all that, juggle all that. . . . And then she goes and has babies.

Of course, Rachel's difficulties were only compounded when she became a teenage mother. So, knowing that Rachel would need ample parenting support, Grace provided housing and childcare.

Conflict ensued when Rachel routinely left the children with Grace to spend time with friends and romantic interests, causing Grace to assume more responsibility for her grandchildren than she wanted.

> She never really wanted responsibility, so she wouldn't do that much with the kids. And the kids always minded me. They saw me as the first

nurturer 'cause I was there, I'm the one that they would come to for everything. Homework. . . . I enrolled them in school. Go to the school to see
about their progress. . . . In fact, it's me that the teachers and the principals
knew at all the schools.

Although Grace shouldered the bulk of responsibility for her first two
grandchildren, she resisted when Rachel had her third child, Dwayne: "I
kept fighting' her tooth and nail." Grace would leave the house before
Rachel, not intervene or voice concern when Rachel left Dwayne in different people's care, and, like other grandmothers in her situation, call DCFS
when Rachel left Dwayne for extended periods. She wanted Rachel "to
make a conscious effort to keep her legs closed and not keep bringing kids
into this world." This, she reasoned, was a way to put more of the "burden
on her" and take "away some of her freedom."

When a desperate Grace contacted DCFS for help with her daughter
and her grandchildren, they did send caseworkers but asked if she had
given Rachel a "pep talk" or would take her to "see somebody," meaning a
psychologist. Grace had done both. "And they said, 'Well, we can tell you
that not much is going to be done.' Now, this is why I always felt alone in
my plight." Two of her grandchildren's fathers "come around periodically,
sporadically" and the other grandchild's "father been missin' in the pic-
ture." Alone as her grandchildren's only viable care option, Grace was
effectively coerced into mothering.

> They [CPS] once told me there's no such thing as intervention in the sys-
> tem. . . . No support system unless they got the kids in the system. And that's
> it. I never wanted them to take my kids [grandchildren] out my house and
> put 'em nowhere. In nobody's house. 'Cause that's a difference between
> something happening to 'em and them actually staying safe. . . . So that was
> a downer for me, for them to tell me that. But the report will always come
> back unfounded. Why? Because . . . as long as grandmamma was there,
> grandmamma was that second parent. They know grandmothers are saving
> the system a lot. . . . Okay? This is the way they setting it up. You're not
> gonna help grandmamma financially because they feel like grandmamma's
> supposed to be that second parent. Okay? That's how they feel.

Like so many grandmothers in her predicament, Grace understood
personally and politically that she had to become the intervention she
sought. To both her daughter and DCFS, her role as a grandmother

ensured the foregone conclusion that she would succumb to coerced mothering to keep her grandchildren safe. Grandmothers like Grace saw the state's reliance on Black grandmothers for what it was: a lack of reciprocity and a gross devaluing of their contributions.

Another daunting aspect of coerced mothering involved challenges to opting out once caregivers assumed the role. Grace learned this the hard way. She started a new job and needed Rachel to take care of the children. Rachel told her that she was on her way, so Grace secured the children, who were five years old, three, and less than one, in a room, and "left on her word that she would be right behind me." Rachel never arrived. Grace got a call from a policewoman, who had the three children in her care.

A devastated Grace was eventually able to find some humor in the story—laughing at five-year-old Ava having called 911 and telling the operator she was tired of being in the house by herself. But it was a source of deep pain for her. And it was one of many incidents that conspired to prevent her from abandoning her caregiving responsibilities. Grace had been written up by DCFS in a report that she said read: "The grandmother left the kids in the house and this, that, and the other."

> They not trying to hear my story. They gonna write what they see. Okay? . . . It was more hurtful than anything. Because I'm thinking, "I can't even go to work." I can't depend on her and I'm tryin' to go to work and tryin' to make it better for all of us. . . . I look back on those days and I say, "Thank you, Jesus." . . . They was such trying times for me.

The experience with DCFS reinforced for Grace that she had little choice but to abandon her role expectations for grandmotherhood and mother her grandchildren. A decade later, Grace left Rachel in the apartment where she had raised her children and grandchildren for most of their lives. When she moved out, Grace took one of her grandsons with her. So Rachel wasn't responsible for all three children. But neither was Grace.

In contrast, fifty-two-year-old Cheryl increased responsibility for five of her grandchildren, whose mother, Khandice, struggled with substance addiction, even as she begged her daughter to get help and do the minimum for her children. This increasing responsibility catalyzed Cheryl from anticipatory responsibility into coerced mothering.

Khandice was fifteen years old when she developed a crack-cocaine addiction; the father of her child "was selling stuff and he was giving it to her." At the time, she lived in a multigenerational household with Cheryl. By the time Khandice went into rehab at sixteen, she had one child and was in a relationship characterized by intimate-partner violence with the child's father. Khandice tried unsuccessfully to maintain her sobriety. "She got clean. She came home. But he [child's father] wouldn't leave her alone. . . . He'd jump on her all the time and do her so bad."

Over the next decade, Khandice had four more children. Although the circumstances varied, all of the children ended up in their grandmother's care for the same reason—Khandice's substance addiction.

> When Tevin [Khandice's firstborn] was born, she was running the streets with the baby's father. She wouldn't get out and do nothing for him. I had to take care of him because she wouldn't do it. She wouldn't do nothing for him. She won't come down here and sign no papers to get no money for him, for him to get his shots and for him to get food stamps. I couldn't make her do this.

Unable to "make" Khandice take care of her then one child, Cheryl was compelled to take parent-like responsibility for him. The transition from grandmothering to mothering happened gradually, as Khandice's mothering became more sporadic, including disappearing for extended periods from the multigenerational home she shared with her mother, sometimes with the kids in tow, but most often leaving them in Cheryl's care. Cheryl eventually found herself defaulting to mothering another generation.

This pattern continued with Khandice's other children, though her negligence escalated as she started taking the children's resources.

> When she had Keith, the same thing happened. She would get his little check. She would come home for two or three days before the checks would come, and clean the baby up. The day the check would come, she would go to the currency exchange . . . and then she was gone. I wouldn't even see her no more. She wouldn't come home and give me no money, she wouldn't buy the baby no clothes. . . . I could do it at the time because I was working as a bartender, but I just got tired of it!

Khandice's first three children, Cheryl explained, "always been with me. . . . But the last two she had 'em down South," when at some point,

Khandice went to New Orleans to live with relatives. She took her youngest two children [Jamal and Shandra] with her, but they, too, eventually ended up with Cheryl when Khandice came to visit and left the children in her care.

Like so many women in her position, Cheryl's discrete role as a grandmother could not withstand the pressure of Khandice's substance addiction, and she too found herself forced into the default position of mothering another generation effectively on her own. While her grandchildren's fathers were involved, their involvement was dictated by their circumstances—one was drug addicted, two were incarcerated for drug-related offenses, and two held stable jobs. They all made contributions as and when they could; the incarcerated fathers visited and gave their children money before going to prison, as did the two fathers with full-time jobs, one of whom made more formal payments through his job's pension. Still, their involvement did not extend to full-time child-rearing and, with no acceptable alternatives, the responsibility fell to Cheryl.

At the time of the interview, Khandice had gotten clean. But she still wasn't stable enough to raise her five children—Tevin, nineteen; Keith, sixteen; Quincy, thirteen; Jamal, ten; and Shandra, eight—and, at any rate, they were unwilling to leave the grandmother who had cared for them for much of their lives. So Khandice supported her mother as she was able.

To sum up, then, as is brutally evident from the stories of Virginia, Mavis, Martha, Grace, and Cheryl, the phenomenon of coerced mothering is an unacknowledged pattern in which Black women, many of whom already engage in intensive grandmothering, are forced to provide even more care. The factors commonly identified as contributing to an over-representation of grandparent-headed households among African Americans are in fact forms of coercion that affect families across multiple generations. When grandmothers' efforts to support mothers failed, when teenage and single mothers engaged in drive-by mama behavior, when parents' substance abuse or addiction undermined their ability to parent, and when parents' own history of child maltreatment was intergenerationally transmitted, grandmothers had no choice but to intervene to thwart actual or potential child maltreatment of their grandchildren. In many cases, they intervened using the only options they had—the criminal justice and child welfare systems.

The struggles experienced by parents in this study are not unique. They are unaddressed challenges faced by many parents in the United States, but that society at large and policy makers could address by creating and investing in resources like jobs that pay a living wage, affordable housing and childcare, and expanding access to mental health and substance addiction treatment among low-income and poor individuals. Without these structural supports, at best too many parents' child-rearing responsibilities will continue to be pushed up the generational ladder, crowding the top rung with two vulnerable populations—children and largely poor, aged women of color. At worst, parents' child-rearing shortcomings will be "resolved" by the child welfare and criminal justice systems. Both "solutions" create a vicious cycle that undermines healthy development and stability across the generations.

HOW GRANDMOTHERS MAKE DECISIONS ABOUT CAREGIVING ARRANGEMENTS

The next stage in the evolution from grandmothering to coerced mothering was the formalization (or lack thereof) of the mothering role—a transition that in some cases legalized grandmothers' relationships with grandchildren. As previously discussed, the law distinguishes coerced mothering from mothering. Grandmothers are required to grapple with their legal marginalization relative to parents not only when care shifts to them but also when deciding the best caregiving arrangement in which to provide that care. Therefore, grandmothers' relationship to the legal system becomes the mechanism transforming coerced mothering into specific caregiving arrangements.

In determining whether they would keep or take their grandchildren, these grandmothers' decision-making was shaped by: (1) their ability to take care of their grandchildren without legal authority, (2) parents' willingness to leave children in grandparent's care, and (3) negotiating their personal lives. In general, keeping involved caring for grandchildren privately (unless grandmothers were unable to access resources and services) and wasn't as permanent as taking, which involved legal guardianship to prevent parents from removing children from their care. As yet another testament to strategic inventiveness in overcoming their lack of legal rights, grandmothers took grandchildren from parents not only with and without consent but also with and without parents' knowledge.

Grandmothers' decision-making about caregiving arrangements were also influenced by the fourth aspect of coerced caring—"the degree to which caregivers surrender certain aspects of their personhood, such as violating valued aspects of their identity and giving up their own projects."[10] As Nakano Glenn argues, "All caregivers who are enmeshed in full-time care find their autonomy restricted as their schedules are dictated by the needs of the care receiver, with little time to dedicate to their own pursuits."[11] Being coerced into taking their grandchildren from their own children often violated grandmothers' self-identity as both protective, supportive mothers and grandmothers who valued the parent-child relationship, and who were expecting and willing to grandmother (even intensively), but not mother, their grandchildren. These women were forced to forego activities vital to both their sense of self and their self-care—grave losses for women who struggled financially, grappled with poor health, and lacked sufficient formal and informal support. Grandmothers leveraged caregiving arrangements both to safeguard their grandchildren's welfare *and* to mitigate the dominance of caregiving on their lives. These tension-permeated narratives are heart-wrenching: Black grandmothers' deep love for and commitment to their grandchildren challenged or precluded practicing the same love and commitment for themselves. The role of racism cannot be erased from this equation, as these choices are not required of all grandparents and middle-aged/older adults.

Grandmothers' decision-making about caregiving arrangements also transformed the meaning they associated with grandmotherhood, specifically by emphasizing protecting their grandchildren over other meanings they associated with the grandmother role. But it was more than just a reconfiguration of energy: the processes and strategies associated with coerced mothering catalyzed the grandmother-to-mother shift. The harder grandmothers fought with parents, the state, and others to act in their grandchildren's best interest and to scaffold the structure (e.g., the specific caregiving arrangement) needed to provide care, the more they resembled mothers. The more time, energy, and resources they poured into their grandchildren, and the more their grandchildren related to them as mothers—in most cases calling them "mama" or some version of mother, even when others challenged their use of the term—the more they became de facto mothers, though with different legal rights.

Keeping Their Grandchildren

Although Black grandmothers play a crucial role in maintaining and stabilizing Black families, their assuming primary caregiving responsibilities doesn't preclude conflict, as we have seen. In other words, though malleable and fluid, Black grandmothers' parental surrogacy isn't always seamless, and to suggest otherwise romanticizes their experiences. This romanticization, perpetuated by scholars, the Black community, and society at large, erases the magnitude of the emotion-work, problem-solving, and family conflict associated with the call for grandmothers to "keep" their grandchildren in private kinship arrangements. It also ignores the impact on the psychological and physical well-being of these women. While grandparent caregivers are vulnerable to the strictures of the state, which determines whether and how they care for their grandchildren, they are also vulnerable to parents. Legal custody conflict with parents prevented some grandmothers in this study from formalizing their relationship with grandchildren even when desired or necessary. Others, like Virginia whose story began this chapter, resisted formalizing caregiving arrangements because parental surrogacy jeopardized what they wanted and needed for themselves.

Even though Grace had cared for her fifteen-year-old grandson, Shemar, his whole life, she did not become his legal guardian when she set up a skipped-generation household with him: "It's not a typical . . . grandmother-and-grandson thing in such that I took him from her and pursued legal papers or what have you . . . she wanted me to take all three of 'em" [*Laughter*]. In clarifying that she did not become Shemar's legal guardian, Grace characterized her relationship as atypical because she raised him as a mother, but without the legal rights to do so. She was fulfilling the legal aspects of motherhood, but, after her experience with the child welfare system, eschewed legal responsibility. While she accepted raising Shemar, by not parenting all her grandchildren into adulthood, she also resisted being consumed by carework—no small feat for the grandmother whose grandchildren "look at me as their mother. All three of 'em."

Grace devised strategies to obtain the resources and services Shemar needed without obtaining legal guardianship and without the assistance of his parents. Since she had been unable to rely on her grandchildren's parents, Grace had long figured out the bureaucracy of child-rearing institutions. As a result, she was able to get a medical card and TANF child-only benefits. She was also able to enroll Shemar in school because she had done so since he was in pre-K and her name was on all his paperwork.

Like Grace, grandmothers used different strategies to navigate child-rearing institutions without legal guardianship, including building their own trusted relationships with child-rearing institutions, relying on parents, and forging parents' signatures. Among some of the grandmothers I interviewed, medical providers accepted their verbal confirmation of legal authority (even among women who did not have it) and provided care when grandmothers had the child's medical card and it was in the grandmother's name. They acquired the savvy to use private schools, day-care providers they knew, and the Affidavit of Enrollment and Residency, or the McKinney-Vento Homeless Assistance Act to enroll their grandchildren in school.[12]

Grace's reason for resisting formalizing her caregiving arrangement was not her hope that her daughter might resume parenting, but her deferred dreams. For her, as for so many others, parenting her grandchildren silenced vital aspects of her personhood and identity, including education and health. Grace hadn't abandoned her educational goals—"I'm always thinkin' about, 'Well, one day I'm gonna realize the dream and the goal of doin' somethin' that I like to do, and workin' with people and all that,'"—but while she had completed all the credits for her bachelor's degree, her sporadic enrollment prolonged her studies and the university wouldn't award her the degree.

When asked why she felt she needed to care for her grandchildren despite the obvious difficulties and unforeseen sacrifices, Grace provided insight into her motivations and definition of grandmothering (nurturing her lineage):

> To save my grandchildren. I just felt like they would have wound up in the system if I hadn't stepped in. And I think it's somethin' in me, I just cannot see my own, especially my own blood, out there suffering and maybe there was somethin' that I could have done to prevent them from suffering. . . . I

just couldn't see them goin' to no foster home, things happening to 'em. I just felt that they would have been safer around their own. Even if it meant that I had to sacrifice my own ambitions, my own career for the sake of those human beings, those three human beings.

And, like other grandmothers, Grace turned to religion to understand her experience.

Sometimes when I think about how much I had to sacrifice, I get in that mood where I'm downhearted. Because I feel like I missed out on my own life. But, on the other hand, I say, "Well, I think this is what God intended for me to do." You know, invest in these human beings. So I raised my grandchildren and my children. . . . I go back and forth.

Like so many others, Grace's deep love for her grandchildren preempted her own desires. Deprived of the structural, social, and legal supports her family desperately needed, Grace saw God as her only source of help in accepting that her sacrifice was the intervention she had long sought for them. This parallels other research that identified the importance of spirituality for other grandmothers in equally untenable circumstances adjusting to new roles and attendant family difficulties.[13]

Taking Their Grandchildren

In contrast to grandmothers who "keep" their grandchildren, grandmothers who "take" their grandchildren from parents become legal guardians without intentions of returning children to parents' custody unless the parents can demonstrate their fitness to provide care. Among these "takers," two categories emerged: overt and covert pursuers of legal guardianship. Before describing grandmothers' lived experiences, it's important to distinguish the differences in the two processes and in the family and institutional issues compelling grandmothers to use one strategy over another.

When grandmothers took their grandchildren overtly, they did not try to hide their plans from parents, despite the risk of parents deciding to intervene before grandmothers could obtain custody. They saw no need to hide their activities, largely because they assumed enough responsibility for their grandchildren that they felt confident to demonstrate parental unfitness before a judge if necessary. Grandmothers were also disinclined to hide their activities with uninvolved parents who did not threaten legal guardianship or would not resist.

In contrast, when these women took children covertly, it was without parents' knowledge. Grandmothers deployed covert taking primarily to prevent parents from removing children from their care. Covert taking required decoding how the system worked and taking advantage of parental shortcomings. They engaged in the laborious process of what I refer to as "documentation gathering," exercising herculean ingenuity and resourcefulness. First, they educated themselves about the steps required for legal guardianship. They needed primary documentation (e.g., a birth certificate and a social security card), but these necessitated parental consent and involvement. So, they sought secondary documentation—specifically, the paperwork associated with Public Aid benefits (e.g., medical cards, food stamps) or school enrollment—which they then used to obtain primary documentation. Covert takers were not only additionally burdened with time-robbing documentation-gathering, but also with other covert-taking strategies (e.g., hiding pursuits from parents and street-level bureaucrats, and such). But all takers had to navigate lengthy, arduous legal guardianship policies and procedures and to present in court the cases they had built against parents.

Covert and overt takers shared other commonalities. The majority of grandmothers initiated either process by calling the child abuse hotline. Others used CPS and the police to prevent parents from removing their grandchildren. Although some hired a lawyer or filed legal guardianship paperwork themselves, all endured the tension between using or navigating the system by divulging enough information about parents to obtain custody and not losing custody to that very system, or to parents—again demonstrating grandmothers' resourcefulness and commitment to ensuring the safety and well-being of their grandchildren.

Whether grandmothers took children from parents overtly or covertly, obtaining legal guardianship entailed the arduous process of (1) filling out "guardianship of a minor" forms at the clerk of the circuit court, (2) filing the forms, (3) notifying parents that they were petitioning for guardianship and providing the court with proof of that notification, and (4) a minor guardianship court date with paperwork and valid driver's license or state identification card. Any child age fourteen or older also had to attend to tell the judge if they agreed to the guardianship. Parents' rights could be overstepped without their consent only if their inability to adequately parent their children was persuasively conveyed, an emotion-freighted requirement of the guardianship hearing.

Overt and covert takers wrangling legal guardianship were also dependent on street-level bureaucrats, a relationship that might help or hinder them. Street-level bureaucrats could help if they gave clear and easy-to-follow instructions about to-dos and expectations of the legal guardianship process. Guardianship program caseworkers helped by coming to grandmothers' homes to facilitate completing and filing required paperwork; accompanying them to court; and, when facing programmatic or policy barriers, strategizing work-arounds.

By contrast, street-level bureaucrats might substantially hinder the process by providing misinformation, often due to high turnover at DCFS grant agencies. In at least one such case, Cassandra's, this resulted in the paperwork never being filed. While Cassandra assumed that she had legal guardianship, she discovered that she did not. Her grandson's mother, who had once consented, later refused because she wanted the child's resources. So, Cassandra was forced to take her grandson covertly. To add insult to injury, other grandmothers reported being stigmatized during the legal guardianship process—mistreated by caseworkers or judges who blamed them for parents' inability to care for children and questioned their own parenting abilities. Shalonda, an overt taker, recalled the commitment of "going to court a couple of years, I think, before they actually gave me legal guardianship over her [granddaughter]." During the process, the judge gave her a dressing-down: "Why should I give you this kid? You don't look like you did such a good job of raising your own."

OVERT TAKING

Some grandmothers who took children from parents overtly sought out street-level bureaucrats in public assistance programs. Although Cheryl's primary impetus for taking her five grandchildren was to ensure that they stayed in her care, her scarce resources motivated her to obtain legal guardianship. As a single mother raising her own teenagers when care of her grandchildren shifted to her, Cheryl did not earn enough to make ends meet. She combined work income and public assistance for her own children but still struggled financially. Coincidentally, Cheryl and her daughter Khandice had the same caseworker.

> I just went down and sat and talked to her. I told her about the problem: . . . "She will not come down here and sign no papers, won't get no money for him, won't get his shots and his food stamps. . . . I can't make it financially." She said, "You know, Cheryl, since you're taking care of the baby and the baby's staying at your house, I'm gonna put the baby on your card."

And so, Cheryl was able to get her oldest grandson, Tevin, placed on her public aid benefits—receiving his medical card, cash assistance, and SNAP. But more importantly, the caseworker told her how to obtain legal guardianship to get Tevin medical attention—something she could not do without legal authority. Cheryl called DCFS and was given "the number to the guardianship program . . . they come out, fill the papers out, and told me I had to go to court in front of the judge. And that's how I got it." As his guardian, Cheryl was able to get SSI for Tevin.

When Khandice's pattern of neglect continued with her other children, Cheryl "called the guardianship program up. I went right back down there. I got him [Keith] and the little girl [Shandra] at the same time. She didn't have but three then. So, I got all three of 'em." Cheryl did the same when Khandice left the youngest two children in her care. "I didn't want them to go in no system. . . . So I had to get everything turned over to me so I could get some help for them." Cheryl was able to get proper diagnoses and treatment for her grandchildren's developmental disabilities.

Even though her grandchildren had long called her "mama," legal guardianship signaled that Cheryl would now have complete responsibility for them. But she had her sights set on one day being able to work part-time to supplement her disability income. "I'm tired of sitting around this house," she lamented. The mother of three protected her personal life by refusing to raise anymore of her grandchildren even though two of her son's children with whom she was actively involved begged to remain in her care. While Cheryl prioritized these grandchildren in accordance with her definition of grandmotherhood, she told them, "You gotta go home, you gotta go home."

Some grandmothers initiated the legal guardianship process through DCFS after police got involved. For example, Mavis's daughter, Vivica, called the police on her for refusing to relinquish custody of her granddaughter Anika. When Vivica called the police, Mavis "went downtown to court." Getting legal guardianship was relatively easy. "I had proof of everything, which stuff is in my name. Medical—goin' to the clinic and everything is in my name. I had no problems with that." Each time Vivica came to Chicago from Las Vegas, Mavis made her write a letter stating that she was leaving Anika in her custody. "I had all of them letters," Mavis said.

Mavis took Anika from her mother to keep the child in her care, but also to protect her own resources. "Section 8 says . . . for her to be on your lease, you have to have some kind of paperwork. That's all I needed to hear." Mavis had been unable to work after two brain surgeries and two knee surgeries and was unwilling to risk her granddaughter's safety or her Section 8, which she'd had since 1976. Without Section 8, she stated simply, "I can't make it."

Mavis was close to all of her grandchildren, visiting those who lived in other cities. But, she confessed, "I never thought for a minute that I would be takin' care of a little three-year-old child." So raising Anika not only defied Mavis's role expectations but also forced her to deprive her own daughter of her child.

> I'm more disappointed than I am anything. Because I didn't raise her like that. I just knew . . . and she's so good with children, that she would do right. . . . She [Anika] called her "Vivica" one day. I said, "No, that's your mother." She [Anika] loves her so much. . . . I said, "But you put these streets before your baby."

When Mavis's family resisted her tough-love treatment of Vivica, she defended making her daughter accountable for her own child.

> She [Vivica] live over on X Street somewhere. Over to my people. But see, she in and out of my people's house. She can't do that here. And then they try to tell me. That's my child! Can't nobody love her no harder than me, but I'm not gonna help her hurt herself. This is the real world right here. I'm doin' a whole lot for her right now, takin' care of her baby. I don't owe her nothin'. . . . And I don't need your approval for nothin'.

Mavis and others who described loving their children harder than those who objected to their methods were pinpointing the loss of valued self-identity attributable to implementing a high-stakes version of familial love that risked costing them their children in order to protect their grandchildren.

COVERT TAKING

Grandmothers engaged in covert taking when attempts to convince parents to leave children in their care failed or when prior attempts at legal guardianship had failed. Covert takers hid their legal guardianship pursuits from parents, and sometimes from street-level bureaucrats. For example, when Martha's grandson, Kellen, and his partner, Erika, left their three children in her care, she used the opportunity to take them, covertly starting the guardianship process to ensure her great-grandchildren's safety. Local kinship-caregiver support groups provided Martha with the necessary information to obtain legal guardianship of Akram, Akria, and Phallon. Martha's daughter (the children's grandmother) helped obtain birth certificates, which Martha used to procure temporary medical cards. She then used the medical cards to get social security cards.

> Well, I know that the parents wouldn't have consented to it even though they weren't doing the kids right. . . . So when my number was called [at the Social Security office], I went up there and I explained my situation. She [employee] said, "You are those kids' grandmother." She said, "If the welfare took your word enough to give you a medical card for those kids, I'm gonna put in for they Social Security for you."

To learn about the self-education these women invested in on behalf of their grandchildren, I attended a guardianship hearing with Martha for which she had spent months preparing. Martha was living off of her own SSDI and that of an adopted fourth great-granddaughter. Having three additional dependents and being unable to work because she was recovering from lung cancer was taking its toll—as were obstacles concerning bureaucratic regulations and parents' unwillingness to consent. But her persistence and shrewdness paid off. At the guardianship hearing, she had the paperwork in order. She was deliberately vague in explaining the parents' situation to the judge, omitting the abuse, including only that "they hadn't returned for the children" and that she "didn't know where they were." She emphasized meeting the children's needs, especially medical needs.

On reviewing her processed guardianship papers, we saw that the children had been "appointed for the following reasons: Both parents are unemployed and unable to provide for children." Martha's new guardianship status granted her access to the public assistance the children so desperately needed, and, unless the parents could prove they were capable of taking care of the children, Martha had no plans to relinquish them. "I wish they parents would get they self together," she said, "and get they kids and do what they need to do. But until then, as long as I'm living and got that old house over there, I'm gonna see by them."

CONCLUSION

It is important to reiterate that the combination of the historical problems facing Black families and their cultural traditions has meant that, for Black grandmothers, intensive grandmothering is more normative than exceptional, and is certainly not a new phenomenon.[14] What *is* new are the terms and circumstances under which Black grandmothers provide care in the post–civil rights era. This chapter has demonstrated that the factors identified in previous research as contributing to the overrepresentation of grandparent-headed households among African Americans are crucial forms of coercion themselves. Indeed, the parenting struggles of single and teenage mothers, parental substance abuse and addiction, a parent's history of child maltreatment, and other social problems create the context for coerced mothering. Additionally, changes in the kinds of social problems compelling grandparent caregiving, state power to declare parents unfit rather than provide resources—creating a culture of fear among Black families of losing children to the system—and the increasing need for grandmothers to fulfill the legal aspects of motherhood have contributed to the complexities of grandparent caregiving in the twenty-first century, including informal kinship care.

It is no longer sufficient for scholars, policy makers, and society to assume that grandparent caregivers providing informal kinship care— which comprises the bulk of caregiving—simply continue their cultural traditions, family norms, and role expectations. The grandmothers featured in this chapter disrupt assumptions about the expectations and meanings they attribute to grandmothering. It is too often assumed that Black grandmothers raise their grandchildren because they want to. While this is true for some, many do so because they have to. The testimonies of the women in this study reveal that, while they unanimously anticipated playing an active role in their grandchildren's lives, that role varied. While viewing the experiences of grandmothers forced to provide care via coerced mothering is original to this study, Black women's disinclination to be primarily responsible for their grandchildren is not.[15] An imposed view of uncomplicated caregiving robs Black grandmothers of the possibility for others to fathom the totality, difficulty, and complexity of their lived experiences, which by extension means that it robs them and their families of critical resources and support.

Punitive public policy solutions to systemic social problems have fostered an environment in which marginalized grandparents lack nonpunitive options to address their grandchildren's needs—a reality that must be factored into any understanding of grandparent-headed households' experiences. Ironically, using the child welfare system—the very system with a long history of racist policies and practices toward Black families—to dampen parents' legal rights contributes to the overrepresentation of Black families in that system. But when family crises arise and grandmothers are provoked into coerced mothering or coerced to become mothers by default, some use their only option to keep their grandchildren safe—the state or law enforcement. A lack of government supports, mediation services, and nonpunitive options put these grandmothers in a lose-lose predicament. They must proactively use the system to ensure that their grandchildren don't end up in it.

Coerced mothering forced grandmothers into the public sphere in ways parents did not experience. While carework research has focused on the household, the market, and the bureaucracy as primary social modes of caring, less attention has been given to the ways the legal system both facilitates and constrains an individual's ability to provide care. Grandmothers' lack of rights relative to parents and the state was made painfully evident as grandmothers sought to maintain care of their grandchildren, keep them safe, and procure resources and services. In spotlighting the array of strategies women used to overcome their lack of legal rights, I have also illuminated their brilliance and innovation. Carework scholars have long emphasized the ways in which nurturing overshadows the mental acumen required of informal caregivers to perform their carework. This book shows that to get to the nurturing, behind-the-scenes, private-realm activities associated with caring labor, grandmothers must create the necessary structure and conditions to do so—again redefining grandmotherhood. Also overshadowed in existing research are the ways in which coercion affected grandmothers' personal lives. While considering "God's plan" may have helped some cope with deferred dreams, it did not diminish the ache these overburdened women carried.

Even though the fundamental nature of grandparent caregiving has changed in the post–civil rights era, the love and commitment of Black grandmothers for their grandchildren has persisted. Tragically, their ability to demonstrate it has changed. Love, and the very definition of grandmotherhood, takes on painful new meaning when they are forced to build and argue cases against parents, often their own children, to obtain legal custody. Grandmotherhood is redefined when they forge parents' signatures or refuse to divulge the magnitude of their family dynamics and problems to street-level bureaucrats to procure resources and services for their grandchildren. Grandmotherhood is redefined when they call CPS or the police to keep children safe, and when they covertly pursue legal guardianship. It is redefined when they have to defer or forsake self-love and their own pursuits. Grandmotherhood is redefined when grandmothers essentially become mothers to their grandchildren. Indeed, for some Black women, raising grandchildren in the twenty-first century represents a significant departure from anything they have known in their own families or their role as grandmothers to their other grandchildren.

4 How Grandmothers Experience and Respond to Coerced Mothering within Formal Kinship Care

Sixty-three-year-old Nell felt compelled by her daughter Joanna's neglect of her children to protect them, first in a parent support role and then as a licensed foster parent. Nell had long attributed Joanna's not being "quite right" to three brain operations she had had as a twelve-year-old, and to epilepsy that manifested in adulthood. When Joanna became a mother of five, Nell's pattern of "picking her up" intensified. Protecting her grandchildren defined grandmotherhood for Nell. Still, she did not anticipate intensifying her involvement when she noticed "some things that was goin' on that I just didn't really like"—for instance, the parents leaving the children unattended and without sufficient food. Although Nell felt that Joanna "did the best she could with what she had to work with," she asserted, "everybody that can have children is not fit to be a mother." When Nell brought up the "things" she "didn't really like," Joanna was unwilling to take any parental guidance. When she contacted CPS (Child Protective Services), Nell was told that they could not do anything: "Just because she doesn't have food in her refrigerator doesn't mean the children aren't eatin'. Maybe she's takin' 'em out every day to McDonald's or somethin."

Eventually, a neighbor called CPS on Joanna, who had whipped her oldest son, seven-year-old Darrius, reopening a cut near his eyebrow and producing what the investigator identified as a "wound." As a result, Darrius and his four-year-old brother, DeVaughn, were taken to the hospital. When Nell received a call from a caseworker with DCFS (the Department of Children and Family Services) that two of her grandchildren were at the hospital, she and her son came to their aid. On being told that Joanna had been arrested for child abuse, Nell was asked if she had ever witnessed Joanna in the act. Nell told them she had not, but, an hour later, caseworkers showed up with Joanna's other three children and told Nell they were being taken into state custody. She was devastated. The kids were screaming. "Granny don't let them take us, don't let them take us," Nell recollected. "I could remember that as if it was yesterday. . . . I just kind of lost it." Her son grabbed her and said, "Mom, let them take 'em and this time when you get them, she can't come and just take 'em up and just walk out with them." Nell proclaimed, "So I [Nell] had to let them go."

Nell did not anticipate that, instead of immediately releasing the children into her care, DCFS would take them into state custody. Her five grandchildren spent a week dispersed across four nonrelative foster homes despite Nell telling the caseworker that her family was willing to take the children. As instructed, Nell, her daughter Dawn, and her niece Rebecca showed up at the juvenile detention center, where they "signed documents stating that we were willing to take the children." Nell described the process as relatively straightforward. "When we went back to court, they told us that they gave us custody of the kids."

Before becoming her grandchildren's foster parent, Nell reached out to the respective fathers.

> And I gave 'em the date for the court. I said, "If you want to get your kids, you show up in court. And we'll see what happens." So, of course, when we got to court, nobody was there but me and my daughter and my son.

The children were divided among her large family of extended relatives, as Nell knew that she could not handle all five of them and work full-time. Still, Nell ended up raising Joanna's two oldest sons—Darrius and

DeVaughn. Dawn took the two girls—Tysheema, six, and Michiko, fifteen months—and Rebecca took the youngest boy, five-month-old Jarrian.

Although the family was able to take the children into their custody, they were informed by the caseworker that they would need to become licensed to keep the children in their care. "They were just placed with me through the DCFS. . . . And, and we went through training. I got a license. And, so I became a licensed foster home." Nell did her training in the evenings after work, doing six or seven classes over a few weeks.

Nell, Dawn, and Rebecca were given a variety of services for the children, including beds, and vouchers for clothes and anything else they might need. After providing care for about two months, Nell, Dawn, and Rebecca began receiving foster care payments, which increased after they obtained their licenses. For the first five years that the children were in the care of their relatives, the caseworker visited every month, at home and at the children's schools, away from their caregivers.

However, Joanna hadn't fulfilled the case plan that she had been given two years to complete. So, after five years as foster parents, Nell, Rebecca, and Dawn had to obtain subsidized guardianship, adopt, or return the children to DCFS custody. They all chose subsidized guardianship because they wanted Joanna to have the option of getting her children back. But Nell believed that Joanna did not feel urgency about regaining custody because "she knew that, or always felt that, they [the children] were being well cared for and there was never a time that she wasn't able to see them, that she couldn't interact with them, or they weren't around her."

When the kids needed to go to the doctor or have someone come to school, it was Joanna, not Nell, Dawn, or Rebecca who performed those parenting functions. But being involved with her children wasn't the same as being primarily responsible for them, and Joanna's unwillingness to complete her case plan meant that Nell never got to opt out of her caregiving role. At the time I interviewed her, Nell had raised Darrius and DeVaughn for thirteen years, had assumed responsibility for two more of Joanna's children, and was in the process of transitioning the youngest two back to their mother.

I just felt that it was time now for her to step up. . . . A lot can change in thirteen years. Number one, they're no longer five months and fifteen months old. So what she did then would probably not be possible now . . . and I think she really understood what I'm sayin' to her, that "I can't keep fillin' in the gap for you. . . . We've got three of your kids over to the house. So you've gotta weather the storm and do for these two."

During the recent custody hearings, Nell was asked if her grandchildren would be in danger in their mother's care. "They have always been around her [Joanna]!" she said. "I would be lying if I said that they have never been around her because . . . she has always played a part in raising them. . . . During the summertime, they went to her! And each and every last one of them loves their mother to death!" But, while DeVaughn will graduate from high school soon, he has no plans to leave his grandmother's before then. "He likes to go see her," Nell said. "But he don't want to live with her."

Being a mother to her grandchildren wasn't what Nell's experience had prepared her for.

My mother had maybe twenty-five grandchildren. But we were all responsible for our own children. And so she pretty much lived the life that she wanted to live. And with me, I pretty much wanted to do the same thing. Walk in the same shoes. But, of course, it didn't work out like that. So it was always a battle in my mind of "What did I do wrong?" And "What could I have done that could have, maybe, changed that?" But it took me a while to realize it wasn't me. I did the best I could. When I look at it to see all my kids, all raised under the same umbrella, and they're productive, and they're doin' well, and that's what you want. But as mothers, you take the blame and responsibility . . . until you realize that it's not your battle.

For Nell as for other Black women in her position, the notion of linked lives was critical—that is, if their children were doing well or "doing what they are supposed to be doing," the form and tenor of grandmothering would be characterized by choice, not externally imposed and defined. To gauge their own parenting, Nell and other women in this study compared a child who was struggling as a parent to a child who was doing okay. Ultimately, Nell, like many of these women, decided that she would not blame herself. That said, she also did not get to live the life she wanted.

Nell's experience of external state intervention, which I define as state intervention initiated by individuals other than grandmothers, dramatically changed her experience of parenting her grandchildren. Like women parenting their grandchildren in informal kinship care, Nell and others parenting their grandchildren in formal kinship care (tiers one, two, and five of the five-tiered system of kinship care) experienced a transformation in the role expectations and meanings they associated with grandmotherhood and managed the quasi-legal rights associated with their caregiving arrangements. However, unlike grandmothers parenting their grandchildren informally, grandmothers parenting their grandchildren formally had significantly different experiences of coerced mothering. The rest of this chapter is dedicated to exploring those differences in two sections—the first on the impact of external state intervention on coerced mothering, including the significance of grandmothers' pathways to parenting grandchildren with child welfare system involvement, and the second on making difficult decisions about caregiving arrangements within a complex child welfare system and using one's agency to manage involvement with the system.

THE IMPACT OF EXTERNAL STATE INTERVENTION ON COERCED MOTHERING

External state intervention occurred in two ways: through mandatory and nonmandatory reporters (e.g., friends, neighbors, and relatives). Demarcating the two kinds of reporters is important, not only because they demonstrate how families end up in the child welfare system but also because mandatory and voluntary reporters report different allegations.[1] What this means for grandmothers is that the type of child maltreatment a grandmother might be contending with is affected by the type of reporter who initiated the pathway to the child welfare system in the first place. For instance, in this study, all mandatory reporting occurred when hospital personnel contacted DCFS on detecting child maltreatment, including substance abuse during pregnancy.[2] In contrast, the children in grandmothers' care resulting from voluntary reporting were older children who were more likely to be reported to CPS for physical abuse. A final point about the nature of child maltreatment among children being cared for by grandmothers in formal kinship care: consistent with other research, these children were more likely to have experienced more severe child maltreatment—including physical abuse, complications of parental addiction, and other severe forms of neglect—than children being cared for by grandmothers who provide informal kinship care.[3]

Whether by mandatory or voluntary reporting, Black children are more likely than other children to end up in the system. This is due not only to a higher incidence of child neglect associated with higher poverty rates but also to the fact that Black families experience racial discrimination in their interactions with mandatory reporters, including racial disparities in drug-testing newborns for parental drug use and taking substance-exposed infants into state care.[4] Moreover, the racial geography of the child welfare system and lack of other resources available to voluntary reporters means that Black communities disproportionately rely on CPS to resolve potential child maltreatment.[5] Child welfare system factors also contribute to the overrepresentation of Black children in the child welfare system, including lack of resources for families of color and caseworker characteristics.[6]

As Nell's story demonstrates, external state intervention is character-ized by state-mandated (kinship foster care, subsidized guardianship, and kinship adoption) caregiving arrangements. As discussed in the appendix, these caregiving arrangements fall under tiers one and two of the five-tiered system of kinship care, where grandmothers receive more resources and support than those in other tiers, but also manage more state intru-sion (see table 2 in the introduction). External state intervention can also result in state-mediated (kinship diversion and legal guardianship) car-egiving arrangements. These grandmothers are forced to rescue their grandchildren from DCFS according to the constraints outlined in tier five, which for the most part includes no resources and services.

Coerced mothering differed for grandmothers dealing with external state intervention than for those who initiated or avoided state interven-tion. In both scenarios, grandmothers' status position made them more likely than other relatives to raise their grandchildren. However, for grandmothers faced with external state intervention, their status position made them more likely than other relatives to deal not only with the *fear* of running up against state agents on their phone, at their front door, and at the hospital after the births of their grandchildren or during grandchildren's treatment for injuries or illnesses, but with the *reality* of these interactions. Their status position also made them more likely than other family members to receive parents' and family members' frantic and desperate pleas to intervene so that their grandchildren did not end up "in the system." When this happened, grandmothers had to manage kinship foster care or kinship diversion and take on the caregiving arrangements required by the state. When grandmothers were compelled to provide care because of external state intervention it also reinforced for them that their grandchildren had no alternative care options.

Grandmothers managing external state intervention found it more difficult to opt out of caregiving responsibilities because they had to contend with the challenges parents faced as they "got themselves together" as well as the state's assessment of whether that "togetherness" was sufficient. When Nell's daughter, Joanna, failed to complete her case plan and was unable to resume parenting, it did not matter whether or not Nell felt her daughter was ready to take on her parenting responsibilities. DCFS determined the kind of relationship Joanna would have with her children. Grandmothers also found it more difficult to opt out because the state controlled the time frame for how long parents had to get themselves together.

As discussed in the previous chapter, whether providing care in formal or informal kinship care, most grandmothers in this study experienced caregiving as coercive, which also meant that their caregiving cost them aspects of their identity and personhood. But grandmothers raising grandchildren in formal kinship care had to manage more bureaucracy as they fought to preserve or craft their personal lives. If Nell was ever going to be just a grandmother to all of her grandchildren, she would need to transfer custody back to their mother, which meant that she also had to devise strategies to facilitate that outcome, even if it meant contravening DCFS dictates. While some grandmothers accepted that they would likely raise their grandchildren into adulthood, many still hoped that one day children would return to their mother's care. These grandmothers largely believed that for that to happen mothers needed to spend time caring for their children. So, they broke DCFS rules about parental visitations and allowed children to spend time with their mothers, often during the holidays, summers, and weekends. For Nell this was a win-win—her daughter could improve her parenting skills and Nell could get a much-needed respite. But resisting this DCFS policy could jeopardize grandmothers' ability to keep their grandchildren in their care. Ultimately, the strategies grandmothers devised to get, keep, and transition their grandchildren into and out of their care—and the energy they expended keeping their tactics hidden from state agents—increased grandmothers' caregiving demands.

In the two sections that follow, I explore not only *why* (e.g., social problems plaguing a parent generation, state's use of kinship care, and such) grandmothers end up with their grandchildren in their care, but also *how* they experience these forces in the context of coerced mothering. Grandmothers' stories shed light on how they experience coerced mothering when mandatory and voluntary reporters, respectively, initiate their family's involvement in the child welfare system.

Coerced Mothering in the Context of Mandatory Reporting

Sixty-five-year-old Lena Bell was one of several grandmothers whose pathway to the child welfare system began after a mandatory reporter called DCFS because a mother was suspected of child maltreatment. These grandmothers' worst fears had become an impending reality: their grandchildren were about to be or had been taken into state custody. Lena Bell exemplified what happened when women stepped in to prevent grandchildren from being placed in nonrelative foster care.

Feleesha, the mother of two of Lena Bell's twelve grandchildren, returned from work to the home she lived in with her mother, and noticed her infant son Clay was acting "strange." When Feleesha took him to the hospital, DCFS was called. Lena Bell explained why DCFS removed four-year-old Imani and three- to four-week-old Clay from their mother's custody:

> She [Feleesha] left him there with her mother and they had him on the couch. . . . She [maternal grandmother] had Imani and she had her other little grandkids running all around the house. Some kinda way he got hurt. . . . She [maternal grandmother] say she don't know what happened. But anyway, DCFS come in and take him out.

When, because of her status position as a grandparent, Lena Bell received a call from Feleesha imploring her to take the children to prevent them from being taken into state custody, she agreed to do so, explaining: "I didn't want them to go into a home with strangers." At the time, the children's father, Lena Bell's son, was imprisoned. So, despite her poor health, she was her grandchildren's only care option apart from nonrelative foster care.

> I just thank the Lord for giving me the strength to deal with 'em. I didn't want 'em to go into the system so I got 'em. . . . It's so hard. Because you love 'em and you worry about 'em, if you let 'em go to strangers you're gonna worry. So much abuse and everything going on in the world now.

Like many grandmothers unable to opt out of caregiving, Lena Bell needed her spiritual strength. In the seven years that she parented her grandchildren, her son had not been released from prison and Feleesha had been unable to complete her case plan, in part due to her struggle with an opioid addiction that she was managing by taking methadone (though it was unclear whether she had this addiction at the time the children were taken into state custody).

Lena Bell's difficulty in opting out of caregiving was, like many women's, compounded by her child welfare system involvement, because it was DCFS, not grandmothers, who determined if and when parents could resume their child-rearing responsibilities. Lena Bell felt that the injuries Clay sustained while in the care of Feleesha's mother resulted from an accident. Moreover, Feleesha had gotten her addiction under control. Even though Lena Bell felt that the children could be safely cared for by their mother, Feleesha hadn't completed her case plan fast enough to have her children returned to her care. So, like many parents in this study, she lost her children to their grandmother because resolving her personal struggles took longer than DCFS permitted and more resources than DCFS provided. In addition to grandparents, parents in this study also lost their children to other relatives and nonrelative foster care.

Forty-one-year-old Barbara provided another example of a grandmother who stepped in to prevent her grandchild from being placed in nonrelative foster care after hospital personnel contacted DCFS. But unlike Lena Bell, who immediately expressed that she did not want her grandchildren to end up in a "home with strangers," Barbara had to be convinced to assume primary responsibility for her grandson. Many scholars have pointed out that Black families' long tradition of grandparent caregiving is critical to family stability.[7] However, others have complicated this finding by underscoring that women-centered networks and extended families may not be up to the task of supporting mothers in their parenting roles.[8] Barbara's experience illustrates how both of these realities can coexist. She wasn't up to the task and yet found herself parenting another generation anyway.

Barbara's newborn grandson Shaquille came to the attention of DCFS when her seventeen-year-old daughter Talisha left the hospital with the baby after he had been triaged for a high fever. Talisha's strained relationship with her mother led her to turn to her godmother, Merita, for support. Merita encouraged Talisha to take Shaquille back to the hospital to be treated. When she did, DCFS got involved, and Talisha, who suffered from schizophreniform disorder,[9] was charged with medical neglect.[10] In this study, medical neglect occurred among mothers who themselves suffered from untreated mental illnesses or who were caring for children with special needs.

In this instance, DCFS made a safety plan for Shaquille, and he was placed in Merita's care. However, when Merita could no longer care for him, she sought to pass the responsibility to his maternal grandmother, Barbara. So, it wasn't DCFS that contacted Barbara, or even her grandson's parent(s), it was her newborn grandson's godmother—again spotlighting how grandmothers' status position made them overwhelmingly responsible for their grandchildren and, often, their grandchildren's only care option.

Barbara had given up her apartment and was leaving Chicago when the crisis of responsibility for three-month-old Shaquille shifted to her. Taking over the infant's care was Barbara's "first time ever meeting my grandson." Initially, she resisted giving up her own goals to care for him. But Talisha's untreated mental illness made it impossible for her to raise him, and, according to Barbara, Shaquille's father "really wasn't involved in the beginning . . . the father has seen him a couple of times but he was an infant. And the father was in jail in the juvenile system . . . he was in DCFS care himself." Barbara's fiancé, Bobby, convinced her to provide care. When I asked if she would have stepped in if Bobby had not pressed her, Barbara responded:

No, I wouldn't have made the decision. Nope, I would've left him in DCFS care or left him with Merita or whatever. . . . I wouldn't have came and got him. Because it's like, no, this is my life now. I raised my kids. The other two are with their father and Talisha was gone doing her thing. Okay, guess what? It's my turn.

Barbara's experience demonstrates the pressure that grandmothers faced—from multiple directions, including partners, parents, and the state—when their grandchildren experienced actual or potential child maltreatment. Her experience also reveals the resistance of many grandmothers to parental surrogacy—resistance that was most pronounced during transitions, including transitions into their new role, changing their legal status, and relinquishing the role of primary caregiver.

> I feel it's unfair that I do have to take care of my grandchild. Because she's [Talisha's] not doing anything to change her life, but then you're putting my life on hold and you're having your fun. You're doing whatever you wanna do, going wherever you wanna go, this, that, and the other and you don't have nobody else to take with you. You don't have to worry about somebody eating, about nobody having a roof over their head. Just you. I just feel this is kind of selfish. Sometimes I get that way.

Other grandmothers unanimously conveyed the same feelings about the sacrifice required of them, while also asserting their love for their grandchildren and desire to ensure their safety and well-being. They wanted to demonstrate that love in a grandmothering capacity, as mothering forced them to give up long-deferred aspects of their identity and personhood, a loss that was compounded by the constraints of the child welfare system. But grandmothers experiencing coerced mothering within the child welfare system had to contend with significantly more bureaucracy as they tried to manifest their personal lives than grandmothers parenting grandchildren outside the system. In Barbara's case, for example, her involvement with DCFS dashed her dreams of being child free, leaving Chicago, and starting a new life with her partner. In addition to not being permitted to travel without DCFS permission, Barbara had to make her grandson available for parental and caseworker visits. She also had to obtain DCFS-approved housing. So, not only was starting over in a new state itself out of the question but so was living in a basement apartment with her partner to save money to leave Chicago.

Barbara also voiced a common feeling among some grandmothers that the mere fact of mental illness or substance abuse did not absolve parents from contributing to the care of their children. Grandmothers felt that if parents could do the things they wanted to do (e.g., partying, cultivating intimate relationships, traveling, and so on), then they could also do the things they needed to do for their children, or at least some of them. Regardless of her feelings, though, Barbara never got to opt out of her caregiving role.

Coerced Mothering in the Context of Voluntary Reporting

Sixty-year-old Eloise and Mosi, her husband of twenty-six years, were compelled to parent their grandchildren after a nonmandatory reporter reported physical abuse to CPS. Eloise's stepson, Jeremiah, had two children by his girlfriend, Christine—one-and-a-half-year-old Shamicka and nine-month-old LaTrell. Because Eloise and Mosi did not live nearby, they weren't able to prevent their two granddaughters' kinship displacement, which I define as children's risk of being taken away from their family members and placed into state custody. Shamicka and LaTrell had spent a month in nonrelative foster care because their mother was charged with physical abuse (she slapped Shamicka across the room) and none of her relatives could or would fulfill the foster parent eligibility criteria, and their father's drug use and unemployment prevented him from satisfying them too.

Disagreements between Eloise and Jeremiah frequently confirmed that she and Mosi were their granddaughters' only care option. As Eloise talked about these disagreements, she illustrated how coerced mothering manifested, specifically how she was coerced to raise another generation without the legal rights necessary to do so.

> First, he [Jeremiah] want me to take 'em. Then, when he get mad, he'll go to court and say, "No. I don't want her to have 'em. I want to get my kids." But then he doesn't comply with the rules. And I told him, "I want you to have your kids. This is when I should be enjoying my life. Not taking care of little kids." . . . I told him, . . . "I'm doing it for them. I'm not doing it for you. . . . If it wouldn't hurt the kids, I would send them back."

This is how coercion worked with Eloise and her peers—all of the choices were negative ones.

It's been rough. I love 'em to death, but I keep saying I can't do it. I'm getting ready to let 'em go. And then I'm like, ugh! God. Where they gonna go? Nowhere for 'em to go. I'd never let 'em go to a foster home. But if the dad could get 'em back, I would be happy. But I don't think he would do what he's supposed to do. It's been hard. Because my life virtually has stopped.

Many grandmothers expressed the conflicting feelings of not having a choice, but the clarity that it wasn't their duty to raise their grandchildren either, feelings reinforced by those around them. Eloise's friends and family routinely told her they "wouldn't do it" and "hats off" to her for raising her granddaughters; the nurses and doctors who cared for her granddaughters echoed the sentiment. And, like others, Eloise felt that during the four years she cared for her granddaughters, her life was the one that got put on hold. With Shamicka and LaTrell in her care, Jeremiah kept using drugs and working sporadically. Christine had two more children. Mosi still spent his spare time with the various social clubs he belonged to.

Not every grandmother agreed with claims of child maltreatment, including those of caseworkers and mandatory and nonmandatory reporters. Bertha's story is important, in part, because it demonstrates how some grandmothers challenged DCFS's definition of and response to child abuse. Seventy-five-year-old Bertha was compelled by DCFS to care for her sixteen-year-old great-grandson Jamari after his mother, Jessica, struck him and her sister called CPS. In Bertha's eyes, Jessica was a churchgoing woman who believed in "whipping children." Bertha also believed that "the Bible said to spare the rod, spoil the child. And I'm a true believer of that. I don't believe in abuse of any kind, but I believe in that." On the day in question, Jessica and Jamari were having a dispute when, according to Bertha, Jamari started "showing out in front of his company," and Jessica hit him, knocking him down. Jessica's sister, Jasmine, called the police. Jamari told the officers that his mother had knocked him down, causing a head injury. They took him to the hospital and arrested Jessica. Bertha was furious. When DCFS caseworkers came to her house to investigate, Bertha refused to go to the hospital. "I didn't go because I knew that he wasn't hurt!"

Bertha's belief that there was nothing "really wrong" with Jamari was reinforced by a caseworker bringing him to her house instead of keeping him. Despite Bertha's overt disagreement with DCFS's handling of the abuse allegations, Jamari was removed from his mother's custody and placed in his great-grandmother's care. "Honest to God," Bertha said, "there wasn't a scar on that boy. He wasn't hurt. And, I had to pay 250 dollars to get her out of jail. She lost her job. You know, just crazy."

Bertha was tired, but Jamari's biological father was uninvolved and, with their small family, she was Jamari's only care option. Bertha was already caring for her sixty-one-year-old niece, who'd suffered a brain aneurysm, but had still been able to do some of the things she wanted to do. But after assuming responsibility for Jamari, that little diminished to nothing, not only because she had more responsibility but also because DCFS dictated what she could and could not do, including leaving the state and allowing others to care for the boy.

> He's not a bad kid. But I just thought this was the time I could live. I could easily get somebody to keep my niece. I could put her in a home if I wanted to travel. But him, I can't do nothin' with him. Do you understand what I'm sayin'? But I love him. I love my grandkids. I can't say I don't, 'cause I did give up my life for 'em all. But it gets hard sometimes.

Because she did not want to raise a child she could not discipline, Jessica refused to complete the state's case plan, which in turn precluded Bertha's opting out of her caregiving responsibilities. This aspect of caregiving cost Bertha not only the grandparenting role, as grandmothers in other studies have expressed,[11] but also the greater loss of her life. Like other women in this study, Bertha expressed the mixed feelings that coercion produced—she loved her grandson but felt that he should be in his mother's care. And, like other older grandmothers and those grappling with poor health, Bertha expressed concern about having enough life left once her caregiving stint ended to fulfill aspects of her personal life.

External state intervention upped the ante on the way grandmothers experienced coerced mothering: intensifying the urgency to prevent their grandchildren's kinship displacement, illuminating the lack of care options, challenging their ability to opt out, and overwhelming their personal lives with the demands of caregiving amid bureaucracy. When mandatory and voluntary reporters initiated their family's child welfare system involvement, grandmothers had little to no time to minimize or strategize around dealing with the child welfare system. So, when they received calls and home visits from parents, relatives, and caseworkers indicating that they were the only measure standing between their grandchildren and nonrelative foster care, these grandmothers made sure that their grandchildren didn't end up "in the system."

HOW GRANDMOTHERS MAKE DECISIONS ABOUT FORMAL CAREGIVING ARRANGEMENTS

When grandmothers were compelled by external state intervention, their decision-making about caregiving arrangements was constrained by the child welfare system, which required that they navigate state-mandated (kinship foster care) and mediated (kinship diversion) kinship care to get and keep their grandchildren. What this meant was that the state determined their ability to prevent their grandchildren from being placed with strangers, staying in nonrelative foster care longer than necessary, and experiencing irreversible kinship displacement. However, parents also influenced these outcomes, specifically, the quality of parents' relationship with grandparents, each other (the coparent), and their children. Finally, like grandmothers parenting their grandchildren in informal kinship care, those in formal kinship care also had to fulfill the duties associated with motherhood while limited to quasi-legal rights (a range of legal rights they shared with parents and the state, depending on the caregiving arrangements).

Federal and state policies mandate that relatives be given preference when children require out-of-home care, but individual states determine (1) requirements for grandmothers to become caregivers for children involved in the child welfare system, (2) caregiving arrangements with their grandchildren, and (3) legal rights, resources, services, and oversight associated with the caregiving arrangements. Like grandmothers in other studies, grandmothers in my study reported rarely receiving options from caseworkers about the most appropriate arrangement for their family and personal needs.[12] They also reported not receiving information about the pros and cons (e.g., available resources and services, legal rights, and degree of state supervision) associated with their caregiving arrangements before agreeing to them. Most grandmothers figured out the boundaries and limitations of their caregiving arrangement after being constricted in some way, including making decisions on behalf of their grandchildren, asserting their right to privacy and autonomy, and managing parental involvement.

Similar to grandparent caregivers in other studies, the grandmothers I interviewed expressed a range of views about their experiences of caseworkers.[13] Most described a lack of support, availability, and consistent or adequate communication about the requirements to enter into, maintain, and transition out of caregiving arrangements. They also identified high turnover levels among caseworkers and "workers" who sought to hinder rather than help them. They complained of caseworkers who dropped in, who arrived late or not at all. And, if they perceived caseworkers as judgmental, bullying, and tied to a script rather than getting to know them individually, they withdrew and felt unsafe sharing their experiences. Conversely, they felt supported and respected when caseworkers used trust versus intimidation to ensure compliance and were mindful of their schedules.[14]

When caseworkers were friendly, gave them critical information and responded to their questions, were "empathetic" and "understanding," and provided material support and advice around child-management issues, some grandmothers in this and other studies saw the child welfare system as a resource.[15] Grandmothers were also inclined to feel that the child welfare system was a resource when social workers provided appropriate resources and services to parents and their grandchildren, including recreational and therapeutic services, learning programs, and counseling to their grandchildren or referrals to other agencies that could supply these and other services.[16]

Regardless of their experiences with caseworkers and DCFS rules and regulations, grandmothers used their agency to actively resist, maximize, and accommodate their family's involvement in the child welfare system. When grandmothers accommodated state involvement, they accepted DCFS practices as is, without modification—a coping response that was driven by their fear of what could happen should they not comply with DCFS protocol, by their sincere agreement with DCFS regulations, or by their lack of knowledge about their rights and responsibilities. Alternatively, when grandmothers maximized their state involvement, they sometimes used DCFS practices and resources in ways that were unintended by the child welfare system, but that benefitted them and their families. Grandmothers maximized state involvement out of necessity, altering the intended use of DCFS practices by (1) using forced parental visitations to monitor parental behavior and (2) using foster care stipends to help parents get on their feet or to facilitate their participation in child-rearing. And finally, when grandmothers resisted state involvement, they rejected DCFS practices altogether. The most common areas of resistance involved (1) physical discipline, (2) household composition and dynamics, and (3) parental participation. Resistance was driven by grandmothers' perceptions of and experiences with state intervention, how they framed parental involvement, and privileged parental rights.

Grandmothers used one coping strategy over another to manage different aspects of their child welfare system involvement. Moreover, their coping strategies were influenced by the tier of the five-tiered system of kinship care within which they provided care. For example, grandmothers forced to take responsibility for grandchildren through kinship diversion had fewer resources and services to maximize in order to facilitate parents' assumption of their parenting responsibilities. But these grandmothers also had less contact with caseworkers than those in kinship foster care. So, they may not have had to develop strategies to manage their relationships with caseworkers in the same way. Thus, the five-tiered system of care shaped not only grandmothers' access to resources and services, exposure to specific DCFS regulations, and degree of state supervision, but also how they formulated coping strategies.

Given all of this, it isn't surprising that raising their grandchildren within the child welfare system transformed grandmothers' role meanings and expectations. Because the system's view of grandmothers' appropriate role was informed by an effort to implement child welfare policies (via workers' practices and interpretations of policies) and by the goals of the case plan (e.g., reunification or adoption),[17] state-driven conceptions of grandmothers' roles and identity often contradicted the women's experiences parenting their grandchildren.[18] In addition, the system's view of grandmothers often contradicted these women's desires for their whole lives, not just the grandmother role. While some Black grandmothers resisted seeing themselves as mothers, it did not change the fact that they were called on to fulfill the social and legal aspects of motherhood.

State-Mandated Kinship Care

Although the child welfare system imposed constraints on grandmothers' caregiving arrangements, grandmothers made the most of the choices within their control, including deciding whether or not to become licensed foster parents, and, when children "timed out" of foster care, whether to become subsidized guardians or adoptive parents. Some grandmothers resisted licensing to minimize the role of the state in their lives and when bureaucratic difficulties stymied the licensing process. Others were misinformed by street-level bureaucrats and through rumors that if they became licensed that they would have to open their homes to children who were not their grandchildren or relatives. In contrast, some grandmothers were motivated to become licensed to maximize resources, and when caseworkers told them that licensing was required to care for their grandchildren.

As foster parents, grandmothers had to contend with the theoretical and practical complications of custodial rights, which allowed the state or the parent to make legal decisions on behalf of the child but gave the grandmother physical custody. More complicated still, when parents failed to fulfill their case plans[19] and grandmothers became their grandchildren's subsidized guardian or adoptive parent, their legal relationships with their grandchildren changed again—as subsidized guardians they held legal rights, and kinship adoption gave them parental rights. What follows is a discussion of grandmothers' experiences of kinship foster care and kinship adoption. Nell, whose story begins this chapter, exemplified grandmothers' experiences of subsidized guardianship, so that caregiving arrangement is not discussed below.

LICENSED AND UNLICENSED KINSHIP FOSTER CARE

When children were taken into state custody, grandmothers had to fulfill the state's eligibility criteria to get their grandchildren in their care. Although grandmothers in this study had successfully fulfilled DCFS eligibility criteria, those parenting their grandchildren in the foster care system still experienced several challenges. For starters, many found the process invasive—for them and, in some cases, for parents—which exacerbated their distrust of the system. Moreover, conflict was sometimes created when DCFS depended on family members to corroborate stories of abuse and neglect. Additionally, when family members who disagreed with the CPS/DCFS assessment were pressured to agree, an adversarial relationship between families and caseworkers was set up. Finally, many grandmothers reported that racism and classism stymied the process of becoming a foster parent or negatively influenced their treatment during interactions with caseworkers and judges.

Grandmothers compelled to raise grandchildren in the foster care system also had to adhere to the child welfare system's rules and regulations to keep their grandchildren in their care, including travel restrictions, sharing medical and educational decision-making, and adhering to parental and caseworker visitations. Because leaving the state was prohibited, DCFS permission was required to take grandchildren to family reunions, funerals, on vacation, and even across the border to Indiana to get cheaper gas and cigarettes. Similarly, grandmothers were unable to make medical decisions for their grandchildren beyond routine medical care. If grandchildren needed to be taken to the emergency room, DCFS had to be notified within twenty-four hours, and if they needed major medical procedures, DCFS had to consent. As foster parents, grandmothers also had to permit caseworker home visits and agree to parental involvement on the state's terms.

When their grandchildren were taken into state custody, Eloise and Mosi had no choice but to become kinship foster parents, which required them to undergo screening and assessment to prove they were capable of providing for the children's basic needs and keeping them safe.

> Once they're under the state, you have to fill out all these papers. You have to go through a police check, background check, a health check. They told me you had to be financially secure before you get 'em. . . . My husband and I both work. So then my daughter had to go through the same check because she was seventeen. . . . Everybody in the house had to go through a background check.

They also had to undergo a home inspection.

> They sent a licensing rep out to the house. And they inspect your house top to bottom. Which I feel is very invasive. Extremely. And when you're licensed, they come out frequently. And they become very obnoxious—most of 'em. I've been in some of the homes where they come in and they want to

push the windowsill up and down. What does that have to do with it? One lady, they told her she had to go get a window fixed.

Although a broken window could pose a hazard to a child or a stuck one a risk in case of fire, the need for these kinds of home repairs is not uncommon among the population most likely to become kinship foster parents.[20] Using home repairs as obstacles is an example of how the child welfare system can (and often does not) support the very women they rely on to care for a substantial number of children in foster care, since paying for minuscule repairs would be a small price to pay given the money these caregivers save the state through their unpaid and underpaid caring labor and the disparities in resources and services received by kinship foster parents (compared with nonrelative foster parents) once those children are in their care.

Eloise expressed what many grandmothers felt: "I didn't know anything about DCFS . . . nothing about them. Because I had never dealt with them." But after becoming her granddaughters' foster parent, Eloise changed jobs and worked at a social service agency that managed DCFS cases. Consequently, she resisted becoming licensed because of her personal and professional experience with caseworkers, who, although she and her husband had a nice home, stable employment, and no criminal records, still made Eloise feel hassled. Eloise expressed that the extra intrusion into their lives was not worth the extra money that came from getting licensed. "I told 'em no. They get very, if you get a bad rep, forget it. They can really try to intimidate you." If it is hard for Eloise, who easily qualified to become a foster parent, the implications for others are strikingly clear.

State agents, meaning caseworkers and judges, had the power to simplify or complicate the process of fulfilling eligibility criteria. The reality of race as a factor for these street-level bureaucrats cannot be overstated and has been corroborated in this and countless other studies.[21] Eloise was one of several grandmothers who felt that racism made rescuing their grandchildren from the grips of state custody more difficult. In recalling how intensely they were scrutinized when they appeared in court to claim Jeremiah's children, Eloise claimed that the qualifications needed to become foster parents were unequally distributed by race, and that, even though she and her husband were squeaky clean, the child welfare system in the small town in southern Illinois where their grandchildren were taken into protective custody discriminated against them, finding ways to hinder their efforts to obtain custody of their grandchildren without legitimate reasons to do so. "When we would go down there . . . tryin' to get the kids, the court . . . was so prejudiced. We had such a hard time in the courts, but we eventually got them."

Eloise's "hard time in the courts" was further complicated by family conflict. And family conflict playing out amid child welfare system involvement provides another set of complex interactions that burden grandparents—in Eloise's case, her relationship with her grandchildren's parents and the parent's relationship with each other. Although Christine, the children's mother, was charged with abuse and the children were taken into state custody, she still influenced who would care for them. Despite Eloise treating her "like a daughter," Christine did not want Eloise caring for her children because she was mad at Eloise's son Jeremiah, the children's father. Eloise and Mosi's "battle" to get their grandchildren from nonrelative foster care was prolonged by the fact that Christine lodged a complaint about them each time they tried, in retaliation against Jeremiah. Eloise's job at the social service agency gave her even more insight into her family's experience with DCFS. She saw the discrepancy between their interactions with Christine as a White mother and with Black mothers.

> Well, they've done a lot of things in court to her favor. Giving her another chance to do this, do that. . . . They've given her services. They've helped her get accommodations. . . . Before I started at X, I saw what they were doing for her.

Eloise also felt they were judged more harshly when Jeremiah could not obtain custody of his own children because he had "dropped hot," or been unable to pass a DCFS drug test. Upon becoming her granddaughters' foster parent, Eloise received $593 monthly. Although Eloise had to manage more state intrusion than grandmothers providing care informally, the financial support she received was substantially higher than that of these grandmothers and those providing care through kinship diversion, but not as high as grandmothers serving as licensed foster parents.

So, Christine complicated Eloise stepping into her role as a foster parent and Jeremiah complicated her stepping out of it. Specifically, for

Christine and Jeremiah to regain custody of their children, they had to complete DCFS-mandated case plans. Christine gave up on fulfilling her case plan for two likely reasons. The first was her history growing up in foster care and the resulting lack of family support she needed to complete the services (e.g., anger management and parenting classes, mental health treatment) associated with her case plan. The second was her unmanaged mental illness. Eventually, Christine acquiesced to the children remaining in Eloise's care. Eloise and Christine also resolved their discord and worked together to do what was best for the children. But the same wasn't true of Eloise and Jeremiah. He vacillated between supervised and unsupervised visits, depending on whether he dropped hot, and thus drew out the reunification process and Eloise's stint as a foster parent. Ultimately, Jeremiah's drug use and sporadic employment precluded his completing his case plan.

The end result was that Eloise was unable to opt out of her caregiving responsibilities. And, she had no choice but to accommodate the child welfare system if she wanted custody of her granddaughters. Despite her custodial rights as a foster parent, it was the caseworker who determined Christine and Jeremiah's parental involvement, and their visitations changed over time as their completion of their case plan services gave them more or less access. Unlike grandmothers who resisted the terms caseworkers set about how much parents should be involved with their children, Eloise enforced DCFS rules about Christine and Jeremiah's limited involvement because she agreed with the state's assessment of their parenting capacity. I asked how it felt to be in that position.

> He [Jeremiah] gets mad. He cuss and scream and holler. And I just close the door on him. . . . My daughter says that's why I got sick this week, because we had a big one last week. . . . He didn't come when he was supposed to, so I had somewhere to go, so I took the kids to a party. And I told him, "I'm not gonna wait all day for you." I used to do that. I got permission [from the caseworker], if he's not there within an hour, leave.

Despite her experience of coerced mothering, Eloise and her granddaughters developed a mother-child bond, changing the meaning she associated with grandmotherhood. "You get attached to them," she said. "And, you don't want to let 'em go." And the youngest one called her "mama." When I asked how it would feel losing her granddaughters, Eloise responded:

> If they were to leave, it would be like somebody had taken my kid away from me. Yeah. As much as I say I'm tired, I know it would hurt me once they go. But . . . kids always want to be with their parents. As much as my babies love me, they want to go to their mama or their daddy.

At the time of the interview, Eloise and her caseworker were discussing her becoming a subsidized guardian. She was hesitant to adopt because she wanted to tend to her personal life, but also because her financial responsibility for her granddaughters would increase and, at her age, she knew she could not afford to send them to college. "I was hoping I didn't have to [adopt], so I could lead my life now. But, if I had to, then I would. Whatever's in the best interest for them. That's always been my goal for them."

While some grandmothers wrestled with the uncertainty of what caregiving arrangement they would assume when their grandchildren timed out of foster care, not all of them did. A variety of factors lessened the burden of unpredictability. Some grandmothers caring for older grandchildren knew they would be doing so into adulthood. Some also understood that when parents refused or were unable to complete their case plan, there was little likelihood of unexpected changes in their caregiving arrangements. On the positive side, many grandparents anticipated that parents would resume parenting and children would transition back to the parental home.

Bertha exemplified what happened when grandmothers did not fret about which caregiving arrangement they would assume when their grandchildren timed out of foster care. Bertha knew that she would raise her great-grandson Jamari through adulthood not only because he was a teenager when she became his foster parent, but also because his mother, Jessica, refused to fulfill the state's mandatory case plan.

> She told 'em that she's not goin' to no classes. She don't want him back. . . . You have to put fear in kids, she said. And she not gonna be able to do that now. So she's not gonna take him back.

Regardless of whether or not Jessica completed the case plan, Bertha had to fulfill the state's eligibility criteria to get Jamari in her care. Bertha was unperturbed by the paperwork and home inspection part of the process of becoming Jamari's foster parent. But two things about becoming a foster parent stood out to her. One was that the caseworker expressed concern about her age. Initially, she was told she was too old. But, according to Bertha, "They must have changed their mind." Bertha's sense was that as Jamari's "nearest relative" she was his only care option, regardless of her age.

The second thing that was memorable about her process of becoming Jamari's foster parent was how she was treated in court when she refused to help the caseworker build a case against her granddaughter, who was charged with abuse. Bertha's unwillingness to help the state make a case against Jessica exacerbated the adversarial relationship between her family and DCFS. Bertha's disagreement with the state's definition of child abuse and their treatment of Jessica soured her to becoming a licensed foster parent. She was only willing to do what was necessary to keep her great-grandson out of nonrelative foster care, nothing more.

Bertha expressed that *keeping* Jamari in her care was more difficult than *getting* him in her care. Although she received more formal support than grandmothers providing care informally ($300/month), Bertha was overwhelmed and dismayed by the initial and continued intrusion into her family's life as well as the constrictions DCFS's protocol placed on her. For starters, Jessica was not allowed parental visitation with Jamari, which also meant that she was unable to visit her grandmother's home. So even though the family understood that Jamari would remain in his great-grandmother's care, family dynamics were still controlled by DCFS.

In addition to being unable to allow parental visits with his mother, Bertha was told by the caseworker that Jamari could not spend time with Scott, the man who had helped raise him (and stayed involved even though he and Jessica were no longer together). When I pressed her about why Jamari was unable to spend time with Scott, Bertha shared:

> He can't be around the dad he's known all his life. . . . But that's the only daddy he know. He loves that man and the man love him. . . . He's been over here to see him—bought him a pair of shoes and coat. . . . He not supposed to go visit him 'cause he's not the daddy. I'm telling you just how it went down. That's so crazy.

Although recent legislative and policy initiatives (e.g., Illinois Fictive Kin Law of 2015) have placed further emphasis on the importance of preserving a child's broader network of significant kin and friends, this isn't enforced by all caseworkers.[22] According to the Illinois Department of Children and Family Services, when caseworkers determine who will be included in the child's visitation and contact plan they should "not only think of parents and siblings but of family members and others who are important in the child's life. Even children who do not have a "return home" goal must have an opportunity to continue relationships that were meaningful to them through visitations with family members."[23] When the caseworker told Bertha that Scott was excluded from Jamari's visitation plan because he was not his biological father, Bertha resisted the directive she saw as unreasonable. This caseworker's unwillingness to approve Scott's visits with Jamari provides an example of the uneven application of DCFS policies and practices with kinship families, forcing them to either accept or break "rules," with negative consequences either way.

Bertha's custodial rights inhibited her assessment of the role Jamari's biological and fictive parents could play in his life, but also her privacy and autonomy. So, while Bertha resisted some DCFS rules and regulations, she acquiesced to what she felt was relentless checking in: "They call here religiously. They always callin' here. . . . I said, 'I get so tired of you all. I done raised a whole three sets of kids.'" She also had to make sure that both she and Jamari were accessible by phone, participated in all support services, and had to be available for surprise visits: "The head lady, she makes sudden appearances sometimes. She just comes. Don't make no appointment. It's okay. But I be doin' hair sometime. I don't have time to talk. But . . . I have to take time." She and Jamari were also subject to strict and unrealistic travel restrictions.

> You can't take him out of town unless you give us two months' notice. . . . If somebody die in my family, how I know when they gonna die or somethin' and I have to go to the funeral and take him? You understand what I'm sayin'? They have some crazy rules.

Bertha's love for Jamari, combined with being coerced to manage DCFS rules and regulations and Jessica's rejection of the services stipulated in her case plan, forced this septuagenarian to come out of retirement and shift from grandmothering to mothering her great-grandson. Her experience reflected the pervading realities of her peers who must share their rights and responsibilities with the state, whether they want to or not.

KINSHIP ADOPTION

All too frequently, caregivers are not provided all of their available options upfront, which prevents them from determining how to fit caregiving into their lives based on their unique needs. This applies particularly to the caregiving arrangements available to kinship foster parents when children will not be returned to their parent's custody. Grandmothers who want to retain custody of their grandchildren have two options—they can become subsidized guardians or kinship adoptive parents. Initially, Lena Bell shifted from proving parental support to raising Clay and Imani so that she did not have to "worry about 'em: It'd been years since I'd raised kids. . . . My other grandkids, I used to see 'em but I never kept 'em. These are the only ones I ever kept." When she assumed responsibility for the children, her caseworker told her that she had to become licensed to be a foster parent. But, after raising them for approximately two years as a licensed foster parent, Lena Bell was informed of the consequences of her grandchildren's mother's failure to complete her case plan.

> The . . . social worker said, "Well if you didn't take 'em we was gonna put 'em in somebody else's home." I said, "Well no, I don't, I didn't want them to go to strange people." . . . And she said, "Well you can adopt them and keep them from going someplace else." I said, "Well okay, I'm gonna adopt 'em." That's when they took us downtown.

When I asked Lena Bell if she had been given an option to become a subsidized guardian, she replied, "Uh, no. I didn't know about that," recalling that the caseworkers "did everything" and all she had to do was show up in court with her grandchildren. Both parents relinquished their rights and were absent from the proceedings.

Lena Bell experienced serious health issues during her seven years as a caregiver. Her blood pressure, which had been maintained before she assumed responsibility for her grandchildren, soared out of control and she was diagnosed with congestive heart failure. As a result, at the time of the interview Lena Bell was in the process of seeing if the children's maternal great-aunt could become their guardian because, with their intellectual and developmental disabilities, they were too much for her to handle. And their great-aunt, who was planning to open up a recovery home for mothers and their children, was going to allow Feleesha and her children to be clients. Lena Bell was talking to someone at "the guardianship place" about reversing her adoption.

> And that way the mama would be able to be with her kids. Because every mother needs to be with her kids. I'm not trying to keep her from 'em. If she's gonna get her life together she can do it. I prefer it like that. That way I can be more laid back and enjoy my years. [*Laughs*]

Had Lena Bell been given the subsidized guardianship option, it would have provided a pathway for the children's care to be more easily transferred back to their parents and other relatives because the guardianship could be vacated. But because she wasn't, Lena Bell was responsible for figuring out how to reverse her adoption. It is possible, but the laws surrounding adoption are very strict. So, while Lena Bell might have been able to reverse the adoption because she had developed health issues that severely complicated her ability to care for her grandchildren, the process of doing so would be far more onerous than vacating a guardianship. Unable to opt of out providing care, Lena Bell's personal life thus receded further out of reach than she could ever have imagined.

Complying with the regulatory guidelines and practices of the child welfare system put grandmothers in the uncomfortable position of monitoring or denying visitation by their grandchildren's parents. Some grandmothers felt that they, instead of the child welfare system, were viewed as the barrier or "enemy" by and between parents and their children, and some resisted being put in the difficult position of "the dual role, as an extension of the state and as family."[24] In Lena Bell's case, for example, before adopting Clay and Imani, she allowed them to spend time with their mother, despite the violation of DCFS policies. As she stated, she believed that "every mother needs to be with her kids." She, like other grandmothers who did not feel that parents posed a threat to their children, resisted DCFS policies prohibiting or limiting parental visitations. But, while her custodial rights meant that Lena Bell had to hide this activity from DCFS, her post-adoption parental rights gave her unmitigated decision-making authority, which was advantageous because Feleesha could help Lena Bell care for the children without fear that they would be removed from her care.

The majority of grandmothers in this study upheld the primacy of mother-child relationships and did what they could, even when it violated DCFS rules and regulations, to facilitate their grandchildren's relationships with their mothers. Lena Bell was no exception. She allowed Feleesha to spend time with her children. She also maximized her family's child welfare system involvement by using the children's adoption payments ($794/month) to facilitate their mother's involvement.

When Lena Bell's health worsened, Feleesha helped by taking her children to school a couple of days a week. Lena Bell described their collaboration.

> In a week, sometimes she'll come two or three days. . . . Sometimes I give her money to get a bus pass . . . when I have money. Or I'll use their money. Because she not working. She don't have any money. But she do what she can do.

State-Mediated Kinship Care

When faced with external state intervention, some grandmothers managed state-mediated kinship care. These mediated arrangements occurred when caseworkers facilitated the relocation of a child from a parent's to a relative's care. In Illinois, when children are diverted to a relative's home as an alternative to formal foster care they are given a safety plan. Although the state placed time limits on how long these caregiving arrangements could last, application of those limits was unevenly applied.[25] After their grandchildren were diverted to their care using safety plans, some grandmothers maintained that they never heard from DCFS again. When this occurred, several grandmothers just "let it be," suspecting that DCFS had resolved the issue with their grandchildren's parent(s). In other cases, grandmothers contacted DCFS to terminate their grandchild's safety plan so that it wasn't hanging over their heads. Other grandmothers contacted DCFS not because they tired of child welfare system involvement or of being in limbo, but because they needed proof of legal guardianship to obtain resources and services for their grandchildren.

Because caregivers in safety plans do not have a legally binding relationship to the child in their care and therefore do not hold educational, medical, or custodial rights or obligations, it did not take long for grandmothers in these arrangements to confront the limitations of their lack of legal rights. When they did, the women in my study sought legal guardianship of their grandchildren. So, for the majority of grandmothers, kinship diversion was a bridge to legal guardianship, as these children rarely ended up back in the care of parents.

The Extended Family Support Program (EFSP) factored prominently into grandmothers' journeys to legal guardianship. The EFSP—to which grandmothers either reached out to on their own or were referred by the caseworkers who handled the termination of their safety plan—helps relative caregivers obtain legal guardianship through probate court, including educating and helping the caregiver negotiate the probate court system, assisting caregivers to obtain required documents, and arranging for legal counsel in counties where legal counsel is necessary. The program pays for these services and may provide cash assistance to get the child basic goods and services needed to acclimate to the relative's home. The EFSP also assists families to obtain TANF child-only grants, subsidized daycare and other entitlements (e.g., medical card), and to enroll children in school.[26]

FROM KINSHIP DIVERSION TO LEGAL GUARDIANSHIP

Managing Shaquille's safety plan meant that Barbara was charged by the state to do "the basic things that a mother is supposed to do for they child." Her experience demonstrates why I have placed kinship diversion in tier five—caregivers are given no legal rights, have no guarantee of resources and services, and must still manage child welfare system involvement, albeit to a lesser degree than those in kinship foster care.

Since she was not a part of Shaquille's original safety plan, the first thing that Barbara had to do was contact DCFS to discern her rights and responsibilities.

When I ended up going to get Shaquille from Merita, I called DCFS and . . . I said, "Look, I don't wanna be bothered with y'all because I don't want y'all coming to my house looking under peek holes. . . . I don't need that in my life. I can take care of him without no problem." So they was like, "Okay, well we can sign off on this." Yes, sign off on it and I'm through. We signed off on it and that was it.

What Barbara eventually "signed off on" was the "Safety Plan Termination Agreement."[27]

In actuality, Barbara did not immediately sign off on Shaquille's safety plan, because she was not a part of it. Caseworkers first had to assess whether Shaquille was, in fact, safe in his grandmother's care. So, when Barbara became a part of his plan, she was required to demonstrate that she could provide for his basic needs.

> He has to have his own room. Just like it was your own kid. With DCFS, they had to have their own room, gas and lights gotta be on. They gotta go to school, they gotta be clean, nourished. You know, going to the doctor and stuff like that. Just the basic things that a mother is supposed to do for they child.

But as Barbara struggled to care for herself and her grandson, she resisted the DCFS housing and space requirements because even after moving multiple times she could not afford a larger dwelling: "So, it was like, well, he little, he really don't need a room. Even though I was supposed to, but I'm in my house. DCFS ain't there."

Barbara also had to agree to parent Shaquille in adherence with DCFS policies and practices, including not using physical discipline. She resisted this requirement, invoking a rationale for "spanking" Shaquille that was similar to other Black parents who sought to instill respect for authority figures so that they would avoid trouble due to anti-Black racism and "the streets":[28] "It's far and few in between [spankings], but . . . I'd rather for me to do it than the police knock him upside his head out there or the gangs knock him upside his head out there."

As another part of the safety plan, Barbara had to comply with the supervised visits Talisha was given. When Barbara first got Shaquille, "she [Talisha] came by and she saw him. And then she would come and go. She'll see him one day and then she'll be gone two weeks and then she'll come back and see him then she'll be gone four weeks. This was happening really regular." Weeks stretched into months and eventually a year. When Talisha was present, Barbara found her involvement more harmful than helpful to Shaquille. For instance, she once left the house while he was in the bathtub. In another incident, Barbara acquiesced to Talisha's pleas to care for her son over the summer, only to return Shaquille to Barbara "filthy" and sick. Talisha resisted parental guidance and getting the help she needed to effectively parent her child.

Barbara's experience demonstrated the paradox of coerced mothering—grandmothers were charged with fulfilling the social and legal functions associated with motherhood but without the legal rights to do so. Motivated by Talisha's inability to adequately parent Shaquille and her own lack of legal authority to navigate child-rearing institutions and obtain resources and services for him, Barbara decided to become Shaquille's legal guardian.

> Now I tried to keep her in his life but . . . she just wasn't doing it. So when I decided to get guardianship it was like if something happens to her, even though I'm his maternal grandmother I can't do anything. I couldn't sign nothing or none of that or put him in school or anything because I would need her. It's like, no. I got to count on me because if she do something then I'm in trouble. They're not gonna look for her, they're gonna look for me.

After terminating the safety plan, a caseworker connected Barbara to the EFSP, which connected her to Catholic Charities. Catholic Charities helped her "go through guardianship" by giving her a caseworker who went to court with her and did "all the things. And after everything's done, they give you like a gift certificate. I think it was like $75 from Target, just a little thing to say, hey, here's something to help." Barbara remembered the exact date in 2004 when she became Shaquille's legal guardian.

> They came by and they talked to me about the process of going through guardianship. They said they'll write out everything about Talisha and how she's not doing what she's supposed to be doing as a mother and that I've been doing it all—making sure he goes to school. Well, he was going to work with me so it really didn't make a difference, but going to school. How he's fed and just the basic things of being a parent. . . . So, making sure he's fed and changed and everything even as an infant. Making sure he's going to the doctor and everything. Just the whole nine yards. So she [caseworker] would write all this stuff out. . . . They went to court with me and everything. They drew up all the papers at the Daley Center and got everything rolling and that was it.

When Barbara worked with the EFSP to become Shaquille's legal guardian, she had to demonstrate yet again that she would do "the basic things of being a parent." And Talisha's inability to adhere to the conditions of the safety plan made it easier to demonstrate her unfitness and for Barbara to become her grandson's legal guardian.

Although legal guardianship could be reversed, most grandmothers saw it as permanent. They surrendered to the reality that they were primarily, and in some cases, solely responsible for raising another generation. After becoming his legal guardian, Barbara was asked by people in her social network why she didn't let DCFS take Shaquille into state custody and become his foster parent, which would have entitled her to more resources and services (she received a monthly $107 TANF child-only payment). She responded, "See I didn't know the process and everything to do with all this because this was just dropped in my lap. I'm just going through the motions." As for Barbara, the sudden and unexpected assumption of grandparent caregiving made it difficult for grandmothers to ascertain their caregiving arrangement options. They relied on caseworkers to help them navigate "the system," but, if caseworkers fell short, grandmothers often lacked the necessary knowledge to choose the best caregiving arrangement for their family and individual circumstances.

Barbara's relationship with Shaquille had transformed in the nearly five years she'd raised him: "I mean I guess I had to learn to like it even though my life had to stop basically. And I had to learn to enjoy having him and having an infant at thirty-six." She had grown to accept that she was going to mother, not grandmother, her grandson, but her journey to that acceptance wasn't easy. The more she "put into him"—meaning fulfilled the social, emotional, and legal functions associated with motherhood and developed a mutual emotional bond with him—the more her role shifted. When I interviewed her, Barbara was considering adopting Shaquille.

CONCLUSION

In this chapter, I underscore how coerced mothering manifested within the context of the child welfare system. External state intervention changed the nature of coerced mothering as DCFS rules and regulations made it more difficult for women to opt out of caregiving, reinforced that their grandchildren had no alternative care solutions, exploited that grandmothers assumed a disproportionate share of responsibility for their grandchildren, and exacerbated lost aspects of their personhood and identity. More than in the case of grandmothers raising their grandchildren outside of the child welfare system, the caregiving arrangements associated with the child welfare system armed grandmothers with a range of quasi-legal rights to fulfill the legal aspects of motherhood. As they shared their rights with the state, grandmothers fulfilled DCFS eligibility criteria to *get* their grandchildren in their care, and they adhered to most, if not all, DCFS policies and practices to *keep* their grandchildren in their care.

Grandmothers' caring labor filled gaps in the social safety net for the parent generation and the child welfare system's responsibility for and accountability toward the children they serve. But grandmothers used their agency to devise strategies to manage their child welfare system involvement. When grandmothers feared what could happen should they not comply with DCFS protocol, agreed with DCFS regulations, or lacked knowledge about their rights and responsibilities, they accommodated their child welfare system involvement. When grandmothers sought to provide parents with the support they needed to get themselves together and raise their own children, they maximized state involvement by using DCFS practices and resources in unintended ways. When grandmothers disagreed with DCFS practices such as the degree to which parents should be involved, their household composition and dynamics, and using physical discipline, they resisted aspects of state involvement. Depending on the coping strategies they used, grandmothers' strategies for managing the child welfare system could compromise their ability to care for their grandchildren. In some ways, grandmothers' coping strategies reflect cultural practices, for instance, the use of physical discipline. However, in many ways, they reflect the insufficiency of the child welfare system to address issues facing the families they serve and to create policies and practices that honor how families operate (e.g., providing parental resources and guidance to mothers trying to get on their feet) and experience kinship (e.g., the importance of fictive kin).

As grandmothers became mothers, their role expectations and meanings were transformed and renegotiated. When their grandchildren's biological mothers tried to assert their rights, like Barbara, grandmothers informed parents that should something happen to their grandchildren, it was they, not parents, who would be held accountable. While grandmothers checked parents, state agents checked grandmothers. The state's rights superseded those of grandmothers, who had little say in the duration of their child welfare system involvement, parents' involvement in their children's lives, children's medical care, and others aspects of their caregiving experiences. As these grandmothers' accounts reveal, the more grandmothers fought parents and/or the state to ensure the safety and well-being of their grandchildren, the more they poured their resources, time, and energy into their grandchildren, and the more their grandchildren related to them as mothers, the more they shifted away from a blending of the mother and grandmother role that has historically characterized Black grandmotherhood and toward a mother role.

Existing research has brought attention to the resentment, anger, resignation, grief, and mixed emotions Black grandmothers experience from being thrust into raising their grandchildren. Black grandmothers in this study confirm these findings.[29] What they wanted for themselves was put off, lost, or barely held on to. By centering the processes associated with coerced mothering, I lay out how women come to experience their roles as grandmothers in ways they could not have anticipated, replete with unexpected responsibilities, legal rights, and emotions.

5 "He Don't Get Enough Money to Do All That. And I Don't Either"

GRANDMOTHERS' ECONOMIC SURVIVAL STRATEGIES

Primary caregiving affected not only grandmothers' relationships with family members and the state but also women's fragile financial statuses. To make ends meet, many grandmothers resorted to survival strategies to fulfill their most pressing financial needs—sufficient income and housing. Other expenses—utilities, food, clothing, personal and household goods, transportation, and education—became secondary priorities. I refer to the tactics they devised to circumvent or lessen loss and harm as "risk-negotiation strategies." These strategies reflect not only personal circumstances but also the overall marginalization of Black women raising their grandchildren by the labor market and the welfare state, which makes it difficult, and in many cases impossible, for them to access necessary resources and services. And the risk-negotiation strategies they devised to confront this sobering reality—shifting or forgoing work, brokering deals, and defying safety net program eligibility criteria and intended uses, to name a few—transformed what it meant to be a grandmother.

In this chapter, I discuss risk-negotiation strategies in three policy settings critical to grandparent-headed households and low-income households broadly: cash assistance; subsidized childcare; and subsidized housing. I reveal that, instead of being a safety net, the complex web of safety net programs and requirements depressed access and withheld support. The state, therefore, often further burdened grandmothers' existing struggles to meet their family's economic needs. Finally, I argue that, even as they prioritized caregiving and negotiated risks in pursuit of resources, grandmothers resisted the devaluation of their caring labor, devised strategies to allow for the fluidity and complexity of grandparent-headed households, and redefined what grandmotherhood means.

HOW AND WHY THE ENDS DON'T MEET

One reason the ends do not meet is that grandparent caregivers are highly likely to be economically vulnerable and already struggling financially when they assume care of grandchildren. It is not surprising, therefore, that most grandmothers raising grandchildren find the additional financial burden to be the most stressful part of caregiving.[1] The majority of families I interviewed experienced several structural constraints that contributed to their economic fragility: (1) gendered racism in the labor market, a decline in earnings from midlife through old age, and overrepresentation among the poor, especially for Black women sixty-five and older;[2] (2) the prohibitive cost of formal childcare (poor families spend on average 30 percent of their income on childcare);[3] necessity for subsidized childcare, or reliance on family, friends, and neighbors (FFN) for childcare (reliance on FFN for childcare is more difficult for grandmothers who are often asked by parents to provide childcare);[4] (3) difficulty acquiring affordable housing and obtaining subsidized housing, contributes to Black women (along with Latinas) being among the most rent-burdened (spending over 30 percent of income on rent) of all racial and ethnic groups; and (4) the inadequate response of neoliberal social welfare policy to parents and children, itself driven by systemic racism, notions of deserving, and an emphasis on private over public responsibility.[5]

Policy Rules and Regulations

Another reason the ends don't meet is because the state provides inadequate support to grandparent-headed households, stratifying households by need and caregiving arrangement. As discussed in the appendix, a grandmother's type of caregiving arrangement determines the level of state support. Caregivers providing care in the top tiers (one and two) of the five-tiered system of kinship care receive more resources and services (through the child welfare system) than those in the bottom tiers (three, four, and five). The majority of grandparents raising their grandchildren do so in informally, which means that they have access to only a handful of programs, of which three are important in supporting these families:· TANF (Temporary Aid to Needy Families), subsidized childcare and subsidized housing (see table 4 at the end of the chapter).

TANF

Grandparent caregivers applying for TANF family grants must participate in work activities no later than twenty-four months after receiving assistance.[6] Although many states provide age-based exemptions from work requirements, that age varies and typically ranges from fifty-five to sixty-five. In Illinois it is sixty. When health issues, caregiving demands, and other reasons prevent applicants from working, the TANF child-only grant is another option. In general, TANF child-only grants are the most accessible form of financial assistance for relatives because the eligibility criteria exclude caregivers' income, guardianship status, or ability to fulfill work and education requirements. Still, while child-only cases have increased dramatically since the passage of welfare reform, they are underused by kinship caregivers.[7] The reasons grandmothers participating in this and other studies failed to receive public assistance were complex and included family dynamics, a lack of awareness of available rights and resources, difficulty satisfying eligibility criteria, obfuscation of the eligibility criteria by street-level bureaucrats, and stigma and discrimination.[8]

SUBSIDIZED CHILDCARE

The Child Care and Development Fund helps low-income parents pay for childcare so they can work or participate in education and training. Because the program is so poorly funded, however, in 2015, just 15 percent of all children in the United States who qualified for childcare assistance under federal eligibility parameters received it.[9] In 2017, the United

States ranked third from the bottom in spending on early childhood education and care compared to other Organisation for Economic Co-operation and Development countries.[10]

Childcare subsidy programs vary greatly across states, including who is eligible for assistance, how much parents must pay and providers will be paid, which providers parents can use, and the quality standards providers must meet.[11] Illinois approves searching for a job as a qualifying activity for the Child Care Assistance Program only if a caregiver *already* receives subsidized childcare when they are unemployed.[12] In contrast, nineteen states and territories consider job search a qualifying activity for both initial and continuing eligibility, which helps relative caregivers who often have little, if any, time to prepare for their new role and need childcare to obtain and maintain employment.[13] Further, Illinois is among nearly half of states that include TANF benefits and Supplemental Security Income (SSI) as countable income when establishing eligibility. It is also one of the majority of states that consider Social Security Disability Insurance (SSDI) as countable income, but that does not count foster care income towards determining Child Care Assistance Program eligibility.[14] Counting TANF but not foster care income is another policy rule that contributes to inequities in the kinship care system.

Children living in grandparent-headed households often miss out on early childhood education and care because their caregivers face unique challenges accessing subsidized childcare. The grandmothers I interviewed were unable to secure the subsidy because they failed to satisfy eligibility criteria—they may not have already been employed when care of their grandchildren shifted to them, and the program required work and school participation. The program also failed to consider women's place in the life course, including stipulating school requirements that fail to support advanced degrees, which was problematic for grandmothers with a bachelor's degree. The income eligibility requirement also confounded some grandmothers.[15] Although many worked low-wage jobs, they'd done so long enough to earn somewhat more than was allowed by this means-tested program. Finally, some grandmothers who met eligibility criteria didn't apply for childcare subsidies because the process was complex and confusing.

SUBSIDIZED HOUSING

Subsidized housing provides support for families struggling to find quality affordable housing by preventing the housing expenditures of recipients from exceeding 30 percent of their household income, thereby significantly reducing a family's financial strain. The Fair Housing Act "makes clear that grandparents and other relatives cannot be required to have legal custody of the children in their care in order to qualify for assisted housing."[16] Yet some housing authority officials and landlords of privately operated subsidized housing unlawfully required grandmothers to demonstrate proof of legal guardianship in order to maintain or obtain subsidized housing. Finally, while senior housing is an option for some older caregivers, children are usually excluded from this type of housing.[17] Still, some elderly residents in this and other studies raised children in housing not designed for them and thus risked losing their housing in the process.[18]

Based on the aforementioned social welfare policy and program-related impediments, it is unsurprising that, by almost every available measure, the level of need experienced by grandparent-headed households is not reflected in their overall benefit-receipt patterns.[19] Fewer than 12 percent of kinship families receive TANF assistance, and only 6 percent of children living with relatives receive TANF child-only payments.[20] Moreover, because most kinship caregivers fail to receive TANF, they miss opportunities to connect to other critical safety net programs, as TANF can be an important gateway program for low-income households because it often entails categorical eligibility for other in-kind programs. For example, 17 percent of low-income working kinship caregivers receive subsidized childcare assistance and only 15 percent receive public housing assistance (compared to 21.8 percent of parent-child families and 37.8 percent of single-parent families). Fewer than half (42 percent) receive assistance from SNAP (compared to 51.6 percent of parent-child families and 66.4 percent of single-parent families), although most report food insecurity.[21] Table 4 outlines the eligibility criteria of safety net programs available to kinship care providers, the barriers grandmothers participating in this study faced accessing public support, and the number of grandmothers receiving *and* eligible for benefits.[22] For clarification, the cash payments provided to grandmothers providing care within the child welfare system are not considered safety net programs.

Beyond these structural impediments, family conflict also impeded women's access to the resources and services they so desperately needed. In some cases, grandmothers' and their families' limited access to resources and services fostered family conflicts that prohibited grandmothers from getting the financial support they needed. When parents were unwilling to relinquish the child's public assistance and threatened to remove children from grandmothers' care if they were made to do so, many grandmothers simply did without or used risk-negotiation strategies to bypass or subdue parents' legal authority. Similarly, parental refusal to allow grandmothers legal guardianship forced grandmothers to devise risk-negotiation strategies to access resources and services. These family dynamics made parents "draining ties"—ties "that drain one's household of resources through frequent requests for assistance with food, money, or other assistance that is not reciprocated, as well as ties to people that bring one down emotionally with constant complaining or involvement in their problems."[23] In this study, draining ties (1) failed to contribute (e.g., money; time so grandmothers could run errands, have respite, and such; childcare; services such as "doing hair," washing the children's clothing); (2) took resources intended for children, forcing grandparents to forgo such resources; (3) stole money and material possessions; and (4) needed more support than grandparents could provide.

WHEN THE ENDS DON'T MEET

Care for grandchildren further complicates grandmothers' already complicated financial situations. The vast majority of families in this study scraped by on meager incomes from their own, and in some cases, their partner's work, Social Security and retirement benefits, and financial contributions from their social support systems. Working grandmothers, many of whom already provided childcare to grandchildren,[24] shifted from being a family childcare provider to needing access to childcare resources; if they were to continue working, they had to secure formal center-based care and childcare subsidies or obtain informal childcare. Nonworking grandmothers receiving public assistance also experienced complications as they tried to maintain their benefits even as their grandparent caregiving roles undermined their efforts and eligibility. Next to generating income, keeping a roof over their expanding family's heads was most important to these grandmothers, who, to acquire new housing, moved from one bad neighborhood or building to a less bad one. Grandmothers with subsidized housing strategized to hold on to their housing *and* their grandchildren, while those providing care within the child welfare system fulfilled state-mandated housing requirements or risked losing their grandchildren to state custody. In the next section, I discuss how grandmothers devised risk-negotiation strategies to maintain and supplement their income and housing.

Making Changes in Work and Income

Caring for grandchildren posed a number of new challenges to grandmothers' labor-force participation. Caregiving arrangements changed grandmothers' calculations around work schedules, finding the right occupation, and the ability to keep a "good job." The impact of grandparent caregiving on women's paid work also resulted in multiple secondary stressors, including lost income, pensions, and desirable work shifts as well as health problems exacerbated by unaffordable health care.[25]

In the three sections that follow, I explain (1) the employment changes grandmothers made to accommodate caregiving, (2) the related issue of childcare for grandmothers caring for non-school-aged children, and (3) acquiring additional income through public assistance.

SHIFTING THEIR WORK

Efforts by grandmothers to decrease labor-market participation often involved relinquishing a second job—typically a job that predated providing care—and keeping the job that allowed them to accommodate their new caregiving responsibilities. Other grandmothers went from working full-time to part-time in the same job. Jobs with suitable hours and flexible schedules usually paid less and had no or minimal benefits. Bobbie Joe was one of nine grandmothers to drop a job to accommodate caregiving responsibilities.

I was teaching in the daytime, and in the evenings I was working as a pharmacy technician at a medical center. But then when [my granddaughter] came on board, I stopped the pharmacy job so I could devote all my time to her. . . . We don't have any health benefits, but this is a great working environment. . . . I have flexibility to do most of the things that I want. . . . I kinda overlook the money.

Bobbie Joe still worked full-time as a private-school teacher and relied solely on work earnings to care for her granddaughter Cherelle. When she needed childcare for Cherelle, Bobbie Joe paid a neighbor to watch her during the day.

It also was common for grandmothers to increase their employment when care shifted to them. Eleven grandmothers interviewed indicated they had made such decisions. For example, Bertha came out of retirement and resumed working as a hair stylist (in her basement) when care of her sixteen-year-old grandson shifted to her. Like other unlicensed foster care parents, she received $100 to $150 less per month than grandmothers who were licensed, but still needed to work to fill the gaps that remained after using the $301 foster care payment. When asked when she was going to stop working, Bertha replied,

Well, I got another child now. I can't. I told you, I have to give him bus fare, lunch money. He don't get enough money to do all that. And I don't either. . . . He eat up three hundred dollars. He's a big boy. A tall, big boy. His clothes is very expensive because he can't wear everything; he wear a 13 shoe. And you can't find them everywhere.

Bertha also made plain the link between caregivers' efforts to meet the economic demands of caregiving and the exacerbation of health conditions, doing fewer "heads" because of her age and arthritis. "I don't do a lot of hair. I used to do twenty and twenty-one heads on a Saturday. But now, I'm down to five. But it gives me change to give this boy to get to school and little extras."

When Marian became her newborn great-granddaughter's surrogate parent, she rejoined the labor market after having been retired. After twenty-six years of employment and a short two-year break from the labor force, she described accepting a lower paying job (half of her pre-retirement earnings) to give her great-granddaughter the best education and extracurricular activities she could.

I didn't care [about making less], I just needed enough . . . to help . . . pay for
Milena's expense. Thank God I work. [*Laughter*] I had to come to work. . . .
I could pay that money when I was working. . . . But after I stopped working,
I still paid it, but it reduced my cash flow. . . . And I didn't want to take
Milena out of this environment [her day care] she was in.

Marian received no formal resources for Milena. She was among those
older grandmothers who wanted to retire but had to work in order to provide for their grandchildren.

While grandmothers raising grandchildren in state custody received
larger monthly stipends compared to TANF recipients (and grandmothers
who received no cash assistance) and had an increased likelihood of
receiving subsidized childcare, they also made changes to their paid work.
Eloise was an unlicensed foster parent and one of four grandmothers who
changed their type of work to care for their grandchildren. Assuming care
of her two non-school-aged granddaughters precluded continuing the
varying shifts and extensive travel of her twenty-nine-year stint with a
major airline. Although Eloise was forced to change occupations to care
for her granddaughters, unlike some grandmothers she did not have to
forfeit paid work altogether, qualifying for subsidized childcare if she
worked or attended school.

Grandmothers fortunate enough to work in pension-providing jobs
risked losing their pension benefits if they left. In some cases, they were
able to keep the whole pension or to leave pension money where it was
and apply for it on retirement. In others, if an employer contributed to the
pension plan, they might get to keep their contributions but forfeit the
employer's—as happened to Eloise. When Eloise landed a job in social
services, she took a pay cut and a major blow to her pension. "I get almost
sixteen [hundred]–fifteen-ninety-five. . . . I took it five years early, so I lost
half my pension. [*Laughter*] That's what I was tellin' 'em at Catholic
Community Charities [employer]. I ain't never worked for this little
money before." While all older workers face potential penalties for taking
early retirement, caregivers experience substantial income loss compared
to non-caregivers. In addition to lost wages and Social Security benefits,
they lose private pension savings. Pension plans typically require a set
number of years with an employer for vesting, and workers receive no
benefits for extended absences.[26]

Grandmothers who worked in the informal economy also experienced unique challenges. With the added demands of providing care, some grandmothers engaged in "off-the-books" work: selling dinners and cigarettes, making and selling clothing, styling hair, bartending, and providing childcare and home health care assistance. Nearly a fifth of grandmothers engaged in off-the-books work, but negotiated risk to do so: if grandmothers' informal work was disclosed to caseworkers, they risked losing public assistance; if they didn't provide for their grandchildren, they risked losing them.

MANAGING CHILDCARE

Grandmothers made decisions about optimal childcare for their grandchildren by considering not only their personal preferences but also their financial and employment situations, lack of legal rights, ability to qualify for subsidized childcare, access to formal and informal childcare, and grandchildren's needs. But a lack of affordable childcare and difficulty accessing subsidized childcare forced grandmothers to negotiate risks (e.g., choosing between work and staying at home to care for their grandchildren, deciding whether to keep caregiving arrangements private or seek legal guardianship), broker deals with potential childcare providers, navigate or try to bypass bureaucratic regulations for the Child Care Assistance Program, and experience immense financial losses as they forfeited jobs or paid for childcare expenses.

The exorbitance of formal childcare excluded the bulk of grandmothers who needed it in order to maintain their labor-market participation.[27] As a result, only four were able to sustain paying for unsubsidized childcare, these grandmothers spent $400–700/month on childcare. While grandmothers spent less on childcare than the market rate, it was a substantial expenditure given their financial circumstances. Subsidized childcare was used by only six grandmothers raising grandchildren outside of the child welfare system and two grandmothers raising grandchildren within it.

When grandmothers were unable to access childcare, they managed by giving up or forgoing work and staying home with their grandchildren, as was the case with forty-eight-year-old Kathleen, who was forced to quit her job because she was unable to afford formal childcare, qualify for subsidized childcare, or find reliable informal childcare. When Kathleen's granddaughter, Tayauna, was born with developmental delays, Cynthia, the child's mother, would do nothing for or with her, ashamed of the child's disability. Kathleen immediately assumed care for her granddaughter, using her own income. She even tried to rotate childcare between her three other school-aged children by "taking turns taking 'em outta school." At the time, Kathleen was not Tayauna's legal guardian so she couldn't force Cynthia to relinquish the child's public assistance. As long as Cynthia received Tayauna's public assistance, Kathleen would be unable to obtain subsidized childcare because only one person could receive the child's public assistance. Thus, family dynamics impeded Kathleen from applying for subsidized childcare. Kathleen eventually lost her job, forcing her to rely on unemployment income and her personal network.

Fifty-one-year-old Lenora typified grandmothers who paid for formal childcare when they could do so and pursued subsidized childcare when they could not. When her twenty-four-year-old daughter died of childbirth complications, Lenora was left to care for a newborn and a toddler. At that time, she paid for formal childcare. Shortly thereafter, she lost her high-earning job, making it impossible to afford childcare. "I worked all my life. So, I have never been in the system and never had to have any public assistance or anything." But she needed a job to afford childcare and she needed childcare to work. So, she turned to public aid, facing policies ill-suited to her circumstances. "You cry, 'Oh why should I need childcare?' [*Laughter*] Because you're not working or you ain't in school. I said, 'Well how do you think I'm gonna get a job if I don't have any childcare? I can't go for a job interview. . . . I got infants. I can't go anywhere, and I can't leave them and no one can babysit because everybody else works." Eventually, Lenora had a certification program approved to satisfy the Child Care Assistance Program school requirement and was able to enroll the children in formal childcare. After her unemployment ended (during this time she only received WIC), she fell behind on her mortgage. As someone who had never been on public assistance, she described trying to get "some assistance" as a job. She eventually qualified for SNAP and a TANF family grant, but it took months and required the help of a judge.

Helen, forty-eight, also tried to obtain subsidized childcare and to pay for formal childcare, to no avail. She was already struggling to provide for her daughter when her grandson was born. Initially, she changed her work schedule to be home with him, one of several grandmothers who modified their labor-market participation because they couldn't afford childcare. When she didn't qualify for subsidized childcare, Helen was furious: "What's the purpose of applying . . . if y'all gonna tell me I'm not approved . . . because I make too much?" Although she had a job in social services, Helen qualified, "believe me, social service make the least money, almost less than the poverty level." Until two months before the interview, the uninsured grandmother had paid nearly $700/month for childcare, but she could no longer afford to pay the fees.

Unable to afford formal childcare or rely on the child's father, Helen had to move to a less desirable shift. "I switched to nights because I didn't have nobody to watch him. If Felicia [niece] didn't watch him then I had no one." While she was unable to obtain subsidized childcare, Helen did receive a medical card and TANF child-only for her grandson.

Grandmothers raising grandchildren in state custody experienced fewer barriers to accessing childcare than those caring for children informally. Their advantage was their ability to obtain the childcare subsidy with fewer obstacles and to maintain employment without worrying about affordable childcare. In this study, five of the ten kinship foster care providers and all three of the subsidized guardians were employed when care shifted to them. However, access to affordable childcare was a vital resource for employed and unemployed grandmothers alike. For instance, having DCFS subsidize her childcare enabled Eloise to find a new job when care of her granddaughters shifted to her.

> The youngest [child] couldn't go to a daycare until she was, like, two. They didn't take 'em before two. . . . The other one [oldest child] I did put in a daycare. . . . DCFS will pay for it. . . . So by the time I put the other one in daycare, I was back to work. They will pay for the daycare if you're working or in school.

As previously mentioned, when Eloise returned to work, she changed occupations entirely to support her new role, her transition eased by subsidized childcare. She also received a $593 monthly foster care payment.

Grandmothers' childcare experiences illustrate the real and grave consequences of the disparities within the five-tiered system of kinship care as subsidized childcare was more difficult to access by grandmothers providing care informally than those doing so formally, exacerbating their financial strain and contributing to their high rates of poverty.

For grandmothers trying to supplement their income from work, pension and retirement, and disability benefits, obtaining public assistance (cash benefits) was complicated.

Grandmothers wanted what was best not only for the grandchildren in their care but also for the child's parents (especially when parents had additional children), which too often meant going without or using public aid in unintended ways. Most understood that public assistance benefits had declined, jobs failed to pay living wages, and housing and childcare subsidies offsetting the high cost of living and childcare were in short supply. As such, most grandmothers felt that scarce public assistance should be reserved for the greatest need. When their and their grandchildren's struggles exceeded those of parents, grandmothers felt the greatest need was in their own households. But, if they felt that mothers raising additional children needed the formal resources more than they did, grandmothers had no compunction about allowing mothers to keep the public aid of children *not* in their care or about channeling it to mothers struggling to regain custody of their own children. Still, when grandmothers felt that they alone were making sacrifices, they gauged whether they could keep their grandchildren *and* strategize to take the resources they were entitled to—even if it meant engaging in illegal tactics. What this and other studies demonstrate is that when families must resort to defrauding the state by breaking program eligibility rules in order to survive, more is said about the failure of our social safety net to meet the needs of parents and children than about the measures families take to survive.[28]

Since the state provides aid for a child to only one caregiver, grandmothers can access public assistance only if parents aren't already claiming these funds. When parents refused to relinquish children's resources, grandmothers had to provide proof of physical or legal custody to get the resources their grandchildren deserved.[29] Many grandmothers in these circumstances feared doing so because they didn't want the mother to retaliate by removing the child from their custody.[30] So the decision to forgo resources to protect grandchildren was complicated and coercive, preventing some grandmothers from receiving the only form of cash assistance for which they were eligible.

Cassandra, forty-seven, exemplified the inability to supplement her income with public assistance because of family dynamics, specifically, parents using their rights to take or threaten to take children from grandmothers lacking legal guardianship in order to receive the child's resources. Cassandra had been caring for seven-year-old Kwan Jr. (KJ), her son's child, since he was three months old. Because she knew KJ's mother "didn't want him" but only wanted to access resources for herself, Cassandra continued to refuse her attempts to resume her parenting status:

> She trying to get Section 8 and she trying to get an apartment. . . . But like I told her, "I don't care about you putting him on the lease because they ain't gonna do nothing to me with you putting him on. . . . He gonna stay right here where he is and he's gonna stay in the school he's at."

By allowing KJ's mother to receive his formal resources, including her son's child support for a child who wasn't in her care, Cassandra prioritized protecting her grandson over receiving much-needed resources.

Some grandmothers were willing to forgo public assistance so their financially struggling daughters could buttress their fragile financial status. Victoria allowed her daughter to receive the granddaughter's public assistance, requesting only that she keep the child clothed, which for the most part she did. For Victoria and others, brokering deals with parents was a small price to pay for ensuring the safety and well-being of their grandchildren. Cheryl did so with her daughter, Khandice, too, devising a system for sharing public assistance. She had raised Khandice's five children as their mother grappled with substance addiction, and was able to receive public assistance after Cheryl became the children's legal guardian (which allowed her to thwart Khandice receiving the benefits). However, once her daughter entered recovery, Cheryl allowed her to receive assistance for her youngest child. "I got the Link card. She got the cash card. . . . She give me $150/month to help around here."

Although some grandmothers were willing to broker deals with mothers or allow them to keep formal resources, others resorted to illegal tactics to obtain public assistance intended for their grandchildren. When caregiving responsibilities cost Kathleen her job, she collected unemployment. However, when her unemployment benefits ended, Kathleen resorted to trickery to get her daughter to sign the necessary legal guardianship documentation:

> I let her mama get her [granddaughter's] Social Security check. . . . So once my unemployment ran out I told Cynthia I had to have the check. And she didn't wanna give it to me . . . [b]ecause she didn't want the baby but she just wanted the check. So I had to go to court and file a petition so I could get legal guardianship. . . . I had to . . . tell her it was something pertaining to school with Tayauna and that I needed her signature.

At the time of the interview, Kathleen and her granddaughter lived on the child's disability benefits and SNAP. While grandmothers like Kathleen shouldn't have had to go to such lengths to get the resources the children in their care deserved, without other options, they had little choice but to exploit loopholes in the system or to take advantage of parents' disengagement with their children. Importantly, though, even when grandmothers were driven to such measures, it lessened but didn't eliminate their financial struggles.

Grandmothers reported that the majority of parents able to contribute financially failed to do so, not only impeding grandmothers from accessing public assistance but also exhausting grandmothers' scarce resources. These draining ties took an emotional toll, often manifesting as fear, anger, resentment, sadness, and guilt. Helen provided an example of the financial and emotional toll to already struggling grandmothers when parents stole things. Her son grappled with a crack-cocaine addiction. Although stealing from loved ones is commonplace among those with a substance addiction, her story about his actions the Christmas she'd bought gifts for all of her grandchildren was especially heartbreaking:

> Took shoes, brand new boots, . . . clothes outta the boxes and . . . he had wrapped 'em back up with all this old stuff. My other son got two daughters and I bought 'em a bunch of stuff. . . . They came to get they stuff and it was all gone. Took the things out the box and put my shoes back in the box like I wasn't gonna notice.

Furious after that incident, Helen left all Christmas gifts at a niece's house until Christmas day. But when her son also stole her car, which was found broken down in another neighborhood, she had finally had enough and decided to press charges against him. "He stole my keys. This is the kind of stuff I gotta go through. I leave here eight hours going to work. He got eight hours to search this bastard down [her home], which he has done. That's it! He went to court today. I got papers . . . for grand auto theft."

By contrast, despite their own financial struggles, there were also countless examples of the ways in which grandmothers, and sometimes their partners, helped their grandchildren's parents by providing financial support, ranging from helping with bills to providing groceries, household items, and cash. Grandmothers also paid for transportation to facilitate many mothers' involvement with their children, as seventy-year-old Sharon identified in the following incident involving her two grandchildren's drug-addicted mother:

> Her girlfriend . . . brought her to my house. And she said, "Mom, you got a few dollars you can give us so she can put some gas in?" I said, "I'm really kinda broke myself," but I gave her a couple of dollars.

Like other grandmothers in her predicament, Sharon understood that this mother could "barely take care of herself," sometimes arriving with "little cheap gifts." But, since Sharon's son had died of a heart attack, she did what she could—and sometimes what she couldn't—so that, despite the financial drain, her grandchildren could spend time with their mother.

As if family dynamics weren't enough for grandmothers to contend with as they sought to hold on to their income or supplement it with public assistance, they also faced institutional challenges, specifically the stigma and discrimination associated with being poor and unfair treatment based on their family structure. In these scenarios, grandmothers reported being blamed by street-level bureaucrats for having to raise their grandchildren, which was attributed to having raised their own children poorly. In fact, some grandmothers were questioned about their capacity to care for their grandchildren, given how their own children turned out. Sometimes state agents gave grandmothers faulty information about a program's eligibility criteria, including the need for legal guardianship to access certain resources (SNAP, TANF child-only, Medicaid, subsidized guardianship), the requirement of work or school enrollment to receive TANF child-only, and the need to divulge their own incomes for specific programs (TANF child-only, Medicaid). So, to minimize the risk of losing children and maximize the likelihood of receiving public assistance, grandmothers acquiesced when confronted with bias or confounding eligibility processes, satisfied eligibility criteria when possible, bypassed bureaucratic regulations when it wasn't possible, and did without when all else failed.

When forty-one-year-old Shalonda decided to care for her newborn granddaughter, Dana, it was because of the home conditions of Dana's parents. To protect her granddaughter, Shalonda eventually called Child Protective Services and pursued legal guardianship. When, during the guardianship hearing, Shalonda asked about available resources, the response she received from the judge was not only stigmatizing but also stopped her from asking for anything more: "When I first got Dana . . . trying to get assistance . . . was just like the hardest thing because they wouldn't give me assistance for her and the judge made me feel like *this* little. She was like, 'Well, if you need assistance for her, if you can't afford to take care of her, why should we give her to you?'" A few years later, she tried again and received TANF child-only. Other grandmothers also expressed frustration about not receiving benefits not because they lacked the proper paperwork but because staff questioned their doing so as *grandparent* caregivers.[31]

Marian, who came out of retirement to care for her great-granddaughter, did not mince words about her poor treatment trying to access public assistance.

> The man that I was talking to told me to my face, "I didn't ask you that question. Speak when you're spoken to." I am seventy-two years old and he's telling me to speak when spoken to. So you have to swallow your pride, if you think you're going to get some food stamps or a medical card. . . . He never looked at me when he was writing my information down; he never looked at me. It was just questions. I was not visible, I was not there, I was truly disposable.

And so, rather than deal with the indignities of public aid, Marian went back to work, her experience demonstrating the difficulties grandmothers had accessing the few available resources.

Street-level bureaucrats who conveyed TANF eligibility criteria in erroneous and onerous ways were a common impediment. In fact, next to parental receipt of public assistance, confusion about the legal-guardianship requirement was a chief barrier to TANF access, and, due to such barriers, less than half of eligible grandmothers in this study received the $107 monthly stipends (see table 5 at the end of the chapter for study participants' household sources of income). Although relative caregivers are eligible for TANF child-only grants without being legal guardians of the children in their care, many reported being told otherwise, as May encountered when seeking public assistance in light of accumulating costs in caring for her granddaughter, McKayla.

> I went to the aid office and they told me I couldn't get anything because I'm not her legal guardian yet. But I showed 'em, I said, "Look, I got her in school. She started school October the 12th. . . . And I got her in school but I'm having a hard time getting school supplies because I'm only working part-time. And I got bills to pay. It's coming outta my pocket, using my credit cards buying things for her that I should be buying for me, but I'm looking out for her." So they gave me a $200 voucher to get her some clothes. . . . Because I went through the guardianship on my own, it's nothing they can do about it as far as helping me out.

For women seeking an alternative to TANF child-only grants, obtaining TANF assistance for themselves and the child was even more out of reach. Kinship caregivers in family TANF cases were subject to time limits and employment and training requirements.[32] Additionally, the benefit calculation had to include grandmothers' incomes. Unfortunately, aging and health-related issues often made it difficult to fulfill the work and training requirements. For instance, when Susan applied for a TANF family grant, her caseworker explained that she needed to satisfy work and training requirements, so Susan's age and frail health precluded participating in the program. "It was hard. I mean I would take them to school and then I had to go to school. See? . . . It was hard just for that little $377 I actually got out of it. I pretended like I had gotten hit in the arm because I was tired of going. [*Laughter*] So, I just called 'em up one day and told 'em I had a job." When the grant agency learned that she had not completed the program or secured a job, they reduced her TANF family grant

($377/month) to a child-only grant of $190/month. Although she turned sixty-five shortly thereafter and was able to qualify for SSI, she still fell short of affording private-market housing and supporting her two grandchildren, whose mother was in prison. So they lived with Susan's son until she could secure subsidized housing.

Although she desperately needed the medical card that came with public assistance, Grace also found it difficult to sustain her participation. In order to fulfill the program's work and training requirement, she participated in the Workfare program, which assigns recipients of public assistance to employment without compensation and is required for persons who do not participate in job-search training and work programs but who are not exempt from registration with the Job Service. As a result, Grace was given a volunteer assignment at a social service organization for thirty hours a week: "I guess it became a little bit difficult for me. Again, when I have family problems or whatnot, it's hard on me. And with the osteoarthritis, the pain that sometimes I get . . . weighs me down." When Grace's health precluded her participating in the program, her resources were terminated, including access to medical coverage and the $292/month cash assistance she received for her and her grandson, Shemar. Indeed, only two grandmothers I interviewed who applied for a TANF family grant qualified for the program.

In addition to family dynamics, grandparent-headed households underuse public assistance benefits because they are differentially incorporated—the unequal treatment and differential access of marginalized populations to society's economic, social, political, and cultural rewards—into safety net programs.[33] Grandparent-headed households experience differential incorporation not only because of the disproportionate number of BIPOC (Black, Indigenous, and people of color), low-income women providing care but also because of their family structure. Institutional agents were too often ill-informed about the eligibility requirements for families not headed by parents. Still others let their own personal biases about caregivers obstruct the services they provided such families. Further exacerbating their difficulty accessing formal resources, grandparent-headed households experience a structural lag[34] between their families and safety net programs geared toward parents and not other caregivers.

In the face of public assistance that failed to support families in general, and grandparent-headed households in particular, grandmothers became deal brokers (e.g., splitting resources with parents), risk negotiators (e.g., forgoing resources in order to keep children in their care, resorting to trickery to obtain legal guardianship), safety net navigators, and in some cases, more impoverished as they failed to procure resources to offset caregiving costs.

Keeping a Roof over Their Heads

Maintaining and securing housing that could adequately accommodate their grandchildren was critical to grandmothers thrust into the primary caregiving role. They confronted several housing issues found in other studies, including acquiring new housing to accommodate their grandchildren, fulfilling the child welfare system's housing requirements, violating lease agreements, and overcoming barriers to accessing and maintaining subsidized housing.[35] Certainly, many of the grandmothers interviewed had limited housing options prior to assuming responsibility for their grandchildren. However, housing their grandchildren exacerbated and complicated those constraints.

ACQUIRING NEW HOUSING

Grandmothers acquired new housing when their existing housing was insufficient for raising their grandchildren, either because they were cohabitating with others, their grandchildren weren't allowed, or their dwellings were too small or located in an unsafe neighborhood or building. When fifty-eight-year-old Sandy assumed primary responsibility for two-year-old Sophia after the child's forty-year-old mother died of a heart attack, Sandy knew that she would need legal guardianship to access child-rearing institutions and receive public assistance. However, becoming Sophia's legal guardian required demonstrating to the judge and caseworker that she could provide adequate housing. Because Sandy lived in a friend's house prior to her daughter's unexpected death, Sandy's sister and twenty-four-year-old granddaughter agreed to share an apartment with her to demonstrate that Sophia would have a stable home: "We pay $900 a month; $300 apiece." Sandy used her disability check to pay her part of the rent and household expenses, and to raise her granddaughter.

Fifty-two-year-old Pamela, another grandmother who had to combine resources with others to secure and maintain housing for her grandchildren, lived with her sister and shared expenses to ease the demands of caregiving. Pamela worked as a program director at a daycare center and compensated for her sister's change to a lower-paying job.

> We split down the middle, my sister and I. Well, really not half . . . since she had lost her job. . . . The mortgage is like $1,300. She'll give me $575 dollars. She'll pay the cable bill, which is about . . . $150 or so. We each pay our own cell phone bills, and I have the gas bill and the other part of the mortgage.

In addition to pooling resources with her sister, Pamela relied on her income and SNAP benefits to raise her two granddaughters (ages eleven and five). Sandy and Pamela were among twelve grandmothers acquiring new housing to pool resources on assuming primary caregiving responsibility.

In order to accommodate their suddenly larger families, grandmothers often opted for substandard housing or housing in unsafe neighborhoods whose space was offset by rampant problems. Cheryl, a Section 8 recipient,[36] exemplified grandmothers trying to upgrade housing with limited income, time, and resources. Her experience also revealed mobility constraints on grandmothers trying to leave decaying neighborhoods, including finding places that accepted subsidized housing vouchers:

> I moved from 54th and Lovejoy, right down the street. . . . I had to. . . . You see drugs in the hallway, everything in the hallway. I come from work at night, I couldn't even get through the hallway. Fifteen or twenty people . . . was smokin' dope, doing everything. . . . But this building is cleaner. . . . Big change.

Affording safe housing was nearly impossible for many grandmothers. Although Cheryl felt her new apartment was an improvement, she shared safety concerns with many grandmothers, in her case vulnerability to violence due to a neighbor's drug-trade involvement:

At a certain hour of the night y'all [grandchildren] get up and stay on the porch. Somebody comin' through the alley shootin.' Three guys come right down here [apartment below her] with a gun and put the gun on this woman and her grandkids. . . . Looking for her son. . . . A drug dealer. . . . Went . . . and ransacked the [son's] room. . . . That's scary shit.

Similarly, Sharon moved when she became a surrogate parent to her two grandchildren (ages nine and five).

I tried to find a better neighborhood for the children . . . because the house next door to me, the people there were selling drugs. We couldn't come out our door without hearing a lotta profanity and I didn't want them to think that was normal. So I moved to Woodlawn. . . . I had a real nice place there, but it was . . . big, . . . very cold. I couldn't heat it up. . . . And then someone broke in . . . and stole some things. . . . So where I am now, it's better.

Like Cheryl's, Sharon's new neighborhood and apartment building were better in many ways; still, she confided, "Once in a while I hear some shooting. Yeah, unfortunately I do occasionally. [*Laughter*] Not often. But it's a nice building. The area is nice too."

While some grandmothers who relocated rated their new neighborhoods as "nice" or "better" because they were plagued with less violence, not all of them did. Forty-nine-year-old Joan didn't like her neighborhood. In fact, she didn't even claim it.

I really cannot describe this neighborhood. I can tell you what I can see from inside and I don't even look out my windows. At night, I see police fly through here every night. You hear gunshots. . . . I think I'm in the middle of a war zone. . . . You got one set of gangs over here and one set of gangs over there. . . . When I go outside, I walk out this door, get in the car or get on PACE and go away. I don't live in this neighborhood; I live in this house.

Joan's restriction to her house described a common coping strategy of parents raising their children in concentrated poverty.[37] She also demonstrated the limited mobility of poor families seeking safe, affordable housing. Like Cheryl, Joan was also a Section 8 recipient, raising five grandchildren (ages one to sixteen) on her disability check ($700/month), and the food their mother bought with the SNAP benefits she received because the state assumed the children lived with her. As one would expect, modifying their housing was disruptive for most caregiving grandmothers, many at a life stage normally characterized by decreasing rather than expanding housing needs.

MANAGING THE STATE'S HOUSING REQUIREMENTS

Grandmothers providing care under the aegis of the child welfare system had a higher stake in maintaining and improving housing. Not only were they internally driven to provide adequate housing for their grandchildren, but they also faced external pressure to do so or lose their grandchildren to nonrelative foster care. Although non-safety-related foster home licensing standards can be waived on a case-by-case basis for kinship foster care homes, grandmothers still experienced challenges fulfilling the state's housing requirements, including needing to move to satisfy space requirements and make home repairs with limited resources.

When her oldest daughter entered a battered women's shelter, and DCFS gave sixty-two-year-old Miriam her three grandchildren, she encountered difficulty passing the DCFS home inspection required of kinship foster care providers.

> They came by and they did a house inspection and they worried the hell outta me.... You see the ledging around the door? That came off on the door. It wore out. It's a raggedy old house. And they told me that it was structural damage and if I could not repair it they could not pay me.

Then, when another housing problem surfaced, Miriam temporarily lost her grandchildren to nonrelative foster care: "My bathroom floor had a hole in it.... They had me release custody of these children to somebody else until the ... floor was finished."

Similarly, if less vividly, Louise recalled:

> They look at your house and then they, uh, I don't know whether they measured the rooms or what, but ... they license your house ... for how many [children] you can have in your house.

Based on her housing specifications, Louise was licensed to accommodate her three grandchildren, whom she almost lost when a caseworker misrepresented the state of her housing. Although she kept her youngest grandson, a toddler at the time, in a baby bed near her bed because he often escaped from his own, the caseworker reported otherwise.

> They come out and they told some lies and said that I had Cole sleeping downstairs and he was all full of cold and all that. He was in my room right there with me. . . . I had a small bed [in his room in the basement] and had a baby bed for him [near her bed].

Louise avoided an investigation by explaining to a DCFS supervisor that she didn't heat up her grandson's basement bedroom because he didn't use it. But the experience left a bitter taste in her mouth and reinforced that she couldn't trust her "workers."

In general, caseworkers lacked sensitivity about grandmothers' struggles to provide their grandchildren housing. While the state relied heavily on these women to provide care, they provided nominal support to families that they *knew* struggled to make ends meet, including difficulty finding safe and affordable housing. Instead of working with potential or actual kinship foster care providers to ensure that their homes posed no risks to children, some caseworkers looked for shortcomings and, in the majority of cases, provided no support to address them. They also determined what was "wrong" based on their own socioeconomic class values and cultural identity—not those of the communities they served.

Advocates for grandparent-headed households argue that some categories of the child welfare system's standards may not be necessary at all, including arbitrary and strict square-footage requirements.[38] Grandmothers terrified of losing custody of their grandchildren scrambled to fulfill the state's housing requirements even when it meant redirecting already stretched dollars toward home repairs and lying about the number of occupants.

KEEPING AND GETTING SUBSIDIZED HOUSING

Because subsidized housing was hard to come by, grandmothers used risk-negotiation strategies to keep both their housing subsidy and their grandchildren in their care. Twenty-one of seventy-four grandmothers in the study received some form of housing assistance, but the rules of subsidized housing often caused problems for the grandmothers, who had to specify and stick to the number of people listed on the lease. It was not uncommon for grandchildren to move between their grandmothers' and parent's homes.[39] Most grandmothers therefore simply refused to divulge their housing composition to landlords and housing authority officials. Fifty-year-old Dorothy models the use of this risk-negotiation strategy. She had lived in subsidized housing for eleven years but she'd been caring for her grandson for only four: "Technically he [grandson] don't [live here], but he came back in. He's not on the lease." Although she didn't jeopardize her subsidized housing by adding him to her lease, the once-unemployed grandmother got a full-time job to provide for him.

Grandmothers like Sharon were forced to obtain legal guardianship when housing authority officials and landlords of privately operated sub-sidized housing unlawfully required them to have legal guardianship of grandchildren to qualify for subsidized housing. "I had to show them my custody papers and things like that. And that's basically it, show that I had the kids—that was one of the requirements [for Section 8 benefits]." Similarly, Beulah was told by housing authority officials that she needed legal guardianship to add her two grandchildren to her lease. She then had to devise a plan to get legal guardianship of her grandchildren with-out her daughter's consent. As discussed earlier, grandmothers gave a lot of consideration to "taking" their grandchildren from parents. But, ulti-mately, they did so out of necessity—either to keep their grandchildren safe or to access desperately needed resources and services. Because they were forced to mother rather than grandmother their grandchildren, they didn't feel bad about doing what was needed to carry out this increased responsibility—even when it meant going against parents. In Beulah's case, keeping a roof over her grandchildren's heads superseded worrying about her daughter's feelings.

Misinformation about legal guardianship from housing authority offi-cials and landlords of privately operated subsidized housing impeded grandmothers trying to both use *and* access subsidized housing. For example, when asked why she applied for legal guardianship of her three grandchildren to obtain Section 8, fifty-eight-year-old Lottie explained, "I wanted a house because with three kids an apartment just ain't gonna get it. . . . 'Cause they told me I couldn't . . . unless I had guardianship papers."

Despite misinformation from street-level bureaucrats, Lottie and her disabled husband tried to hold on to their grandchildren *and* obtain subsidized housing by satisfying eligibility criteria. When care transferred to her, she was working full-time, but her hours were cut during the Great Recession, causing additional financial strain.

Lottie's application for subsidized housing outside Chicago exemplified a tactic for accessing housing during the Section 8 freeze:

> That's what made me opt for putting in for an application in the suburbs. . . .
> [But] we didn't have transportation to get out there to search for an apartment or a house because my husband's disabled and then by me working there was . . . no time to . . . look like I wanted to.

Although she was awarded Section 8, living in Chicago made it difficult to find Section 8 eligible housing in the suburbs, which also signaled to Lottie that it would be difficult to get to her job in the city without transportation. Thus, they spent half of their income paying private market rent.

Family dynamics also impeded grandmothers' attempts to use and access subsidized housing. In these cases, grandmothers strategized in yet other ways to obtain public assistance or to make the most of a housing subsidy. While most adhered to CHA regulations, some ignored bureaucratic strictures. For example, when the gravity of her family problems kept her co-residing with her son, developmentally disabled daughter, and grandchildren, Grace allowed a friend to use her Section 8 voucher until she could use it herself. "It's where I first utilized my Section 8. And I say utilized it because I didn't actually live there. . . . Someone else did. I was still livin' in X. . . . I was so desperate because I didn't want to lose that subsidy for future purposes."

While some grandmothers forswear senior housing that doesn't allow grandchildren, studies indicate that some grandparents live in senior housing with their grandchildren anyway, risking eviction, the loss of housing subsidies, and the loss of their grandchildren.[40] In this study, senior housing forbidding children was an issue for renters *and* homeowners who wanted to give up the homes in which they'd raised their children or take advantage of the publicly subsidized senior housing for which they qualified and retire there to accommodate changes in their economic and health status.

While some of the housing issues described are unique to Black grandmothers raising grandchildren in or near inner cities (e.g., living near crime and violence, a limited rental market overrun with dilapidated housing, and such), other housing concerns are associated with grandparent caregiving more generally. Indeed, previous research has found that a lack of affordable housing is one of the most critical access issues for grandparents and other relatives raising children.[41]

CONCLUSION

Grandparents raising grandchildren in skipped-generation households find themselves in a marginal position relative to judicially favored parents and the state. Inasmuch as family dynamics and state agents hinder grandparents' efforts to retain the resources to provide for themselves, their families, and their grandchildren, risk negotiation helps them overcome barriers. Risk negotiation enables people to use strategies appropriate to their circumstances to offset their marginalization as they interact with individuals and institutions with more power and privilege. For some grandmothers in this study, risk negotiation involved resorting to trickery when parents refused to relinquish children's resources and when formal resources were inadequate and difficult to access. Their experiences clarify that while parents and the state rely heavily on grandmothers as a safety for their grandchildren, there is no safety net for these caregivers. Grandmothers shouldn't have to resort to such measures in order to survive. Indeed, as grandmothers experienced financial burden and loss, brokered deals, negotiated risks, navigated safety net programs, and negotiated state supervision in pursuit of income, childcare, and housing, they experienced a transformation in the role meanings and expectations they associated with grandmotherhood.

The grandmothers I interviewed struggled with the housing-authority prerequisite of legal guardianship to add children to leases or apply for subsidized housing—despite an FHA mandate that protects them from such action. They weighed the fluidity and uncertainty of grandparent caregiving against a tight subsidized-housing market, and some would not divulge their household composition to landlords or housing authority officials for fear of losing their subsidies. If landlords or housing authority officials found out that their housing composition had changed, grandmothers could lose their housing subsidy, be asked to move, or undergo a rent increase. Others, like Beulah, Sharon, and Lottie, assumed guardianship to keep children in their care, add them to their leases, or apply for Section 8 status. Still others found caregiving responsibilities blocked access to the publicly subsidized senior housing market. While grandmothers demonstrated impressive agency, their efforts were no match for structural constraints, so several bypassed regulations to expedite receiving public housing or by illegally remaining in such housing.

Although thirteen grandmothers in this study were income eligible for the TANF family grant, only two satisfied the welfare programs' eligibility criteria. These programs did not align with the lived experiences of grandparent caregivers, many of whom were unable to work due to poor health and caregiving responsibilities. Their experiences demonstrate the structural lag between grandparent-headed households and safety net programs, as well as their differential incorporation.

When grandmothers are principal childcare providers, their role as childcare consumers is largely ignored in current childcare policy, even though most remain in the labor market.[42] While these women had slightly higher wages because of their work longevity, few earned enough to pay directly for childcare. I found that, paradoxically, as a result of modifying their labor-market participation to care for grandchildren, some grandmothers lost the income needed to meet the economic demands of providing such care. While mothers' experiences are similar, grandmothers' are direr, as they have higher rates of poverty, poorer health, age-limited job prospects, and—often—more caregiving responsibilities, many are still raising children and caring for aging parents, spouses, or ill relatives. Lacking access to childcare challenged custodial grandmothers' efforts at economic self-sufficiency or escaping impoverishment. Indeed, paying for childcare made it difficult to afford health insurance, rent, and utilities. Since safe, reliable childcare is expensive, grandmothers understood why some grandparent caregivers decline to report their full income or devise other strategies to qualify for childcare subsidies and other forms of public assistance. Some grandmothers in my study who were unable to pay for childcare were compelled to quit their jobs or were unable to secure employment.

In some cases, the structural lag between grandparent-headed households and safety net programs was compounded by inadequate and punitive welfare policies that engender family conflict over who will receive the child's scarce resources. By acting in the best interests of their grandchildren, grandparent caregivers too often fell short. Without legal protections or publicly recognized authority as parents, accessing safety net programs was difficult. While some grandmothers devised strategies to take legal guardianship from parents, others negotiated with them to share resources. Still, others simply did without, though that was less problematic for grandmothers raising grandchildren as foster care parents, subsidized guardians, and adoptive grandparents. In short, the disparities within the five-tiered system of kinship care thus have severe consequences for grandparents raising grandchildren.

Table 4 Safety Net Programs, Eligibility Criteria, Study Participants Receiving Benefits, and Barriers

Types of safety net programs	Eligibility criteria for informal kinship caregivers in Illinois	Study participants receiving/eligible for* benefit (N = 74)	Barriers to receiving benefit
TANF Child-Only Grant ($107 per month for one child, $211 for two, $261 for three)	(1) Low-income assistance program that doesn't count grandparent's income and assets in child's eligibility; (2) Exempt from work and time limits; (3) Legal guardianship not required	16/41	(1) Obfuscation about eligibility criteria (e.g., legal guardianship) by street-level bureaucrats; (2) Family dynamics; (3) Stigma and discrimination
TANF Family Grant ($292 per month for family of two, $396 for three, $435 for four)	(1) Low-income assistance program for income eligible grandparents that are included in assistance unit; (2) Subject to work participation and 5 year time limit; (3) Age exemption-60; (4) Legal guardianship not required	2/13	(1) Obfuscation about eligibility criteria (e.g., legal guardianship) by street-level bureaucrats; (2) Family dynamics; (3) Inability to satisfy work, education or training requirements
Subsidized Housing (Housing expense limited to 30% of income)	(1) Household income may not exceed 50% of median income of area or 80% for those displaced by rental rehabilitation; (2) Assets not in excess of limitation set by Chicago Housing Authority; (3) Physical custody, not legal custody of child required; (4) Limited due to funding restrictions	21	(1) Erroneous information regarding legal guardianship; (2) Family dynamics

Program	Number	Eligibility criteria	Barriers
Subsidized Child Care (No cost or co-payment for formal child care)	8 (6 outside of child welfare system; 2 within it)	(1) Grandparent must be income eligible for Illinois Child Care Assistance Program; (2) Employed grandparents receiving a child-only grant eligible for daycare assistance; (3) Subject to work, education or training requirements; (4) Limited to subset of eligible households due to funding restrictions	(1) Erroneous and onerous information about income eligibility requirements for employed grandparents who receive TANF child-only grant; (2) Obfuscation about eligibility criteria (e.g. legal guardianship) by street-level bureaucrats; (3) Family dynamics
Supplemental Security Income	28	(1) Entitlement program wherein grandparent or grandchild eligible if meet disability guidelines, including countable income less than benefit amount and individual assets less than $2,000; (2) Guardianship required to obtain birth certificate and social security card	(1) If for grandchild, family dynamics (e.g., conflict over legal custody); (2) Difficulty obtaining birth certificate and social security card
SNAP ($189 per month maximum for one person, $347 for two, $497 for three, $632 for four)	34/42	(1) Low-income assistance program when net household income does not exceed 130% of the federal poverty level; (2) Grandchildren counted when determining the grant amount; (3) Exempt from employment and training	(1) Obfuscation about eligibility criteria (e.g., legal guardianship) by street-level bureaucrats; (2) Family dynamics (e.g., conflict over legal custody)

* Eligibility is defined as study participants that are income eligible for safety net programs but are *not* receiving benefits. Study participants eligible for TANF Family Grants are not receiving SSI or SSDI and have not timed out of the TANF program.

Table 5   Household Income Sources/Financial Changes

Study participant name	Income package	Financial change
Sylvia	Housing Subsidy, SNAP	Decreased work
Angela	Housing Subsidy, SNAP	
Susan	SSI, Housing Subsidy, TANF Child-Only, SNAP	Increased work Changed housing
Dorothy	Earnings, Housing Subsidy, TANF Child-Only	Increased work
Otha	SSI, SSDI	Decreased work
Cassandra	SSI, Child Care Subsidy, SNAP	
Kathleen	SSI, Housing Subsidy, SNAP	Decreased work
Helen	Earnings, TANF Child-Only	
Shalonda	Earnings, TANF Child-Only	
Donna	Earnings, Foster Care Payment ($560 for 2 children)	
Laverne	SSI, Housing Subsidy, TANF Child-Only, SNAP	
Barbara	Earnings, TANF Child-Only	Changed housing
Victoria	SSI, Housing Subsidy, SNAP	
Rose	Earnings, SNAP	Changed type of work
Pearl	Pension, SSI, TANF Child-Only	
Tamara	SSI, Adoption Room & Board Payment ($1,683 for 4 children), SNAP, Housing Subsidy	Changed housing
Martha	SSDI, SNAP	Increased work
Eliza	SSDI, Pension, SNAP	Decreased work
Bobbie Joe	Earnings only	Decreased work
Kathryn	SSDI only	
Judy	SSI, Earnings, SNAP	
Virginia	SSDI, Pension, TANF Child-Only	Increased work
Sonya	None	
Miriam	SSI, SNAP	Increased work
Maxine	Earnings, Childcare Subsidy	
Beulah	Earnings, TANF Child-Only	
Nancy	Earnings, Childcare Subsidy, TANF Family Grant	
Faith	SSI, TANF Child-Only, SNAP	
Lottie	Earnings, SSI	Changed housing

Table 5   (Continued)

Study participant name	Income package	Financial change
Lena Bell	Pension, SSI, Adoption Room & Board Payment ($794 for 2 children), Housing Subsidy	
Cora	SSI, Housing Subsidy, SNAP	
Lonna	Earnings, Adoption Room & Board Payment ($384), Housing Subsidy, SNAP	
Opal	Pension, SSI, Adoption Room & Board Payment ($445)	
Nell	SSI, Subsidized Guardianship Payment ($376, $444)	Increased work
Sandy	SSI, SNAP	Changed housing
Cheryl	SSI, Housing Subsidy, TANF Child-Only, SNAP	Increased work Changed housing
Grace	Housing Subsidy, TANF Child-Only, SNAP	Increased work Changed housing
May	SSDI, SNAP	
Ruby	SSI, Pension, Foster Care Payment	
Gloria	SSDI	
Ida	Pension, SSI, Foster Care Payment	
Eloise	Earnings, Foster Care Payment ($593 for 2 children), Child Care Subsidy	Changed type of work
Latoya	Earnings, Subsidized Guardianship Payment ($300-$380), Child Care Subsidy	
Bertha	SSI, Foster Care Payment	Increase work
Viola	SSI, Subsidized Guardianship Payment ($1,464 for 3 children), Section 8	Decreased work
Frances	SSI only	Changed housing
Alice	Earnings, Foster Care Payment	
Josephine	SSI, Foster Care Payment	
Louise	SSI, Foster Care Payment	
Janet	Earnings, Foster Care Payment	Changed type of work
Carolyn	Housing Subsidy, TANF Family Grant, SNAP	

Table 5   (Continued)

Study participant name	Income package	Financial change
Lenora	Child Care Subsidy, TANF Child-Only & SNAP in process	Decreased work
Nicole	SSDI only	Changed housing
Michelle	Earnings, Child Care Subsidy, TANF Child-Only	
Velma	SSI, Adoption Room & Board Payment	
Connie	SSI, SNAP	Changed housing
Mavis	SSI, Housing Subsidy, SNAP, TANF Child-Only in process	
Chandra	Housing Subsidy, SNAP	
Natalie	Earnings only	Increased work
Claudette	SSDI, SNAP	
Pamela	Earnings, SNAP	
Marian	Earnings only	Increased work Changed type of work
Joan	SSDI, SNAP	
Sharon	Section 8, SSI	Changed housing
Jacky	SSDI, Earnings, Housing Subsidy, TANF Child-Only, SNAP	
Joyce	SSDI, Housing Subsidy, SNAP	Decreased work
Vivian	SNAP only	
Brenda	SSDI	
Norris	None	
Regina	SSDI, SNAP	Decreased work Changed housing
Denise	SSDI, Housing Subsidy, SNAP	
Waneda	Earnings, Housing Subsidy, SNAP	
Penny	Earnings only	
Rachel	Earnings, Child Care Subsidy	

6 Managing the Burden and the Blessing

As already suggested, grandmothers face an array of dilemmas and stressors associated with raising grandchildren. In addition to the normal and predictable child-rearing challenges, the women I interviewed were raising another generation in the context of coerced mothering and a complex and unequal system of kinship care. They had to make extremely difficult decisions about appropriate interventions when their grandchildren experienced actual or potential threats to their safety and well-being and whether to use punitive institutions to overcome their lack of legal authority. Like grandparents in other studies, the women in my study withstood enormous stress because of financial hardships, family conflict, legal issues, housing insecurity, stigmatization, managing unpaid carework and paid work, managing multiple caregiving responsibilities, and problems associated with child-rearing.[1]

In this chapter, I focus on the toll of grandparent caregiving on women's personal lives, including restricting their freedom, impairing their romantic relationships, and impeding their retirement. I then demonstrate the impact of grandparent caregiving on grandmothers' physical and mental health. Next, I show that grandmothers relied on social support networks and religion to cope with caregiving consequences. I end the chapter on the rewards of raising grandchildren, including grand-mothers' desires for companionship and intimacy, an opportunity to reparent, and a sense of purpose.

THE COST OF RAISING A GRANDCHILD

Parenting their grandchildren deprived women of time, energy, and resources to devote to their personal lives. At the most basic level, women articulated the unexpected loss of freedom. Grandparent caregivers in this and other studies also report decreased social interaction and socialization with their peers.[2] Additionally, grandparent caregivers may experience emotional distress because of decreased leisure time and respite from caregiving responsibilities,[3] fractured peer and familial relationships,[4] and social isolation.[5] Finally, their mid- or late-life plans and expectations are disrupted.[6]

Another impact on their personal lives is their romantic relationships. Although Black grandmothers are more likely than other caregivers to parent their grandchildren without parental or partner presence, a quarter of the women in my study were in intimate relationships and more wanted to be. Few studies have examined the influence of raising grandchildren on caregivers' romantic relationships, even though half of US grandparents primarily responsible for their grandchildren are married.[7] My study findings support the burgeoning literature on this topic, including that marriage reduces psychological distress and caregiving strain and buffers some of the hardships of raising grandchildren.[8] Still, caregivers report the potential relationship strain of raising grandchildren.[9] Like grandparent caregivers in other studies (in their research on grandparent caregivers in New Zealand, Shirley Ann Chinnery and Jill Worrall document separations and divorces resulting from child-raising pressures),[10] women in my study reported having less attention for their partners and relationship tension when a partner expected an empty-nest retirement.[11] That said, another study reported both increased and decreased marital satisfaction among grandparent caregivers.[12]

The literature on the impact of caregiving on grandparents' personal lives has tended to focus on physical and mental health. Raising grandchildren can thwart healthy, active aging, resulting in a decrease or discontinuation of health practices.[13] After transitioning into surrogate parent roles, grandparents in this and other studies report being less likely to prioritize their own health over grandchildren's needs. In contrast, grandparents also describe the increased activity associated with raising grandchildren as leading to better health practices, with some grandparents feeling motivated to cultivate health practices that increase longevity so that they can provide care.[14]

Although the findings on the impact of grandparent caregiving on health practices are mixed, it is widely recognized that the stress of caring for grandchildren is associated with negative mental and physical health outcomes, especially among those with inadequate finances and diminished social support.[15] Grandparent primary caregivers have poorer mental and physical health outcomes than do non-caregivers, even when controlling for age, race/ethnicity, economic status, education, and marital status. They also have poorer mental and physical health than filial and spousal caretakers, custodial grandparents who provide less care, or members of the general population.[16] Grandparent caregivers have been shown to experience higher rates of arthritis, hypertension, insomnia, pain, hearing problems, diabetes, and limitations on daily-life activities than do their age-related peers.[17] Many grandparent caregivers also report an exacerbation of chronic diseases.[18] Finally, grandparents in skipped-generation households are more likely than those in three-generation households to experience limitations in their daily-life activities than do their non-caregiving peers.[19]

These poor health outcomes are compounded for Black women, who experience persistent and severe preexisting health disparities, including the second-lowest life expectancy and the highest age-adjusted death rates for heart disease, stroke, cancer, diabetes, and Alzheimer's disease among women.[20] Black women also face poor outcomes across nearly all domains of reproductive health—from sexually transmitted disease to pregnancy to gynecologic cancers.[21] Like those in other studies, women in my study experienced significant health issues, including diabetes, high cholesterol, obesity, and hypertension;[22] strokes, heart attacks, kidney disease, and various cancers were also widespread. Finally, like Black women in the general population, those in my study experienced disparities in access to and quality of health care and health insurance.

Previous research has identified clinically significant levels of psychological distress among grandparent caregivers, with a constant finding of elevated symptoms of depression, especially among those caring for special-needs children,[23] and Black women are more likely to report increased psychological distress than their White counterparts,[24] which also exacerbates the role of psychological stress on the health of Black women.[25] School of Nursing professor Susan Kelley and colleagues found that nearly 40 percent of African American grandparents scored in the clinical range on psychological distress, the main contributing factors being grandchild behavior problems, diminished grandmother physical health, and lack of family resources.[26] Contravening the conventional saying among African Americans that "Black women don't have the luxury of being depressed," many grandmothers in my study were candid about their vulnerability to depression, reflecting higher rates of depression than White women in the general population.[27] Black women's expression of depression also differs from traditional clinical symptoms and from that of White women due to multiple stressors—a greater number of acute life events, socioeconomic status, racism, perceived discrimination, multiple role obligations, misogynoir in health care, geographic location, high unemployment rates, and underaccess to resources.[28] Research highlights that depression among Black women is often more difficult to detect "because they present with multiple comorbidities, emphasize more somatic symptoms and physical functioning impairments, report symptoms of anger or irritability, and even deny their illness."[29]

When asked how caregiving changed their lives or what they would otherwise be doing, grandmothers in this study identified the aforementioned aspects of their personal lives as the hardest hit by the demands of providing care. The next section examines these frequently articulated aspects of grandmothers' personal lives, along with others that emerged from the data.

Restricted Freedom

> JUDY: I just don't wanna be tied down with little babies no more. I wanna go to school. You know what I'm saying? I wanna be a pharmacy

technician. And I wanna be free to do it. . . . And . . . after seven kids I'm ready. I'm tired.

LASHAWNDA: So you're ready for a break?

JUDY: I'm ready for a life.

Fifty-one-year-old Judy was raising her youngest of seven children when she was coerced into providing care for her heroin-addicted daughter Chanté's first child, four-month-old Simone. Judy had been caring for others most of her life. Not only had she raised herself while growing up in the projects, but also she and her older brother had been charged with raising their four younger siblings. Although their mother didn't abandon them entirely, "she was out a lot." Their mother left them grocery money and, in her absence, they attended school only when they wanted.

Judy married and had her first child at sixteen. She didn't reveal much about her children's fathers, except that they had succumbed to tragic deaths and drug addiction. She'd been with her current husband for nearly a decade. All of Judy's children except Chanté took care of their own children. But raising her granddaughter while she was still raising the last of her seven children meant that Judy had experienced no break in child-rearing since she began raising her younger siblings. So, being "tied down with little babies" not only prevented Judy from getting a break from child-rearing but also thwarted her desire to have "a life," which for her meant going back to school. Her exasperated declaration, "I wanna be a pharmacy technician. And I wanna be free to do it," illustrated a common hunger—freedom was not only the conduit to a life, however these women defined it, it was a prerequisite: they needed to be free *in order to* tend to their personal lives. Freedom seemed to be characterized by two primary traits—choice (having and using options) and movement (being able to come and go at will).

Raising children required significant time, energy, and resources, which tethered women to the home front, restricting their ability to fulfill their own needs. Before assuming responsibility for their young grandchildren, women with their own adolescent children at home might still have factored them into their plans, but their day-to-day lives and schedules hadn't been dominated as they were about to be by resuming care for younger children. Many of these women talked about counting down to freedom based on the age of their youngest child. As Sylvia put it, "Girl, I got about four more years [before her teenage children were grown and out of the house]. I'm all geeked up!" But parenting another generation changed all those calculations.

VICTORIA: Well, my fourteen-year-old, in four more years she'll be gone. But . . . since Nia [six-month-old granddaughter] is here, I won't have the freedom.

ELOISE: This is my time. My daughter had just made eighteen and I was like jumping for joy. . . . Free at last. Free, free. And then, two months later, I get the kids [granddaughters].

In the last season of their lives, older women (and partners present during the interview) expressed hope for enough time to do the things they wanted to do before they no longer had the time and energy to do so.

BERTHA: I got two more years and I'll be headin' for eighty. But I still hope I have some more spunk and stuff to do something, to go somewhere.

ELIZA: So I think just to enjoy some freedom. A different kind of freedom. Not having always to take care of somebody else. We'll be taking care of each other because I'm taking care of him now. He has a lung condition. And he had to take disability leave from his job.

LASHAWNDA: So you all would have less responsibility?

VIRGINIA AND NORMAN (IN UNISON): Yeah, no responsibilities!

NORMAN: Responsibilities would be to each other, doing what we wanna do.

Basically, women wanted what one grandmother articulated as the freedom to "go when I wanna go . . . and just do what I wanna do"—a stay against the dominance of Black women's social worlds, a reprieve from being mothers, grandmothers, wives, girlfriends, workers, daughters, activists, othermothers, and community workers. In fact, what they "wanna do" and where they "wanna go" didn't need to be defined, figured out, or tied to a role or identity. Women didn't feel the need to accomplish anything in particular—just to be able to do whatever, whenever they were so moved.

Being able to "do" and "go" took them myriad places: the skate rink, trips with and to see loved ones, visits with other seniors, their beds and couches to convalesce, the boat [casino], family reunions, hanging with friends, non-caregiving support groups, God, restaurants, and doctors' offices. It allowed for rest, recovery, discovery, adventure, reflection, healing, socializing—or the luxury of doing nothing at all.

Building on age and stage theories, sociology professors Gunhild Hagestad and Linda Burton contend that "the entry into grandparent-hood has become a normal expectable part of middle age, a time when daily involvement in the demands of parenthood have ceased. When the transition does not come in the expected life context, it may disrupt resolution of developmental tasks and hamper involvement in other roles."[30] From a developmental psychology and life-course perspective, "the normal expectable life" is regarded as "a set of seasons, with characteristic preoccupations, changes, challenges, and rewards."[31] Developmental psychology emphasizes the series of developmental tasks with which a combination of developmental changes and societal context presents individuals, while the life-course perspective focuses on role transitions, which follow timetables and established sequences.[32] Grandmothers' accounts provide insight into their "normal expectable life" and restrictions on their ability to fulfill these developmental tasks and role transitions.

Lena Bell exemplified women thwarted in their desire to do what they "wanna do" and go where they "wanna go." Before parenting two of her twelve grandchildren, Lena Bell spent time visiting relatives, both locally and out of state: "It was surprising that the mother had caught me that day [calling for Lena Bell's intervention when the children were taken into state custody]. I'd come home to get some clothes to go back over to my cousin's. Because I didn't hardly ever stay at home. I wasn't here a lot." After becoming her grandchildren's sole and primary caregiver, Lena Bell and her cousin, both widows, no longer spent time visiting various churches to "hear the good singing and stuff" or caught the Pace bus to "go places. Go out to Evergreen Plaza, going shopping, going out to eat. You know, just doing something to keep our lives going." The activities that Lena Bell and her cousin engaged in to keep their "lives going" expressed their capacity for whimsy when unencumbered by carework, kin-scripts,[33] and family obligations. "Well," Lena Bell said, when asked what she would be doing if not raising her grandchildren, "I would just try to be relaxed, go when I wanna go, go on some trips and just do what I wanna do. . . . I don't think I'd be with the kids but the seniors. [*Laughs*] . . . They go on a lot of trips and stuff. Just enjoy doing that." Often, grandmothers' ability to tend to their personal lives boiled down to childcare. If another adult or an in-house teenager was willing to babysit, they could maintain varying degrees of engagement with the things and people that they had previously enjoyed. Eloise yearned for the life she had before assuming responsibility for her two granddaughters. "My friends, we don't go out and do stuff, 'cause I got to keep the kids . . . I used to go roller-skating all the time. I like to roller-skate" [*Laughter*]. Now, if she wanted to go anywhere, Eloise had to get a babysitter. Eloise's husband refused to watch his granddaughters, refuting her right to complain because of the monthly foster care payment "she" received. Like a lot of women, Eloise didn't want to make her only daughter the de facto babysitter; she wanted her to have a life, even if it meant giving up her own. "People just stopped calling . . . 'cause it's hard to get a babysitter. . . . My friends, sometimes they call and the kids be in the background and they go, 'Girl, let me talk to you later.' So, a lot of my friendships have changed. A lot has changed in my life. I can't really do anything."

Eloise's experience highlights the impact of grandparent caregiving on peer relationships. Burton has extensively studied the impact of the timing of family role transitions among Black grandmothers and found that when the younger generation pushed child-rearing responsibilities up the generational ladder to grandmothers who "did not expect, nor were they prepared for, the roles into which they had been propelled," these lineages were "thrown off track."[34] Not only were these grandmothers "thrown off track" within their family's timetables and the expected sequence and rhythm of their own lives, but they were also out of sync with their peers who were past the parenthood stage. Eloise's friends were done with crying babies and talkative young children in the background; they wanted to have uninterrupted adult conversation. Consequently, not only was Eloise spending less time with her friends, but she was also talking to them less, increasing her social isolation and negatively affecting her emotional well-being.

"I'm tired," Eloise confided. "I find myself getting angry. . . . Everybody's life has gone on. Mine's the only one that changed." Similarly, many grandmothers felt that their lives had "changed" or "stopped" after becoming primary caregivers, their lives dominated again by child-rearing demands that allowed little time for anything else. Some grandmothers felt their children and grandchildren did not appreciate the lives they had given up, as revealed by this snippet of an argument one woman had with the nineteen-year-old granddaughter she rescued from nonrelative foster care when she was eleven: "I had a life. I gave up my life for y'all and you think you're gonna stand in my face and talk shit to me?" She wasn't alone. These grandmothers expressed feeling "hurt" by and resentful of the disrespect and ingratitude of grandchildren oblivious to their sacrifices.

For the women in this study, the less their freedom to go when they wanna go and do what they wanna do, the greater the negative implications to their emotional and physical well-being. So, having their personal lives, not just their caregiving responsibilities, supported by their social support networks cannot be overstated.

Impaired Romantic Relationships

The majority of the women in this study, whether part of older couples, part of married couples, or women who were dating, all wanted more time to cultivate romantic relationships—and not just moments eked out of a day, but a span in their lives where they could drop anchor and build deeper connections with their partners. Still, others had to contend with tension or rejection in their romantic relationships with partners who would not make the sacrifices necessary for raising another generation.

Sixty-three-year-old Eliza and her husband, Tony, had cared for six of their grandchildren for a total of seven years as the children's mother struggled with substance addiction. They dreamed that their daughter, who had recently gotten clean, would eventually raise her own children. Married for forty-three years, what Eliza most wanted at this stage of her life was to focus on herself and her husband: "I've never been alone because I was still home when I got married. . . . I've never had a me. [*Chuckles*] . . . I don't even know what it's like to just be concerned about me." When asked if she thought that she might someday be able to have a "me," Eliza responded,

> I think it's gonna happen in a sense to where maybe I will never be alone but just my husband and I. I will say that. Not the collection of others. . . . I think just he and I being together or just some "us" time. We've not had that. Just a little peace to where we could do whatever we wanna do.

Sylvia also wanted more time for romance. When she assumed care of her newborn granddaughter, the never-married mother of four was counting down to her youngest child reaching adulthood so that she would be free to do what she wanted.

> I was looking forward to . . . finding me a husband, get married, and live my happy little life after all. And then me and my husband buy us a house. I was thinking about . . . as you get older . . . and you see how all the older people be. And the husband and wife, they have they car, they have they house, and, you know, they be all right. They have they little room for they grandkids whenever they *visit*! [Sylvia's emphasis]

At the time of the interview, Sylvia had been with her current partner for three years and wanted time to parlay the moments of privacy stolen from responsibilities for Zoe into a more serious relationship.

Grandmothers' romantic relationships were affected in myriad ways. For women like Eliza and Sylvia, caregiving responsibilities made it difficult to cultivate intimacy with their partners; still, in the majority of cases, women's partners, whether their grandchildren's biological grandfathers or not, supported and/or shared caregiving responsibilities. For others, caregiving created conflict and tension in their romantic relationships, as illustrated in Lottie's recap of a conversation with her husband about assuming care of her three grandchildren: "He [husband] said, 'You didn't even ask me about it.' I said, 'Well at that particular time we was just living together. . . . If you said 'no' then there would be no me and you.' So, he was like, 'Okay, baby, we'll do it for a little while but just so she [Lottie's daughter] can get herself together.'" She never did. So Lottie and her partner stayed together *and* shared financial responsibility for her grandchildren, despite ongoing resultant tension and conflict.

Bertha's partner, someone she described as "real good to me," left her after she became her grandchildren's surrogate parent. They were together for decades, after her husband died of cancer when they were in their thir-

ties, and during that time, he took her "all over the world." They even pur-
chased a home together. But when her daughter died prematurely from
cancer, leaving two granddaughters in Bertha's care, he left her.

> I had to put in time. They were young. And I would've had sympathy for
> anybody, young people lose their mama. That's hard. . . . Sometime he would
> want to go and I couldn't go. I couldn't leave those kids. My daughter was
> not his. It makes a difference. If they were his, he would have saw things
> differently.

Years later, he got sick and the younger woman he left Bertha for left
him. He had displayed romantic interest in Bertha again, being so nice
Bertha called it "pitiful." When probed about her inability to forgive him
and take him back, Bertha confessed: "It just was a big letdown. And it
hurt. It hurt me real bad and I'm not gonna lie to you. I was . . . upset." She
didn't want another relationship, despite getting "plenty offers." "I'm okay
now. I'm doin' fine. I don't even want a boyfriend. I don't wanna be let
down no more."

Some grandmothers reported that their caregiving responsibilities
made it difficult to find time to date. Cassandra shared, "I wasn't in a rush
to date because I wanted to make sure I gave him [grandson] the time
that he needed. So, I wasn't in a rush to date." Similarly, Bobbie Joe shared:

> As far as plans and going out, I had minimized that so I could try and devote
> total energy to her [granddaughter]. . . . And even she said "Mama, why
> don't you get you a boyfriend?" I said, "But if I did then that would be less
> time that you and I would be hanging out." She said, "Oh, never mind."

Precluded Retirement

Caregiving costs some grandmothers the ability to retire or to prepare to.
Older women often worked past retirement age or came out of retirement
to provide for their grandchildren, while middle-aged women were forced
to abandon maximizing (e.g., working more, improving their financial
status) their remaining time in the workforce before eventually leaving
it altogether. Grandmothers desiring retirement also wanted to downsize
housing, as raising grandchildren entailed maintaining housing that

contravened their stage in the life course—the fact of aging and being an empty-nester. Older women and couples shared their dreams for retiring and relinquishing their current housing for senior housing, while middle-aged women wanted to relocate preemptively in order to put down roots and phase out of working.

Virginia and Norman were raising their two great-grandchildren but desperately wanted to sell their home and move to a senior apartment.

LASHAWNDA: What do you all think you would be doing if you weren't raising grandchildren?

NORMAN: You know what I'll be doing?

VIRGINIA: Traveling or whatever he wanna be.

NORMAN: I'll be at a senior apartment.

LASHAWNDA: You all want to go to a senior's apartment?

VIRGINIA AND NORMAN (LOUD, EXCITED, AND IN UNISON):   Yes!

NORMAN: What would I need this [house] for, do you know what all work I have to do to maintain this? . . . I don't need all that, I need a senior apartment where I can look out the window.

VIRGINIA: I like those in River Oaks that we just passed the other day, the seniors go over to the Country Buffet for dinner, for lunch, and eat. And they stroll and they shop . . . and they relaxing, you see?

NORMAN: We worked hard and what we was looking forward to was retirement.

VIRGINIA: But there is no retirement.

NORMAN: I ain't never been retired. I don't even know what it is to be retired. I can't even take a vacation.

VIRGINIA: I should have kept working [meaning full-time; she still worked as a nurse through contract jobs]. At least I was getting paid for it. . . . My patients loved me. We can't even participate with the seniors at the church. They talking 'bout going on a boat trip or something like that. My friend call me yesterday, . . . she said, shall I get tickets for you and Norman? I say, Jean Anne, now the only way that I can do this would be . . . if I can get someone to keep him [grandchild].

Despite knowing that they would likely raise one of their great-grandsons to adulthood and would need to transfer child-rearing responsibilities for the other back to his mother, the eighty-something-year-olds dreamed. Meanwhile, Norman would have to settle for the pleasure of gambling the allowance Virginia gave him after paying bills, and she'd have to play some of her favorite jazz tunes after dusting off her old saxophone.

Nell had raised two of her grandchildren for thirteen years and a third grandchild for one year, and was mid-process in transferring custody of the youngest back to her mother. Having cared for people most of her life, Nell was ready for a life undefined by carework: "It started with me being the oldest of five ... responsible for my sisters and brothers.... I went from that to gettin' married and having kids of my own, and from that to grandchildren." Nell had retired after years in the formal care-work sector and wanted to move from her rented house into senior housing. When asked about her life plans, Nell responded:

> Well, I wanted to travel, which I did do some before Darrius and DeVaughn came to live with me. But just to be able to get up and go when I got ready, and do the things I wanna do.... When DeVaughn finish school, hopefully he'll go away to college. I'm gonna go to a senior building.

She looked forward to spending time with friends, engaging in community-facilitated extracurricular activities, traveling, and controlling her visitors through an electronic monitoring system—she was tickled by her dream of having a television-like screen to see who was buzzing her, shaking her head "no," and declining company.

Donna, fifty-four, provided a stark contrast to Virginia and Norman, who were raising great-grandchildren after also raising grandchildren, and to Nell. As a middle-aged woman, Donna had set her sights on retiring and tried to control how much caregiving dominated her life and undermined her desire to "live" it. Donna kept her thirteen- and fifteen-year-old grandsons from nonrelative foster care, but agreed to do so for only a year. "They on contract," she clarified to her daughter Theresa. She laughed: "I'm vibrant, I'm energetic. And I want my life and they, they got me on hold for a year." As she raised her own five children, she told them, "I'm not giving up my life unless somebody get sick, killed, or you get in jail." She meant it. "I got about twenty grandbabies and one great-grandbaby and one in the oven" and with the exception of Theresa, all of Donna's children were doing well and parenting their own children. When

DCFS took Theresa's children due to her substance addiction, Donna was living in Minnesota and refused to return to Chicago to care for her grandchildren. So, Theresa's friend Ramiro agreed to care for her two sons, and her two daughters were placed in nonrelative foster care.

The children had been in foster care for two years when, missing her mother, Donna returned to Chicago. Ramiro decided he could no longer handle the two boys. Donna became a licensed foster parent to her two grandsons, but not her three and five-year-old granddaughters. "I didn't want to, but I say, 'I'll give 'em a year.'" Donna used the foster care payments for her grandsons' needs, but also her daughter's, as she supported her efforts to resume parenting. "I don't want that [foster care payments], I want my life back. [*Laughs*] All money ain't good money. . . . It's good money for them, but baby I'd rather live by myself. . . . I been single with no kids in my house for nineteen years. Just imagine me taking care of some kids in my house. I'm going crazy." Donna told Theresa, "If you go back, or you regress, you backslide, or whatever, they going into the system and that's it." Donna's tough love approach worked. Theresa was within a couple of months of getting her own place and her four children back.

Donna was unapologetic about feeling entitled to her life. Drawn to the South because of the warm weather and her changing health, she planned to move to North Carolina, where another daughter lived. She had already secured a job as a director of a childcare center—the field she had been in for years.

> I'm getting older and everything—now my ankle done swole up for no reason. I say, "See, it's letting me know you're getting older, live your life. Take care of your business, take care of yourself. Live your life." So I'm getting ready to leave. . . . I'm going to Charlotte this summer.

Donna was in the minority in this study, though; although many grandmothers hungered to retire or to plan for retirement, they conceded that it was unlikely.

Virginia, Nell, and Donna provide only a few examples of the impact of caregiving on grandmothers' retirement plans; specifically the losses grandmothers suffer when unable to retire, including the ability to tend to their changing health, to turn inward, to socialize with peers, and for couples to spend time caring for each other. Knowing that retirement was unrealistic didn't stop their yearning for the life that retirement would bring—from wanting to look out the window of a senior apartment to leaving the frigid climate of the Midwest for warmer weather, to controlling their potential visitors through an electronic monitoring system.

Exacerbated Mental and Physical Health Issues

Being primarily, and in some cases solely, responsible for raising a second and third generation contributed to or exacerbated grandmothers' mental and physical health issues; specifically, by (1) playing a part in their social isolation, (2) increasing their financial and housing-related hardship, and (3) requiring that they function as parental surrogates even as they managed significant health challenges.

Grandmothers' conversations about the impact of grandparent caregiving on their emotional well-being were often tempered by comments like "not being the same" or "not being myself" after a traumatic event, or "I don't care" after prolonged exposure to stressors. Although many grandmothers cloaked their depression, grief, and anxiety in coded language, some talked explicitly about their emotional struggles. For example, Sylvia's depression resulted from a life upended by grandparent caregiving responsibilities; this led to difficulty working, social isolation, and a barrage of conflicting emotions toward her daughter, whose child she was raising. "To me it be feeling like I just be wanting to go ... just get away. Go outta here, just go and don't never come back." Sylvia knew that she couldn't follow her impulses. "One time I did that. I went to rent me a [hotel] room. . . . I think it was just for a couple of hours because I just needed it. . . . Um, I have had suicidal thoughts though, before. . . . But I be like, 'Ooh, this girl [granddaughter], who, where will she be then?'" She found herself saying "I don't even care" about her appearance. "But that's depression though, it do get me bad because I started cutting all my hair off. . . . I cut it off, cut it. . . . I pick it in the middle and I just cut, I just grab me some scissors and cut all my hair."

The majority of women in this study who divulged experiencing depression identified the financial struggles associated with being responsible for their grandchildren as the primary cause. Miriam, a mother of twelve, assumed care of her three grandchildren when their mother, Attallah, took her infant to the hospital because something "wasn't right" with him. Attallah went to multiple hospitals before getting a head-injury diagnosis. Attallah knew that the injury occurred in the father's care, having left the infant with him while she worked two jobs. Despite Miriam explaining to DCFS that her overworked daughter had done everything she could to discover what was wrong with her son and that she was a domestic-violence victim, they took Attallah's three children into state custody. Miriam became their foster parent. At the time, she was also raising two of her other eighteen grandchildren. Even working full-time and receiving foster care payments, Miriam couldn't make ends meet: "Money will kick you. There are times I have gone to bed depressed."

Another grandmother suffered great anguish from being tied to her current Section 8 apartment until the lease ended. After being gouged by her landlord, who hooked up the entire building's utilities to her meters, resulting in utility bills she couldn't pay, Kathleen called Section 8. "Ever since then, he became the landlord from hell." He called her "all kinds of names," lied to others in the building and to the Section 8 staff about her children and grandchildren, and "did a lot of things" in the six months she had lived there, including cutting off heat to her apartment. Kathleen had never dealt with these kinds of problems anywhere she had lived, including in the projects. "He just torturing us up here," she said. When Kathleen shared the magnitude of her stress with her doctor he prescribed her anti-depressants. Her anxiety about what the landlord might do to her family ran wild (she was caring for a grandchild with intellectual and developmental delays): "I don't sleep in this house. I sleep in the daytime; I don't sleep at night." She tried to wean herself off of the antidepressants because of the side effects: "It's hallucinations, dry mouth, dry tongue, vomiting, diarrhea. . . . Hair loss. Girl, it's whole lotta stuff."

Kathleen experienced depression not only because of her housing-related hardship, but also, like so many grandmothers, because of health issues that hindered her ability to care for her grandchild and to adequately care for herself. Her health issues confined her to the house. "I live with pain every day of my life. And I walk, I mean my feet hurt every day, all day. . . . And my knees and my feet they hurt every day, all day. They burn just like fire." Before her untreated plantar fasciitis and bad knees immobilized her, she said, "Summer come at my house, I'm gone, I'm out. . . . So, I be doing this and I be doing that." But now, "I feel like I'm ninety years old. . . . I'm too young . . . I see old people getting around better than me." While she once regularly checked on her granddaughter during the school day, she now significantly reduced that time.

> I go up to the school sometimes . . . [but] some days I can't walk. . . . So I can't, I don't get to her school or go to church no more. Because I will be like, "I'm gonna go on trips" and I can't get up on the school bus because they steps too high.

Miriam provided another example of how grandmothers were required to function as parental surrogates even as they managed significant health challenges. Miriam lived in chronic pain for a decade, raising her five grandchildren with undiagnosed and untreated spinal stenosis: "I was wetting in the bed. I would get out the bed and my leg give out and I'm falling on the floor and I'm dragging my body to the toilet. Sometimes I make it, sometimes I don't." She epitomized the impact of poor health on depression among grandmothers.

> I got down when I couldn't control the pain, . . . so bad I started crying in the doctor's office. "I'm gonna write you a prescription for some depression medicine." I said, "You take that pen, you take that pad, and you shove it. You're not gonna give me—I take twelve medicines now; you're not gonna give me any more medicine. I'm not gonna let you."

She was treated for problems with her legs, and when the treatment didn't work her doctor told her that her issues were psychosomatic. Another doctor prescribed pain medication that made her a "space cadet," unable to care for her grandchildren. "The one [son] told my husband, 'Mama can't function. She can't do this.' [*Laughs*] . . . They was scared to leave the babies." Fed up, Miriam said, "I had to go and find out how to get rid of the pain by myself." She went to an acupuncture clinic and experimented with natural pain remedies. She eventually received appropriate treatment at the University of Chicago, despite being "poor and . . . Black." She had only begun to get some relief in the last year but was told, "whatever was wrong with me ten years ago might've been curable. But now I'm beyond cure." So doctors helped her manage her pain with alternative therapies (e.g., physical therapy, aquatics).

Cassandra exemplified the mental and physical health effects of financial stress as the inability to provide for herself and her grandson exacerbated health-related vulnerabilities. When care of her newborn grandson KJ shifted to her, Cassandra was working as a case manager for a social service agency. She worked at the agency for several years before being offered another job that paid twice as much. Unfortunately, she was laid off after only a couple of months. Cassandra was already heavyset, but she gained seventy-five stress-related pounds. Despite completing two certification programs in computer and office-aide training, she experienced job discrimination because of her weight.

> I've had so many interviews. . . . They would look at my résumé and so that tells them that I was qualified for the position. So I would go in for the interview and then they'd look at my size. . . . I got so depressed until my health really started failing and I started getting arthritis in my knees. I've always had asthma, but it just started getting real worse. . . . Because I couldn't get a job, . . . it depresses me and it angers me because I know that I'm qualified.

Beleaguered by health-related depression, Cassandra had been unemployed for five years. Although her children contributed financially, being primarily responsible for making sure that her grandson's needs were met exacerbated Cassandra's mental and physical health issues.

> I went from buying just about anything I wanted for me and my children to not being able to buy anything. . . . I went about three years without having an income period and that was very stressful. And then they started giving me some cash assistance . . . for KJ. But then it was still very stressful because they were only giving me $107 a month . . . and I tried to make sure he had everything that he needed.

Joan, forty-nine, also experienced health-related depression. The mother of two and grandmother of six suffered a back injury while working for the post office. "I did get it treated, and the situation got worse, and since then I've had two back surgeries, bypass surgery in my leg." She also had a heart attack and open-heart surgery.

> Those are just the major surgeries. Because I'm diabetic, I got hypertension, congestive heart failure, peripheral artery disease, degenerative back dis-

ease. It's really depressing when I talk about my life. . . . I'm in stage IV kidney failure right now. My kidneys are not working and it's because of the diabetes, and the hypertension damages my kidneys. . . . It's stressful but just like anything else, you just deal with it and move on.

Joan struggled to raise her three grandchildren, even as she described her health as "extremely hard to deal with on a daily basis. I take so many pills, I don't even think they know what they all supposed to do. I take like 15 pills in the morning, 11 at night. I take insulin twice a day, so that is rough."

May had recently had a heart attack but left the hospital prematurely to get back to the granddaughter she was raising.

When I was in the hospital, I had all her clothes together but I was still worried about her. Because I mean I left the hospital before I was supposed to leave because I was too worried about her. Everybody kept telling me don't worry about her. I mean I had my girlfriends saying don't worry about it, I'll do her hair, I'll do this, don't worry about it. . . . I don't want her to think that I wasn't coming back, because that's what she kept thinking. I wasn't coming back. You know I didn't want her to worry.

Leaving the hospital early was not without consequence. According to May, she "wound up going again."

COPING WITH THE COST OF RAISING A GRANDCHILD

The grandmothers in this study coped with child-rearing costs by relying on their social support systems and religion. African Americans have a long history and tradition of creating and using informal social support networks to adjust to and cope effectively with adverse circumstances. Social support refers to emotional (e.g., friendship, empathy, compassion), instrumental (e.g., material aid, childcare, transportation), and informational (e.g., guidance, advice, referrals) assistance from others. In the case of informal support, assistance is provided by family, friends, or personal confidants. Carol Stack's *All Our Kin* illuminates the importance of insular, local, and extended family-based networks to mostly female-headed poor Black families. Stack found that locally based social networks revolving around extended family and friends allowed families living in "the Flats," a pseudonym for a poor Black neighborhood, to survive on a day-to-day basis through mutual support despite extreme poverty. Such studies suggest that Black women learn to be resourceful, devising creative strategies for coping with the historical and continuous racism and poverty that pervades their lives. More recent studies have continued to document the significant role played by informal support systems in the lives of poor families.[35]

Social support has been shown to improve grandparent caregivers' self-rated health and role satisfaction, to lessen surrogate parent role-strain and depression, and to increase tolerance of a grandchild's disruptive or irritating behavior.[36] Unfortunately, many studies have found that grandparent caregivers report inadequate social support,[37] which has been linked to their risk of depression and lowered self-esteem.[38] Social support is not only crucial to the physical and mental health of grandparent caregivers but also to their ability to cope with parenting demands.[39] In contrast to the grandmother caregivers in other studies, those in my study drew heavily on their social support networks for instrumental and emotional support.

Like Black grandmothers raising grandchildren in other studies, these women also relied heavily on religious coping, which includes the use of religious/spiritual beliefs, individual behaviors, social rituals, and religious/spiritual practices.[40] Previous research has found that religious participation among family caregivers and older adults facilitates stress management and provides a sense of purpose. Religious participation also helps caregivers develop a sense of peace.[41] Extensive research among older African American caregivers has shown that faith and its expressions help manage stress.[42] Finally, spirituality as a coping strategy has been associated with greater well-being among grandparent caregivers.[43]

Reliance on Social Support

Grandmothers relied on family members for cash, childcare, housing assistance, and emotional support. In fact, unlike grandmothers' experiences with parents, nearly every grandmother reported receiving emotional and instrumental support from their social support networks, including biological and fictive family, partners, and friends. Concerning emotional support, some grandmothers reported not having friends or only having one "good girlfriend," by choice or because of their life circumstances. However, all women shared that they had someone with whom to share their struggles, seek advice, and to turn to during difficult times.

Although nearly every grandmother identified family members and close friends as a monetary safety net, experiences with financial assistance varied. I observed three distinct styles of cash assistance: (1) installments (e.g., monthly, biweekly, weekly financial contributions), (2) specific needs (e.g., school shopping, holiday gifts, extracurricular activities), and (3) bailouts (e.g., helping with an inability to pay a bill, an unexpected expense).

Sylvia's family helped her by contributing installments. "Every month my sister give me like $100, $50 or whatever I might need." Although some installments were used as needed, others targeted something specific. Cassandra experienced both:

> Because outta the five years [of being unemployed] I've never went hungry. My bills were paid and it's all due to God. He did it through my children. Because my children turned around and started taking care of me. They paid my rent. They pay half my rent right now. . . . It's a blessing. Any time I fall short I can call any one of 'em. Every time he [the grandchild's father] gets paid, he come in and just put money in my hand. And not just him but all the rest of 'em. They just, it's just awesome. And I thank God.

In the case of forty-one-year-old Rose, her siblings tried to lighten her financial load by taking care of her grandchildren's wants while she worked to provide for their needs:

> My brother do a lot of shopping for them for me. Like for Christmas. I bought 'em something but I didn't have to because my brother went and spent $400 apiece on both of 'em. Yeah. He does that. I gotta give it to him. He'll call me and say, "Well I bought so-and-so, I'm gonna drop it off." Yeah, he helps out a lot. Between him and my sister, they help out a lot.

Grandmothers' adult children also pitched in to fill specific needs, including funding their nieces' and nephews' school fees and extracurricular activities and buying items they knew their mothers couldn't afford (e.g., clothing, diapers, sporting equipment, bikes). As Lena Bell explains:

Well, he [son] would always babysit and buy 'em Pampers, they [sons] did all kinds of stuff. . . . When he wasn't working, he'd take care of 'em. If they didn't do it, the girlfriends did it. Because they knew it was just something for me to deal with a baby. So they did it. The girlfriends and the wives, they always helped out. Whatever I needed they would, they was right there.

Lena Bell also spoke extensively of how vital her three sons' contributions were as she cared for her grandchildren with special needs. She was not alone. Most grandmothers knew that if they were in a financial crunch and unable to meet the economic demands of caregiving, they could call on their parents, adult children, grandchildren, and siblings.

As she shared how her church and mother helped her pay for the children's school expenses, Lavern provides an example of how bailouts worked:

My church give so much, my mama give some money. I got a waiver on some of the fees for Chastity [granddaughter]. The day of graduation they weren't gonna give them their diplomas because I owed $50, so my mother went in the office and paid 'em because she got very upset. Don't do that to kids, that don't make sense. And at the beginning they was telling me, "Oh it's okay." They was gonna work with me. And then got all the way up to that day and said they couldn't waive no more fees. So my mother paid and I later paid her back.

But it was partners who, when present, offered the strongest and most consistent monetary support. Almost all partners made major economic contributions to rent or other expenses such as utilities, food, transportation. Partners were either employed full-time or receiving retirement or disability payments. Although Rachel worked full-time in social service, her wife, who worked as a police officer, took care of their family's major expenses. "No utility expenses," Rachel said. "My mate takes care of all of that." And the same was true of rent. Judy and her husband lived on her disability income and his earnings from his job at Greyhound. She did not have the resources to take care of her family: "Because once I pay rent I got a few dollars left. He takes care of everything else. We just always broke. He gets his little seven-day bus pass and the toiletries and stuff for the house." Similarly, Eliza and her husband pooled resources to care for their six grandchildren. Initially, they relied on their shared work earnings, but as they aged and dealt with health issues, they depended on her pension and Social Security and his long-term disability. Next to God, Eliza credited her husband with her ability to provide for their family.

Grandmothers who were dating or single were generally worse off economically than their married counterparts because they could not pool resources. Instead, they received modest economic support from the men they dated, as Dorothy explained: "He tell me all the time, 'I want you to ask me if you need anything or whatever.'" However, these male partners were generally less economically stable than spouses because of other financial obligations, including caring for their own homes and children from previous relationships. Sylvia's partner of three years, "forty-some-year-old" Roy, was a school bus driver and father of three young children. Still, he did what he could to support her:

> I ask my friend Roy first and if he ain't got it, then I'll try to go to see my sister nem'. See, he got a car; he can take me to do anything I need to do. Or he can take me over there to get some money from my sister nem'. He'll come get me if I say I need to go grocery shopping or to go to get some WIC. And by him driving the busses here, he be coming through on the bus. Everybody be like, "You on that bus." I be like, "I'm going to do what I gotta do. Bus full of groceries."

Elsewhere in this book, I address grandmothers seeking childcare in order to stay in or enter the labor market; here I discuss the importance of childcare to grandmothers' maintaining their personal lives. Social support networks are critical to grandmothers' ability to maintain connections to the activities and people that, as Lena Bell comments above, help "to keep our lives going." Yet these activities or connections may be overlooked or dismissed as not urgent or essential by the women's partners, children, other family members, and friends. Subsequently, women are often left alone to devise strategies to afford them time and space for their personal lives. For instance, while Lena Bell's sons and their wives and girlfriends did provide vital support to the needs of Lena Bell and her grandchildren and to the *children*'s wants (e.g., extracurricular activities, leisure), it did not extend to *Lena Bell*'s wants and desires. Women in this study varied in their ability to attend to their personal lives. Women caring for non-school-aged children had the least flexibility, which was exacerbated for those without childcare. Although parents often turned to grandparents for childcare, grandmothers had fewer options and couldn't easily pass children on to anyone else. While childcare did not afford them complete freedom to orchestrate their days, it did provide some breathing room.

Susan relied on her social support network to "watch" the two grandchildren she'd raised for eleven years, while she participated in various social activities. Struggling with substance addiction and domestic violence, their mother was imprisoned for stabbing her partner. Susan "didn't go out too much" before assuming responsibility for the children, but to maintain even her low-key social life and "get out of the house," she relied on family for childcare. Family support enabled her to visit friends and ensured that she and the two grandchildren had rides (she doesn't drive) to family members' homes for weekends, holidays, and summers.

Martha was already raising an adopted great-granddaughter when she was forced to take responsibility for three more great-grandchildren who were being abused. She relied on a daughter who was living with her to maintain her personal life.

> I go to my sister's house once in a while. I'll sit and talk with her and drink a few beers and come back home. That's it. I got a girlfriend; I go to her house and I talk to her once in a while. I'm in the Order of the Eastern Star. . . . We have our meetings and . . . I interact with them. . . . But I'm not unhappy. I'm not unhappy at all.

Grandmothers without access to childcare held on to child-friendly activities, but foreswore others. For instance, when care of Cassandra's infant grandson shifted to her seven years ago, five of her six children were grown.

> Like I had a couple of friends that I used to go hang out and play cards with them a lot because I had no [young] children. So I didn't need no babysitters. All of a sudden, any time I needed to go somewhere I needed a babysitter. I would have to call one of the kids and say could you come and get him and take care of him. And . . . if they had something to do . . . I had to stay at home.

Like many grandmothers, Cassandra was able to participate in family gatherings and church, where she could take her grandson. Once her grandson started attending school, Cassandra's children began to take her out to prevent her being stuck in the house all day.

Religious Coping

To manage grief, depression, anxiety, and other burdensome emotional states, the grandmothers in this study often used religion, specifically, (1) prayer, (2) their intimate relationships with God, (3) surrender, and (4) reframing. Prayer reinforced the belief that God would get them through that difficult moment, just as in the past. As Faith, forty-eight, described it, "When things get rough, I just go somewhere and pray." Surrendering meant that grandmothers entrusted to a deity and/or their ancestors (especially deceased parents and grandparents) burdens they could not manage alone. They also used reframing, which Minkler and Roe define as "getting a new perspective on the problem, or on one's relationship to the problem."[44] Although these frequently articulated types of religious coping were used in response to emotional and physical health issues and caregiving-related stressors, due to space constraints, I focus on how they were employed to lessen the negative effects of financial stress on grandmothers' mental health.

Cassandra relied not only on her children and extended family but also on prayer to manage her financial hardships and depression: "I talk to my pastor, my sisters, and I pray." Similarly, although Joan's doctor had given her medication, it made her sleep all day, which Joan didn't consider treatment. So, choosing "not to take it because it just makes things worse to me," she too coped with financial and health-related stress, as well as depression, by talking to people and praying:

> Every day is a challenge. . . . But you just do it and get it over with and move on. I would have nearly lost my mind if I thought about the fact that I have to do this every day. . . . I would probably not be able to do it. . . . I kind of used to take myself away from the world. I would be satisfied in my bed by myself, turn my phone off, and I'm not going to answer my door. Then you realize your world becomes darker when you do that. So if I'm depressed and it's something I can talk about, I'll do that. I pray a lot.

And, as Dorothy elaborated:

I be depressed sometimes when things get a little bit unbearable. Like if I need extra money to do something and then if I don't have it, especially when it's something of importance. But then I try not to worry about it because I tell you, God is good and He always make a way. So I have that to stand on. I've faced eviction. . . . And I was able to stay. . . . God has seen me through. And during those depression times I just ask for strength from above and . . . and He helps me with that.

Grandmothers who used religious coping unanimously treated God as a companion in their struggle; many reported conversing with God much as they would with a confidante. After assuming responsibility for her granddaughter, Sylvia relied *more* on God to help her cope with her struggles and depression, as evidenced by the palpable urgency in her cries for help:

My . . . spirituality got stronger. Because at first you pray for the little things, but since her [granddaughter], I be praying even more now because help me, help me, help me. You know what I'm saying? You know, help me and help them. Now I just pray, pray, pray for my children, grandchildren, all my children.

Although spirituality helped Sylvia, as for so many women who relied on a deity, family, and friends, these coping resources couldn't allay her depression. She wanted to see a therapist but couldn't afford it. Similarly, when the economic hardships associated with providing care overwhelmed Barbara, she used her intimate relationship with God and her church family as sources of emotional support.

I got a great pastor. And his first lady. I go to them. . . . And talk to the man upstairs. I can't do no better than that. . . . I just talk to Him. Just like I'm talking to you. Just talk to Him. "Thank you. Thank you, Lord, I don't know how I'm doing it but I'm doing it!"

Grandmothers not only talked to God, but they gave their burdens to God too. Miriam coped with her money worries by relying not just on "everybody, everybody"—her social support system—but also surrender.

I learned a lesson . . . when you go to the Creator and ask for help, turn it loose and let him do it. I used to hold on to that and I'd come back with the same problems I went with. But when you turn loose, then it's gonna be okay. If you don't let it go, you'll be unhappy. . . . I ain't got time for no lingering on one problem. Turn it loose and keep going. I say, "God, you gotta take care of this." [*Laughs*] I say, "Allah is the greatest, not me."

Linked to surrender were both the act of giving "the glory to God"—or giving God credit for outcomes that seemed impossible without divine intervention—and the need to trust what God offered, even if a disadvantageous outcome. In either case, grandmothers viewed God as orchestrating both realities. Thus, when they were able to stretch their meager earnings, depend on their informal social support networks, and receive formal support, it was God's work not theirs. Faith captures this sentiment, "Baby how I take care of this is God. God do it. That's who do it—God. I can't do nothing without him," and Barbara provides a more explicit account of God as responsible for her ability to survive:

> God has been paying my bills because ain't nothing been turned off. Even though I've been getting that disconnection notice, ain't nothing been turned off. Nothing. . . . Jesus found me another job. . . . So it was like, "Thank you, thank you, Lord." And it's like I've just been more appreciative and more appreciative and more appreciative because I know I'm not doing this by myself! It got to be a higher power.

Similarly, they attributed any inability to make ends meet to God's deeming it unnecessary that they have whatever they were doing without. Some grandmothers even took it a step further by claiming that God must have something even better in store for them than what they had just lost.

As for using religious coping to reframe their burdens, grandmothers rationalized that if God allowed "it" (an adverse outcome) to happen, then God must know they could bear it, that they were strong enough to handle it. Kathleen expresses this use of religion to reframe the financial burden associated with caregiving:

> It was hard. [*Chuckles*] It was extremely hard. . . . It was just hard. That's all that I can say. Just pray a lot. I just prayed the grace of God to get me through it. Take me through it, carrying us through it. I just kept saying, "Lord, you ain't gone put too much on us than we can bear." I just made it that way. I don't like thinking back on it because it kinda tears me up. It was really hard. [*Cries*]

Similarly, Eliza provided an example of reframing as she accepted that she "wasn't gonna be in a place where I'm gonna be left to myself or just feeling overburdened."

> It [grandparent caregiving] changed my life but probably drew me closer to God to trust Him more and to know and realize that He's the one that arranges things in our lives. You know, a lot of times we think, "Oh woe is me, why is this happening to me?" And He lets things happen for a reason and a purpose.

THE REWARDS OF RAISING A GRANDCHILD

Research suggests that grandparents derive substantial rewards from raising their grandchildren.[45] Like grandparents in other studies, grandmothers reported that parenting another generation yielded a sense of purpose[46] and provided companionship and intimacy.[47] For some grandmothers, raising their grandchildren allowed them a second-chance to parent, including amending parenting mistakes with their own children and leveraging increased knowledge, time, and attention to grandchildren.[48] Finally, for some grandmothers, raising grandchildren of deceased parents allowed them to keep a part of the deceased with them.

Reparenting

Fifty-two-year-old Pamela exemplified both reparenting and purpose as rewards associated with raising her three grandchildren. Unable to get clean before her mother raised her son to adulthood, her grandchildren gave her the ability to parent in ways she wished she could have with her own child. Her grandchildren also gave Pamela what she and many grandmothers described as a sense of purpose. For some, this included a reason "to get up every morning," something to keep their mind off their poor health, and—as in Pamela's case—a reason to stay home and out of the streets. Pamela described getting her granddaughters as "fun." "Matter of fact," she said, "I think it slowed me down." Although she had given up "hangin' out, just goin' in and out, comin' home when I feel like it," she credited the necessity to do so with potentially saving her life because "there's so much happening out there [in the streets]."

Rose also experienced both reparenting and purpose as rewards associated with raising her two grandchildren. Rose married at sixteen and
divorced at thirty-one because of her husband's incarceration for murder.
Rose had Xavier, her first of three children, at seventeen. As a dominant
family figure and community othermother, Rose did what was necessary
to care for her family and others, including working in the underground
economy. She kept her illegal work activities secret, but her son still
learned the drug trade at her knee.

> I sold drugs, worked two jobs to raise my kids. That's why I say, the drug-
> dealing? My son basically got it from me. . . . I tried to hide it from them
> because I didn't want them to be out here trying to do it. But with boys it's
> hard. It's hard for a Black woman to raise a boy. But I did it to the best of my
> knowledge.

When her twenty-five-year-old son was murdered, he left two daughters, Sveva and LaKeithia, in Rose's care. After paying off her house, her
granddaughter LaKeithia gave her a wake-up call one day that she couldn't
ignore.

> When she was two years old, which I was still selling drugs when she was
> two years old, and I was trying to keep it from them because they so small.
> That's what really made me quit. Besides, my job pay enough I can take
> care of everything now. But the people would come to buy the drugs and she
> used to be like, "Granny, there's some hypes [drug addicts] out here in your
> yard."

Rose gave up working in the underground economy to parent her granddaughters in a way that she had been unable to parent her own children.
    Sveva and LaKeithia also provided Rose some consolation and a sense
of purpose. When I asked, "How's it been raising your granddaughters?"
she responded:

> A blessing. A blessing. I'm gonna put it to you like this: they daddy is gone.
> They all I got that's a part of him. So I would rather they be right here with
> me than to be way in Atlanta with their other grandmother and I never see
> them again. . . . Because I believe deep in my heart if something was to hap-
> pen to those children it would be the end of me. Seriously. It would be the
> end of me. Because that's what I hold on to every day—my babies running

around here. "Granny this, Granny." . . . They get on my nerves with it, but honey, please. I think I would go crazy if I couldn't hear it.

A Sense of Purpose

Grandparent caregiving yielded a sense of purpose when it was seen as a part of God's plan to ensure that their grandchildren received the care they deserved, allowed grandmothers to express love, and kept grandmothers active. Dorothy connected raising her grandson with God's will.

> If I had to do it all over again I would. . . . It just adds to [my life]. Joy. And every night when I turn over and look at him, I kiss him and I thank God for "Whatever reason you assigned me to be over this life, thank you."

Dorothy's sense of God's will resonated with findings from other studies that grandmothers derived a sense of purpose from being protectors, mentors, and helpers.[49]

Like other grandmothers imbued with a sense of purpose by loving their grandchildren, Miriam described loving and being loved by her grandchildren:

> That's unconditional love. They love you when you stink, they love you if you ain't brushed your teeth, they love you if you ain't took a bath. They don't care. It's the purest love in the world. Can't no man love you like that. [Laughs] And all you can do is give them love, and love begets love. Love generates love.

Similarly, Bobbie Joe described the pleasure she experienced from being a part of her granddaughter's happiness: "And just seeing her happy and laughing and having a good time with the children . . . that's a turn-on to me . . . to see her happy . . . and just to see kids happy in general."

Raising grandchildren gave some grandmothers a reason to get out of bed, especially those in poor health. As Joan's health worsened, she felt life's pleasures were "few and far between." Raising her grandchildren gave her something else to focus on.

> My grandbabies, they are my life. They're everything to me. . . . They keep me going, make me want to get up in the morning. Halfway through the day, I want to choke them, but at night when I lay them down, and kiss them on

the cheek and say goodnight, . . . [and] when I lay down and take that breath before I fall asleep, I just thank the Lord for making it through this day and, if you want me to, wake me up in the morning. But I love my grandkids. I love them to death.

Companionship and Intimacy

Children not only staved off loneliness but also offered intimacy, as Martha's care for her great-granddaughter exemplified.

> You know when you get sick and you can't do the things you used to do. . . . Your kids are grown and gone, you got nobody, and, in my case, husband walked out on me. . . . I'd be sitting up there in that big ole eight-room house by myself going crazy. I probably would've been going crazy if I hadn't . . . adopted Kennedy. She keeps me going.

Forty-nine-year-old Kathryn stepped in when her daughter Tichina's postpartum depression impeded her ability to care for her newborn child. Kathryn and her grandson grew attached to each other, so attached that when her daughter recovered, Kathryn wouldn't let him go. At the time of the interview, Tichina had married and was expecting another child.

> She [Tichina] said, "What's the chances of me getting Tyler back?" I said, "Slim to none. [*Laughter*] Because now I'm attached to him and he's attached to me." . . . Like I told her, "If you wanna, come and take him out. . . . You can . . . I'm not telling you you can't see him. It's just that he's your baby, but he's my baby, too . . . and he's been with me all his life. Ain't no need to change anything now." . . . I don't have custody of him. But I told her if she ever tried to take him, then we're going to court.

Although she could legally have taken action, Tichina left Tyler in her mother's care in the face of this family conflict. "We don't have to go through this, Ma," Tichina told her mother, "My son is where he wants to be, with you. I trust you."

Kathryn was, however, an anomaly in this study. An overwhelming majority of grandmothers expressed that parents should raise their children whenever possible, regardless of the blurred historical and actual lines between motherhood and grandmotherhood. Even grandmothers who had grown deeply attached to their grandchildren or who had raised them for years felt that children were best off in the care of capable parents. This was not only because these women respected parent-child ties, but also because they feared that the emotional development of children who were not raised by their parents could be undermined, specifically their sense of worth and self-esteem.

Kathryn was also breaking an unspoken rule about grandparent caregiving—namely, that when parents "got themselves together," no matter how long it took, and children wanted to return to their care, grandparents supported the transition. Kathryn's story is important because it shows that caring labor involves just that—caring—and that the intimacy associated with care could, and in Kathryn's case, did make it hard for some grandmothers to let go. While not all were able to, most grandmothers coped with this loss for the greater good of the family and of the grandchild. Finally, for some grandmothers, the loss of these relationships was exacerbated by their sense that while they had made great sacrifices to raise these children, often giving up jobs and adult relationships, and compromising their health and well-being, everyone else's life had continued uninterrupted. Their relationships with their grandchildren were evidence that their sacrifices weren't made in vain.

CONCLUSION

At the heart of Black grandmothers' conflicted personal lives was their desire for freedom, characterized by choice—the ability to do what they "wanna do"—and movement—the ability to go where they "wanna go." They counted down to their adolescent children's reaching adulthood and contemplated how much life might remain after raising a second and third generation. For the majority of grandmothers, the restricted freedom of becoming primary, and in some cases sole, caregivers, shrank their worlds. Grandmothers like Susan, Cassandra, and Martha were able to maintain some freedom by relying on their social support networks for childcare, while others, like Eloise and Lena Bell, resigned themselves to the curtailment of their lives. Some women, like Kathryn and Martha, were undeterred by their caregiving responsibilities, as what they "wanna do" included enjoying the companionship of their grandchildren. Others viewed caregiving as also having a chance to raise another generation "right" (Pamela and Rose) and appreciated that their grandchildren gave them a reason to "get up every morning" (Joan, Rose), someone to love on (Miriam, Bobbie Joe), and a reminder of God's will (Dorothy).

For the majority of grandmothers, freedom was a prerequisite to their ability to experience other wants, including time, energy, and resources, to devote to romantic relationships, retirement, and health. Sadly, the costs of raising a grandchild rang out in my interviews with the women in my study. Grandparent caregiving contributed to and exacerbated financial fragility and emotional and physical health issues, manifesting in grief, anxiety, sadness, depression, chronic and acute pain, and illness. While some stigmatized therapy, many felt they would benefit from talking to somebody—a threshold they likely arrived at because, although most relied heavily on social support networks and religious coping, they were combatting persistent, emotional overload.

Conclusion

In a tradition dating back to the late 1880s, canaries were used in coal mines to detect carbon monoxide and other toxic gases before they could hurt humans. By the time the practice ended in the mid-1980s, when electronic sensors replaced the birds, the term "canary in a coal mine" had become an idiom to describe someone or something that is an early warning of danger. Black grandmothers are canaries in the coal mine, amplifying how centuries of perilous social injustice imperil how families form and function. They are an early warning sign to policy makers and grandparents from other racial and ethnic backgrounds of the ways in which the social problems undermining the parent generation's ability to care for their own children become forms of coercion that compel grandparents into parental surrogacy. They are an early warning sign that the added layer of state intrusion into—rather than support for—the family lives of historically marginalized communities contributes to their chronic fear of losing their grandchildren to the system, itself an additional form of state coercion. They are a warning sign to policy makers and grandparents of the danger of not having nonpunitive options to deal with family crisis and conflict. They are a warning sign of the dangers of raising a second and third generation with inadequate resources and of the ways in which an increasingly complex and unequal kinship care system changes the nature and meaning of grandparenting. Finally, Black grandmothers are an early warning sign to other grandparents of what they sacrifice to raise their grandchildren.

With the exception of American Indian/Alaska Native (AI/AN) grandmothers, Black grandmothers have been where many other grandparents have only more recently begun to go. The sociodemographic trends in the post–civil rights era that contributed to the reliance on intensive grandmothering among White grandmothers arrived earlier and were more pronounced among African Americans. These trends continued Black women's long history of intensive grandmothering and reinforced their own and others' normative expectations about the grandmother role among African Americans as one defined by a sense of responsibility for their grandchildren's safety and well-being.

However, the 1980s marked a significant turning point in the prevalence and nature of grandparent caregiving among Black women. Between 1970 and 1990, the number of children living in grandparent-headed households nearly doubled, from 3.2 to 5.5 percent. In 1990, Black children were significantly more likely than other children not just to live with grandparents but to live with grandparents who were primarily responsible for them—13.5 percent, compared with 5.8 percent of Latino children and 3.6 percent of White children.[1] Asian children had a similar likelihood of living with grandparents but, unlike Black children, the majority of Asian children were not being raised by the grandparents they lived with. In fact, both parents were usually present. The prevalence of grandparent caregiving in AI/AN families was not systematically documented until the American Community Survey/Census 2000 Supplementary Survey, when it was found that grandparent caregiving among AI/AN was on par with the experiences of African Americans (9.5 percent of AI/AN grandparents lived with their grandchildren).[2]

The social and economic gains of the civil rights era came to a screeching halt as neoliberal economic and social policy impeded Black progress. In the 1970s, wages began to stagnate despite increased productivity by workers. The productivity-pay gap was exacerbated by deindustrialization, rising inequality, multiple recessions, and the passage of the 1996 welfare reform. While most Americans have been negatively affected by these economic trends (except the elite and upper class, where wealth is concentrated), racial disparities in income and wealth make Black, Indigenous, and other people of color (BIPOC) more susceptible than Whites to experiencing unemployment, impoverishment, and a fragile middle class. By shifting social welfare responsibility from the federal government to the private sector (privatization), neoliberalism changed the social safety net available to those who earn too little or nothing. Additionally, the social safety net became more punitive, linking public assistance and the criminal justice and child welfare systems in unprecedented ways through new digital infrastructure that targets, tracks, and punishes poor people. Neoliberalism both increased economic hardship, social problems, and privatization of services and subjected families relying on government assistance to more government control, surveillance, and punishment.

Black grandmothers are no strangers to weathering economic storms. In greater numbers than their White counterparts, they lived in multigenerational and skipped-generation households before, during, and after the Great Depression and also during periods when African Americans received few, if any, government benefits (e.g., Social Security, Aid to Families with Dependent Children). But after the 1970s, Black progress became further impeded by residential segregation, redlining, reverse redlining, the establishment and demolishment of vertical ghettos, increased poverty concentration, and racially targeted subprime lending. While other people of color have also been affected by these manifestations of systemic racism, African Americans have been especially hard hit. As Black grandmothers bolstered their families by helping to raise or by raising their grandchildren amid these systemic barriers rooted in structural racism, they began their journey as canaries in the coal mine demonstrating the impact of centuries of accreted social injustice on how families form and function. And too many began it alone.

Black grandmothers penetrated deeper into the coal mine as the HIV/AIDS epidemic disproportionately devastated Black communities. They went deeper in as the changing nature of poverty transformed some of the most vulnerable Black communities into open-air drug markets. They went deeper in as drug epidemics plagued Black communities, and a punitive government response to substance abuse and addiction, as well as low-level drug dealing, made African Americans the most overrepresented racial and ethnic group in the country's jails, prisons, juvenile detention centers, and foster care system. By the time American sentiment and policy makers called for more humane, compassionate, and less punitive solutions to the opioid epidemic, millions of African Americans had been traumatized and retraumatized by the carceral state and child welfare system. Millions of Black families had been shattered. As some policy makers acknowledged in hindsight, the disparate impact of punitive policies and practices, the damage to Black communities and families had been done. Black grandmothers' caregiving as an intervention to remedy centuries of systemic racism and state-sanctioned violence was an early warning of danger that was ignored by policy makers. Consequently, White families—for whom the public health approach was being touted as the best or most appropriate response to substance-use disorder caused by the opioid crisis—confronted a lack of public health infrastructure.

Since 2000, the share of Black children living with grandparents has shrunk, while the share of White and Latino children living with grandparents has increased, though White children are still least likely to live with and be raised by their grandparents. In 2017, the fastest-in-the-nation increase in number of children being cared for by grandparents was in South Dakota, concentrated in counties with large American Indian populations.[3] Shockingly, 58.7 percent of grandparents living on the Pine Ridge Indian Reservation are raising their grandchildren.[4] The impact of the Great Recession (2007–2009) and the abuse of opioids and other substances on the middle generation have contributed to these increases.[5] Fortunately, awareness about the insensitivity and stigma associated with calling substance-exposed infants "oxytots" and "meth babies" impeded these tropes from causing the mass hysteria of so-called crack babies. Unfortunately, despite a shift toward providing "in-home services" and leaving families intact,[6] the foster care system has absorbed many children affected by these social problems.

As of 2017, the number of children in foster care had increased 11.6 percent since 2012, when the number began to rise after more than ten years of decline. The percentage of children entering the foster care system in 2017 because of parental drug use was 36 percent, compared with 15 percent in 2000. The percentage of children under five entering foster care in 2017 was 9 percent more likely to be White and 14 percent more likely to be from the southern United States than in 2000.[7] Still, racial and ethnic disparities and disproportionalities in the child welfare system persist. According to 2018 data, Black children were 13.71 percent of the child population, yet 22.75 percent of children in foster care. AI/AN children accounted for not even 1 percent of the child population yet comprised 2.4 percent of children in foster care. Although the number of White and Latino children in the foster care system has increased, they continue to be underrepresented in the foster care system (White and Latino children are 50.50 and 25.41 percent of the child population and 43.7 and 20.84 percent of the foster care population, respectively), as are Asian children, who are 5.01 percent of the child population and 0.73 percent of the foster care population.[8]

The increase in the foster care population has resulted in an increase in states' reliance on kinship foster care and kinship diversion. Deep in the coal mine, Black (and AI/AN) grandmothers have been the canaries garnering firsthand experience of the changing nature of grandparent caregiving stemming from the transformation of kinship care, a historically informal system of care, into a formal part of the child welfare system. Offered as a service available to children receiving out-of-home care, kinship care has complicated women's relationships with their children and grandchildren, including the quasi-legal rights that frame their relationships, the rights and responsibilities associated with specific caregiving arrangements, and the financial support and services that caregivers are and should be provided by the state.

Black grandmothers have also been at the forefront of using legal guardianship in unanticipated ways to ensure their grandchildren's welfare, and to satisfy the increasing need for legal authority as they interact with child-rearing institutions and parents who refuse to relinquish custody of children for whom they are unable to adequately care. Black grandmothers' experiences of coerced mothering reveal that, despite their innovative practices and strategies, grandparent caregiving taxes their already fragile economic, social, mental, and physical well-being. Researchers are documenting similar consequences of grandparent caregiving among AI/AN, Latino, and White grandparents.[9]

White grandparents have been increasingly affected by grandparent caregiving and intensive grandparenting, and researchers, policy makers, and practitioners (e.g., nonprofit employees, social workers, caseworkers,

mental health and health care providers, attorneys, and so on) have broad-
ened their perspectives, spotlighting the marked shift in their experiences
of the role. And yet, bolstered by a common belief among Black (and other)
communities, policy makers, practitioners, and academia that Black
grandparents "have always" raised their grandchildren and that it is merely
a continuation of these cultural practices under different conditions, the
perspectives on Black grandparenthood have not been equally complicated. Despite significant evidence that Black grandparents have struggled
to provide care amid the changing circumstances affecting Black families
in the post–civil rights era. I assert that Black grandparents haven't
"always" experienced caregiving in its current iteration. Perpetuating this
idea erases their lived experiences, denying them and their families the
resources and services they so desperately need, and obfuscating an accu-
rate, comprehensive, and nuanced story. Below, I review insights based on
Black grandmothers' positionality as canaries in the coal mine, illuminating their experiences and providing critical information about grandparent caregiving in the twenty-first century.

MUCH MORE THAN THE LOSS OF GRANDMOTHERHOOD

Eliza told her daughter Mignon, whose six children she was raising
because of her substance addiction, "You're forcing me to be a mother to
your children and I should be their grandmamma. I should be able to love
them and send them home. But I gotta instruct. I gotta teach." As for Eliza,
surrogate parenting affected not only how grandmothers and their grandchildren experienced (or didn't experience) the grandmother role but also
other aspects of grandmothers' lives, including fulfilling their own developmental needs.

I've shown that untimely entry into the surrogate parenting role significantly affected the "normal expectable life" of grandmothers in this study.
I've explored women's expectations for the grandmother role and the family crises that "represent breaches of such expectations."[10] I have revealed
the concerns of grandmothers regarding what they were missing by being
thrust into a parenting relationship with their grandchildren. Here, I
examine the impact of surrogate parenting on two time-related aspects of

grandparenthood and on women's ability to resolve age-related developmental tasks and capacities.

A time-related aspect of African American grandparenthood disrupted by surrogate parenting involved intergenerational transmission. It is believed that grandparental wisdom, coupled with a less intensive role in a child's life than parenting, enables grandparents to pass down the stories, beliefs, values, and lessons of a family's and a racial/ethnic group's lineage. The West African scholar and writer Dr. Malidoma Somé explains that the relationship between grandparents and grandchildren is among the most prized in West Africa because children are coming from where elders are going. Therefore, it is critical that their paths cross so that they can exchange information about this side (the earthly or societal realm) and the other side (the spiritual realm). I have shown that, in the course of managing parents, the state, financial pressures, and the demands of care work, grandmothers are ill-positioned to share in this sacred exchange with their grandchildren. In some cases, grandmothers expressed being too busy and exhausted to share in this exchange with the grandchildren that they *weren't* raising, begging the question of what will become of these rich legacies, sacred information, and distinct bonds as such deprivation increases.

Another sacrificed dimension of grandparenthood was indulgence. Time spent mothering rather than grandmothering their grandchildren impeded women's ability "to just have fun and not having to not instruct, or to teach, or to correct, or readjust, or reaffirm." Eliza illustrated being deprived of this important part of grandparenthood.

> I can't be so free with you [grandchildren in her care] because you're here with me every day and there are certain things that you have to learn that you can't get away with. But if you were not . . . you could get away with the world. . . . So I miss that.

Women lamented the loss of not only grandmotherhood but also personhood. Developmental theorist Erik Erikson asserts that each life phase is characterized by a fundamental tension. The midlife years, when most people become grandparents, are marked by the developmental tension between generativity and stagnation. Generativity involves exercising one's freedom to actively channel one's energy into specific activities and roles. Individuals who have completed their child-rearing obligations return to previous, or develop new, opportunities to explore and express themselves. They are driven to engage in generativity—or risk stagnation.[11] The middle years are characterized by a shift from "time spent" to "time left."[12]

The developmental tension associated with older age is between either despair or ego integrity, the latter involving accepting one's life and impending death. Interestingly, this transition has ramifications for grandparents as well as grandchildren. Family members look to older relatives for comfort and the "assurance that in the long run, people turn out okay."[13] When the younger generation (parents) fall behind in their life course progress, grandparents and great-grandparents can be thrown off as well and may not experience the freedom that is central to achieving generativity and the time and space needed to accept impending death. Midlife grandmothers participating in this study complained that they were missing out on their long-anticipated freedom, while older grandmothers began to fear death rather than make peace with it because they worried about what would become of their grandchildren should they die. Eliza went from raising her five children, to caring for her terminally ill mother-in-law, to raising her six grandchildren. She had "never had a me." Eliza longed for some "us time" with her husband, without "the collection of others." Until then, she thanked God for giving her the relatively good health she needed to raise her grandchildren. "God still is giving me strength to go on and to endure and I'm thankful that I'm able to do it. I could be laid up sick. But I thank and praise Him that I'm able to do it."

I argue that the inability of increasing numbers of Black grandmothers to complete age-appropriate developmental tasks is detrimental to this subset of our society's elderly population. When faced with a seemingly endless cycle of relentless caregiving, they are unable to achieve generativity, ego integrity, or other important developmental milestones.

BEYOND CPS AND THE POLICE

I've shown the negative effects of the racial geography of the criminal and child welfare systems, making these punitive institutions those most available to resolving family conflict, including battles over legal authority of children.

The killing of George Floyd and 2020 Black Lives Matter protests sparked a never-before-seen reckoning about the role of police in public safety, centering on defunding (reinvesting in social services and community groups), abolishing, "and other measures aimed at shrinking the footprint of policing in American life."[14] Calls to defund or abolish the police came after decades of police reform have failed to improve the tense relationship between the police and many racially and economically isolated communities, and to eradicate racial disparities in police brutality. Although the George Floyd Justice in Policing Act of 2020 (H.R. 7120) emerged out of these debates, it is one more in a long line of public policies and laws that fail to link the structural factors (e.g., concentrated poverty and racial inequality) causing legal estrangement—African Americans' persistent distrust of the police—with concrete reforms to policing.

Law professor Monica Bell offers several important suggestions for the federal government to force local departments to change or eliminate structurally exclusive policies and to dismantle legal estrangement, including paying and reorganizing the police, using Fourth Amendment jurisprudence to correct racial discrimination in the conduct of police investigations, shrinking and refining the footprint of the police, and democratizing the police.[15]

Beyond impelling various levels of government to improve policing, investing in community efforts to keep their own neighborhoods safe is a very real, but underfunded and understudied solution. Sociologist Patrick Sharkey points out that "decades of criminological theory and growing evidence demonstrate that residents and local organizations can indeed 'police' their own neighborhoods and control violence—in a way that builds stronger communities."[16] He continues, "And yet we have never made the same commitment to these groups that we make to law enforcement—we ask residents of low-income neighborhoods to do the crucial work of building safe spaces on the cheap, often without any resources or compensation."[17] Similarly, Bell states: "there has never been a well-funded, institutionally embedded alternative with *primary control* over violence reduction." If we invest in community-based institutions the way we invest in the police and CPS, we can begin to transform a neighborhood.[18] For the purposes of this study, such neighborhood transformation would reduce not only the number of parents unable to raise their own children but also the number of families using the police and CPS to resolve family crises related to raising children.

Similar debates about reforming or abolishing the child welfare system exist. While some scholars argue that the child welfare system doesn't disproportionately harm Black and AI/AN children by oversurveilling, over-removing, and overpolicing them, ample research, including my own, suggests otherwise. As with policing and other aspects of the carceral state, racial inequality and poverty need to be systemically addressed to reduce family- and community-contact with the child welfare system. Put another way, families need resources and services to *prevent* maltreatment. An overwhelming body of research on the negative effects of poverty on children tells us that root-cause investments in child welfare would drastically reduce child maltreatment, including increasing the minimum wage and enacting aggressive job-creation policies that ensure a guaranteed income;[19] enacting public policies to address residential segregation and a lack of affordable housing; and "providing high-quality childcare, preschool education, and paid parental leaves for all families."[20]

Such investments would also change the focus of the child welfare system—to provide for children's well-being, not just remove them from their parents.[21] This forcible and involuntary separation of children from their parents has been normalized as an acceptable form of intervention but harms the most vulnerable families, which is reflected in the child welfare system's racial disparities and disproportionalities. Additionally, the child welfare system is adversarial, pitting social workers and parents against one another and requiring a judge to render a decision based on evidence and arguments from both parties.

By contrast, child protection mediation (CPM) programs have aimed for "a collaborative problem-solving process involving an impartial and neutral person who facilitates constructive negotiation and communication among parents, lawyers, child protection professionals, and possibly others, in an effort to reach a consensus regarding how to resolve issues of concern when children are alleged to be abused, neglected or abandoned."[22] Children's voices are also a part of this decision-making process. The benefits of CPM have been well-documented, including increased involvement of parents and extended families in case planning, effectively addressing problems a court hearing rarely deals with, such as communication issues among the mediation parties and an opportunity for parents to have their concerns heard by others, and expediting permanency, to name a few. However, CPM programs are underfunded, serving a minuscule number of children and families. A review of children involved in mediated cases in Cook County showed that over the course of a year, 165 cases involving 314 children were mediated (approximately 2.25 percent of children in state custody).[23] Finally, CPM is only triggered on contacting CPS, which is not preventative.

While CPM and other approaches (e.g., differential response, Family Group Decision-Making) aim to improve families' experiences of the child welfare system, some scholars and activists have argued that it is time to consider a new framework that reimagines the meaning of child welfare and the ways in which we as a society support child and family safety and well-being. This reimagining would be intentionally and inherently anti-racist. Proposed approaches range from shifting control of child welfare back to the communities they serve[24] to the upEND Movement, which calls for "the abolition of child welfare through the creation of new, anti-racist structures and practices to keep children safe and protected in their homes" by "collectively tackling the core stressors that make children vulnerable to unnecessary family separation."[25]

Making root-cause investments in families and communities would drastically reduce the need for the child welfare system in whatever iteration. So too would providing resources and services for families in crisis *outside of* the child welfare system. Black children have the highest estimated lifetime risk of maltreatment investigations of all children (53 percent compared to 37.4 percent of all US children). Black children are almost twice as likely to be investigated as White children.[26] Given the high prevalence of CPS investigations of Black children, there is a critical need for family-crisis support *before* these families are reported to CPS. Although federal spending on child welfare was 11.2 billion dollars in 2021, the majority of federal dollars supported state child protective and foster care services, with more limited funding for family preservation services, family support services, adoption promotion and support, services for transition-aged youth, and training for child welfare professionals.[27] Even less funding goes to prevention services, including home-visitation programs,[28] parenting programs,[29] and community-based family support initiatives.[30]

In addition to increasing the availability of resources and services outside of child protection agencies, families need an alternative to triggering CPS involvement when children are low risk for child maltreatment. When they were unable to keep their grandchildren safe on their own, the grandmothers in this study called CPS or the police. It was all they knew to do, in the absence of anyone else to call. But a recent report by the Annie E. Casey Foundation maintains that helplines, or "warmlines," provide "other pathways to support and strengthen families when a call to the child protection hotline is not warranted."[31] Not only are CPS hotlines not equipped or designed to effectively deal with the overwhelming number and variety of underlying conditions presented in the reports they receive, most calls fail to result in confirmed victims of maltreatment. It is also critical to change the culture of asking for help in communities with only lose-lose options at their disposal. The Casey Foundation has studied the recent implementation of hotlines in several states, including various models of care, potential partners, funding and cost-benefit analyses, marketing strategies, and using data to guide development of service infrastructure.[32]

MAKING A DIFFERENCE FOR GRANDFAMILIES

Existing research has shown that grandparent caregivers are more vulnerable than parents or other substitute caregivers, and that the children in their care suffer greater vulnerabilities than is typical among US children. I have shown that the differential treatment of grandfamilies based on caregiving arrangements reinforces the vulnerabilities experienced by grandparents and the children they care for. Our failure to provide adequate resources, services, information, and supports to two of society's most vulnerable populations—children and elders—when they form families not only illuminates what and who we value in American society but also demonstrates a lack of societal commitment to child well-being in general by failing to recognize the public good that grandparent (and other kin) caregivers provide. The child welfare system assumes responsibility for those children they take into custody and is increasingly using kinship diversion to reduce the number of children they are responsible for, effectively redirecting that responsibility into the laps of families.

When I talked to then director of the Illinois DCFS Erwin McEwen, he emphasized that when custody cases can be safely handled outside of the overburdened state system, relatives are advised to handle their cases in probate court. However, he acknowledged that some cases are going to the wrong court. He also asserted that while he understood the need for increased services and resources, children shouldn't "be brought into state care just because families are suffering from poverty." McEwen's comment represents the conundrum of child welfare in America—the state will assume responsibility for children in its custody but has little accountability for those outside it. This bears out in fact, as, compared to other Organisation for Economic Co-operation and Development (OECD) countries, the United States spends a nominal amount of its GDP on family-benefits spending, including financial support that is exclusively for families and children (0.625 percent of GDP in 2017, compared to 2.115, which was the average of all OECD countries). The only country that spent less was Turkey (0.479 percent of GDP).[33] This is an issue that transcends grandfamilies but affects them because their place in the five-tiered system of kinship care determines the degree of responsibility and accountability the state assumes for their welfare. That is, kinship foster care merits more resources and services, and kinship diversion, legal guardianship, and private kinship care receive fewer resources and services.

If the child welfare system operated with accountability for the millions of grandfamilies in America, it would invest in capacity building to help these families systematically connect with the resources available to them (e.g., Temporary Assistance for Needy Families [TANF] programs), especially families seeking legal guardianship, providing care in private kinship arrangements, and experiencing kinship diversion (tiers three, four, and five, respectively). In Illinois, the Extended Family Support Program (EFSP) is a pathway to do more of this work. So too are Kinship Navigator Programs (KNP), designed to help caregivers navigate the formal support system by increasing awareness of services and clarifying eligibility procedures.[34] Initially started as demonstration projects authorized by the Fostering Connections to Success and Increasing Adoptions Act of 2008, funding was not available to all states or localities. In 2012, only fourteen states had KNP. The Family First Prevention Services Act of 2018 made KNP more widespread, appropriating $20 million to KNP in 2018 and

2019. In 2018, forty-six states, eight tribes, and two territories applied for and received funds. Importantly, children are not required to meet Title IV-E income eligibility requirements and are not required to meet the definition of a candidate for foster care, so the program is available to all caregivers. There are currently approximately seventy programs.[35]

KNP represent a promising federal policy initiative to assist grandparent caregivers providing care outside the child welfare system. As safety net programs targeting the poor continue to be politically vulnerable, KNP might be able to connect vulnerable families to scant available resources, improving their take-up rates and outcomes for children, caregivers, and families in the process. The grandmothers in this study reveal that a lack of information about available resources and services is only one of a multitude of issues that impede access to formal support systems. KNP offer a mechanism for systematically assessing family dynamics, which often impede caregivers' public assistance receipt. By considering intra- and interfamilial dynamics, KNP could help caregivers pursue available resources, operating as a critical feedback loop between individuals *experiencing* and those *formulating* and *implementing* policies and programs, specifically by reporting structural lags between grandparent-headed households needs and the social welfare policy designed to meet those needs.

KNP also have the capacity to keep pace with rapidly changing state-driven program availability and eligibility criteria. States that impose caregiver income requirements when awarding child-only grants, which are in most states based on the child's income, vary. The Urban Institute Welfare Rules Databook shows that, as of 2019, Arizona and Nevada include income requirements in eligibility determination for child-only grants, and Texas includes it for caregivers who are legally responsible for the children in their care.[36] Similarly, while most states impose no time limits on child-only grants, some do. KNP could monitor such changes and also increase take-up rates by providing correct information about eligibility criteria. State agents routinely—but mistakenly—tell relative caregivers that legal guardianship is required to receive TANF assistance, subsidized housing, and childcare, preventing them from receiving available resources.

National cross-site evaluations indicate that caregivers receiving KNP assistance need less intervention and enjoy better access to public supports.[37] Evaluations also found that children in the care of relative caregivers receiving navigation services had higher rates of permanency through legal guardianship and reunification with parents. Moreover, relative caregivers receiving navigator services achieved identified safety goals for their families. Finally, KNP were found to improve the well-being of grandfamilies by ameliorating their unmet needs.[38] Based on these results and on findings from this study and others, programs should have strong information and referral, outreach, advocacy, and education/training components as well as strong family-intervention components to help caregivers and parents negotiate.

Additional policy changes that would make safety net programs more accessible to these highly vulnerable families include training and education through both HUD and the Fair Housing Initiatives Program, for front line workers who may be misinterpreting policies that affect these families.[39] Training and education could also extend to TANF and Child Care Assistance Programs. To prevent caregivers from being confused about eligibility criteria and their rights, correct information regarding the legal requirements necessary for grandparent-headed households to receive these public benefits should be disseminated to state agents, owners of privately operated subsidized housing, and relevant support groups.

Interventions that would support employment stability among grandparent-headed households include providing childcare subsidies for grandparent caregivers. Providing a period of subsidized childcare would enable them to maintain or obtain employment. Additionally, work requirements could be reduced to reflect aging and health issues; part-time work could be accepted to fulfill work-eligibility criteria.

Policy consistency would also be beneficial to grandfamilies. Policies and practices pertaining to grandparents' rights, responsibilities, and access to resources and services vary widely, based not only on their caregiving arrangements but also on where they live. Berrick and Hernandez suggest that policy consistency be achieved by creating similar guidelines relating to mandated care for all kin subject to any time of mandated care. "Similarly, the rules relating to mediated care should be relatively similar across all types of care within that care arrangement." Moreover, "the obligations of the state vis-à-vis caregivers in state-mediated care should be relatively similar, regardless of the type of mediated care, and these obligations should be somewhat greater than the obligations seen in state-independent care, but somewhat less onerous than what is found in state-mandated care."[40]

The compelling stories in this book illustrate, in heartbreaking detail, the need for major policy changes that prioritize supporting children and shoring up their caregivers, regardless of who they are. Policy and programmatic approaches must also directly address the unique needs of BIPOC families, including systemic barriers rooted in structural racism that disproportionately affect people of color, especially African Americans. Like being canaries in the coal mine, warning us of the dangers of transmitting social injustices from one generation to the next, Black grandmothers pay an incredibly high cost to ensure their grandchildren's safety and well-being. At the same time, women's stories illustrate, time and again, how their love and perseverance make it possible to do so.

The Five-Tiered System of
Kinship Care

In the late 1970s and 1980s, as more children entered foster care, states began
to consider kin a viable child-rearing option.[1] Several lawsuits, combined with
advocacy efforts, contributed to changes in statutory[2] and administrative[3] laws
that established relatives as the preferred placement when children were taken
into state custody.[4] This appendix provides a brief overview of the ways in which
these public policies transformed kinship care—a historically informal system of
care—into a formal part of the foster care system. Unfortunately, while these
public policies did provide relatives a way to prevent children in their family from
being placed, or remaining, in nonrelative foster care, they also produced inequities in resources and services *between* relative and nonrelative caregivers, and
among relative caregivers. Although there is considerable variability in the financial assistance available to kinship caregivers across the states, both the policies
and five-tiered system of kinship care discussed in this appendix affect the experiences of all grandparents parenting their grandchildren in skipped-generation
households—regardless of a grandparent's race and ethnicity, of where a grandparent lives, and of whether they experience caregiving as coercive or not.

Despite the similar challenges faced by kinship caregivers inside and outside of
the child welfare system, the support these caregivers receive is very different—
inequities I will demonstrate by means of a five-tiered system of kinship care I
have developed. As I have conceived it, the five-tiered system of kinship care is the
outcome of three aspects of child and social welfare system policies and
practices.

First, the child and social welfare systems influence the level of benefits and services available to children living with relatives. Grandmothers who parent grandchildren in the foster care system are generally eligible for greater benefits and services and receive more child welfare system oversight than children in other living arrangements, who may receive support through public assistance programs. In 2010, the average monthly foster care payment for a licensed caregiver was $511 for one child, while the average TANF (Temporary Aid for Needy Families) child-only payment was $249 (these payments are lower in the state of Illinois).[5]

Second, child welfare system policies and practices also determine the structure of the caregiving arrangements available to families with child welfare system involvement, including state agents (e.g., caseworkers) who make decisions about what approach to take when intervening on behalf of a child (e.g., kinship diversion versus kinship foster care). Moreover, while most relatives provide care in private kinship arrangements, they are increasingly seeking court appointment as the child's legal guardian to access resources and services, and to keep a parent from reassuming custody of the child. Thus, the state—primarily through probate codes and courts—shapes this legal designation and caregiving arrangement. I bring attention to the ways in which this unequal system of kinship care has produced a daunting range of challenges and quasi-legal rights for care-providing relatives. Most grandmothers found the kinship care system difficult to understand and to navigate, especially amid family crises.

Third, child welfare system policies and practices determine three aspects of caregivers' experiences of agency and control: their ability to make decisions on behalf of the children in their care, the level of privacy and autonomy they will experience, and the way they manage parents' involvement with their children.

I now will dive deeper into the five-tiered system of kinship care. I begin with the evolution of kinship care policy overall, then move on to tiers one and two— kinship foster care (both licensed and unlicensed), subsidized guardianship, kinship adoption, and voluntary placement agreements. Next, I break down tier three to discuss legal guardianship and private adoption, and tier four to discuss private kinship care. And I wrap up with a discussion of tier five, which focuses on state-mediated kinship diversion.

THE EVOLUTION OF KINSHIP CARE POLICY

In the 1970s, the Indian Child Welfare Act (ICWA) was being deliberated and then was passed, in response to the overrepresentation of American Indian/Alaska Native (AI/AN) children in the foster care system. This 1978 law stated that in American Indian placements, a child should be "within reasonable proximity to his or her home," and that states should aim to place the child with "a member of the

Indian child's extended family."[6] While ICWA was instrumental in curbing the overall number of AI/AN children taken into state custody and placed outside of their families and tribes, they are still overrepresented in the child welfare system.[7] That said, while ICWA set the stage for a model of family preservation for AI/AN children, it also paved the way for preservation legislation for non-Indian children.

In 1980, another family-centered policy was passed as a response to the increased overall number of children in foster care, the increased time they spent in foster care, and the reduced chances of their adoption or reunification with their families of origin. As part of its mission to establish a comprehensive federal scheme to reform the nation's foster care system, the Adoption Assistance and Child Welfare Act (AACWA, Public Law 96–272) required that state agencies make "reasonable efforts" to prevent the removal of children from their home, to reunify a child with parent(s), and to ensure that children are placed in the least detrimental and restrictive environment.[8] To further their goals, many states interpreted this act as a preference for the use of kin as foster care providers, and several states began to enact laws that explicitly preferred kin.[9] AACWA provided federal subsidies to encourage the adoption of children from the foster care system. It required states to provide adoption assistance to individuals who adopt children whose parents had low incomes (were eligible for Aid to Families with Dependent Children [AFDC]) and who were deemed to have special needs.[10] The *Miller v. Youakim* (1979) Supreme Court decision ruled that relatives were entitled to the same federal foster care benefits received by nonrelative foster parents if the placement is AFDC-eligible. Consequently, relative caregivers benefited from the passage of AACWA. In 1988, Illinois amended its Children and Family Services Act to require that relatives "be selected as the preferred caregiver" when "placement of children outside of the parental home is considered necessary by the child welfare system. The statute required that children be placed with close relatives after an immediate preliminary approval process."[11]

As states increasingly came to rely on relatives to care for children unable to remain in the care of parents the number of foster children living with relatives increased. Between 1986 and 1990, children in kinship foster care increased from 18 to 31 percent in twenty-five states. According to law professor Dorothy Roberts, "by 1997, there were at least as many relative caregivers as traditional foster parents in California, Illinois, and New York."[12] This increase was exacerbated by the passage of the Personal Responsibility and Work Opportunity Reconciliation Act of 1996 (P.L. 104-193), which eliminated AFDC's open-ended entitlement, placed a five-year time-limit on cash assistance, imposed work requirements for most recipients, and required unmarried teens to stay in school and live at home or in an adult-supervised setting. As discussed in the introduction, reductions in cash welfare benefits played a dominant role in explaining the growth in foster care caseloads from 1985 to 2000, and consequently the number of children being cared for in kinship foster care.[13]

The 1997 Adoption and Safe Families Act (ASFA, Public Law 105–89) continued this preference for "relatives first."[14] But it also swung "the pendulum of child welfare philosophy . . . decisively in the opposite direction."[15] In contrast to the focus on preventive and reunification programs associated with AACWA, ASFA shifted the orientation toward support for children being adopted into new families. ASFA mandated that children be removed from their homes when their safety and health was compromised and that permanency be accelerated. In order to "free" children for adoption, the new law established swifter timetables for terminating biological parents' rights.

The law mandates that states file a petition to terminate the rights of parents whose child has been in foster care for fifteen of the previous twenty-two months. The law allows states to exempt cases where a relative is caring for the child, where a compelling reason exists that termination would not be in the best interests of the child, or where the agency did not make reasonable efforts for reunification. By 1999, all fifty states had passed legislation that mirrored or was tougher than the federal law. Some states imposed even shorter deadlines and expanded the grounds for severing biological ties.[16]

But policy makers passed this law without providing comprehensive services to Black families, which were most affected by these policies. In fact, this law was passed one year after welfare reform, which also disproportionately harmed Black families. Black parents whose children were taken into state custody had less time and fewer resources to address deeply structural issues, or risk losing their children. Two components of the move toward adoption were financial incentive to states to get more children adopted within and outside of their families of origin and concurrent permanency planning.[17]

ASFA required relatives to meet the same licensure standards as those of nonrelative foster parents, though states could waive these requirements on an individual basis for issues not related to children's safety.[18] Research conducted by the Urban Institute found that this rule contributed to twenty-seven states changing their licensing policies. Eighteen of these implemented stricter licensing standards for relatives than they had previously.[19]

The Fostering Connections to Success and Increasing Adoptions Act of 2008 (FCA, Public Law 110-351) prioritized permanence for children in foster care by incentivizing adoption and providing adoption assistance rather than prioritizing efforts to keep children in the care of their parents.[20] It also provided new supports for relatives caring for children in state custody, including notice to relatives when children enter care; a state option for federal reimbursement under Title IV-E for subsidized guardianship payments; new allocations for states to develop kinship navigator programs, which provide information, referral, and follow-up services to grandparents and other relatives raising children to link them to critical benefits and services; and flexibility in foster care licensing for relatives (e.g., waiving nonsafety licensing standards on a case-by-case basis in order to eliminate barriers to placing children safely with relatives in licensed homes).[21] FCA required states to explain foster parent requirements to relatives and describe the services available to licensed providers.[22]

It wasn't until 2018 that a drastic turnabout in the approach of the child welfare system occurred—one that sought to eliminate unnecessary removal of children from parents. The Family First Prevention Services Act (FFPSA, Public Law 115-123) was passed to address the needs of children at-risk of or experiencing out-of-home care. FFPSA allowed states to "use federal funds available under parts B and E of title IV of the Social Security Act to provide enhanced support to children and families and prevent foster care placements through the provision of mental health and substance abuse prevention and treatment services, in-home parent skill-based programs, and kinship navigator services."[23] Although various factors fueled the passage of FFPSA, including years of advocacy by stakeholders for reforms to help keep children safely with their families and avoid the traumatic experience of entering foster care, the opioid epidemic's intensification of family separation was key among them.[24] Media coverage of White families affected by the opioid epidemic differed from media coverage of Black and Latino experiences of the opioid and crack-cocaine epidemics and contributed to a symbolic, and then a legal, distinction between the groups, including racially divergent criminal justice and child welfare system policies and practices.[25] A number of researchers have documented the fact that when the racial and ethnic composition of children in the welfare system changes, the child welfare system's approach to child welfare changes, including services to families and the system's punitive functions.[26]

Nevertheless, children from all racial and ethnic backgrounds benefit from this long-overdue historic reform to help children stay with their families safely and avoid the trauma of foster care. FFPSA supports kinship caregivers by: (1) providing "evidence-based" prevention services, including placing children with kinship caregivers, to avoid foster care; (2) requiring states to improve their standards and procedures for licensing foster parents with related children in their care; (3) allowing states to receive federal support to establish or maintain kinship navigator programs; and (4) promoting family engagement for children who live in group settings.[27]

Table 1 (at the end of the introduction) is a first step in clarifying how caregivers' initial caregiving arrangement may differ from the caregiving arrangement they occupied at the time of the interview. By doing so, it demonstrates the difficulty researchers have determining the size of the kinship care population because the changing nature of caregiving arrangements over the life of the caregiving experience makes it hard to grasp how many caregivers are providing care in specific caregiving arrangements at any one time.[28]

I developed the five-tiered system of kinship care shown in the introduction to this volume (table 2) as a framework for understanding the multiple caregiving arrangements available to grandparent-headed households, and which I base on prominent models in the field.[29] This framework categorizes distinctions between state-independent, state-mediated, and state-mandated care and exposes disparities among kinship caregivers—namely, caregiving arrangements in the upper tiers of the system are associated with more resources and services. Demonstrating the huge disparities that exist within kinship care—whereby some families are offered more resources, services, and oversight than others—is important to any understanding of the perpetuation of this type of inequality and the devaluation of caring labor by society at large and by lawmakers. It is also important in improving policy making pertaining to kinship care.[30] Finally, this system of kinship care reveals the complicated relationship between caregiving arrangements and the rights of parents, the state, and relative caregivers.

TIERS ONE AND TWO: KINSHIP FOSTER CARE, KINSHIP ADOPTION, AND SUBSIDIZED GUARDIANSHIP

The first tier consists of (1) licensed foster parents, (2) licensed subsidized guardians, (3) kinship adoptive parents, and (4) voluntary placement agreements. In the second tier are (1) unlicensed foster parents and (2) unlicensed subsidized guardians. I discuss tiers one and two together because they are both part of the foster care system and to demonstrate that when children are taken into state custody, relatives living in certain states can choose whether or not they would like to become licensed—since licensure has implications for the kinds of eligibility criteria relatives must fulfill, the amount of the subsidies they receive, and ongoing oversight by the child welfare system.

While grandmothers refer to all child welfare system involvement generically as "the system" or "DCFS [the Department of Children and Family Services]," or "the state," a great deal of nuance exists within the kinship care system. For instance, researchers and policy makers refer to the caregiving arrangements in these first two tiers as formal or public kinship care, or, in the work of social welfare professor Jill Duerr Berrick and law professor Julia Hernandez, as state-mandated care.[31] These categories may not be apparent to the women to whom they apply, but they matter because they determine how DCFS handles each case. For instance, state-mandated care arrangements occur when the state requires that children live in a relative's home due to a substantiated allegation of maltreatment in the birth parent's care. In Illinois, to be "substantiated," the investigator will have made this determination by conducting a "CERAP" (Child Endangerment Risk Assessment Protocol). However, DCFS policy currently provides that the mere fact of certain allegations automatically results in an "unsafe" CERAP determination and requires either a safety plan or that the child be taken into protective custody. If a DCFS investigator takes a child into protective custody, the investigator must start a court case within forty-eight hours.[32]

Even though the goals and structure of the child welfare system in the United States disproportionately affects BIPOC (Black, Indigenous, and people of color) families, these communities have had little say in the way the system operates. We see this lack of community (and often family) involvement in state-mandated kinship care decision-making, where the state (e.g., child welfare workers) initiates the caregiving arrangement, imposes mandated responsibilities on both caregivers and parents, and extends certain rights to the caregiver. Moreover, the juvenile court can make the determination about these caregiving arrangements without parental consent.[33] In order to regain custody of their children, parents are required to participate in a case plan. Case plans, developed for children in foster care, typically include descriptions of the problems that led to the family's involvement with the child welfare system and the services that will be provided to the parents to address those problems. The plans also include goals and objectives that the parent(s) must meet in order to ensure that they can provide a safe home for the child and time frames for achieving those goals. Parents are not provided services after children shift to subsidized guardianship or kinship adoption.[34]

Although children being cared for in the kinship foster care system comprise a small fraction of the children being cared for in kinship care overall, they are an increasing segment of the foster care system. Indeed, data from the National Survey of Children in Nonparental Care (NSCNC) suggest that in 2013, an estimated 196,000 children in kinship care were being cared for by foster parents.[35] Approximately 9 percent of all children in kinship care were being cared for by licensed or unlicensed foster parents, and 20 percent were in kinship adoption arrangements.[36] Finally, research has found that "reliable estimates of the number of children served by subsidized kinship guardianship are not presently available. Federal data indicate that over 17,000 children exited foster care to guardianship in 2013; however, these figures include both kin and nonkin guardianships."[37]

Licensed and Unlicensed Kinship Foster Care

In Illinois, prior to having a child placed in their care, relatives must satisfy conditions that many biological parents are unable to meet, including: (1) participate in a home inspection (e.g., home must be free from observable hazards, have operational utilities, provide sleeping arrangements suitable to the age and sex of the children, and so on); (2) provide basic necessities for themselves and their own children; (3) have no communicable disease "that could pose a threat to the health of the related children or an emotional or physical impairment that could affect the ability of the caregiver to provide routine daily care to the related children or to evacuate them safely in an emergency";[38] (4) display no evidence of current drug or alcohol abuse by any household member; (5) have the ability to contact the agency, if necessary, and to be contacted; (6) have immediate access to a telephone when the related child has medical or other special needs; and (7) cooperate with the supervising agency's educational and service plan for the child. To be licensed, relatives fulfill these requirements, plus: (1) undergo a social assessment (references); (2) provide proof of financial stability; (3) complete a health screening that includes verification that immunizations are up-to-date; and (4) complete twenty-seven hours of training focused on foster care and the needs of children who are in foster care.[39]

Both licensed and unlicensed kinship foster parents must complete a criminal background check of all household members and a child abuse and neglect registry check.[40] While states may use waivers and variances to more easily place children in kinship foster care arrangements, the criminal background and child abuse and neglect registry checks cannot be waived, according to 471(a)(20) of the Social Security Act and as amended by the Adam Walsh Act.[41] Waivers are case-by-case exemptions from compliance with a non-safety-related standard,[42] and allow the state flexibility in applying licensing standards without jeopardizing its Title IV-E eligibility.[43] A variance occurs when a state licenses a "kinship foster family home that meets a standard for licensure through an alternative method that is equivalent to that specified in the state's licensing standards."[44] For example, if the home inspection requires that windows have locks, a relative might be permitted to complete a home repair that satisfies this criterion. Federal guidance permits IV-E reimbursement for children living in homes licensed in this manner.[45]

In Illinois, kinship foster parents may be licensed or unlicensed, but licensing standards and processes for relatives differ in two key ways from those for nonrelatives—timing and urgency.[46] In contrast to nonrelatives, who generally seek licensure first and placement second, relatives pursue licensure because they want a specific child placed with them. Thus, an expedited time frame is necessary when licensing relatives.[47]

To make the process easier for kinship caregivers, who are overwhelmingly low-income, impoverished, and/or BIPOC, at least twenty-nine states, including Illinois and the District of Columbia, provide "provisional licensing." Provisional licenses allow a relative or a nonrelative to care for a child after certain basic safety checks have been completed on the home and household members. These licenses allow the adult to complete the licensing process during the time period of the provisional license. In the event the adult does not meet licensing requirements, the child is removed.[48] Illinois allows children to be placed with relatives without formal licensing but relatives must later apply for licensure in order to receive foster care maintenance payments and other services and supports.[49]

Both licensed and unlicensed foster parents have custodial rights only, which give grandmothers physical custody but provide the parent or the state the right to make legal decisions on behalf of the child. When relatives become licensed as a foster family home, they are paid the full foster care board rate. In Illinois, unlicensed relatives caring for children in state custody are supported at the state standard of need—higher than TANF child-only payments but lower than foster care payments.[50] The standard of need rate varies depending on the number of related children relatives care for and the county where they live.[51] The only financial assistance available to unlicensed relatives in most states is TANF child-only grants or Supplemental Security Income (SSI) if eligible. While foster care payments increase equally for each child, TANF only increases incrementally for each additional child. Consequently, the huge gap between levels of financial support for children in licensed versus unlicensed foster care (and children being cared for outside of the child welfare system) becomes even larger as caregivers raise additional children.[52] At the time that I collected data for this book, unlicensed kinship foster parents received approximately $270 to $300 a month for one child and those with a license received approximately $380 to $450. Grandmothers caring for a child with special needs received more.

In Illinois, licensed kinship foster parents are required to meet with caseworkers at least every thirty days, or more often on an as-needed basis, in order to provide consultation and support. If the caregiver is an unlicensed relative, they are required to have in-home, face-to-face visits and consultations at least twice per month.[53]

Nationally, it is estimated that more than half of kinship foster parents serve as unlicensed caregivers.[54] In 2009, an average of 16 percent of all children in foster care—living in thirty-two states—were placed with licensed relatives and 14 percent with unlicensed relatives.[55] For the nine states that calculated the percentage of children in unlicensed versus licensed kinship foster care, an average of 38 percent of children were placed with licensed relatives and 62 percent with unlicensed relatives.[56] In 2012, there was roughly an equal number of licensed and unlicensed kinship foster homes in Illinois. But unlicensed relative homes in the state grew 59 percent by mid-2018, while licensed relative homes declined 7 percent.[57]

Children who are the most marginalized are the most affected by the child welfare system, yet when their caregivers are family members, the caregivers experience payment and service disparities, which exacerbates the struggles of those families. Although the payment inequities between kinship foster parents and nonrelative foster parents have diminished considerably in recent years,[58] available data suggest that service and support opportunities for kinship caregivers remain inequitable.[59] Previous research found that kinship foster parents were offered and received fewer services (e.g., respite, support groups, training, and specialized training [caring for a drug-exposed infant]) from child welfare agencies, had less contact with child welfare workers, and received less money to care for children than nonrelatives.[60] Children in nonrelative foster care were also more likely to receive mental health services than those cared for by a relatives.

Subsidized Guardianship

In Illinois, if a parent does not fulfil the reunification program (also referred to as the case plan, or permanency plan),[61] kinship caregivers can become subsidized guardians or kinship adoptive parents instead of surrendering their custodial rights. Subsidized guardianships, also referred to as kinship guardianships, have several advantages. Subsidized guardianships provide financial assistance to caregivers who assume legal guardianship of a child for whom they have cared as a licensed or unlicensed foster parent and for whom they have committed to care on a permanent basis.[62] In contrast, private legal guardianship (tier three) has no guarantee of formal support, though resources may be acquired from public assistance programs. Subsidized guardianships are also a viable permanency option for relatives who are hesitant or unwilling to terminate parental rights by adopting the children in their care. As subsidized guardians, caregivers gain legal rights for the children in their care, which allows them to make decisions on their behalf, but birth parents can petition the juvenile court to reverse a subsidized guardianship placement.

While subsidized guardianships were already being used by thirty-eight states and the District of Columbia, the Fostering Connections Act (FCA) of 2008 offered states the option to use funds through Title IV-E to finance a guardianship assistance program.[63] Illinois is one of twenty-six states that allow children who are not Title IV-E eligible to exit foster care into subsidized permanent homes with relatives.[64] As of March 2020, forty states, the District of Columbia, and fourteen tribes have used subsidized guardianships to achieve permanency for children in state custody.[65] However, in order to become a subsidized guardian, the child welfare worker must recommend this caregiving arrangement and the court orders it following a six-month minimum stay in foster care. Grandmothers are screened and/or assessed prior to shifting to this new caregiving arrangement just as when they became foster parents, so they adhere to the same standards as traditional foster care.

Typically, guardianship subsidies are similar in amount to foster care subsidies, and grandmothers who are foster parents can become subsidized guardians in two ways. The first is through the Kinship Guardianship Assistance Program (KinGAP), which was established with the passage of FCA. The second is the option for unlicensed kinship foster parents. In Illinois, they can also become subsidized guardians through the state funded option,[66] though unlicensed subsidized guardians in this state receive lower payments via the state-funded option than those who are licensed subsidized guardians and receive payments through Title IV-E KinGAP. As a point of reference, subsidized guardians participating in this study received from $380 to $480 a month for one child if they were licensed and approximately $300 to $380 a month for one child if they were not.

A last word on subsidized guardians: unfortunately, they do not typically receive the supports they received as foster parents, though some jurisdictions offer post-guardianship supports. Illinois does provide post-guardianship services.[67] Ongoing review of placement/caregiving appropriateness requires that the caregiver complete an annual form to attest to the child's continued residence in the home.[68]

Kinship Adoption

Many relatives in this and other studies report reluctance to adopt the children in their care. However, kinship adoption has increased, from 20 percent of children adopted from foster care in 2000 to 30 percent in 2010.[69] In fact, the majority of adoptions of children by relatives occurs following placement in out-of-home care through the child welfare system—so, through kinship adoption rather than through private adoption.[70] Some states require state agencies to give relatives preference when making adoption decisions.[71]

Kinship adoption gives grandmothers parental rights to their grandchildren, a caregiving arrangement that, unlike foster care and subsidized guardianship, is permanent. However, like other caregiving arrangements discussed so far, in general, relatives undergo some screening and/or assessment prior to entering this caregiving arrangement. Here, too, relatives receive an adoption assistance payment equivalent to foster care. Although they don't typically receive postadoption services, some jurisdictions do offer some services. An advantage of kinship adoption is that relatives no longer have to undergo ongoing review of placement/caregiving appropriateness.

As for the relative financial benefits of this caregiving arrangement, in Illinois, if a relative is a licensed foster parent, they may still be eligible to receive a monthly subsidy payment once they adopt the children in their care. Whether they receive the adoption assistance payment is based on the needs of the child and the family circumstances. In Illinois, relatives *do* receive post-adoption resources and services for the children in their care, including a Medicaid card; payment or reimbursement for any physical, emotional, and mental health needs that are not covered through insurance or public resources; employment-related day care payments for children under the age of three; therapeutic day care; and respite care for children with special needs.[72] Grandmothers participating in this study received from $389 to $445 a month for one adopted child in their care, including a child with special needs.

Voluntary Placement Agreements

In general, voluntary placement agreements (VPAs) "can be voluntarily agreed upon by parents or guardians without formal removal of children from their homes and placement into kinship care; or when children are 'constructively' removed from their parent's or guardian's home while they are being looked after by another caregiver on a temporary basis."[73] Temporary care is restricted to six months and the caregiver must be licensed, approved, or certified as a foster parent in order to receive federal Title IV-E matching funds, including foster care, kinship guardianship, and adoption subsidies. Thus, VPAs provide an option for states to support children without a court-ordered removal and to support the child's caregiver (relative and nonrelative) by providing a pathway to the formal foster care system.[74]

Illinois defines VPAs as a time-limited written request and consent from a parent for placement of the child out of the home.[75] The Illinois DCFS agrees to provide child welfare services, which include placement.[76] VPAs are offered when the Illinois DCFS "has determined that family preservation services are not appropriate because such services are not in the child's best interests or would not protect the child from imminent risk of harm."[77] A VPA may be entered into for a maximum of sixty days. A VPA also requires prior written approval of the administrator in charge of the department region or designee. It may be renewed for an additional sixty days only with the prior nondelegable[78] written approval of the administrator in charge of the department region.

In general, relatives undergo the same screening/assessment standards as traditional foster care. In Illinois, relatives are vetted to determine their appropriateness for care and are eligible for foster care funds if they are licensed. The relative caregiver must pass a basic safety check to care for children without a foster care license. Payments to relatives for the care of state wards are paid by DCFS and the Illinois Department of Public Aid at the level of the AFDC standard of need. They can become licensed to receive more resources and services.

VPAs differ from kinship foster care in that they circumvent a court review when child welfare agencies help arrange placing a child with a relative.[79] VPAs also differ from safety plans. Under VPAs, the DCFS takes temporary custody of the child, which is not the case with a safety plan. Finally, while some safety plans allow the child to remain home, VPAs place the child out of the home.

TIER THREE: LEGAL GUARDIANSHIP AND PRIVATE ADOPTION

The third tier of the five-tiered system of kinship care as I am defining it consists of legal guardianship and private adoption, which are both categorized as state-mediated care. State-mediated care falls between state-mandated and independent care. These caregiving arrangements are mediated by government agents (e.g., probate or civil court, the child welfare system). State-mediated arrangements may be initiated by a relative (legal guardianship, private adoption) or by "a child welfare worker or other professional, acting on behalf of the state" who facilitates "the relocation of a child from a parent's to a relative's home (e.g., kinship diversion)."[80]

The resources available to legal guardians and adoptive parents are less than those provided to grandparents raising grandchildren in tiers one and two. However, their ability to more easily navigate bureaucracies and to restrict parents from keeping resources intended for children means that they often receive more resources and services than those in private arrangements (tier four). What follows is a more in-depth discussion of each of these two categories of caregiving arrangements.

Legal Guardianship

Legal guardianship, which has been referred to as "private child protection" or private guardianship, has seen an increasing number of relatives seeking legal authority for the children who come into their care.[81] By the turn of the twenty-first century, legal guardianship was transformed from its original function of managing the property of legal orphans to being used as a form of private child protection.[82] Legal guardianship falls under tier three not only because of the direct access it permits relative caregivers to resources and services for the children in their care, but also because of the power it gives them to thwart parents' receipt of these resources and parents' ability to keep children in their care.

Relatives seek legal guardianship for two primary reasons: first, to access resources and services that are difficult or impossible to ascertain without legal guardianship, and second, "to obtain some measure of enforceable rights of their own, given that parents otherwise would have an unlimited authority to end the caregiving arrangement."[83] Legal guardianship grants relatives' enforceable legal rights—not as a full "parent," but in a legally defined role.[84] Additionally, legal guardians are assigned specific duties by the courts, which may include care and protection and medical and educational rights. Finally—unlike with adoption, but like subsidized guardianship—parental rights are not terminated and parents' full custodial rights may be reinstated under petition.

Although most public benefits can be obtained without legal guardianship, legal guardianship does make it easier for relative caregivers to access these resources—both in the face of street-level bureaucrats, who too often provide misinformation about eligibility criteria, especially their insistence that legal guardianship is required to access TANF benefits, and in the face of parents who will not relinquish the child's benefits (dependent children can only receive benefits via one caregiver). Compared to other caregiving arrangements, little attention has been given to caregivers who serve as legal guardians.[85]

In Illinois, relatives can obtain TANF and related resources and services (e.g., Medicaid, SNAP, WIC, childcare assistance) for the children in their care without legal guardianship. However, these programs have different eligibility rules and access to these resources is not universal. Several states do not allow nonparent caregivers to receive TANF family grants, and TANF allowance amounts vary by state.[86] When data for this study was collected, TANF child-only payments in Illinois were a paltry $107 per month for one child, $211 for two children, and $261 for three children. Family grants were $292 per month for a family of two, $396 for three, and $435 for four.

Other resources are similarly sparse and conditional. If one or both of a child's parents are disabled, retired, or deceased, a child may be eligible for Social Security benefits. Disabled children whose parents have little income or resources may be eligible for SSI benefits.[87] Legal guardianship is not needed to obtain these resources; however, the child's birth certificate, and the parent's and child's social security numbers are needed to procure Social Security benefits,[88] and a social security card or number, proof of age (a birth certificate), and medical sources are needed to apply for SSI.[89] Thus, grandparents who are legal guardians have a much easier time procuring necessary documentation and available resources than those in private kinship arrangements (tier four).

In Illinois, obtaining a child's birth certificate requires that relatives demonstrate they are "legal representatives" of the child.[90] Similarly, obtaining a social security card for someone under age eighteen requires that the child be old enough to sign the application for her/himself or that it be signed by a parent or legal guardian.[91] If grandparents want grandchildren to receive their Social Security benefits grandparents must demonstrate that the grandchild is a dependent, that both parents are disabled or deceased *or* that the child has been legally adopted. So, without parental assistance, legal guardianship is needed to obtain the documents necessary to apply for Social Security and SSI benefits, and in some cases, adoption is needed to include grandchildren in Social Security benefits.

Social Security and SSI benefits are not the only resources difficult to obtain without legal guardianship. Legal guardianship is helpful for facilitating a grandparent's receipt of Family and Medical Leave Act (FMLA) leave to care for a grandchild. FMLA may be available to relatives who can demonstrate to their employer their *in loco parentis*—acting as a child's parent, even though she may not be biologically or legally the parent—or legal guardianship status. Grandparents raising grandchildren may be disinclined to request FMLA because care for a grandchild is not specifically listed in the law, and a declined FMLA request therefore means that the individual grandparent has to overcome limitations in the law. That said, *Gienapp v. Harbor Crest* (2014) provides a possible loophole for grandparent caregivers living in Illinois, Indiana, and Wisconsin (states under the jurisdiction of the Seventh Circuit)—namely, the Seventh Circuit case opened the door for grandparents to receive FMLA leave to take care of grandchildren, as long as the grandparent can show that the care for the grandchildren is also providing "care" to the grandparent's own child (the grandchildren's parent).[92]

Private Adoption

Private adoption occurs when grandparents adopt grandchildren who are not in state custody. I categorize it in the third tier because it gives grandparents the legal rights needed to navigate child-rearing institutions and access certain resources (e.g., Social Security benefits, federal adoption tax credit) and services for their grandchild that they cannot access as legal guardians: specifically, an adopted grandchild may have access to certain benefits they might not otherwise have access to, including better insurance benefits (coverage under private plans versus CHIP)[93] and inheriting from adoptive parents without the inheritance being stipulated in a will.[94] Unlike those providing care via kinship adoption, grandparents electing private adoption receive no adoption subsidy, which means they assume complete financial responsibility for the child in their care. I have therefore included private adoption in the third tier because caregivers are responsible for paying the legal fees associated with adoption, whereas in contrast, the legal fees associated with kinship adoption are paid for by the state. To further contextualize, private adoption also terminates parental rights and transfers those rights to relative caregivers.[95]

TIER FOUR: PRIVATE KINSHIP CARE

The majority of caregiving happens at the fourth level of my kinship care system, in private kinship arrangements (state-independent care). These are caregiving arrangements without the involvement of the child welfare system. It is estimated that nearly 40 to 60 percent of all children in kinship care are being cared for by relatives (including grandparents) in private kinship arrangements. Estimates in the lower range are associated with studies providing a more nuanced breakdown of caregiving arrangements than those that simply categorize care types as formal versus informal.[96] Caregivers in private kinship care have no legal relationship with the grandchildren in their care, which is why I have assigned this type of caregiving arrangement to tier four. Without legal rights, these caregivers are contending with the greatest barriers to resources and services for their grandchildren and to preventing their grandchildren from being removed from their care.

The tenuous nature of private kinship care can make it difficult for grandparents to care for their grandchildren. But this wasn't always the case. Twenty-first-century consent policies and practices, and erroneous information provided by street-level bureaucrats, make it increasingly difficult for contemporary grandmothers to navigate child-rearing institutions. Additionally, caregivers in private kinship care are only eligible to receive allowances from public assistance programs. Social Security benefits (through a deceased parent) and SSI benefits can be obtained if they can access children's birth certificates and children's and parent's social security numbers. Finally, without a legally defined role, they are at the whims of parents who may change their minds about the informal arrangement.

TIER FIVE: KINSHIP DIVERSION

Tier five consists of caregiving arrangements involving diversion, meaning that children are diverted to kinship care as an alternative to being brought into state custody (formal foster care). While "kinship diversion" is used interchangeably with a variety of terms—including safety planning, voluntary kinship care, parental placement, redirection, informal kin care, and prevention services, among others[97]—it describes situations in which children are brought to the attention of child welfare agents because of alleged abuse or neglect. If an investigation determines that a child cannot remain safely with parents, the child welfare agent facilitates that child's care by a relative instead of bringing the child into state custody. Diversion also occurs as a result of "a negotiated agreement with family members following a family team meeting."[98] Either way, the child welfare system has a role in arranging, sanctioning, or supporting these caregiving arrangements without seeking court action to take custody of the child. Researchers, policy makers, and child welfare practitioners often use the term "safety plans" to describe state-mediated kinship.[99] Further on, I discuss the controversial nature of these caregiving arrangements, in part, because of their coerciveness and lack of resources and services for caregivers.

States are economically motivated to promote kinship diversions because, in most kinship diversions, the relative caregiver receives little or no financial compensation.[100] A major drawback of kinship diversion observed in this and other studies is that caregivers must contend with state involvement without a guarantee of resources (e.g., IV-E matching funds for formal kinship care, TANF and related benefits) and services. In Illinois, the caseworker is supposed to provide the caregiver with "information for how to obtain medical care for the child, . . . information on how to notify schools and day care providers of safety plan requirements."[101] However, caseworkers may or may not link them with such services.

Kinship diversion policy and practice affect a significant number of children and families who come to the attention of the child welfare system, although data on the extent of these practices are not readily available because they are not systematically tracked. Estimates about the number of children living with caregivers under kinship diversion range from 135,000 to 400,000.[102]

Safety Plans

In Illinois, if a child is declared unsafe in their family, removal from the unsafe situation is not the only course of action. Under certain circumstances, caseworkers develop a safety plan. While there is no universal definition for a safety plan, in general, it is a "plan developed for a family in a traditional investigatory response after a risk assessment of the home is completed."[103] Illinois defines a safety plan as "a voluntary, short-term safety plan designed to address serious and immediate threats to children's safety."[104] In these cases, the Illinois DCFS has grounds to take protective custody of a child—meaning that DCFS investigators use their authority to take children from their parents without a court order or warrant—and the safety plan is used as an alternative.[105] An emergency refers to a situation in which a child is in immediate danger, and there is not enough time for the investigator to go to court to request a warrant or a court order. According to the Illinois DCFS, the safety plan "must be adequate to ensure the child's safety and be as minimally disruptive to the child and family as is reasonably possible."[106] The idea behind safety plans is that they offer an intermediary step between unrestricted custody by parents and protective custody[107] by DCFS.

According to the Illinois DCFS policy and procedure manual:

> Safety plans can take a variety of forms and are developed with the input and voluntary consent of the children's legal caregivers and other family members. Safety plans are typically short-term environmental manipulations to ensure child safety; they are not interventions designed to change behaviors over the long term.[108]

Possible safety plans include in-home safety plans, in-home safety plans with a protective caregiver, in-home safety plans with the removal of the alleged perpetrators, and in-home or out-of-home safety plan requirements for alternate protective caregivers (e.g., the home of a relative or friend).[109] Put another way, the child welfare system may open a family case and provide services to the child and family and monitor the child's safety, or not open a case and instead refer the family for services with no additional monitoring.

The parent can "voluntarily" enter the safety plan as an alternative to protective custody and choose the individual(s) responsible for supervising or monitoring the safety plan if such person(s) is/are determined to be qualified by DCFS. I have placed the term "voluntarily" in quotes because it is consistent across this and other studies that this practice is rarely perceived by parents or relative caregivers as voluntary. Rob Geen, an expert on child welfare programs and policies, notes that "both the parent and the relative are likely to know that if the parent refuses, the agency may petition the court to obtain custody."[110]

Safety plans vary in terms of duration and the terms of the plan according to the discretion of the caseworker. Often throughout the duration of the safety plan communication between the parent and the child is at least restricted, if not completely halted.[111] In most cases, parents are required to complete the services required of them before resuming parenting, such as anger management, parenting class, and therapy.

To qualify, all adult members are subjected to an assessment of the caregiver's home, for safety hazards, among other things.[112] According to the Illinois DCFS policy, every safety plan must specify the conditions under which the safety plan is to be terminated, a time frame when this can be expected to occur, and an explanation of consequences if the caregiver does not agree to implement or fails to carry out the terms of the safety plan.[113] If the safety plan is not carried out, a reassessment of the home, possible protective custody, and/or referral to the State's Attorney's Office for a court order to remove the children from the home may occur.[114] Caregivers with safety plans do not have a legally binding relationship to the child in their care and therefore do not hold educational, medical, or custodial rights or obligations; biological parents, on the other hand, maintain all of their rights.[115]

CONCLUSION

The evolution of kinship care policies and practices in the post–civil rights era represent a drastic turnabout from the child welfare system's historical treatment of kin. When the Adoption Assistance and Child Welfare Act formed the basis of federal foster care policy, kin were very rarely formally designated as foster parents for related children. By 2018, when the Family First Prevention Services Act was passed, nearly all states gave preference to relatives when children were placed in foster care. Relatives' experiences of the child welfare system are contingent on the state they live in: some states allow relatives to care for children without formal licensing, and some offer waivers and variances to more easily place children in kinship foster care. To further complicate matters, states are increasingly using kinship diversion to bypass the formal foster care system, which reduces their budgets by providing fewer resources and services to families who come into contact with the child welfare system but whose children are not taken into protective custody. Kinship diversion policies and practices also vary widely by state. Finally, relatives are increasingly formalizing their relationships with the children in their care by using legal guardianship as a form of private child protection to bypass parental rights.

The ways in which Black grandmothers make decisions about their caregiving arrangements have imperfect parallels to the available legal options. Furthermore, families may get directed into caregiving arrangements based on how they enter the system, as opposed to being able to choose the best option for them. This appendix provides an overview of kinship laws and policies that exposes crucial but often overlooked differences between the complexities facing contemporary grandmothers raising their grandchildren and those of their foremothers, many of which previous generations did not experience and that few could have imagined. The importance of the stories in this book cannot be overstated because of the frequency with which many current scholars and social critics have overlooked the ways in which grandparents themselves make sense of, and decisions within, this complex kinship care system. It therefore follows that more examination is also needed of the ways in which inequities within the five-tiered system of kinship care influences grandmothers' caregiving experiences.

Notes

INTRODUCTION

1. African American and Black are used interchangeably in this book.

2. Meyer, *Grandmothers at Work*.

3. Kaplan, *Not Our Kind*; McDonald, "Black Activist Mothering"; Burton, "Age Norms."

4. *Grandmothering* is defined as the implementation, enactment, or execution of the grandmother role.

5. Kinship care refers to the care of children by relatives or, in some jurisdictions, close family friends (often referred to as fictive kin, defined as nonkin relationships that are as important as or more important than comparable relationships created by blood, marriage, or adoption).

6. Wu, *Grandchildren Living*; Wilson, *Coresident Grandparents*.

7. Carlson, *Grandchildren Living*.

8. Amorim, Dunifon, and Pilkauskas, "Magnitude."

9. Amorim, Dunifon, and Pilkauskas, "Magnitude."

10. Amorim, Dunifon, and Pilkauskas, "Magnitude."

11. United States Census, B10051.

12. United States Census, S1002.

13. Except American Indians/Alaska Natives.

14. Amorim, Dunifon, and Pilkauskas, "Magnitude."

15. Ruggles, "Origins."

16. Annie E. Casey Foundation, "Children in Single-Parent Families."

17. Dunifon, Ziol-Guest, and Kopko, "Grandparent Coresidence."

18. Minkler and Roe, *Grandmothers as Caregivers*.

19. Hanlon, Carswell, and Rose, "Research on the Caretaking"; Travis, McBride, and Solomon, "Families Left Behind."

20. Centers for Disease Control and Prevention, "Opioid Data"; Jamison, "Opioid Epidemic."

21. Swann and Sylvester, "Foster Care"; Johnson and Waldfogel, "Parental Incarceration."

22. Swann and Sylvester, "Foster Care"; Johnson and Waldfogel, "Parental Incarceration."

23. Swann and Sylvester, "Foster Care."

24. Abramovitz, "Economic Crises."

25. US Department of Health and Human Services, "Report to the Congress."

26. Testa, "Kinship Foster Care."

27. Fuller et al., *Conditions of Children*. Child Trends found that in 2019, 46 percent of children in foster care in Illinois were placed with a relative (Williams, *State-Level Data*). However, according to Fuller and colleagues (*Conditions of Children*), 57.1 percent reflects the percentage of all children in substitute care at the end of the fiscal year that were placed in kinship foster homes.

28. Roberts, *Torn Apart*; Roberts, *Shattered Bonds*.

29. Gleeson et al., "Becoming Involved"; Harden et al., "Kith and Kin"; Berrick, "Assessing Quality."

30. Herring et al., "Evolutionary Theory"; Cuddeback, "Kinship Family"; Cole, *Security of Attachment*; Berrick et al., *Tender Years*.

31. Font, "Is Higher Placement."

32. Nesmith, "Factors Influencing"; Wilkerson and Davis, "Grandparents in Kinship Care."

33. Malm, Sepulveda, and Abbott, *Variations*; Wu and Snyder, "Factors Associated."

34. Berrick and Hernandez, "Developing Consistent"; Murray, Ehrle, and Geen, *Estimating Financial*; Geen, *Foster Children*; Scarcella, Macomber, and Ehrle, *Identifying*.

35. Beltran and Epstein, *Improving Foster Care*; Palacios and Jiménez, "Kinship Foster Care"; Geen, *Kinship Care*.

36. Gleeson et al., "Becoming Involved."

37. Murphy, Hunter, and Johnson, "Transforming Caregiving."

38. See www.webmd.com/connect-to-care/addiction-treatment-recovery/difference-between-substance-abuse-and-addiction for the difference between substance abuse and addiction.

39. Dunifon, Ziol-Guest, and Kopko, "Grandparent Coresidence."

40. Pittman, "Safety Net Politics"; Pittman, "How Well"; Park, "Economic Well-Being."

41. Dunifon, Ziol-Guest, and Kopko, "Grandparent Coresidence."

42. United States Census Bureau, "America's Families."

43. Dunifon, Ziol-Guest, and Kopko, "Grandparent Coresidence," 118.

44. Pittman, "Safety Net Politics"; Pittman, "How Well"; Baker and Mutchler, "Poverty and Material"; Brandon, "Welfare Receipt."

45. Chen et al., "Race/Ethnic Differentials"; Scommegna and Mossaad, "Health and Well-Being"; Leder, Grinstead, and Torres, "Grandparents Raising."

46. Rapoport et al., "Family Well-Being"; Dunifon, Ziol-Guest, and Kopko, "Grandparent Coresidence"; Schwartz, "Nobody Knows"; Bachman and Chase-Lansdale, "Custodial Grandmothers'"; Billing, Macomber, and Kortenkamp, *Children Cared.*

47. Chen et al., "Race/Ethnic Differentials."

48. Meyer and Abdul-Malak, *Grandparenting Children*; Dunifon, Ziol-Guest, and Kopko, "Grandparent Coresidence"; Pittman, Nodvin, and Howett, "Grandparents"; Strong, Bean, and Feinauer, "Trauma."

49. Dunifon, *You've Always.*

50. Ellis and Simmons, *Coresident Grandparents.*

51. Ruiz, *Amazing Grace*, 111.

52. Minkler and Roe, *Grandmothers as Caregivers*, 5.

53. Nakano Glenn, *Forced to Care*, 6.

54. Nakano Glenn, *Forced to Care*, 6.

55. Nakano Glenn, *Forced to Care*, 6.

56. Nakano Glenn, *Forced to Care.*

57. Fisher and Tronto, "Toward a Feminist," 37.

58. Fisher and Tronto, "Toward a Feminist," 40.

59. Smith, "Keeping It."

60. Smith, "Keeping It."

61. Fisher and Tronto, "Toward a Feminist."

62. Mason, *From Father's Property.*

63. Atkinson, *Obtaining Visitation.*

64. Atkinson, *Obtaining Visitation.*

65. Smith, "Keeping It."

66. Roberts, *Shattered Bonds*, 9.

67. Testa, "Kinship Foster Care," 117.

68. Testa, "Kinship Foster Care," 117.

69. Williams and Sepulveda, *Share of Children.*

70. Soine, "Kinship Foster Caregivers."

71. Alabama, California, Connecticut, Delaware, Georgia, Hawaii, Indiana, Louisiana, Maryland, Massachusetts, Montana, New York, North Carolina,

Ohio, Oklahoma, Oregon, South Carolina, South Dakota, Tennessee, Texas, Utah, Virginia, Washington, and Wyoming (Grandfamilies, "Education").

72. Iowa, Michigan, New Jersey, and Rhode Island (Grandfamilies, "Education").

73. Arkansas, Arizona, Colorado, District of Columbia, Florida, Idaho, Kansas, Kentucky, Mississippi, Missouri, Nevada, New Mexico, North Dakota, Pennsylvania, and Wisconsin (Grandfamilies, "Education").

74. US Department of Education, "Education for Homeless Children and Youths."

75. Illinois General Assembly, "Education for Homeless Children Act."

76. Illinois State Board of Education, "School Wellness"; Illinois State Board of Education, "Non-Regulatory Guidance"; US Department of Education, "National Center for Homeless Education."

77. Illinois State Board of Education, "Affidavit of Enrollment."

78. Harris, "Criminalization of School Choice."

79. Rooks, *Cutting School.*

80. Rooks, *Cutting School.*

81. Harris, "Criminalization of School Choice"; Rooks, *Cutting School*; Gustafson, "Degradation Ceremonies."

82. Generations United, "State Educational."

83. The process and importance of obtaining parental consent to provide medical care to children has evolved and solidified over time (see Faden, Beauchamp, and King, *History and Theory*).

84. Szinovacz, "Research on Grandparenting."

85. Szinovacz, "Research on Grandparenting."

86. Szinovacz, "Research on Grandparenting," 265.

87. Kivnick, *Meaning of Grandparenthood.*

88. Sudarkasa, *Strength of Our Mothers.*

89. Stryker, "Traditional Symbolic," 219.

90. Turner, "Role-Taking."

91. Hunter and Taylor, "Grandparenthood."

92. Burton and Dilworth-Anderson, "Intergenerational Family."

93. Burton, "Age Norms."

94. Ruiz, *Amazing Grace*; Minkler and Roe, *Grandmothers as Caregivers.*

95. Horton, "Disproportionality in Illinois."

96. Annie E. Casey Foundation, "Children in Foster Care"; Williams, *State-Level Data.*

97. Roberts, *Torn Apart*; Roberts, *Shattered Bonds.*

CHAPTER 1. MOTHERING WHILE BLACK

1. Collins, *Black Feminist Thought*, 136.

2. Moynihan, "Negro Family," 30.

3. Collins, *Black Feminist Thought*, 136.

4. In 2017, the Black homeownership rate, at 41.8 percent, was not only the lowest of all racial and ethnic groups but was at its lowest level in fifty years. While the Black-White homeownership gap is somewhat attributable to differences in parental wealth and homeownership, income, credit score, age distribution, and marital status, structural racism plays a significant role (Choi et al., *Explaining*).

5. The National Labor Relations Act of 1935 strengthened the right of workers to organize.

6. Bhutta et al., *Disparities in Wealth*.

7. DuMonthier, Childers, and Milli, *Status*.

8. Jones, *Labor of Love*.

9. Goldin, "Female Labor."

10. Paul et al., *Returns*, 19.

11. Institute for Women's Policy Research, "Lost Jobs."

12. Shrider et al., *Income and Poverty*.

13. Black women's earnings are lower than White women and men, and Black men.

14. National Partnership for Women and Families, "Black Women."

15. DuMonthier, Childers, and Milli, *Status*.

16. DuMonthier, Childers, and Milli, *Status*.

17. Paul et al., *Returns*.

18. Misogynoir—the specific hatred, dislike, distrust, and prejudice directed toward Black women.

19. Merling, *Black Women*.

20. Seefeldt, *Working after Welfare*; Edin and Lein, *Making Ends Meet*.

21. "Man in the house" rules sought to ensure only women with children, who at the time were expected not to work, benefited from welfare. Households with an adult male were viewed as undeserving of assistance because adult males were expected to provide for their families through work. The rules, enforced through highly invasive inspections, forced many families to choose between maintaining welfare supports and keeping their families intact (Kurwa, "New Man").

22. Gustafson, *Criminalization*.

23. Sharkey and Faber, "Where, When, Why."

24. America's Health Rankings, "Public Health Impact."

25. Byerly, "Residential Segregation"; Parisi, Lichter, and Taquino, "Multi-Scale Residential."

26. Sharkey, "Spatial Segmentation."

27. Sharkey, "Spatial Segmentation," 907.

28. Light and Thomas, "Segregation and Violence."

29. Alleyne and Wood, "Gang Involvement."

30. Owens, "Income Segregation."

31. Taylor, *Race for Profit*; Rothstein, *Color of Law*; Boustan, *Competition in the Promised Land*; Bell, *Hate Thy Neighbor*; Massey and Denton, *American Apartheid*.

32. By contrast, White neighborhoods were often outlined in blue and green and were subsequently favored for investment. Rothstein, *Color of Law*.

33. California Newsreel, "Race—The Power."

34. Massey and Denton, *American Apartheid*.

35. Massey and Denton, *American Apartheid*, 46.

36. Massey and Denton, *American Apartheid*, 62.

37. Massey and Denton, *American Apartheid*, 48.

38. Massey and Denton, *American Apartheid*.

39. Electronic Encyclopedia of Chicago, "West Englewood."

40. Chicago Metropolitan Agency for Planning, "Community Data Snapshot."

41. Boustan, *Competition in the Promised Land*.

42. California Newsreel, "Race—The Power."

43. Gounder, S2E11.

44. Gounder, S2E11.

45. Tonry and Melewski, "Malign Effects."

46. Williams, "Toward a Theorization," 18.

47. Electronic Encyclopedia of Chicago, "Englewood" and "West Englewood."

48. Bursik and Grasmick, "Economic Deprivation," 15.

49. Raley, Sweeney, and Wondra, "Growing Racial."

50. Iceland and Hernandez, "Understanding Trends."

51. Kneebone and Holmes, *U.S. Concentrated Poverty*.

52. Iceland and Hernandez, "Understanding Trends."

53. Iceland and Hernandez, "Understanding Trends."

54. Sastry and Pebley, "Family and Neighborhood."

55. Sastry and Pebley, "Family and Neighborhood."

56. Pattillo, *Black Picket Fences*.

57. Husock, "How Brooke."

58. National Equity Atlas, "Neighborhood Poverty."

59. Wilson, *Black Unemployment*.

60. Williams, "Laid Off More." This includes the 1973–75 recession, 1980–82 recession, Great Recession (2007–9) and COVID-19 recession.

61. Annie E. Casey Foundation, "Children Living in High Poverty."

62. Husock, "Up from the Poorhouse"; Husock, "How Brooke."

63. McDonald, "Black Activist Mothering."

64. Ziemba, "CHA Work."

65. The 1985 relocation was part of the short-lived Comprehensive Improvement Assistance Program (CIAP), which expired in 1989, when further funding was not approved by the Reagan administration, which instead continued what has been decades of dwindling federal contributions to urban budgets (Ziemba, "CHA Work"). Not soon after the expiration of the CIAP, displacement of public

housing residents resumed through poverty deconcentration programs (see Pittman and Oakley, "It Was Love").

66. Sastry and Pebley, "Family and Neighborhood."

67. Anderson, *A Seat at the Table.*

68. "Hostility is typically considered the conceptual opposite of warmth and refers to behaviors marked by harshness, over-reactivity, irritability, and explosiveness; it also includes overt communication of criticism, derision, disapproval, and sarcastic remarks [Skinner et al., 2005]" (in Rious, Cunningham, and Spencer, "Rethinking the Notion," 36).

69. Rious, Cunningham, and Spencer, "Rethinking the Notion," 43.

70. Washington Post, "Fatal Force."

71. Turner, "Black Mothering"; Dow, "The Deadly Challenges."

72. Pillemer et al., "Capturing the Complexity."

73. Cichy et al., "You Are Such," 893; Ryff, Schmutte, and Lee, "How Children."

74. Cichy et al., "You Are Such," 893.

75. Jones, *Between Good*; Venkatesh, *Off the Books*; Anderson, *Code of the Streets*; Kaplan, *Not Our Kind.*

76. Pattillo, *Black Picket Fences*, 109.

77. A subprime loan is a loan offered to individuals, who do not qualify for conventional loans, at an interest rate above prime. Such individuals may have low income, limited credit history, poor quality collateral, or poor credit. In an insidious form of reverse redlining, the secondary mortgage system systematically channeled otherwise qualified Black and Latino borrowers into subprime and high-cost loans, regardless of whether they qualified for a conventional loan. On the eve of the Great Recession, a scandalous 62 percent of subprime borrowers actually qualified for prime loans, and roughly one out of every two loans made to Black borrowers were high-cost, compared to fewer than one out of five loans made to White borrowers (Steil et al., "Social Structure," 4). The ripple effects of the subprime lending scandal resulted in a greater loss of wealth (47.6 versus 26.2 percent) and net worth (53 versus 16 percent) among African Americans compared with White Americans, respectively. It also widened the racial homeownership gap between Black households and White households. That gap is more than 30 percentage points, which, inconceivably, is greater than it was *before* the passage of the 1968 Fair Housing Act (McKernan et al., "Disparities in Wealth").

78. Allen, "African American Family," 572.

79. Williams, "Toward a Theorization."

CHAPTER 2. BLACK GRANDMOTHERING

1. Otha's grandparents separated sometime in the 1930s when most (three-fifths) Black workers resided in the South and were employed in agriculture or

domestic service. In 1935, when the Social Security Act was passed, the combined effect of the Old Age Assistance and Old Age Insurance programs excluded African Americans almost entirely (Quadagno, *Transformation*, 115).

2. Hunter and Taylor, "Grandparenthood"; Jimenez, "History of Grandmothers."

3. Von Hentig, "Sociological Function."

4. May, Mason, and Clarke, "Being There"; Cherlin, "On Single Mothers."

5. Cherlin, "On Single Mothers."

6. White, *Ar'n't I*.

7. Ruggles, "Origins."

8. Jimenez, "History of Grandmothers."

9. McDonald and Armstrong, "De-Romanticizing"; Kaplan, *Not Our*; Burton, "Age Norms."

10. Hunter and Taylor, "Grandparenthood," 79.

11. Role enactment is the execution or implementation of the grandparent or parent role.

12. Sadruddin et al., "How Do Grandparents."

13. Martin and Martin, *Black Extended Family*.

14. Although low-income families where unmet need is greatest are more likely to trigger intensive grandmothering or surrogate parenting, sociologist Andrew Cherlin asserts, "the greater role of Black grandparents is not just limited to the low-income population. At every income level, even among households with annual incomes of $200,000 or more, Black households are at least twice as likely to be extended as White households" (Cherlin, "On Single Mothers," 801).

15. Schneider, "Single Mothers," 82.

16. McLanahan and Percheski, "Family Structure," 259.

17. Sedlak et al., *Fourth National*.

18. Schneider, "Single Mothers."

19. Schneider, "Single Mothers."

20. Berger et al., "Income and Child."

21. Scannapieco and Connell-Carrick, "Correlates of Child."

22. Office of Population Affairs, "Trends in Teen Pregnancy."

23. Misra et al., "Family Policies."

24. McLanahan and Percheski, "Family Structure."

25. Brand and Thomas, "Job Displacement."

26. Murry et al., "African American."

27. Dominguez and Watkins, "Creating Networks"; McDonald and Armstrong, "De-Romanticizing."

28. Staton-Tindall et al., "Caregiver Substance."

29. Staton-Tindall et al., "Caregiver Substance."

30. Nation's Health, "Behind Bars II."

31. Nation's Health, "Behind Bars II."

32. Nation's Health, "Behind Bars II."

33. Thornberry, Knight, and Lovegrove, "Does Maltreatment."

34. Chamberlain et al., "Parenting After."

35. Valentino et al., "Intergenerational Continuity."

36. Savage et al., "Maternal History."

37. Hoyert, "75 Years."

38. Jimenez, " History of Grandmothers."

39. Burton, "Age Norms."

40. James, "Mothering," 47.

41. Meyer, *Grandmothers at Work.*

42. Martin and Martin (*Black Extended Family*) define the dominant family figure as one who "resides at and controls the extended family base household and is central to the continuing existence of the family network" (17).

43. Concerted cultivation is a parenting practice marked by a parent's attempts to foster their child's talents by incorporating organized activities in their children's lives (Lareau, *Unequal Childhoods*).

44. Kivnick, *Meaning of Grandparenthood.*

CHAPTER 3. HOW GRANDMOTHERS EXPERIENCE AND RESPOND TO COERCED MOTHERING WITHIN INFORMAL KINSHIP CARE

1. Fisher and Tronto, "Toward a Feminist Theory," 48.

2. Street-level bureaucrats are public service workers who interact directly with the public, representing the frontlines of government policy. They have substantial discretionary authority and interpret policy on a case-by-case basis (Lipsky, *Street-Level Bureaucracy*).

3. Letiecq, Bailey, and Porterfield, "We Have No Rights"; Jendrek, "Grandparents Who Parent: Circumstances and Decisions."

4. Roberts, *Torn Apart*; Bell, *Black Security*; Roberts, "Racial Geography."

5. Bell, *Black Security.*

6. Roberts, *Torn Apart*; Dettlaff et al., "It Is Not," 509.

7. Sadruddin et al., "How Do Grandparents."

8. "The motivation to form and sustain kin support networks for young mothers is understood to be derived from a conjunction of empathy for other Black women who suffer or have suffered similar social disadvantages and of African American norms of solidarity, responsibility, and accountability" (McDonald and Armstrong, "De-Romanticizing," 214).

9. Burton, "Age Norms."

10. Nakano Glenn, *Forced to Care*, 159.

11. Nakano Glenn, *Forced to Care*, 159.

12. Illinois State Board of Education, "Affidavit of Enrollment."

13. Standing, Musil, and Warner, "Grandmothers' Transitions."

14. Hunter and Taylor, "Grandparenthood."

15. Other authors (Ruiz, *Amazing Grace*; Minkler and Roe, *Grandmothers as Caregivers*; Burton, "Age Norms") have also noted that some Black women feel that they have no choice but to assume a caregiver role for their grandchildren if they want to ensure their safety and well-being.

CHAPTER 4. HOW GRANDMOTHERS EXPERIENCE AND RESPOND TO COERCED MOTHERING WITHIN FORMAL KINSHIP CARE

1. McDaniel, "In the Eye"; Giovannoni, "Reports of Child."

2. In Illinois and twenty-two other states and the District of Columbia, substance abuse during pregnancy is considered to be child abuse under civil child-welfare statutes (Guttmacher Institute, "Substance Use").

3. Bramlett, Radel, and Chow, "Health and Well-Being."

4. Harp and Bunting, "Racialized Nature"; McDaniel, "In the Eye."

5. Roberts, "Racial Geography."

6. Child Welfare Information Gateway, "Racial Disproportionality."

7. Jimenez, "History of Grandmothers"; Hunter and Taylor, "Grandparenthood."

8. McDonald and Armstrong, "De-Romanticizing."

9. Schizophreniform disorder is a type of psychotic illness with symptoms similar to those of schizophrenia but lasting for less than six months. Like schizophrenia, schizophreniform disorder is a type of "psychosis" in which a person cannot tell what is real from what is imagined (WebMD, "What Is Schizophreniform Disorder?").

10. The child welfare system defines medical neglect as the failure of a parent or other person with responsibility for the child to provide needed medical care (Child Welfare Information Gateway, "Child Neglect"). It accounts for 2.3 percent of all substantiated cases of child maltreatment (Jenny, "Recognizing and Responding").

11. Waldrop, "Caregiving Issues."

12. Simpson and Lawrence-Webb, "Responsibility Without."

13. Simpson and Lawrence-Webb, "Responsibility Without"; Stevenson, Henderson, and Baugh, "Vital Defenses."

14. These findings are consistent with research that shows that relative foster parents receive fewer resources and services and less support than do nonrelative foster parents (Sakai, Lin, and Flores, "Health Outcomes").

15. Gladstone and Brown, "Grandparent Involvement."

16. Gladstone and Brown, "Grandparent Involvement"; Murphy, Hunter, and Johnson, "Transforming Caregiving."

17. Murphy, Hunter, and Johnson, "Transforming Caregiving."

18. Murphy, Hunter, and Johnson, "Transforming Caregiving," 80.

19. As grandmothers served as foster parents, children's biological parents (mostly mothers) were given case plans to reunify with their children. Although most children reunify with their biological parents, certain child, family, and system-related factors are predictive of reunification or nonreunification, including age, race/ethnicity, type of abuse, and type of services offered (Roberts, *Torn Apart*; Roberts, *Shattered Bonds*).

20. Kinship caregivers are more likely to be single, unemployed, and older, less educated, and poorer than foster parents. Kin caregivers report more health problems, a higher level of depression, and less marital satisfaction than foster families, and such families receive fewer services and less training and financial support (Cuddeback, "Kinship Family").

21. See Roberts, *Torn Apart*.

22. The Illinois Fictive Kin Law expanded the definition of family to include any individual, unrelated by birth or marriage, who is shown to have close personal or emotional ties to the child or the child's family. Illinois General Assembly, "DCFS-Child Custody."

23. Illinois Department of Children and Family Services, "Part 301," 242.

24. Murphy, Hunter, and Johnson, "Transforming Caregiving," 81.

25. When data for this study were collected, safety plans lasted for indefinite periods. Existing research shows that in extreme cases, a safety plan can last for over a year. Although the length of kinship diversion arrangements is difficult to obtain, a recent report by the nonprofit organization, Child Trends found that kinship diversion cases can be relatively short term (three months or less) or range from four to six months (Malm and Allen, *Qualitative*).

26. Illinois Department of Children and Family Services, "Extended Family Support Program"; Illinois Department of Children and Family Services, "Family Preservation Services."

27. Illinois Department of Children and Family Services, "Safety Plan Termination Agreement."

28. Turner, "Black Mothering."

29. Conway, Jones, and Speakes-Lewis, "Emotional Strain"; Minkler and Roe, *Grandmothers as Caregivers*; Ruiz, *Amazing Grace*.

CHAPTER 5. "HE DON'T GET ENOUGH MONEY TO DO
ALL THAT. AND I DON'T EITHER"

1. Pittman, "Safety Net Politics"; Pittman, "How Well"; Dunifon, Ziol-Guest, and Kopko, "Grandparent Coresidence"; Park, "Economic Well-Being."

2. NAACP, "Aging While Black"; DuMonthier, Childers, and Milli, *Status.*

3. Rice, Schmit, and Matthews, *Child Care.*

4. Lumsdaine and Vermeer, "Retirement Timing."

5. The United States is one of thirty-eight high-income countries in the Organsation for Economic Co-operation and Development (OECD), and compared to other OECD countries, it is third from the bottom on spending for family benefits (Organisation for Economic Co-operation and Development, "Public Spending on Family Benefits").

6. Smith and Beltran, "Role of Federal Policies."

7. TANF child-only cases have risen from only 10 percent of the overall caseload in 1988 to 41 percent in 2009 (Falk, *Temporary Assistance*).

8. Pittman, "Safety Net Politics"; Pittman, "How Well."

9. Rice, Schmit, and Matthews, *Child Care.*

10. Organisation for Economic Co-operation and Development, "Public Spending on Childcare and Early Education."

11. Dwyer et al., *Key Cross-State.*

12. Dwyer et al., *Key Cross-State.*

13. Dwyer et al., *Key Cross-State.*

14. Dwyer et al., *Key Cross-State.*

15. Income guidelines are based on working families whose monthly incomes are at or below 185 percent of the most current Federal Poverty Guidelines (Dwyer et al., *Key Cross-State*).

16. Generations United, *A Place to Call Home.*

17. Kolomer and Lynch, "Challenges for Grandparent."

18. Little, "Grandparents Raising."

19. Baker, Silverstein, and Putney, "Grandparents Raising."

20. Beltran, *Improving Grandfamilies'.*

21. Annie E. Casey Foundation, "Stepping Up"; Foster and Rojas, "Program Participation."

22. It does not include free (Medicaid) or subsidized health insurance for children (Children's Health Insurance Program [CHIP]).

23. Curley, "Draining or Gaining?"

24. Meyer, *Grandmothers at Work.*

25. Sociologist Leonard Pearlin and colleagues ("Caregiving and the Stress Process") defined secondary strains as "spillover" effects or the ways in which being a caregiver can produce stress proliferation in other areas of life.

26. US Department of Labor, "What You Should Know."

27. In 2007 when data collection began, licensed childcare centers in Cook County charged between $1,020 and $1,740 per month for childcare and licensed home providers charged between $750 and $810 each month—the younger the child, the higher the rate (Garnier and Hickman, "Market Rate").

28. Seefeldt, *Working after Welfare*; Edin and Lein, *Making Ends Meet*.

29. Flint and Perez-Porter, "Grandparent Caregivers."

30. Pittman, "Safety Net Politics"; Pittman, "How Well."

31. Henderson and Cook, "Grandma's Hands."

32. Pittman, "Safety Net Politics"; Pittman, "How Well."

33. Henry, *Caribbean Diaspora*.

34. Structural lag occurs when there is a mismatch between people's capacities and needs and the surrounding societal structures that grant opportunities to express those capacities and meet those needs.

35. Generations United, *A Place to Call Home*.

36. Section 8 awards vouchers to low-income households to housing apartments on the private market. Tenants generally pay 30 percent of their income toward rent, while the federal government covers the difference, up to a specified maximum payment standard. The voucher program is the largest housing subsidy program for low-income households (Pittman, "Safety Net Politics"; Pittman, "How Well").

37. Kimbro and Schachter, "Neighborhood Poverty"; Furstenberg, "How Families."

38. Grandfamilies.org, "Housing."

39. Letiecq, Bailey, and Porterfield, "We Have."

40. Generations United, *A Place to Call Home*.

41. Generations United, *A Place to Call Home*.

42. An estimated 1.3 million custodial grandparents are in the labor force (United States Census Bureau, "Grandparents Still Work to Support Grandchildren").

CHAPTER 6. MANAGING THE BURDEN AND THE BLESSING

1. Kelley et al., "The Mental Health"; McLaughlin, Ryder, and Taylor, "Effectiveness of Interventions"; Grinstead et al., "Review of Research."

2. Grinstead et al., "Review of Research."

3. Williams, "Changing Roles."

4. Minkler, "Intergenerational Households"; Jendrek, "Grandparents Who Parent: Effects on Lifestyle."

5. Grinstead et al., "Review of Research."

6. Langosh, "Grandparents Parenting Again."

7. Matzek and Cooney, "Spousal Perceptions."

8. Bachman and Chase-Lansdale, "Custodial Grandmothers."

9. Chinnery and Worrall, "Rocking the Cradle"; Grinstead et al., "Review of Research."

10. Chinnery and Worrall, "Rocking the Cradle."

11. Robinson and Wilks, "Older but Not Wiser."

12. Jendrek, "Grandparents Who Parent: Effects on Lifestyle."

13. Scommegna and Mossaad, "Health and Well-Being"; Jendrek, "Grandparents Who Parent: Effects on Lifestyle."

14. Gibbons and Jones, "Kinship Care."

15. Kelley et al., "The Mental Health"; McLaughlin, Ryder, and Taylor, "Effectiveness of Interventions"; Scommegna and Mossaad, "Health"; Leder, Grinstead, and Torres, "Grandparents Raising"; Blustein, Chan, and Guanais, "Elevated Depressive"; Grinstead et al., "Review of Research."

16. Kelley et al., "The Mental Health"; Musil et al., "Grandmothers and Caregiving."

17. McLaughlin, Ryder, and Taylor, "Effectiveness of Interventions," 510.

18. McLaughlin, Ryder, and Taylor, "Effectiveness of Interventions," 510.

19. Minkler and Fuller-Thomson, "Health of Grandparents."

20. Chinn, Martin, and Redmond, "Health Equity."

21. Alson et al., "Incorporating Measures."

22. Whitley, Kelley, and Sipe, "Grandmothers Raising."

23. McLaughlin, Ryder, and Taylor, "Effectiveness of Interventions," 510.

24. Kelley et al., "Psychological Distress"; Minkler et al., "Grandparent Caregiving."

25. Woods-Giscombé and Black, "Mind-Body."

26. Kelley, Whitley, and Campos, "Grandmothers Raising Grandchildren."

27. Bailey, Mokonogho, and Kumar, "Racial and Ethnic"; Dumonthier, Childers, and Milli, *Status*.

28. Walton and Boone, "Voices Unheard," 302.

29. Walton and Boone, "Voices Unheard," 302.

30. Hagestad and Burton, "Grandparenthood," 471.

31. Hagestad and Burton, "Grandparenthood," 473.

32. Hagestad and Burton, "Grandparenthood," 472.

33. Kinscripts encompasses three culturally defined family domains: kin-work, which is the labor and the tasks that families need to accomplish survive from generation to generation; kin-time, which is the temporal and sequential ordering of family transitions; and kin-scription, which is the process of assigning kin-work to family members (Stack and Burton, "Kinscripts," 157).

34. Burton, "Age Norms," 205.

35. Stack, *All Our Kin;* Pittman and Oakley, "It Was Love"; Dominguez and Watkins, "Creating Networks."

36. Simpson et al., "Social Support"; Leder, Grinstead, and Torres, "Grandparents Raising."

37. Ruiz, *Amazing Grace*; Minkler and Roe, *Grandmothers as Caregivers.*

38. Hayslip and Kaminski, "Grandparents Raising."

39. Gerard, Landry-Meyer, and Roe, "Grandparents Raising."

40. Koenig, "Religion, Spirituality, and Health"; Harrison et al., "Epidemiology."

41. Minkler and Roe, *Grandmothers as Caregivers.*

42. Pickard, Witt, and Aitch, "Resilience"; Dilworth-Anderson, Boswell, and Cohen, "Spiritual and Religious."

43. Wilmoth et al., "Contributions."

44. Minkler and Roe, *Grandmothers as Caregivers*, 127.

45. Freeman, Elton, and South, "A Second-Chance"; Fuller-Thomson, Serbinski, and McCormack, "Rewards of Caring."

46. Langosch, "Grandparents Parenting Again"; Ross and Aday, "Stress and Coping."

47. Waldrop and Weber, "From Grandparent"; Minkler and Roe, *Grandmothers as Caregivers.*

48. Freeman, Elton, and South, "A Second-Chance."

49. Fuller-Thomson, Serbinski, and McCormack, "Rewards of Caring."

CONCLUSION

1. Uhlenberg and Kirby, "Grandparenthood Over Time"; Minkler and Roe, *Grandmothers as Caregivers.*

2. Mutchler, Baker, and Lee, "Grandparents Responsible"; Fuller-Thomson and Minkler, "American Indian."

3. Van Dam, "How These Grandparents."

4. Richards, "Grandparents Raising Grandchildren."

5. Although rural and suburban White families have been hard hit by synthetic opioid addiction and deaths, since 2014, the national rate of fatal drug overdoses has increased more than twice as fast among African Americans as among Whites. Heroin laced with the powerful synthetic opioid fentanyl has killed thousands of drug users in the past several years, driving a largely overlooked urban public health crisis (Jamison, "Opioid Epidemic"). Austin, "Native Americans."

6. Child Welfare Information Gateway, "In-Home Services."

7. Monitor on Psychology, "More Kids."

8. National Conference of State Legislatures, "Disproportionality."

9. Montoro-Rodriquez and Ramsey, "Grandparents and Race/Ethnicity"; Whitley and Fuller-Thomson, "Latino Solo"; Fuller-Thomson and Minkler, "American Indian."

10. Hagestad and Burton, "Grandparenthood," 473.

11. Hagestad and Burton, "Grandparenthood," 476.

12. Hagestad and Burton, "Grandparenthood."

13. Hagestad and Burton, "Grandparenthood," 478.

14. Bell, *Black Security*.

15. Bell, "Police Reform."

16. Sharkey, "Why Do We."

17. Sharkey, "Why Do We."

18. Bell, *Black Security*.

19. Roberts, *Shattered Bonds*, 268.

20. Roberts, *Shattered Bonds*, 268.

21. Roberts, *Shattered Bonds*, 14.

22. Association of Family and Conciliation Courts, *Guidelines for Child*, 6.

23. Shack et al., "Child Protection."

24. See Roberts, *Shattered Bonds* for an in-depth discussion of ways to give clients more say in the way the system operates.

25. See https://upendmovement.org/ for a fuller discussion.

26. Kim et al., "Lifetime Prevalence."

27. First Focus on Children, "Children's Budget 2020."

28. Peacock et al., "Effectiveness of Home."

29. Prinz et al., "Population-Based Prevention."

30. Annie E. Casey Foundation, "Community-Based Family."

31. Annie E. Casey Foundation, "How Can Helplines."

32. Annie E. Casey Foundation, "How Can Helplines."

33. Organisation for Economic Co-operation and Development, "Family Benefits."

34. Beltran, "Supporting Grandfamilies."

35. Beltran, "Supporting Grandfamilies."

36. Urban Institute. "Welfare Rules Database Project."

37. Lin, "Evaluating Services."

38. Rushovich et al., "A Kinship Navigator Program."

39. Generations United, "A Place to Call Home."

40. Berrick and Hernandez, "Developing Consistent," 30.

APPENDIX: THE FIVE-TIERED SYSTEM OF KINSHIP CARE

1. US Department of Health and Human Services, "Report to the Congress."

2. Written law enacted by a legislative body. Statutes may originate with national and state legislatures or local municipalities.

3. A body of law that governs the activities of administrative agencies of government. In this case, the child welfare system.

4. Gleeson, "Kinship Care," 30.

5. United States Government Accountability Office, "Child Welfare."

6. National Indian Child Welfare Association, "About ICWA"; "Understanding ICWA."

7. National Indian Child Welfare Association, "What Is Disproportionality."

8. Murphy, Hunter, and Johnson, "Transforming Caregiving"; McGowan and Walsh, "Policy Challenges."

9. Murphy, Hunter, and Johnson, "Transforming Caregiving"; McGowan and Walsh, "Policy Challenges."

10. Child Welfare Information Gateway, "Adoption Assistance."

11. Gleeson, "Kinship Care," 31.

12. Roberts, *Shattered Bonds*, 24.

13. Swann and Sylvester, "Foster Care."

14. Murphy, Hunter, and Johnson, "Transforming Caregiving"; Smith and Devore, "African American Children"; McGowan and Walsh, "Policy Challenges."

15. Roberts, *Shattered Bonds*, 105.

16. Roberts, *Shattered Bonds*, 110.

17. "This policy places foster children on two tracks at the same time—one track focuses on reuniting them with their parents; the other seeks to find them a permanent home with another family. Caseworkers must pursue both goals simultaneously. The point of this policy is to ensure that there will be a permanent home waiting for children in the event that reunification efforts fail. Concurrent permanency planning is supposed to keep children from being stranded in foster care. But this policy puts caseworkers in a schizophrenic position. It intensifies the conflict already inherent in child welfare practice between preserving families and seeking adoptive homes" (Roberts, *Shattered Bonds*, 111).

18. Malm and Allen, *Qualitative*.

19. Grandfamilies.org, "Foster Care Licensing."

20. Stoltzfus, *Child Welfare*.

21. Stoltzfus, *Child Welfare*.

22. Malm and Allen, *Qualitative*.

23. US Government Publishing Office, "H.R. 1892."

24. Garcia, "Replacing Foster Care"; Waite, Greiner, and Laris, "Putting Families First."

25. Netherland and Hansen, "The War"; Cicero et al., "Changing."

26. Roberts, *Torn Apart*; Roberts, *Shattered Bonds*; Billingsley and Giovannoni, *Children of the Storm*.

27. Grandfamilies.org, "New Opportunities."

28. Testa, "Introduction."

29. For example, Berrick and Hernandez's framework ("Developing Consistent and Transparent Kinship Care Policy and Practice") and Testa's typology of kinship care ("Introduction").

30. Importantly, regardless of where caregivers are located within the five-tiered system of kinship care, they can access support through Departments or Divisions of Aging kinship programs. Although these programs are not readily available and are poorly funded, they provide some funding for support groups, mentoring programs, respite care, educational programs, and other caregiver support programs.

31. Social work professor Mark Testa refers to licensed and unlicensed kinship foster care as public kinship care and subsidized guardians and adoptive parents as permanent kinship care ("Introduction"). Berrick and Hernandez, "Developing Consistent," refer to these caregiving arrangements as state-mandated.

32. Ascend Justice, "Understanding and Responding."

33. Berrick and Hernandez, "Developing Consistent."

34. Berrick and Hernandez, "Developing Consistent."

35. Bramlett, Radel, and Chow, "Health and Well-Being."

36. Testa, "Introduction."

37. Berrick and Hernandez, "Developing Consistent," 28.

38. Illinois Department of Children and Family Services, "Section 301.80."

39. Consult the Illinois Department of Children and Family Services, "Section 301.80" for more information about how placing workers assess a relative as a placement resource.

40. Illinois Department of Children and Family Services, "Foster Care."

41. Grandfamilies.org, "Relative Foster Care."

42. Grandfamilies.org, "Relative Foster Care," 4.

43. Grandfamilies.org, "Relative Foster Care," 4; Illinois Department of Children and Family Services, "Waiver of Licensing Standards."

44. Almost half of states have provisions allowing for some type of non-safety-related waivers, and almost twenty states allow for variances from non-safety related requirements. Of these, about fifteen states have waivers for specific licensing standards, such as age requirements (Grandfamilies.org, "Report to Congress," 5).

45. Grandfamilies.org, "Report to Congress," 5.

46. Beltran and Epstein, *Improving Foster Care*, 16.

47. Beltran and Epstein, *Improving Foster Care*, 16.

48. Beltran and Epstein, *Improving Foster Care*, 16.

49. "Provisional licenses are typically time limited and allow a relative or a non-relative to care for a child after certain basic safety checks have been com-

pleted on the home and household members. These licenses generally allow the adult to complete the licensing process during the time period of the provisional license; and in the event they are unable to be licensed, the child is removed. About 35 states have these licenses, and only a couple—Arkansas and the District of Columbia—specifically limit them to kin. Rather than providing for 'provisional licensing,' a few states—California, Connecticut, Minnesota, New Jersey, New York, Oklahoma, Rhode Island, and Utah—call for the same type of background checks, time limitations, and applications for full licensure, but rather than 'licensing' the home, albeit it provisionally, the states simply call it an emergency or temporary placement. Almost all of these states limit these placements to relatives or kin. In Connecticut, emergency placements are also open to children where the adult is a relative of a sibling" (Beltran and Epstein, *Improving Foster Care*, 16).

50. The growth in kinship foster care, in the overall Illinois Department of Children and Family Services (DCFS) caseload, and in the Illinois DCFS budget led to the passage of the 1995 Home-of-Relative (HMR) Reform Plan. HMR eliminated separate approval standards and required relatives to meet the same foster care standards as non-kin (those approved under previous home-of-relative approval standards were given six months to meet foster home licensing standards) (Leos-Urbel, Bess, and Geen, "Evolution"; Gleeson, "Kinship Care," 43).

51. Leos-Urbel, Bess, and Geen, "Evolution"; Gleeson, "Kinship Care," 43.

52. Beltran and Epstein, "Standards," 365.

53. Illinois Department of Children and Family Services, "Part 301."

54. Berrick and Hernandez, "Developing Consistent," 27; Annie E. Casey Foundation, "Stepping Up."

55. Grandfamilies.org, "Report to Congress."

56. Grandfamilies.org, "Report to Congress."

57. Shelton, "Kin Prop Up."

58. "In 2014, California's governor made equal the subsidy amount for non-kin and kin foster parents" (Berrick and Hernandez, "Developing Consistent," 27).

59. Berrick and Hernandez, "Developing Consistent," 27.

60. Berrick, Barth, and Needell, "Comparison."

61. These permanency plans are controversial, with some arguing that they have little to do with services for the family or whether a child may be safely returned home. Dorothy Roberts notes, instead, they become about "whether the mother has attended every parenting class, made every urine drop, participated in every therapy session, shown up for every scheduled visitation, arrived at every appointment on time, and always maintained a contrite and cooperative disposition" (*Shattered Bonds*, 80). Many courts apply a rule that failure to complete the permanency plan is prima facie evidence that children should not be reunited with their parents (Roberts, *Shattered Bonds*).

62. Illinois General Assembly, "Section 302.410"; Grandfamilies.org, "Guardianship Assistance."

63. Compared to "state or local funds, Temporary Assistance for Needy Families (TANF) monies, Title XX Social Services block grant funds, or through a waiver from the U.S. Department of Health and Human Services (HHS) that specifically allowed them to use Title IV-E funds for their subsidized guardianship programs" (Grandfamilies.org, "Guardianship Assistance").

64. To be eligible for federal Title IV-E adoption assistance, the child must qualify as a child with special needs and meet IV-E eligibility rules (North American Council on Adoptable Children). Prior to FCA, Illinois used a Title IV-E federal waiver to fund its subsidized guardianship program. Illinois has used its subsidized guardianship program to transition increasing numbers of children to permanence, significantly reducing the number of children in long-term foster care. Between 1999 and 2003, the number of foster children living with relatives for more than twelve months decreased by 45.5 percent in Illinois (Grandfamilies.org, "Guardianship Assistance").

65. Grandfamilies.org, "Guardianship Assistance."

66. Illinois General Assembly, "Section 302.410."

67. Illinois Department of Children and Family Services, "Post Adoption."

68. Berrick and Hernandez, "Developing Consistent."

69. Hernandez and Berrick, "Kinship Probate Guardianship"; Child Focus, "Kinship Adoption."

70. Berrick and Hernandez, "Developing Consistent."

71. Berrick and Hernandez, "Developing Consistent," 28.

72. Illinois Department of Children and Family Services, "Post Adoption."

73. Child Welfare League of America, "New Directions," 150.

74. Child Welfare League of America, "New Directions," 150.

75. Illinois Department of Children and Family Services, "Part 301."

76. Illinois Department of Children and Family Services, "Part 301"; "Voluntary Placement Agreement."

77. Illinois Department of Children and Family Services, "Part 301."

78. A nondelegable duty is an obligation that cannot be outsourced to another party by contract. This prevents a party from contracting out of an obligation or duty of care that belongs with that party by law.

79. Berrick and Hernandez, "Developing Consistent."

80. Berrick and Hernandez, "Developing Consistent," 25.

81. Smith, "Keeping It."

82. Smith, "Keeping It," 276.

83. Smith, "Keeping It," 297.

84. Smith, "Keeping It," 297.

85. Smith, "Keeping It"; Berrick and Hernandez, "Developing Consistent."

86. Urban Institute, "Welfare Rules Database Project."

87. See Social Security Administration, "Benefits for Children," for more information about this program.

88. Social Security Administration, "Benefits for Children."

89. Social Security benefits are based on earnings, financed by employers and wage contributions. Supplemental Security Income benefits are based on need and funded by general tax revenue. Social Security Administration, "Understanding Supplemental Security Income."

90. See Illinois Department of Public Health, "Application for Illinois Birth Record," for more information about the requirements to request for a copy of a birth record.

91. Social Security Administration, "Application."

92. The Seventh Circuit stated that "care" for a child can include psychological assistance. Specifically, the Seventh Circuit stated, "A combination of assistance to one's daughter, plus care of grandchildren that could take a load off the daughter's mind and feet, counts as 'care' under the [FMLA]" (*Gienapp v. Harbor Crest*).

93. North American Council on Adoptable Children, "How to Cover."

94. Hg.org, "Rights of Lineal Relatives."

95. Berrick and Hernandez, "Developing Consistent," 26.

96. Testa, "Introduction"; Berrick and Hernandez, "Developing Consistent."

97. Malm, Sepulveda, and Abbott, *Variations*.

98. Berrick and Hernandez, "Developing Consistent," 26.

99. Testa nuances our understanding of kinship diversion by distinguishing between CPS involvement wherein a brief home visit or background check is conducted and those that involve opening up a CPS case and providing ongoing intervention and treatment services. Bramlett and colleagues found that in 2013 an estimated 374,000 (17 percent) of children in kinship care were in voluntary kinship care and had an open CPS case and 335,000 (15 percent) were in voluntary kinship care without an open case but with other CPS involvement in the placement (a background check or home visit or CPS had arranged for the child's placement). These estimates have been changed to reflect Testa adding adopted children to the calculation ("Introduction").

100. Wu and Snyder, "Factors Associated."

101. Illinois Department of Children and Family Services, "Principles of Permanency Planning."

102. Berrick and Hernandez, "Developing Consistent," 26.

103. McGrath, "Differential Response," 675.

104. Chiu and Fuller, *Understanding Safety Assessment*, 4.

105. Illinois Department of Children and Family Services, "Principles of Permanency Planning."

106. Illinois Department of Children and Family Services, "Principles of Permanency Planning."

107. Illinois Department of Children and Family Services, "Principles of Permanency Planning."

108. Illinois Department of Children and Family Services, "Principles of Permanency Planning."

109. Illinois Department of Children and Family Services, "Principles of Permanency Planning."

110. Geen, *Kinship Care*, 279.

111. Redleaf, *They Took the Kids*.

112. "Five key components should be included in every written safety plan: (1) the actions that have or will be taken to protect each child in relationship to indicated safety threats; (2) the person(s) responsible for ensuring the safety of each child in relationship to the indicated safety threats; (3) the actions or conditions that must occur in order for this safety plan to be terminated; (4) the time frame imposed by the safety plan; and (5) information pertinent to care of child" (Chiu and Fuller, *Understanding Safety Assessment*, 4).

113. Illinois Department of Children and Family Services, "Safety Plan"; "Safety Plan Rights."

114. Illinois Department of Children and Family Services, "Safety Plan"; "Safety Plan Rights."

115. Berrick and Hernandez, "Developing Consistent," 26.

Bibliography

Abramovitz, Mimi. "Economic Crises, Neoliberalism, and the U.S. Welfare State: Trends, Outcomes and Political Struggle." In *Global Social Work Education: Crossing Borders and Blurring Boundaries*, edited by Carolyn Noble, Helle Strauss, and Brian Littlechild, 225–41. Sydney: Sydney University Press, 2014.

Allen, Walter R. "African American Family Life in Societal Context: Crisis and Hope." *Sociological Forum* 10, no. 4 (1995): 569–92.

Alleyne, Emma, and Jane L. Wood. "Gang Involvement: Social and Environmental Factors." *Crime and Delinquency* 60, no. 4 (2014): 547–68.

Alson, Julianna G., Whitney R. Robinson, LaShawnDa Pittman, and Kemi M. Doll. "Incorporating Measures of Structural Racism into Population Studies of Reproductive Health in the United States: A Narrative Review." *Health Equity* 5, no. 1 (2021): 49–58.

America's Health Rankings, "Public Health Impact: Residential Segregation—Black/White." Minneapolis, MN: United Health Group, 2021.

Amorim, Mariana, Rachel Dunifon, and Natasha Pilkauskas. "The Magnitude and Timing of Grandparental Coresidence during Childhood in the United States." *Demographic Research* 37 (2017): 1695–706.

Anderson, Elijah. *Code of the Street: Decency, Violence, and the Moral Life of the Inner City*. New York: W. W. Norton, 2000.

Anderson, Meredith B.L. *A Seat at the Table: African American Youth's Perceptions of K-12 Education*. Washington, DC: UNCF, 2018.

Annie E. Casey Foundation Kids Count Data Center. "Children in Foster Care by Race and Hispanic Origin in the United States." April 2022. https:// datacenter.kidscount.org.

———. "Children Living in High Poverty Areas by Race and Ethnicity in the United States." May 2022. https://datacenter.kidscount.org.

———. "Children in Single-Parent Families by Race in the United States." December 2020. https://datacenter.kidscount.org.

———. "Community-Based Family Support Exemplars with Implementation and Evaluation Strategies." May 2016. https://www.casey.org/community -based-family-support.

———. "How Can Helplines Serve as a Better Pathway for Families to Access Support?" July 13, 2020. www.casey.org/helplines-vs-hotlines.

———. "Stepping Up for Kids: What Government and Communities Should Do to Support Kinship Families." January 1, 2012. https://www.aecf.org/resources /stepping-up-for-kids.

Ascend Justice. "Understanding and Responding to Department of Children and Family Services' Abuse and Neglect Investigations in Illinois: A Basic Guide for Illinois Parents and Other Caregivers." Chicago: Ascend Justice, April 2016.

Association of Family and Conciliation Courts. *Guidelines for Child Protection Mediation*. Madison, WI: Association of Family and Conciliation Courts, 2012.

Atkinson, Jeff. *Obtaining Visitation with or Custody of Grandchildren*. Washington, DC: American Bar Association, 2012.

Austin, Algernon. "Native Americans Are Still Waiting for an Economic Recovery." Washington, DC: Economic Policy Institute, 2013. www.epi.org /publications.

Bachman, Heather J., and Lindsay Chase-Lansdale. "Custodial Grandmothers' Physical, Mental, and Economic Well-Being: Comparisons of Primary Caregivers from Low-Income Neighborhoods." *Family Relations* 54, no. 4 (2005): 475–87.

Bailey, Rahn Kennedy, Josephine Mokonogho, and Alok Kumar. "Racial and Ethnic Differences in Depression: Current Perspectives." *Neuropsychiatric Disease and Treatment* 15 (2019): 603–9.

Baker, Lindsey A., and Jan E Mutchler. "Poverty and Material Hardship in Grandparent-Headed Households." *Journal of Marriage and Family* 72, no. 4 (2010): 947–62.

Baker, Lindsey A., Merril Silverstein, and Norella M. Putney. "Grandparents Raising Grandchildren in the United States: Changing Family Forms, Stagnant Social Policies." *Journal of Societal and Social Policy* 7 (2008): 53–69.

Bell, Jeannine. *Hate Thy Neighbor: Move-in Violence and the Persistence of Racial Segregation in American Housing*. New York: New York University Press, 2013.

Bell, Monica C. *Black Security and the Conundrum of Policing*. New York: Just Security, July 15, 2020.

———. "Police Reform and the Dismantling of Legal Estrangement." *Yale Law Journal* 126, no. 7 (2017): 2054–150.

———. "Situational Trust: How Disadvantaged Mothers Reconceive Legal Cynicism." *Law & Society Review* 50, no. 2 (2016): 314–47.

Beltran, Ana. *Improving Grandfamilies' Access to Temporary Assistance for Needy Families*. Washington, DC: Generations United, 2014.

———. "Supporting Grandfamilies: Federal and State Policy Reforms." *Grand-Families: The Contemporary Journal of Research, Practice, and Policy* 5, no. 2 (2019): 1–12.

Beltran, Ana, and Heidi Redlich Epstein. *Improving Foster Care Licensing Standards around the United States: Using Research Findings to Effect Change*. Washington, DC: Generations United and the American Bar Association Center on Children and the Law, 2012.

———. "The Standards to License Kinship Foster Parents around the United States: Using Research Findings to Effect Change." *Journal of Family Social Work* 16, no. 5 (2013): 364–81.

Berger, Lawrence M., Sarah A. Font, Kristen S. Slack, and Jane Waldfogel. "Income and Child Maltreatment in Unmarried Families: Evidence from the Earned Income Tax Credit." *Review of Economics of the Household* 15, no. 4 (2017): 1345–72.

Berrick, Jill Duerr. "Assessing Quality of Care in Kinship and Foster Family Care." *Family Relations* 46, no. 3 (1997): 273–80.

Berrick, Jill Duerr, Richard P. Barth, and Barbara Needell. "A Comparison of Kinship Foster Homes and Foster Family Homes: Implications for Kinship Foster Care as Family Preservation." *Children and Youth Services Review* 16, no. 1–2 (1994): 33–63.

Berrick, Jill Duerr, and Julia Hernandez. "Developing Consistent and Transparent Kinship Care Policy and Practice: State Mandated, Mediated, and Independent Care." *Children and Youth Services Review* 68 (2016): 24–33.

Berrick, Jill Duerr, Barbara Needell, Richard P. Barth, and Melissa Jonson-Reid. *The Tender Years: Toward Developmentally Sensitive Child Welfare Services for Very Young Children*. New York: Oxford University Press, 1998.

Bhutta, Neil, Andrew C. Chang, Lisa J. Dettling, and Joanne W. Hsu. *Disparities in Wealth by Race and Ethnicity in the 2019 Survey of Consumer Finances*. Washington, DC: Board of Governors of the Federal Reserve System, September 28, 2020.

Billing, Amy, Jennifer Ehrle Macomber, and Katherine Kortenkamp. *Children Cared for by Relatives: What Do We Know about Their Well-Being?* Washington, DC: Urban Institute, 2002.

Billingsley, Andrew, and Jeanne M. Giovannoni. *Children of the Storm: Black Children and American Child Welfare*. San Diego: Harcourt College Publishers, 1972.

Blustein, Jan, Sewin Chan, and Frederico C. Guanais. "Elevated Depressive Symptoms among Caregiving Grandparents." *Health Services Research* 39, no. 6, pt. 1 (2004): 1671–90.

Boustan, Leah Platt. *Competition in the Promised Land: Black Migrants in Northern Cities and Labor Markets*. Princeton, NJ: Princeton University Press, 2016.

Bramlett, Matthew D., Laura F. Radel, and Kirby Chow. "Health and Well-Being of Children in Kinship Care: Findings from the National Survey of Children in Nonparental Care." *Child Welfare* 95, no. 3 (2017): 41–60.

Brand, Jennie E., and Juli Simon Thomas. "Job Displacement among Single Mothers: Effects on Children's Outcomes in Young Adulthood." *American Journal of Sociology* 119, no. 4 (2014): 955–1001.

Brandon, Peter D. "Welfare Receipt Among Children Living with Grandparents." *Population Research and Policy Review* 24, no. 5 (2005): 411–29.

Bursik, Robert J., and Harold G. Grasmick. "Economic Deprivation and Neighborhood Crime Rates, 1960–1980." *Law and Society Review* 27, no. 2 (1993): 263–83.

Burton, Linda M. "Age Norms, the Timing of Family Role Transitions, and Intergenerational Caregiving among Aging African American Women." *The Gerontologist* 36, no. 2 (1996): 199–208.

Burton, Linda M., and Peggye Dilworth-Anderson. "The Intergenerational Family Roles of Aged Black Americans." *Marriage and Family Review* 16, no. 3–4 (1991): 311–30.

Byerly, Jack. "The Residential Segregation of the American Indian and Alaska Native Population in US Metropolitan and Micropolitan Areas, 2010." *Demographic Research* 40 (2010): 963–74.

California Newsreel. "Race—The Power of an Illusion, Episode Three: The House We Live In." San Francisco: California Newsreel, 2003.

Carlson, Lisa. *Grandchildren Living in Grandparent-Headed Households, 2019*. Bowling Green, OH: National Center for Family and Marriage Research, Family Profiles, FP-21-07.

Centers for Disease Control and Prevention. "Opioid Data Analysis and Resources." Page reviewed June 1, 2022. www.cdc.gov/opioids/data/analysis-resources.html.

Chamberlain, Catherine, Graham Gee, Stephen Harfield, Sandra Campbell, Sue Brennan, Yvonne Clark, Fiona Mensah, Kerry Arabena, Helen Herrman, and Stephanie Brown. "Parenting after a History of Childhood Maltreatment: A Scoping Review and Map of Evidence in the Perinatal Period." *PLoS ONE* 14, no. 3 (2019): 1–41.

Chen, Feinian, Christine A. Mair, Luoman Bao, and Yang Claire Yang. "Race/Ethnic Differentials in the Health Consequences of Caring for Grandchildren for Grandparents." *Journals of Gerontology Series B: Psychological Sciences and Social Sciences* 70, no. 5 (2015): 793–803.

Cherlin, Andrew J. "On Single Mothers 'Doing' Family." *Journal of Marriage and Family* 68, no. 4 (2006): 800–803.

Chicago Metropolitan Agency for Planning. "Community Data Snapshot, Englewood, Chicago Community Area July 2022 Release." July 2022. www.cmap.illinois.gov/documents/10180/126764/Englewood.pdf.

Child Focus. "Kinship Adoption: Meeting the Unique Needs of a Growing Population." April 2010. www.grandfamilies.org/Portals/0/Documents/Adoption/Kinship%20Adoption.pdf.

Child Welfare Information Gateway. "Adoption and Foster Care Analysis and Reporting System (AFCARS) FY 2020 data." September 26, 2022. www.acf.hhs.gov/sites/default/files/documents/cb/afcarsreport28.pdf.

———. "Adoption Assistance for Children Adopted from Foster Care." June 2020. www.childwelfare.gov/pubPDFs/f_subsid.pdf.

———. "Child Neglect: A Guide for Prevention, Assessment and Intervention." 2006. www.childwelfare.gov/pubPDFs/neglect.pdf.

———. "Child Welfare Practices to Address Racial Disproportionality and Disparity." April 2021. www.childwelfare.gov/pubPDFs/racial_disproportionality.pdf.

———. "In-Home Services to Strengthen Children and Families." April 2021. www.childwelfare.gov/pubPDFs/inhome_services.pdf.

Child Welfare League of America. "New Directions for Kinship Care Policy and Practice: A Position Paper from the Kinship Summit at Albany, New York, September 2016." *Child Welfare* 95, no. 4 (2017): 137–65.

Children's Bureau. "Report to Congress on States' Use of Waivers of Non-Safety Licensing Standards for Relative Foster Family Homes." Administration for Children and Families, June 15, 2015. www.acf.hhs.gov/archive/cb/report/report-congress-states-use-waivers-non-safety-licensing-standards-relative-foster.

Chinn, Juanita J., Iman K. Martin, and Nicole Redmond. "Health Equity among Black Women in the United States." *Journal of Women's Health* 30, no. 2 (2021): 212–19.

Chinnery, Shirley Ann, and Jill Worrall. "Rocking the Cradle or the Boat? Assessing Grandparent Partner Relationships." *Families in Society* 98, no. 2 (2017): 156–64.

Chiu, Yu-Ling, and Tamara L. Fuller. *Understanding Safety Assessment in Illinois: The Child Endangerment Risk Assessment Protocol (CERAP).* Champaign: University of Illinois, Children and Family Research Center, August 2018.

Choi, Jung Hyun, Alanna McCargo, Michael Neal, Laurie Goodman, and Caitlin Young. *Explaining the Black-White Homeownership Gap: A Closer Look at Disparities across Local Markets*. Washington, DC: The Urban Institute, 2019.

Cicero, Theodore J., Matthew S. Ellis, Hilary L. Surratt, and Steven P. Kurtz. "The Changing Face of Heroin Use in the United States: A Retrospective Analysis of the Past 50 Years." *JAMA Psychiatry* 71, no. 7 (2014): 821–26.

Cichy, Kelly E., Eva S. Lefkowitz, Eden M. Davis, and Karen L. Fingerman. "You Are Such a Disappointment!": Negative Emotions and Parents' Perceptions of Adult Children's Lack of Success." *Journals of Gerontology Series B: Psychological Sciences and Social Sciences* 68, no. 6 (2013): 893–901.

Cole, Susan A. *Security of Attachment in Infants in Foster Care*. Presentation at the 14th Annual Symposium on Doctoral Research in Social Work, April 20, 2002. Ohio State University, College of Social Work. https://kb.osu.edu/handle/1811/36963.

Collins, Patricia. *Black Feminist Thought: Knowledge, Consciousness, and the Politics of Empowerment*. New York: Routledge, 1990.

Cuddeback, Gary S. "Kinship Family Foster Care: A Methodological and Substantive Synthesis of Research." *Children and Youth Services Review* 26, no. 7 (2004): 623–39.

Curley, Alexandra M. "Draining or Gaining? The Social Networks of Public Housing Movers in Boston." *Journal of Social and Personal Relationships* 26, no. 2–3 (2009): 227–47.

Dettlaff, Alan J., Kristen Weber, Maya Pendleton, Reiko Boyd, Bill Bettencourt, and Leonard Burton. "It Is Not a Broken System, It Is a System That Needs to Be Broken: The upEND Movement to Abolish the Child Welfare System." *Journal of Public Child Welfare* 14, no. 5 (2020): 500–517.

Dilworth-Anderson, Peggye, Gracie Boswell, and Monique D. Cohen. "Spiritual and Religious Coping Values and Beliefs among African American Caregivers: A Qualitative Study." *Journal of Applied Gerontology* 26, no. 4 (2007): 355–69.

Dominguez, Silvia, and Celeste Watkins. "Creating Networks for Survival and Mobility: Social Capital among African-American and Latin-American Low-Income Mothers." *Social Problems* 50, no. 1 (2003): 111–35.

Dow, Dawn Marie. "The Deadly Challenges of Raising African American Boys: Navigating the Controlling Image of the 'Thug.'" *Gender and Society* 30, no. 2 (2016): 161–88.

DuMonthier, Asha, Chandra Childers, and Jessica Milli. *The Status of Black Women in the United States*. Washington, DC: Institute for Women's Policy Research, 2017.

Dunifon, Rachel E. *You've Always Been There for Me: Understanding the Lives of Grandchildren Raised by Grandparents*. New Brunswick, NJ: Rutgers University Press, 2018.

Dunifon, Rachel E., Kathleen M. Ziol-Guest, and Kimberly Kopko. "Grandparent Coresidence and Family Well-Being: Implications for Research and Policy." *ANNALS of the American Academy of Political and Social Science* 654, no. 1 (2014): 110–26.

Dwyer, Kelly, Sarah Minton, Danielle Kwon, and Kennedy Weisner. *Key Cross-State Variations in CCDF Policies as of October 1, 2019*. Washington, DC: Urban Institute, December 2020.

Edin, Kathryn, and Laura Lein. *Making Ends Meet: How Single Mothers Survive Welfare and Low-Wage Work*. New York: Russell Sage Foundation, 1997.

Electronic Encyclopedia of Chicago. "Englewood." Chicago Historical Society, 2005. https://encyclopedia.chicagohistory.org/pages/426.html.

———. "West Englewood." Chicago Historical Society, 2005. https://encyclopedia.chicagohistory.org/pages/1337.html.

Ellis, Renee R., and Tavia Simmons. *Coresident Grandparents and Their Grandchildren: 2012 Population Characteristics*. Washington, DC: United States Census Bureau Report, 2014.

Faden, Ruth R., Tom L. Beauchamp, and Nancy King. *History and Theory of Informed Consent*. New York: Oxford University Press, 1986.

Falk, Gene. *Temporary Assistance for Needy Families (TANF): Size and Characteristics of the Cash Assistance Caseload*. Washington, DC: Congressional Research Service Report 43187, 2014.

First Focus on Children. "Children's Budget 2020." Washington, DC: First Focus on Children, 2020.

Fisher, Berenice, and Joan Tronto. "Toward a Feminist Theory of Caring." In *Circles of Care: Work and Identity in Women's Lives*, edited by Emily K. Abel and Margaret K. Nelson, 35–62. Albany: State University of New York Press, 1990.

Flint, Margaret M., and Melinda Perez-Porter. "Grandparent Caregivers: Legal and Economic Issues." In *Intergenerational Approaches in Aging: Implications for Education, Policy, and Practice*, edited by Robert Disch and Kevin Brabazon, 75–88. New York: Routledge, 2013.

Font, Sarah A. "Is Higher Placement Stability in Kinship Foster Care by Virtue or Design?" *Child Abuse and Neglect* 42 (2015): 99–111.

Foster, Ann, and Arcenis Rojas. "Program Participation and Spending Patterns of Families Receiving Government Means-Tested Assistance." *Monthly Labor Review, US Bureau of Labor Statistics*, January 2018.

Freeman, Jessica D., Jessica Elton, and Andrea Lambert South. "A Second-Chance at Being a Parent": Grandparent Caregivers' Reported Communication and Parenting Practices with Co-Residential Grandchildren." *Journal of Family Communication* 19, no. 3 (2019): 261–76.

Fuller, Tamara, Martin Nieto, Kyle A. Adams, Michael Braun, Yu-Ling Chiu, Laura Lee, Steve Tran, Satomi Wakita, and Shufen Wang. *Conditions of Children in or at Risk of Foster Care in Illinois*. ACLU of Illinois, 2018.

Fuller, Tamara, Martin Nieto, Kyle A. Adams, Yu-Ling Chiu, Theodore P. Cross, Cady Landa, Laura Lee, Steve Tran, Satomi Wakita, and Shufen Wang. *Conditions of Children in or at Risk of Foster Care in Illinois: FY2021 Monitoring Report of the B. H. Consent Decree*. University of Illinois at Urbana-Champaign and the Illinois Department of Children and Family Services, October 27, 2021.

Fuller-Thomson, Esme, and Meredith Minkler. "American Indian/Alaskan Native Grandparents Raising Grandchildren: Findings from the Census 2000 Supplementary Survey." *Social Work* 50, no. 2 (2005): 131–39.

Fuller-Thomson, Esme, Sarah Serbinski, and Leanne McCormack. "The Rewards of Caring for Grandchildren: Black Canadian Grandmothers Who Are Custodial Parents, Co-Parents, and Extensive Babysitters." *Grand-Families: The Contemporary Journal of Research, Policy, and Practice* 1, no. 1 (2014): 4–31.

Furstenberg, Frank F. "How Families Manage Risk and Opportunity in Dangerous Neighborhoods." In *Sociology and the Public Agenda*, edited by William Julius Wilson, 231–58. Newbury Park, CA: Sage Publications, 1993.

Garcia, Caitlyn. "Replacing Foster Care with Family Care: The Family First Prevention Services Act of 2018." *Family Law Quarterly* 53, no. 1/2 (2019): 27–49.

Garnier, Phillip C., and Laura L. Hickman. *Market Rate Survey of Licensed Child Care Programs in Illinois FY08*. Springfield: Illinois Department of Human Services, 2009.

Geen, Rob. *Foster Children Placed with Relatives Often Receive Less Government Help*. Washington, DC: Urban Institute, 2003.

———. *Kinship Care: Making the Most of a Valuable Resource*. Washington, DC: Urban Institute Press, 2003.

Generations United. "A Place to Call Home: Building Affordable Housing for Grandfamilies," 2019. www.gu.org/app/uploads/2019/11/19-Grandfamilies-Report-APlacetoCallHome.pdf.

———. "State Educational and Health Care Consent Laws." American Bar Association, June 1, 2014. www.americanbar.org/groups/public_interest/child_law/resources/child_law_practiceonline/child_law_practice/vol-33/june-2014/state-educational-and-health-care-consent-laws/.

Gerard, Jean M., Laura Landry-Meyer, and Jacqueline Guzell Roe. "Grandparents Raising Grandchildren: The Role of Social Support in Coping with Caregiving Challenges." *International Journal of Aging and Human Development* 62, no. 4 (2006): 359–83.

Gibbons, Cynthia, and Teresa C. Jones. "Kinship Care: Health Profiles of Grandparents Raising Their Grandchildren." *Journal of Family Social Work* 7, no. 1 (2003): 1–14.

Giovannoni, Jeanne M. "Reports of Child Maltreatment from Mandated and Non-Mandated Reporters." *Children and Youth Services Review* 17, no. 4 (1995): 487–501.

Gladstone, James W., and Ralph A. Brown. "Grandparent Involvement in Child Welfare Intervention with Grandchildren." *Marquette Elder's Advisor* 4, no. 1 (2002): 11–17.

Gleeson, James P. "Kinship Care as a Child Welfare Service: Emerging Policy Issues and Trends." In *Kinship Foster Care: Policy, Practice, and Research*, edited by Rebecca L. Hegar, and Maria Scannapieco, 28–53. New York: Oxford University Press, 1999.

Gleeson, James P., Julia M. Wesley, Raquel Ellis, Claire Seryak, Gwen Walls Talley, and Jackie Robinson. "Becoming Involved in Raising a Relative's Child: Reasons, Caregiver Motivations, and Pathways to Informal Kinship Care." *Child and Family Social Work* 14, no. 3 (2009): 300–310.

Goldin, Claudia. "Female Labor Force Participation: The Origin of Black and White Differences, 1870 and 1880." *Journal of Economic History* 37, no. 1 (1977): 87–108.

Gounder, Celine. "S2E11 / The Opioid Overdose Crisis / This Is America: Race and the War on Drugs." *American Diagnosis with Dr. Celine Gounder*. Podcast Audio. May 22, 2018.

Grandfamilies.org. "Education." www.grandfamilies.org/Topics/Education.

———. "Foster Care Licensing." www.grandfamilies.org/Resources/Foster-Care-Licensing.

———. "Guardianship Assistance." www.grandfamilies.org/Topics/Guardianship-Assistance.

———. "Housing." www.grandfamilies.org/Topics/Housing.

———. "New Opportunities for Kinship Families." www.grandfamilies.org /Portals/0/Documents/FFPSA/new-opportunities-kinship-families.pdf.

———. "Relative Foster Care Licensing Waivers in the States: Policies and Possibilities." www.grandfamilies.org/Portals/0/Documents/Foster%20 Care%20Licensing/Relative%20foster%20care%20licensing%20waivers%20in%20the%20states.pdf.

Grinstead, Linda Nicholson, Sharon Leder, Susan Jensen, and Linda Bond. "Review of Research on the Health of Caregiving Grandparents." *Journal of Advanced Nursing* 44, no. 3 (2003): 318–26.

Gustafson, Kaaryn. *The Criminalization of Poverty*. New York: New York University Press, 2011.

———. "Degradation Ceremonies and the Criminalization of Low-Income Women." *UC Irvine Law Review* 3 (2013): 297–358.

Guttmacher Institute. "Substance Use During Pregnancy." September 1, 2022. www.guttmacher.org/state-policy/explore/substance-use-during-pregnancy.

Hagestad, Gunhild O., and Linda M. Burton. "Grandparenthood, Life Context, and Family Development." *American Behavioral Scientist* 29, no. 4 (1986): 471–84.

Hanlon, Thomas E., Steven B. Carswell, and Marc Rose. "Research on the Caretaking of Children of Incarcerated Parents: Findings and Their Service Delivery Implications." *Children and Youth Services Review* 29, no. 3 (2007): 348–62.

Harden, Brenda Jones, Robert B. Clyman, Dawn K. Kriebel, and Mary E. Lyons. "Kith and Kin Care: Parental Attitudes and Resource of Foster and Relative Caregivers." *Children and Youth Services Review* 26, no. 7 (2004): 657–71.

Harp, Kathi, and Amanda Bunting. "The Racialized Nature of Child Welfare Policies and the Social Control of Black Bodies." *Social Politics* 27, no. 2 (2020): 258–81.

Harris, La Darien, "The Criminalization of School Choice: Punishing the Poor for the Inequities of Geographic School Districting." *Journal of Legislation* 44, no. 2 (2018): 306–37.

Harrison, Myleme, Harold G. Koenig, Judith C. Hays, Anedi G. Eme-Akwari, and Kenneth I. Pargament. "The Epidemiology of Religious Coping: A Review of Recent Literature." *International Review of Psychiatry* 13, no. 2 (2001): 86–93.

Hayslip, Bert, and Patricia L Kaminski. "Grandparents Raising Their Grandchildren." *Marriage and Family Review* 37, no. 1-2 (2005): 147–69.

Henderson, Tammy L., and Jennifer L. Cook. "Grandma's Hands: Black Grandmothers Speak about Their Experiences Rearing Grandchildren on Tanf." *International Journal of Aging and Human Development* 61, no. 1 (2005): 1-19.

Henry, Frances. *The Caribbean Diaspora in Toronto: Learning to Live with Racism.* Toronto: University of Toronto Press, 1994.

Hernandez, Julia, and Jill Duerr Berrick. "Kinship Probate Guardianship: An Important Permanency Option for Children." *Families in Society* 100, no. 1 (2019): 34–51.

Herring, David J., Jeffrey J. Shook, Sara Goodkind, and Kevin H. Kim. "Evolutionary Theory and Kinship Foster Care: An Initial Test of Two Hypotheses." *Capital University Law Review* 38, no. 1 (2009): 291–318.

HG.org Legal Resources. "Rights of Lineal Relatives after Adoption." https://www.hg.org/legal-articles/rights-of-lineal-relatives-after-adoption-36881.

Horton, Arthur. "Disproportionality in Illinois Child Welfare: The Need for Improved Substance Abuse Services." *Journal of Alcoholism and Drug Dependence* 2, no. 1 (2013): 145–52.

Hoyert, Donna L. "75 Years of Mortality in the United States, 1935–2010." *National Center for Health Statistics Brief,* no. 88 (2012): 1–8.

Hunter, Andrea G., and Robert J. Taylor. "Grandparenthood in African American Families." In *Handbook on Grandparenthood,* edited by Maximiliane E. Szinovacz, 70–86. Westport, CT: Greenwood Press, 1998.

Husock, Howard. "How Brooke Helped Destroy Public Housing." *Forbes Magazine,* January 8, 2015.

———. "Up from the Poorhouse: A New Proposal Has the Potential to Remake America's Public-Housing System." *City Journal,* August 2015.

Iceland, John, and Erik Hernandez. "Understanding Trends in Concentrated Poverty: 1980–2014." *Social Science Research* 62 (2017): 75–95.

Illinois Department of Children and Family Services. "Extended Family Support Program." https://www2.illinois.gov/dcfs/lovinghomes/Documents/Extended_Family_Support_Program.pdf.

———. "Family Preservation Services." https://www2.illinois.gov/dcfs/lovinghomes/families/Pages/Family-Preservation-Services.aspx.

———. "Foster Care." https://www2.illinois.gov/dcfs/lovinghomes/fostercare/Pages/index.aspx.

———. "Part 301: Placement and Visitation Services, June 3, 2021—P.T. 2021.06." https://www2.illinois.gov/dcfs/aboutus/notices/Documents/Procedures_301.pdf.

———. "Post Adoption and Guardianship Services." https://www2.illinois.gov/sites/path/Documents/post_a-g_services-cfs-1050.pdf.

———. "Principles of Permanency Planning." https://www2.illinois.gov/dcfs/aboutus/notices/Documents/Procedures_315.pdf.

———. "Safety Plan." https://www2.illinois.gov/dcfs/aboutus/notices/Documents/CFS_1441-A_Safety_Plan_%28Fillable%29.pdf.

———. "Safety Plan Rights and Responsibilities for Responsible Adult Caregivers and Safety Plan Participants." https://www2.illinois.gov/dcfs/aboutus/notices/Documents/CFS_1441-D_Safety_Plan_Rights_and_Responsibilities_for_Parents_and_Guardians.pdf.

———. "Safety Plan Termination Agreement." https://www2.illinois.gov/dcfs/aboutus/notices/Documents/cfs1441b.pdf.

———. "Section 301.80 Relative Home Placement, Joint Committee on Administrative Rules Administrative Code." https://www.ilga.gov/commission/jcar/admincode/089/089003010A00800R.html.

———. "Voluntary Placement Agreement." https://www2.illinois.gov/dcfs/aboutus/notices/Documents/CFS_444_Voluntary_Placement_Agreement_%28Fillable%29.pdf.

———. "Waiver of Licensing Standards." https://www2.illinois.gov/dcfs/aboutus/notices/Documents/cfs_402-1_waiver_of_licensing_standards_for_foster_family_homes_%28fillable%29.pdf.

Illinois Department of Public Health. "Application for Illinois Birth Record." https://dph.illinois.gov/content/dam/soi/en/web/idph/files/forms/form soppsapplication-illinois-birth-record-2018.pdf.

Illinois General Assembly. "DCFS-Child Custody-Fictive Kin (Public Act 098-0846)." www.ilga.gov/legislation/publicacts/fulltext.asp?Name= 098-0846&GA=98.

———. "Education for Homeless Children Act (105 ILCS 45/1–1)." https://ilga .gov/legislation/ilcs/ilcs5.asp?ActID=1013&ChapterID=17.

———. "Section 302.410 Subsidized Guardianship (KinGAP)." http://www.ilga .gov/commission/jcar/admincode/089/089003020C04100R.html.

Illinois State Board of Education. "Affidavit of Enrollment and Residency." https://www.isbe.net/Documents/85-51_affidavit.pdf.

———. "Non-Regulatory Guidance Registration Guidance Residency & Enrollment, Immigrant Pupils, Homeless Pupils and School Fees & Waivers." https://www.isbe.net/Documents/guidance_reg.pdf.

———. "School Wellness: Homeless Education." www.isbe.net/Pages/Homeless .aspx.

Institute for Women's Policy Research, "Lost Jobs, Stalled Progress: The Impact of the 'She-Cession' on Equal Pay." Washington, DC: Institute for Women's Policy Research, IWPR #C505, September 2021.

James, Stanlie M. "Mothering: A Possible Black Feminist Link to Social Transformation." In *Theorizing Black Feminisms: The Visionary Pragmatism of Black Women*, edited by Stanlie M. James and Abena P. A. Busia, 44–54. New York: Routledge, 1993.

Jamison, Peter. "Opioid Epidemic and Its Effect on African Americans." *Washington Post*, December 18, 2018.

Jendrek, Margaret Platt. "Grandparents Who Parent Their Grandchildren: Circumstances and Decisions." *The Gerontologist* 34, no. 2 (1994): 206–16.

———. "Grandparents Who Parent Their Grandchildren: Effects on Lifestyle." *Journal of Marriage and Family* 55 (1993): 609–21.

Jenny, Carole. "Recognizing and Responding to Medical Neglect." *Pediatrics* 120, no. 6 (2007): 1385–89.

Jimenez, Jillian. "The History of Grandmothers in the African-American Community." *Social Service Review* 76, no. 4 (2002): 523–51.

Johnson, Elizabeth I., and Jane Waldfogel. "Parental Incarceration: Recent Trends and Implications for Child Welfare." *Social Service Review* 76, no. 3 (2002): 460–79.

Jones, Jacqueline. *Labor of Love, Labor of Sorrow: Black Women, Work and the Family, from Slavery to the Present*. New York: Basic Books, 2009.

Jones, Nikki. *Between Good and Ghetto: African American Girls and Inner-City Violence*. New Brunswick, NJ: Rutgers University Press, 2009.

Kaplan, Elaine Bell. *Not Our Kind of Girl: Unraveling the Myths of Black Teenage Motherhood*. Berkeley: University of California Press, 1997.

Kelley, Susan J., Deborah M. Whitley, and Peter E. Campos. "Grandmothers Raising Grandchildren: Results of an Intervention to Improve Health Outcomes." *Journal of Nursing Scholarship* 42, no. 4 (2010): 379–86.

Kelley, Susan J., Deborah M. Whitley, Shannon R. Escarra, Rowena Zheng, Eva M. Horne, and Gordon L. Warren. "The Mental Health Well-Being of Grandparents Raising Grandchildren: A Systematic Review and Meta-Analysis." *Marriage & Family Review* 57, no. 4 (2021): 329–45.

Kelley, Susan J., Deborah Whitley, Theresa A. Sipe, and Beatrice Crofts Yorker. "Psychological Distress in Grandmother Kinship Care Providers: The Role of Resources, Social Support, and Physical Health." *Child Abuse and Neglect* 24, no. 3 (2000): 311–21.

Kim, Hyunil, Christopher Wildeman, Melissa Jonson-Reid, and Brett Drake. "Lifetime Prevalence of Investigating Child Maltreatment among US Children." *American Journal of Public Health* 107, no. 2 (2017): 274–80.

Kimbro, Rachel Tolbert, and Ariela Schachter. "Neighborhood Poverty and Maternal Fears of Children's Outdoor Play." *Family Relations* 60, no. 4 (2011): 461–75.

Kivnick, Helen Q. *The Meaning of Grandparenthood*. Ann Arbor, MI: UMI Research Press, 1980.

Kneebone, Elizabeth, and Natalie Holmes. *U.S. Concentrated Poverty in the Wake of the Great Recession*. Washington, DC: Brookings Institution, 2016.

Koenig, Harold G. "Religion, Spirituality, and Health: A Review and Update." *Advances in Mind-Body Medicine* 29, no. 3 (2015): 19–26.

Kolomer, Stacey R., and Karen Y. Lynch. "Challenges for Grandparent Housing Programs." *Journal of Gerontological Social Work* 49, no. 1–2 (2007): 65–79.

Kurwa, Rahim. "The New Man in the House Rules: How the Regulation of Housing Vouchers Turns Personal Bonds into Eviction Liabilities." *Housing Policy Debate* 30, no. 6 (2020): 926–49.

Langosch, Deborah. "Grandparents Parenting Again: Challenges, Strengths, and Implications for Practice." *Psychoanalytic Inquiry* 32, no. 2 (2012): 163–70.

Lareau, Annette. *Unequal Childhoods: Class, Race, and Family Life*. Berkeley: University of California Press, 2011.

Leder, Sharon, Linda Nicholson Grinstead, and Elisa Torres. "Grandparents Raising Grandchildren: Stressors, Social Support, and Health Outcomes." *Journal of Family Nursing* 13, no. 3 (2007): 333–52.

Leos-Urbel, Jacob, Roseana Bess, and Rob Geen. "The Evolution of Federal and State Policies for Assessing and Supporting Kinship Caregivers." *Children and Youth Services Review* 24, no. 1–2 (2002): 37–52.

Letiecq, Bethany L., Sandra J. Bailey, and Fonda Porterfield. "'We Have No Rights, We Get No Help': The Legal and Policy Dilemmas Facing Grandparent Caregivers." *Journal of Family Issues* 29, no. 8 (2008): 995–1012.

Light, Michael T., and Julia T. Thomas. "Segregation and Violence Reconsidered: Do Whites Benefit from Residential Segregation?" *American Sociological Review* 84, no. 4 (2019): 690–725.

Lin, Ching-Hsuan. "Evaluating Services for Kinship Care Families: A Systematic Review." *Children and Youth Services Review* 36 (2014): 32–41.

Lipsky, Michael. *Street-Level Bureaucracy: Dilemmas of the Individual in Public Services.* New York: Russell Sage Foundation, 1980.

Little, Samuel B. "Grandparents Raising Grandchildren." *Journal of Health and Social Policy* 22, no. 3–4 (2006): 167–80.

Lumsdaine, Robin L., and Stephanie J. Vermeer. "Retirement Timing of Women and the Role of Care Responsibilities for Grandchildren." *Demography* 52, no. 2 (2015): 433–54.

Malm, Karin and Tiffany, Allen. *A Qualitative Research Study of Kinship Diversion Practices.* Bethesda, MD: Child Trends, July 2016.

Malm, Karin, Kristin Sepulveda, and Sam Abbott. *Variations in the Use of Kinship Diversion among Child Welfare Agencies: Early Answers to Important Questions.* Bethesda, MD: Child Trends, 2019.

Martin, Elmer P., and Joanne Mitchell Martin. *The Black Extended Family.* Chicago: University of Chicago Press, 1978.

Mason, Mary Ann. *From Father's Property to Children's Rights: The History of Child Custody in the United States.* New York: Columbia University Press, 1994.

Massey, Douglas S., and Nancy A. Denton. *American Apartheid: Segregation and the Making of the Underclass.* New York: Routledge, 2018.

Matzek, Amanda E., and Teresa M. Cooney. "Spousal Perceptions of Marital Stress and Support among Grandparent Caregivers: Variations by Life Stage." *International Journal of Aging and Human Development* 68, no. 2 (2009): 109–26.

May, Vanessa, Jennifer Mason, and Lynda Clarke. "Being There Yet Not Interfering: The Paradoxes of Grandparenting." In *Contemporary Grandparenting: Changing Family Relationships in Global Contexts*, edited by Sara Arber and Virpi Timonen, 139–58. Bristol: Policy Press, 2012.

McDaniel, Marla. "In the Eye of the Beholder: The Role of Reporters in Bringing Families to the Attention of Child Protective Services." *Children and Youth Services Review* 28, no 3 (2006): 306–24.

McDonald, Katrina Bell. "Black Activist Mothering: A Historical Intersection of Race, Gender, and Class." *Gender and Society* 11, no. 6 (1997): 773–95.

McDonald, Katrina Bell, and Elizabeth M. Armstrong. "De-Romanticizing Black Intergenerational Support: The Questionable Expectations of Welfare Reform." *Journal of Marriage and Family* 63, no. 1 (2001): 213–23.

McGowan, Brenda, and Elaine Walsh. "Policy Challenges for Child Welfare in the New Century." *Child Welfare* 79, no. 1 (2000): 11–27.

McGrath, Soledad A. "Differential Response in Child Protection Services: Perpetuating the Illusion of Voluntariness." *University of Memphis Law Review* 42 (2011): 629–85.

McKernan, Signe-Mary, Caroline Ratcliffe, Eugene Steuerle, and Sisi Zhang. "Disparities in Wealth Accumulation and Loss from the Great Recession and Beyond." *American Economic Review* 104, no. 5 (2014): 240–44.

McLanahan, Sara, and Christine Percheski. "Family Structure and the Reproduction of Inequalities." *Annual Review of Sociology* 34, no. 1 (2008): 257–76.

McLaughlin, Beth, David Ryder, and Myra F. Taylor. "Effectiveness of Interventions for Grandparent Caregivers: A Systematic Review." *Marriage and Family Review* 53, no. 6 (2017): 509–31.

Merling, Laura. *Black Women Are the Only Group More Likely to Work Multiple Jobs Now Than a Decade Ago.* Washington, DC: Center for Economic Policy and Research, 2016.

Meyer, Madonna Harrington. *Grandmothers at Work: Juggling Families and Jobs.* New York: New York University Press, 2014.

Meyer, Madonna Harrington, and Ynesse Abdul-Malak. *Grandparenting Children with Disabilities.* Cham, Switzerland: Springer International, 2020.

Minkler, Meredith. "Intergenerational Households Headed by Grandparents: Contexts, Realities, and Implications for Policy." *Journal of Aging Studies*, vol. 13, no. 2 (1999): 199–218.

Minkler, Meredith, and Esme Fuller-Thomson. "The Health of Grandparents Raising Grandchildren: Results of a National Study." *American Journal of Public Health* 89, no. 9 (1999): 1384–89.

Minkler, Meredith, Esme Fuller-Thomson, Doriane Miller, and Diane Driver. "Grandparent Caregiving and Depression." In *Grandparents Raising Grandchildren*, edited by Bert Hayslip Jr. and Robin Goldberg-Glen, 207–19. New York: Springer, 2000.

Minkler, Meredith, and Kathleen M. Roe. *Grandmothers as Caregivers: Raising Children of the Crack Cocaine Epidemic.* Newbury Park, CA: Sage, 1993.

Misra, Joya, Stephanie Moller, Eiko Strader, and Elizabeth Wemlinger. "Family Policies, Employment, and Poverty among Partnered and Single Mothers." *Research in Social Stratification and Mobility* 30, no. 1 (2012): 113–28.

Monitor on Psychology, "More Kids in Foster Care." Washington, DC: American Psychological Association, November 1, 2019.

Montoro-Rodriguez, Julian, and Jennifer Ramsey. "Grandparents and Race/ Ethnicity." In *Grandparenting: Influences on the Dynamics of Family Relationships*, edited by Bert Hayslip Jr. and Christine A. Fruhauf, 313–30. New York: Springer, 2019.

Moynihan, Daniel Patrick. "The Negro Family: The Case for National Action." Office of Policy Planning and Research, US Department of Labor, 1965.

Murphy, S. Yvette, Andrea G. Hunter, and Deborah J. Johnson. "Transforming Caregiving: African American Custodial Grandmothers and the Child Welfare System." *Journal of Sociology and Social Welfare* 35, no. 2 (2008): 67–89.

Murray, Julie, Jennifer Ehrle, and Rob Geen. *Estimating Financial Support for Kinship Caregivers.* Washington, DC: Urban Institute, 2004.

Murry, Velma McBride, Mia Bynum, Gene Brody, Amanda Willert, and Dionne Stephens. "African American Single Mothers and Children in Context." *Clinical Child and Family Psychology Review* 4, no. 2 (2001): 133–55.

Musil, Carol M., Nahida L. Gordon, Camille B. Warner, Jaclene A. Zauszniewski, Theresa Standing, and May Wykle. "Grandmothers and Caregiving to Grandchildren: Continuity, Change, and Outcomes Over 24 Months." *The Gerontologist* 51, no. 1 (2011): 86–100.

Mutchler, Jan E., Lindsey A. Baker, and SeungAh Lee. "Grandparents Responsible for Grandchildren in Native-American Families." *Social Science Quarterly* 88, no. 4 (2007): 990–1009.

NAACP. "Aging While Black: The Crisis Among Black Americans as They Grow Old." The Crisis. June 8, 2021. https://naacp.org/articles/aging-while-black -crisis-among-black-americans-they-grow-old.

Nakano Glenn, Evelyn. *Forced to Care: Coercion and Caregiving in America.* Cambridge, MA: Harvard University Press, 2010.

National Conference of State Legislatures. "Disproportionality and Race Equity in Child Welfare." www.ncsl.org/research/human-services/disproportionality -and-race-equity-in-child-welfare.aspx.

National Equity Atlas. "Neighborhood Poverty: All Neighborhoods Should Be Communities of Opportunity." https://nationalequityatlas.org/indicators /Neighborhood_poverty#/.

National Indian Child Welfare Association. "About ICWA." www.nicwa.org /about-icwa/.

———. "Understanding ICWA Placements Using Kinship Care Research: Family That Children Have Never Known." December 2019. www.nicwa .org/wp-content/uploads/2020/01/2019-Understanding-ICWA-Placements -Using-Kinship-Care-Reasearch-Final.pdf.

———. "What Is Disproportionality in Child Welfare?" 2017. www.nicwa.org /wp-content/uploads/2017/09/Disproportionality-Table.pdf.

National Partnership for Women and Families. "Black Women and the Wage Gap." www.nationalpartnership.org/our-work/resources/economic-justice /fair-pay/african-american-women-wage-gap.pdf.

Nation's Health. "Behind Bars II, Substance Abuse and America's Prison Population." Washington, DC: American Public Health Association, 2010.

Nesmith, Ande. "Factors Influencing the Regularity of Parental Visits with Children in Foster Care." *Child and Adolescent Social Work Journal* 32, no. 3 (2015): 219–28.

Netherland, Julie, and Helena B. Hansen. "The War on Drugs That Wasn't: Wasted Whiteness, 'Dirty Doctors,' and Race in Media Coverage of Prescription Opioid Misuse." *Culture, Medicine, and Psychiatry* 40, no. 4 (2016): 664–86.

North American Council on Adoptable Children. "How to Cover College Expenses for Your Child Adopted from Foster Care." February 9, 2017. www .nacac.org/resource/college-expenses-adopted-child-foster-care/.

Office of Population Affairs. "Trends in Teen Pregnancy and Childbearing." Washington, DC: US Department of Health and Human Services, 2019.

Organisation for Economic Co-operation and Development. "Public Spending on Childcare and Early Education." Paris: OECD Family Database, 2019. www.oecd.org/els/soc/PF3_1_Public_spending_on_childcare_and_early _education.pdf.

———. "Public Spending on Family Benefits." Paris: OECD Family Database, 2019. https://data.oecd.org/socialexp/family-benefits-public-spending.htm.

Owens, Ann. "Income Segregation between School Districts and Inequality in Students' Achievement." *Sociology of Education* 91, no. 1 (2018): 1–27.

Palacios, Jesús, and Jesús M. Jiménez. "Kinship Foster Care: Protection or Risk?" *Adoption and Fostering* 33, no. 3 (2009): 64–75.

Parisi, Domenico, Daniel T. Lichter, and Michael C. Taquino. "Multi-Scale Residential Segregation: Black Exceptionalism and America's Changing Color Line." *Social Forces* 89, no. 3 (2011): 829–52.

Park, Hwa-Ok. "The Economic Well-Being of Households Headed by a Grand-mother as Caregiver." *Social Service Review* 80, no. 2 (2006): 264–96.

Pattillo, Mary. *Black Picket Fences: Privilege and Peril among the Black Middle Class.* Chicago: University of Chicago Press, 1999.

Paul, Mark, Khaing Zaw, Darrick Hamilton, and William Darity Jr. *Returns in the Labor Market: A Nuanced View of Penalties at the Intersection of Race and Gender.* Washington, DC: Washington Center for Equitable Growth, 2018.

Peacock, Shelley, Stephanie Konrad, Erin Watson, Darren Nickel, and Nazeem Muhajarine. "Effectiveness of Home Visiting Programs on Child Outcomes: A Systematic Review." *BMC Public Health* 13, no. 1 (2013): 1–14.

Pearlin, Leonard I., Joseph T. Mullan, Shirley J. Semple, and Marilyn M. Skaff. "Caregiving and the Stress Process: An Overview of Concepts and Their Measures." *The Gerontologist* 30, no. 5 (1990): 583–94.

Pickard, Joseph G., John-Paul R. Witt, and Gina T. Aitch. "Resilience and Faith of African American Caregivers." In *Resilience in Aging*, edited by Barbara Resnick, Lisa P. Gwyther, and Karen A. Roberto, 281–95. Cham, Switzer-land: Springer, 2018.

Pillemer, Karl, Jill J. Suitor, Steven E. Mock, Myra Sabir, Tamara B. Pardo, and Jori Sechrist. "Capturing the Complexity of Intergenerational Relations: Exploring Ambivalence within Later-Life Families." *Journal of Social Issues* 63, no. 4 (2007): 775–91.

Pittman, LaShawnDa. "How Well Does the 'Safety Net' Work for Family Safety Nets? Economic Survival Strategies among Grandmother Caregivers in Severe Deprivation." *RSF: The Russell Sage Foundation Journal of the Social Sciences* 1, no. 1 (2015): 78–97.

———. "Safety Net Politics: Economic Survival among Grandmother Caregivers in Severe Deprivation." In *Relational Poverty Politics: Forms, Struggles, Possibilities*, edited by Vicky Lawson and Sarah Ellwood, 25–42. Athens: University of Georgia Press, 2018.

Pittman, LaShawnDa, Janice Nodvin, and Maeve Howett. "Grandparents as Caregivers for Grandchildren with Intellectual and Developmental Disabilities." In *Health Care for People with Intellectual and Developmental Disabilities across the Lifespan*, edited by Leslie Rubin, Joav Merrick, Donald E. Greydanus, and Dilip R. Patel, 69–77. Cham, Switzerland: Springer International, 2016.

Pittman, LaShawnDa, and Deirdre Oakley. "'It Was Love in All the Buildings They Tore Down': How Caregiving Grandmothers Create and Experience a Sense of Community in Chicago Public Housing." *City and Community* 17, no. 2 (2018): 461–84.

Prinz, Ronald J., Matthew R. Sanders, Cheri J. Shapiro, Daniel J. Whitaker, and John R. Lutzker. "Population-Based Prevention of Child Maltreatment: The U.S. Triple P System Population Trial." *Prevention Science* 10, no. 1 (2009): 1–12.

Quadagno, Jill S. *The Transformation of Old Age Security: Class and Politics in the American Welfare State*. Chicago: University of Chicago Press, 1988.

Raley, R. Kelly, Megan M. Sweeney, and Danielle Wondra. "The Growing Racial and Ethnic Divide in U.S. Marriage Patterns." *Future of Children* 25, no. 2 (2015): 89–109.

Rapoport, Eli, Nallammai Muthiah, Sarah A. Keim, and Andrew Adesman. "Family Well-Being in Grandparent- versus Parent-Headed Households." *Pediatrics* 146, no 3 (2020): 1–10.

Redleaf, Diane L. *They Took the Kids Last Night: How the Child Protection System Puts Families at Risk*. Westport, CT: Praeger, 2018.

Rice, Douglas, Stephanie Schmit, and Hannah Matthews. *Child Care and Housing: Big Expenses with Too Little Help Available*. Washington, DC: Center on Budget and Policy Priorities, 2019.

Richards, Richie. "Grandparents Raising Grandchildren Takes Its Toll." *Native Sun News*, January 6, 2016.

Rious, Jennifer B., Michael Cunningham, and Margaret Beale Spencer. "Rethinking the Notion of 'Hostility' in African American Parenting Styles." *Research in Human Development* 16, no. 1 (2019): 35–50.

Roberts, Dorothy E. "The Racial Geography of Child Welfare." *Child Welfare* 87, no. 2 (2008): 125–50.

———. *Shattered Bonds: The Color of Child Welfare.* New York: Civitas Books, 2002.

———. *Torn Apart: How the Child Welfare System Destroys Black Families—and How Abolition Can Build a Safer World.* New York: Basic Books, 2022.

Robinson, Margaret M., and Scott E. Wilks. "'Older but Not Wiser': What Custodial Grandparents Want to Tell Social Workers about Raising Grandchildren." *Social Work and Christianity* 33, no. 2 (2006): 164–77.

Rooks, Noliwe. *Cutting School: Privatization, Segregation, and the End of Public Education.* New York: New Press, 2017.

Ross, Mary Ellen, and Lu Ann Aday. "Stress and Coping in African American Grandparents Who Are Raising Their Grandchildren." *Journal of Family Issues* 27, no. 7 (2006): 912–32.

Rothstein, Richard. *The Color of Law: A Forgotten History of How Our Government Segregated America.* New York: Liveright, 2017.

Ruggles, Steve. "The Origins of African-American Family Structure." *American Sociological Review* 59, no. 1 (1994): 136–51.

Ruiz, Dorothy Smith. *Amazing Grace: African American Grandmothers as Caregivers and Conveyers of Traditional Values.* Westport, CT: Greenwood, 2004.

Rushovich, Berenice R., Kantahyanee W. Murray, Kristen Woodruff, and Pamela Clarkson Freeman. "A Kinship Navigator Program: A Comprehensive Approach to Support Private and Voluntary Kinship Caregivers." *Child Welfare* 95, no. 3 (2016): 111–31.

Ryff, Carol D., Pamela S. Schmutte, and Young Hyun Lee. "How Children Turn Out: Implications for Parental Self-Evaluation." In *The Parental Experience in Midlife*, edited by Carol D. Ryff and Marsha Mailick Seltzer, 383–422. Chicago: University of Chicago Press, 1996.

Sadruddin, Aalyia F.A., Liliana A. Ponguta, Anna L. Zonderman, Kyle S. Wiley, Alyssa Grimshaw, and Catherine Panter-Brick. "How Do Grandparents Influence Child Health and Development? A Systematic Review." *Social Science & Medicine* 239 (2019): 1–32.

Sakai, Christina, Hua Lin, and Glenn Flores. "Health Outcomes and Family Services in Kinship Care: Analysis of a National Sample of Children in the Child Welfare System." *Archives of Pediatrics and Adolescent Medicine* 165, no. 2 (2011): 159–65.

Sastry, Narayan, and Anne R. Pebley. "Family and Neighborhood Sources of Socioeconomic Inequality in Children's Achievement." *Demography* 47, no. 3 (2010): 777–800.

Savage, Laura-Émilie, George M. Tarabulsy, Jessica Pearson, Delphine Collin-Vézina, and Lisa-Marie Gagné. "Maternal History of Childhood Maltreatment and Later Parenting Behavior: A Meta-analysis." *Development and Psychopathology* 31, no. 1 (2019): 9–21.

Scannapieco, Maria, and Kelli Connell-Carrick. "Correlates of Child Maltreatment among Adolescent Mothers with Young Children." *Journal of Evidence-Informed Social Work* 13, no. 1 (2016): 59–75.

Scarcella, Cynthia A., Jennifer Ehrle Macomber, and Rob Geen. *Identifying and Addressing the Needs of Children in Grandparent Care*. Washington, DC: Urban Institute, 2003.

Schneider, William. "Single Mothers, the Role of Fathers, and the Risk for Child Maltreatment." *Children and Youth Services Review* 81 (2017): 81–93.

Schwartz, Ann E. "'Nobody Knows Me No More': Experiences of Loss among African American Adolescents in Kinship and Non-Kinship Foster Care Placements." *Race and Social Problems* 2, no. 1 (2010): 31–49.

Scommegna, Paola, and Nadwa Mossaad. "The Health and Well-Being of Grandparents Caring for Grandchildren." *Today's Research on Aging* 23 (2011): 1–6.

Sedlak, Andrea J., Jane Mettenburg, Monica Basena, Ian Peta, Karla McPherson, and Angela Greene. *Fourth National Incidence Study of Child Abuse and Neglect (NIS-4): Report to Congress*. Washington, DC: US Department of Health and Human Services, Administration for Children and Families, 2010.

Seefeldt, Kristin S. *Working after Welfare: How Women Balance Jobs and Family in the Wake of Welfare Reform*. Kalamazoo, MI: W. E. Upjohn Institute for Employment Research, 2008.

Shack, Jennifer, Susan M. Yates, Jennifer Spagnolo, and Molly Mcaughey. "Child Protection Mediation: An Evaluation of Services Provided by Cook County Juvenile Court." Chicago: Center for Conflict Resolution and Resolution Systems Institute, 2010.

Sharkey, Patrick. "Spatial Segmentation and the Black Middle Class." *American Journal of Sociology* 119, no. 4 (2014): 903–54.

———. "Why Do We Need the Police?" *Washington Post*, June 12, 2020.

Sharkey, Patrick, and Jacob W. Faber. "Where, When, Why, and for Whom Do Residential Contexts Matter? Moving Away from the Dichotomous Understanding of Neighborhood Effects." *Annual Review of Sociology* 40, no. 1 (2014): 559–79.

Shelton, Deborah L. "Kin Prop Up Illinois' Foster Care System, with Limited Support." *The Imprint*, October 22, 2018.

Shrider, Emily A., Melissa Kollar, Frances Chen, and Jessica Semega. *Income and Poverty in the United States: 2020*. Washington, DC: US Government Publishing Office, September 2021.

Simpson, Gaynell Marie, and Claudia Lawrence-Webb. "Responsibility without Community Resources: Informal Kinship Care among Low-Income, African American Grandmother Caregivers." *Journal of Black Studies* 39, no. 6 (2009): 825–47.

Simpson, Gaynell Marie, Tracy D. Pressley, Dana Carthron, and Kim Stansbury. "Social Support and Survival Strategies of Older African American Grandmother Caregivers." *GrandFamilies: The Contemporary Journal of Research, Practice, and Policy* 4, no. 2 (2017): 24–51.

Smith, Carrie Jefferson, and Ana Beltran. "The Role of Federal Policies in Supporting Grandparents Raising Grandchildren Families." *Journal of Intergenerational Relationships* 1, no. 2 (2003): 5–20.

Smith, Carrie Jefferson, and Wynetta Devore. "African American Children in the Child Welfare and Kinship System: From Exclusion to Over Inclusion." *Children and Youth Services Review* 26, no. 5 (2004): 427–46.

Smith, Deidre M. "Keeping It in the Family: Minor Guardianship as Private Child Protection." *Connecticut Public Interest Law Journal* (2019): 269–356.

Social Security Administration. "Application for a Social Security Card." www .ssa.gov/forms/ss-5.pdf.

———. "Benefits for Children." www.ssa.gov/pubs/EN-05-10085.pdf.

———. "Understanding Supplemental Security Income Documents You May Need When You Apply." www.ssa.gov/ssi/text-documents-ussi.htm.

Soine, Lynne. "Kinship Foster Caregivers—Partners for Permanency." *Social Work Today* 13, no. 5 (2013): 12.

Stack, Carol B., and Linda M. Burton. "Kinscripts." *Journal of Comparative Family Studies* 24, no. 2 (1993): 157–70.

Standing, Theresa S., Carol M. Musil, and Camille Beckette Warner. "Grandmothers' Transitions in Caregiving to Grandchildren." *Western Journal of Nursing Research* 29, no. 5 (2007): 613–31.

Staton-Tindall, Michele, Ginny Sprang, James Clark, Robert Walker, and Carlton D. Craig. "Caregiver Substance Use and Child Outcomes: A Systematic Review." *Journal of Social Work Practice in the Addictions* 13, no. 1 (2013): 6–31.

Steil, Justin P., Len Albright, Jacob S. Rugh, and Douglas S. Massey. "The Social Structure of Mortgage Discrimination." *Housing Studies* 33, no. 5 (2018): 759–76.

Stevenson, Michelle L., Tammy L. Henderson, and Eboni Baugh. "Vital Defenses: Social Support Appraisals of Black Grandmothers Parenting Grandchildren." *Journal of Family Issues* 28, no. 2 (2007): 182–211.

Stoltzfus, Emilie. *Child Welfare: An Overview of Federal Programs and Their Current Funding*. Congressional Research Service, January 10, 2017.

Strong, Deena D., Roy A. Bean, and Leslie L. Feinauer. "Trauma, Attachment, and Family Therapy with Grandfamilies: A Model for Treatment." *Children and Youth Services Review* 32, no. 1 (2010): 44–50.

Stryker, Sheldon. "Traditional Symbolic Interactionism, Role Theory, and Structural Symbolic Interactionism: The Road to Identity Theory." In *Handbook of Sociological Theory*, edited by Jonathan H. Turner, 211–31. Boston: Springer, 2001.

Sudarkasa, Niara. *The Strength of Our Mothers: African and African American Women and Families: Essays and Speeches*. Trenton, NJ: Africa World Press, 1996.

Swann, Christopher A., and Michelle Sheran Sylvester. "The Foster Care Crisis: What Caused Caseloads to Grow?" *Demography* 43, no. 2 (2006): 309–35.

Szinovacz, Maximiliane E. "Research on Grandparenting: Needed Refinements in Concepts, Theories, and Methods." In *Handbook on Grandparenthood*, edited by Maximiliane E. Szinovacz, 257–88. Westport, CT: Greenwood, 1998.

Taylor, Keeanga-Yamahtta. *Race for Profit. Justice, Power, and Politics*. Chapel Hill: University of North Carolina Press, 2019.

Testa, Mark F. "Introduction: Kinship Care Policy and Practice (First Issue)." *Child Welfare* 95, no. 3 (2017): 13–39.

———. "Kinship Foster Care in Illinois." In *Child Welfare Research Review*, vol. 2, edited by Richard P. Barth, Jill Duerr Berrick, and Neil Gilbert. New York: Columbia University Press, 1997.

Thornberry, Terence P., Kelly E. Knight, and Peter J. Lovegrove. "Does Maltreatment Beget Maltreatment? A Systematic Review of the Intergenerational Literature." *Trauma, Violence, and Abuse* 13, no. 3 (2012): 135–52.

Tonry, Michael, and Matthew Melewski. "The Malign Effects of Drug and Crime Control Policies on Black Americans." *Crime and Justice* 37, no. 1 (2008): 1–44.

Travis, Jeremy, Elizabeth McBride, and Amy Solomon, "Families Left Behind: The Hidden Costs of Incarceration and Reentry." Washington, DC: Urban Institute, 2005.

Turner, Jennifer L. "Black Mothering in Action: The Racial-Class Socialization Practices of Low-Income Black Single Mothers." *Sociology of Race and Ethnicity* 6, no. 2 (2020): 242–53.

Turner, Ralph H. "Role-Taking: Process versus Conformity." In *Human Behavior and Social Processes: An Interactionist Approach*, edited by Arnold M. Rose, 20–40. New York: Routledge, 1962.

Uhlenberg, Peter, and James B. Kirby. "Grandparenthood over Time: Historical and Demographic Trends." In *Handbook on Grandparenthood*, edited by Maximiliane E. Szinovacz, 23–39. Westport, CT: Greenwood Press, 1998.

United States Census Bureau. "2019 American Community Survey, B10051: Grandparents Living with Own Grandchildren under 18 Years by Responsibility for Own Grandchildren by Presence of Parent of Grandchildren and Age of Grandparent." 2021. https://data.census.gov/cedsci/table?q= ACSDT1Y2018.B10050&g=0100000US,%2404000%24001&tid=ACSD T1Y2019.B10050.

———. "2019 American Community Survey, S1002: Grandparents." 2021. https://data.census.gov/cedsci/table?q=Grandparents%20and%20 Grandchildren&tid=ACSST5Y2019.S1002.

———. "Grandparents Still Work to Support Grandchildren." August 18, 2022. www.census.gov/library/visualizations/2022/comm/grandparents-work-support-grandchildren.html.

United States Government Accountability Office. "Child Welfare and Aging Programs HHS Could Enhance Support for Grandparents and Other Relative Caregivers." July 2020.

Urban Institute. "Welfare Rules Database Project." https://wrd.urban.org/wrd /Query/query.cfm.

US Department of Education. "Education for Homeless Children and Youths (EHCY) Program." A Brief History of The McKinney-Vento Act. https:// nche.ed.gov/wp-content/uploads/2018/12/ehcy_profile.pdf.

———. "National Center for Homeless Education: Supporting the Education of Children and Youth Experiencing Homelessness Best Practices in Homeless Education Brief Series Students Living with Caregivers: Tips for Local Liaisons and School Personnel Supporting the Education of Children and Youth Experiencing Homelessness." https://nche.ed.gov/.

US Department of Health and Human Services, Office of the Assistant Secretary for Planning and Evaluation and the Administration for Children and Families. "Report to the Congress on Kinship Foster Care." May 31, 2000.

US Department of Labor, Employee Benefits Security Administration. "What You Should Know about Your Retirement Plan." www.dol.gov/sites/dolgov /files/ebsa/about-ebsa/our-activities/resource-center/publications/what-you -should-know-about-your-retirement-plan.pdf.

US Government Publishing Office. "H.R. 1892—Bipartisan Budget Act of 2018." www.congress.gov/bill/115th-congress/house-bill/1892/text.

Valentino, Kristin, Amy K. Nuttall, Michelle Comas, John G. Borkowski, and Carol E. Akai. "Intergenerational Continuity of Child Abuse among Adolescent Mothers." *Child Maltreatment* 17, no. 2 (2012): 172–81.

Van Dam, Andrew. "How These Grandparents Became America's Unofficial Social Safety Net." *Washington Post*, March 23, 2019.

Venkatesh, Sudhir Alladi. *Off the Books: The Underground Economy of the Urban Poor*. Cambridge, MA: Harvard University Press, 2006.

Von Hentig, Hans. "The Sociological Function of the Grandmother." *Social Forces* 24, no. 4 (1946): 389–92.

Waite, Douglas, Mary V. Greiner, and Zach Laris. "Putting Families First: How the Opioid Epidemic Is Affecting Children and Families, and the Child Welfare Policy Options to Address It." *Journal of Applied Research on Children* 9, no. 1 (2018): 1–35.

Waldrop, Deborah P. "Caregiving Issues for Grandmothers Raising Their Grandchildren." *Journal of Human Behavior in the Social Environment* 7, no. 3–4 (2004): 201–23.

Waldrop, Deborah P., and Joseph A. Weber. "From Grandparent to Caregiver: The Stress and Satisfaction of Raising Grandchildren." *Families in Society* 82, no. 5 (2001): 461–72.

Walton, Quenette L., and Camille Boone. "Voices Unheard: An Intersectional Approach to Understanding Depression among Middle-Class Black Women." *Women and Therapy* 42, no. 3–4 (2019): 301–19.

Washington Post. "Fatal Force." www.washingtonpost.com/graphics/investigations/police-shootings-database/.

White, Deborah Gray. *Ar'n't I a Woman?: Female Slaves in the Plantation South*. New York: W. W. Norton, 1999.

Whitley, Deborah M., and Esme Fuller-Thomson. "Latino Solo Grandparents Raising Grandchildren: Health Risks and Behaviors." *Hispanic Health Care International* 16, no. 1 (2018): 11–19.

Whitley, Deborah M., Susan J. Kelley, and Theresa A. Sipe. "Grandmothers Raising Grandchildren: Are They at Increased Risk of Health Problems?" *Health and Social Work* 26, no. 2 (2001): 105–14.

Wilkerson, Patricia A., and Gloria J. Davis. "Grandparents in Kinship Care: Help or Hindrance to Family Preservation." *Journal of Family Strengths* 11, no. 1 (2011): 1–18.

Williams, Jhacova. "Laid Off More, Hired Less: Black Workers in the COVID-19 Recession." Santa Monica, CA: RAND, 2020.

Williams, Molly. "The Changing Roles of Grandparents Raising Grandchildren." *Journal of Human Behavior in the Social Environment* 21, no. 8 (2011): 948–62.

Williams, Rhaisa Kameela. "Toward a Theorization of Black Maternal Grief as Analytic." *Transforming Anthropology* 24, no. 1 (2016): 17–30.

Williams, Sarah Catherine, *State-Level Data for Understanding Child Welfare in the United States*. Washington, DC: Child Trends, October 28, 2020.

Williams, Sarah Catherine, and Kristin Sepulveda. *The Share of Children in Foster Care Living with Relatives Is Growing*. Washington, DC: Child Trends, 2019.

Wilmoth, Joe D., Loriena Yancura, Melissa A. Barnett, and Brittney Oliver. "The Contributions of Religious Practice, Existential Certainty, and Raising

Grandchildren to Well-Being in Older Adults." *Journal of Religion, Spirituality, and Aging* 30, no. 3 (2018): 212–33.

Wilson, Breana. *Coresident Grandparents: Caregivers versus Non-Caregivers.* Bowling Green, OH: National Center for Family and Marriage Research, Family Profiles, FP-12-18, 2012.

Wilson, Valerie. *Black Unemployment Is at Least Twice as High as White Unemployment at the National Level and in 14 States and the District of Columbia.* Washington, DC: Economic Policy Institute, April 4, 2019.

Woods-Giscombé, Cheryl L., and Angela R. Black. "Mind-Body Interventions to Reduce Risk for Health Disparities Related to Stress and Strength among African American Women: The Potential of Mindfulness-Based Stress Reduction, Loving-Kindness, and the NTU Therapeutic Framework." *Complementary Health Practice Review* 15, no. 3 (2010): 115–31.

Wu, Huijing. *Grandchildren Living in a Grandparent-Headed Household.* Bowling Green, OH: National Center for Family and Marriage Research, Family Profiles, FP-18-01, 2018.

Wu, Qi, and Susan M. Snyder. "Factors Associated with the Decision-Making Process in Kinship Diversion." *Journal of Family Social Work* 22, no. 2 (2018): 161–86.

Ziemba, Stanley. "CHA Work to Empty 6 Buildings." *Chicago Tribune*, September 18, 1985.

Index

Founded in 1893,
UNIVERSITY OF CALIFORNIA PRESS
publishes bold, progressive books and journals
on topics in the arts, humanities, social sciences,
and natural sciences—with a focus on social
justice issues—that inspire thought and action
among readers worldwide.

The UC PRESS FOUNDATION
raises funds to uphold the press's vital role
as an independent, nonprofit publisher, and
receives philanthropic support from a wide
range of individuals and institutions—and from
committed readers like you. To learn more, visit
ucpress.edu/supportus.